Untangling the USA

Tom Brady and the "tuck rule"; "Nobody knew health care could be so complicated"; "The financial world has become way too complicated and very secretive." What could Tom Brady, Donald Trump, and Michael Lewis possibly have in common? Complexity. Lewis has analyzed it; Trump has discovered it; Brady has benefited from it. And the USA is entangled in it.

Complex systems are an inevitable part of business and socio-economic structures. We reach a breaking point, however, when social and organizational structures become cumbersome and unintelligible. Entire new systems need to be constructed just to manage this complexity, with questionable or negative value to society at large. The outcome is high costs, poor results, deepening social inequality, and the erosion of public trust. Wholesale changes must be contemplated. This is particularly true in the USA today, where complexity is piled upon complexity in a number of critical sectors, such as health care, energy, finance, and government.

The author takes a common sense, broad-based, and analytical approach to some of the most complicated issues facing the US today. He examines the costs of complexity through a wide-angle lens, provides analysis of the root causes involved, and explains what is necessary to both improve results and lower costs. The ever-increasing level of complexity in the US is compared to that in other developed economies. History is referenced as a guide to show that in many areas, America's success has relied on simple and elegant solutions. These contrasting paths are used to propose alternative approaches and new solutions. Beyond analyzing how incredibly complex socio-economic systems have emerged in recent years in the US, the author steps back, reflects on the fundamental values of this country, and offers a number of actionable proposals to improve the lives of all American citizens.

Etienne Deffarges has enjoyed a successful career, first as a senior strategy consultant to many leading global companies and then as a heath care technology entrepreneur in the US. He is perfectly positioned to observe how complex systems are stifling socio-economic progress. He brings a unique insider view of the issues involved and examines a number of key sectors that impact American society at large, including health care, energy, finance, regulations, taxation, utilities, and welfare.

Etienne Deffarges holds a variety of board positions with companies in aerospace, automotive, construction, energy, food, and health care. Previously, he was part of the founding team, EVP and Vice Chairman at Accretive Health (now R1 RCM); a global managing partner at Accenture; a senior partner with Booz Allen Hamilton; and a general field engineer with Schlumberger.

Untangling the USA

The Cost of Complexity and
What Can Be Done About It

Etienne Deffarges

LONDON AND NEW YORK

First published 2018
by Routledge
2 Park Square, Milton Park, Abingdon, Oxon OX14 4RN

and by Routledge
711 Third Avenue, New York, NY 10017

Routledge is an imprint of the Taylor & Francis Group, an informa business

British Library Cataloguing-in-Publication Data
A catalogue record for this book is available from the British Library

Library of Congress Cataloging-in-Publication Data
Names: Deffarges, Etienne, author.
Title: Untangling the USA : the cost of complexity and
    what can be done about it / Etienne Deffarges.
Description: Milton Park, Abingdon, Oxon ; New York, NY :
    Routledge, 2018. | Includes bibliographical references and index.
Identifiers: LCCN 2018003757 | ISBN 9780815363347 (hbk) |
    ISBN 9781351109796 (ebk)
Subjects: LCSH: United States—Economic conditions—21st century. |
    Business enterprises—United States.
Classification: LCC HC106.84 .D43 2018 | DDC 330.973—dc23
LC record available at https://lccn.loc.gov/2018003757

ISBN: 978-0-8153-6334-7 (hbk)
ISBN: 978-1-351-10979-6 (ebk)

Typeset in Bembo
by Apex CoVantage, LLC

Printed in Canada

This book is dedicated to:

My wife, Ana Paula, for her love, affection, and friendship. Her constant support gave me the enthusiasm I needed to write this book.

My children, Jonathan (who reviewed my prose many times), Charles, Lindsay, David, Hayden, and stepson Pablo (who designed the beautiful cover for the book and helped me with the technical aspects of the photos).

My parents, Marie and Jean-Pierre Deffarges, and siblings Rémi, Geneviève, and François.

Contents

Images and exhibits

Image

Exhibit

About the author

Etienne Deffarges has lived in San Francisco since 1985 and became a U.S. citizen in 1993. He first discovered the Bay Area when studying for his MS in Civil Engineering and Transportation at the University of California, Berkeley, upon graduating as an aeronautical engineer from the ISAE – Sup'Aero in Toulouse, France. A few years later, after working as a general field engineer for Schlumberger in several South American countries, he got his MBA from the Harvard Business School, graduating as a Baker Scholar. Etienne then started a career in management consulting with Booz Allen Hamilton, went through his apprenticeship, and eventually became a senior partner and head of the firm's global energy, chemicals and pharmaceuticals practice. He was a senior advisor to several governments in Asia and South America, and attended the annual meeting of the World Economic Forum in Davos, Switzerland. In 1999, Etienne was recruited by Accenture to be a global managing partner, with leading responsibilities in energy and utilities. He was the company's first global market maker, responsible for large deals with clients, including one well in excess of $1 billion. He founded the Accenture Energy Advisory Board, chaired by Secretary George Shultz, and was a member of the Aspen Institute Energy Forum, since his tenure as a Booz Allen partner. He participated actively in the 2001 Accenture IPO on the New York Stock Exchange. In 2004, Etienne became an entrepreneur and part of the founding team, EVP and Vice Chairman of Accretive Health (now R1 RCM), a health care IT start-up that had its own IPO in 2010, with an enterprise value of $1.2 billion. He got the company to be a global growth, industry shaper and health care partner for the World Economic Forum. Today Etienne holds a variety of board positions with companies in aerospace, automotive, construction, food, energy, and health care. He is an active angel investor and coach to several early stage companies. He speaks five languages, enjoys flying as a private pilot, and is a model railroad hobbyist as well as an avid sports fan.

Acknowledgements

I want to thank and express my gratitude to:

The authors of the forewords to this book, Secretary George P. Shultz and Senator Thomas A. Daschle, with much admiration and appreciation.

My UC Berkeley roommate and friend Steve Marks, now Professor at Boston University, for reading my first draft with great patience, and offering invaluable advice on style and substance for this book.

My friends Olivier Marie and Tom Southern for helping me find a great publisher.

Susan Schendel, for her expert assistance in helping me with the complex permitting process for articles and quotes.

The many friends who gave me great advice and encouragement throughout this writing and publishing journey: William Barboza, Janette Cardoso, Sylvaine and Philippe Cases, Jean-Michel Darroy, Jeane de Freitas and Robert Wicke, Lionel and Pascale de La Sayette, Brian and Sue Dickie, Tom Driscoll, Alain Ducasse, Bonnie Fisher and Boris Dramov, Gilles Guillon, Rebecca Henderson, Laurent Joly, Larry Kelly, Yasemin Besik Kliman, Jean Kovacs and Brooks Stough, Tony Lazar, Bruce and Lynne Pasternack, Alessandro Piol, Joan Plastiras, Phillip Raiser, Patrick Renvoise, Phil Rettger, Pierre Rodocanachi, Jean-Claude and Michelle Sarner, Radhika Shah, Bob Simmons and Kelly Luttrell, Chris Stafford and Eduardo Barbosa, Phil Strause, Anthony St. George, Aladin Stadlin, and Gabe Turner.

And, last but not least, my publishers Rebecca Marsh and Judith Lorton from Routledge – Taylor & Francis Group.

Foreword by George P. Shultz

I have known Etienne for twenty years or so. I was the chairman of the energy advisory board he founded when he was one of the global managing partners at Accenture. A few years later, I joined the board of the health IT company he had helped launch. In half a dozen years, that company grew from a blank piece of paper to a successful $1.2 billion IPO on the NYSE in 2010.

Our energy advisory board included a number of scholars, economists, and CEOs of large energy companies from all around the world. We had stimulating discussions and devised plans to help wean the United States from its dependency on Middle Eastern oil in order to simultaneously improve our economy, environment, and security. In health care, Etienne's IT company helps hospitals navigate the immensely complex US health care reimbursement system in order to improve their financial viability and, thus, their access to the best physicians and leading-edge medical technologies. Over the years, Etienne and I have engaged in frequent discussions about energy and health care, focusing on new solutions for a future full of improvements and breakthroughs.

These themes are at the heart of Etienne's book. Our social and organizational systems in health care, energy, finance, taxation, technology, and government are engulfed in complexity. Etienne analyzes the costs of this complexity, looks at its root causes, and offers practical solutions for improvement. With meticulous documentation, Etienne examines the complexity of the US health care system, an enormous sector of our economy. We have struggled to focus on a few key areas, such as prevention, that would both reduce costs and improve outcomes. Etienne shows why the strong built-in inertia of the whole system makes transformation in health care so challenging, and why changes over the years tend to be incremental, further adding to complexity. This is an industry that is tightly woven into the fabric of our society, and many new directions can lead to unforeseen consequences. For example, we often talk about the cost of health care, but we overlook that this is also one of the few sectors in our economy that has added jobs year after year for at least the last two decades.

In his chapters on electricity and utilities, laws and regulations, and proposed solutions, Etienne mentions several initiatives with which I have been closely involved, such as the political fight in California to preserve our state's Global

Warming Solutions Act, signed by Governor Arnold Schwarzenegger in 2006. I led the opposition to Proposition 23, which was promoted by out-of-state interests and which would have repealed the law. Even though our opponents were well financed, I remember telling Etienne, "We are not just going to win. We will win by a very large margin." In the end, we did win because 62% of Californians agreed with us and voted against Proposition 23. A few years earlier, Schwarzenegger had invited our Energy Advisory Board to Sacramento to test-drive exciting hydrogen fuel cell cars. There were a dozen of them from almost every large automaker selling cars in this country, and they all drove beautifully. The costs of those prototypes? Between $1 and $2 million each. Isn't it remarkable that today both Toyota and Hyundai are ready to launch hydrogen-fueled cars to the broad public, and in the meantime I can drive a fully electric and affordable Chevy Bolt that gives me a battery range of 250 miles?

Etienne also mentions Nobel Prize-winning economist Gary Becker, our late and deeply missed friend. Gary was a member of our energy advisory board, and in one of our meetings he talked about a paper he had authored arguing for a dollar-per-gallon gasoline tax; reduced government budget deficits (the economy); reduced fuel consumption as people would migrate to more economical cars (energy security and the environment); and reduced dependency on oil imports. It was a simple way to achieve significant but elusive national objectives. Today I am a proud advocate of a revenue-neutral carbon tax. In a simple and transparent way, such a tax would help level the competitive playing field for energy producers, taking into account the costs and impacts on health of pollution from fossil fuels. A carbon tax would encourage our producers and consumers to shift toward energy sources that emit less carbon and generate greater demand for electric cars and less demand for conventional gasoline-powered cars. It would also further reduce our already declining oil imports. I have written extensively on this subject, and Etienne's book quotes an opinion piece I wrote with Gary Becker in 2013 as well as an editorial written this year.

Having analyzed prevailing complexity in a number of sectors that together account for a significant proportion of our economy, Etienne makes the case that this complexity is not in our DNA. I like the fact that, as an immigrant to our country, he has obviously learned a great deal about our history during his twenty-five years as a US citizen. And he is right: America's genius has often revolved around simple and effective ideas, inventions, and products. We still benefit from our investments in the railroads in the nineteenth century and Eisenhower's interstate highway system in the 1950s. We won the Cold War, in part, because our extensive dialogue with Soviet leaders convinced them of the superiority of our market-based economy, which is more effective, and also simpler, than any central planning system.

Moving forward, we need to rediscover simplicity in our economic, political, and social decision-making. Fiscal tools like a revenue-neutral carbon tax combine effectiveness with simplicity and provide clear signals to all market participants. Distributed energy can make us more self-sufficient and secure for our daily needs and reduce our reliance on ultra-complex electric grids that may prove to be vulnerable to hackers. And who in America would not want a simpler tax code?

I may not agree with all of Etienne's proposals, but I applaud his determination to offer clear solutions to the problems we face. His main idea that all government and private sector interfaces should be clarified and simplified is a sound one. Etienne's advocacy of simple but strong regulatory incentives to replace today's maze of complex regulations so that our private sector can respond in an optimum way should be well received by all who believe America can find new paths to economic prosperity.

Well written, thoroughly documented, and filled with convincing analyses, engaging anecdotes, and personal stories, Etienne's book and its journey through complexity will appeal to anyone interested in a productive dialogue on ideas to improve our future.

George P. Shultz
October 2, 2017

Foreword by Thomas A. Daschle

It was my good fortune to meet Etienne Deffarges over five years ago as a fellow member of the board of an innovative, leading-edge health care delivery company that focuses on laboratory excellence. I became increasingly impressed with his insightful contributions to our discussions and his unique analytical capacity. With an experience-rich professional background, he combined analysis with lessons learned to offer valuable advice to the company's management.

Over the years, before and after our board meetings, we had many discussions about socio-economics and political trends in the United States. We quickly discovered that we share a common passion about the challenges our country faces and the policies that are necessary to create opportunity and prosperity for all Americans.

We also share a great deal of international experience. Our involvement in Japan, for example, has given us a mutual appreciation of the value of the lessons that can be acquired from learning from what other developed economies are doing in a number of important sectors in business and industry.

Etienne utilizes his characteristic analytical ability in writing this book. He correctly contends that within the United States, we tend to do things in a much more complex way than necessary. The problem is evident across most industries representing much of our economy. The resulting costs are prohibitive. For example, we spend almost $10,000 per year per capita on health care, about twice as much that spent in the average developed economy. However, we rank well below other industrialized countries in terms of major health outcomes such as infant mortality or life expectancy.

Every developed country except the United States has had universal health care for decades. There are many unique systems in countries around the world, each designed to achieve it. But this country not only doesn't have universal health care, it doesn't have a single system of care. Rather, we have a collage of subsystems that span the spectrum of care in the rest of the world. We have a socialized subsystem within the military and Veterans Administration. We have a single payer subsystem in Medicare and a duel payer subsystem involving both the federal and state governments in Medicaid. We have an employer-based subsystem, similar to Germany, for most working Americans, and until 2010, when the Affordable Care Act (ACA) was enacted, we had no system at all for nearly fifty million Americans who had no health insurance. Since then we have had a hybrid subsystem with both public and private sector involvement that now covers approximately twenty million of those previously uninsured.

The national debate over our health care infrastructure has continued for over a century, dating to the early 1900s and the progressive movement, led in part by Theodore Roosevelt. It has largely been a debate about the role of government, with conservatives arguing for less while progressives have wanted more. Over the decades, health care has evolved into a de facto $3 trillion public–private partnership. In 1965 under the leadership of President Lyndon Johnson, both Medicare and Medicaid were enacted into law. President Bill Clinton helped lead the effort in the nineties to create the Children's Health Insurance Program (CHIP). We expanded Medicare to include prescription drugs under President George W. Bush. And the ACA became the latest iteration seven years ago under President Barack Obama's leadership.

With each new addition of another subsystem, our health care infrastructure becomes increasingly entropic. This book examines in informative detail the costs of complexity, an analysis of the root causes involved, and then explains what is necessary to improve our results and lower overall health costs.

The author analyses a number of sectors in addition to health care, including energy, finance, taxation, and utilities. He effectively contrasts them to simpler and oftentimes more efficient systems in other industrialized countries.

A proud immigrant, Etienne is also a keen student of American history. He offers a historical tutorial on the evolution of the country's pervasive complexity. His book also helps us understand why so many Americans feel overwhelmed. They no longer understand why managing one's health, savings, or energy needs to be so complicated. Their frustration oftentimes understandably turns to both fear and anger. As a result, many become increasingly inclined to listen to political demagogues who promise silver bullets and simple solutions. For the past seven years, ACA opponents have had a three-word solution: "Repeal and Replace." Yet, in 2017, Americans have been reminded that simplistic political slogans are deplorable legislative solutions.

In spite of these circumstances, throughout the book the author maintains a positive disposition and offers an impressive array of thoughtful ideas and solutions. Some of them offer a more general application, like his advocacy of streamlined interfaces between the government and the private sector. They could be designed, he argues, to simplify the current patchwork of activities performed by both government agencies and the private sector. This potpourri comes with a myriad of public–private interfaces and a muddled division of responsibilities that is both costly and ineffective.

But the book also includes other solutions that are quite specific, with detailed analyses of both design and associated costs. One example includes an intriguing proposal for a "no-frills" Medicare program that would be made universally available. The federal plan would be administered by the states with universal protections and benefits. Supplemental and alternative plans could be offered in the private sector, similar in design to policies available in the marketplace today but with far greater integration. And the private sector would continue to be encouraged to provide innovation and leading-edge solutions.

We live in a transformational and historic time. The two most catalytic forces are technology and policy. The intersection of these forces has already brought remarkable change, affecting every aspect of the way we live, work, govern, and obtain our health care. Along the way, our infrastructure has become increasingly complex and inefficient. Etienne persuasively argues that in health care as well as in almost every other sector today, we can simplify and reconstruct our systems to be far more productive and capable.

The publication of this book is propitious. It aptly addresses many vital businesses, socio-economic, and public policy challenges in America today. It offers a novel examination of the economic and social issues that have plagued us for decades, drawing on lessons learned from both our history and the experiences of other countries.

The book may also appeal to the majority of Americans who increasingly want a respite from political gridlock. Many of the author's solutions have great potential for bi-partisan support and effectively provide alternatives to the political extremes. Understanding the nature of historical decision-making offers the potential to arrive at practical solutions that are both simple and applicable in today's complex environment. And while some readers and I may not agree with every analysis or proposed solution, Etienne should be enthusiastically applauded for his innovative thinking and for offering many original and well-documented concepts for consideration.

Thomas A. Daschle
September 8, 2017

Introduction

Tom Brady and the "tuck rule"; "Nobody knew health care could be so complicated"; "The financial world has become way too complicated and very secretive." What could Tom Brady, Donald Trump, and Michael Lewis possibly have in common? Complexity. Lewis has analyzed it; Trump has discovered it; Brady has benefited from it. And the U.S. is entangled in it.

I have lived thirty-two years in America, becoming a U.S. citizen in 1993. I first landed in the Bay Area for graduate studies after getting an aeronautical engineering degree from my native France. After a few years as a field engineer in various countries throughout South America, and two years studying in Boston, I settled in California in 1985. Since then, I have been a management consultant, business executive, and entrepreneur, working in industries as diverse as health care, energy, food, aviation, infrastructure, and technology.

My thirty years advising CEOs; managing a very large global technology operation; and launching a health care company with a blank sheet of paper and bringing it to a successful IPO on the New York Stock Exchange allowed me to see a lot of patterns in our country. In the process I interacted with lots of different people. Hourly paid hospital staff in Flint, Michigan; skillful surgeons struggling to cope with their patient accounting and medical records systems in Tennessee; young software programmers in California; technology titans in Silicon Valley; shop floor workers in Pennsylvania; CEOs of businesses struggling under the forces of globalization, or thriving because of them; management consulting partners; university professors with brilliant intellects; powerful officials of government and elected leaders of Congress – I have enjoyed my dialogues with all of them. I learned a lot and validated my observations with data that is both publicly available and easy to digest. When I used to earn my keep as a management consultant, this was what strategy was about: to recognize patterns amidst the fog of data and facts, and describe them clearly. From this, solutions and opportunities would present themselves.

Reflecting upon my experiences, it strikes me that we Americans tend to do things in a much more complex way than needs be, across industries representing much of our economy. This costs us literally trillions of dollars and exacerbates inequality in our society. If we step back and compare with other developed countries, it becomes apparent that major health care, energy, finance, taxation, regulatory, and utility processes are performed in a much simpler and effective manner abroad than at home. We have built this complexity step-by-step, legislation-by-legislation, like a huge construction getting larger and larger. Incremental decisions adding new layers to the construction are easier to take than stepping back and starting from new bases, and so complexity keeps increasing.

This is not sustainable. Many of our citizens feel overwhelmed and no longer understand why managing one's health, savings, or energy needs to be so complicated. With this lack of understanding comes a sense of lack of control in one's life, followed by confusion, and then anger. We need to reverse course. Looking back at major decisions we took during our history and observing how our developed country peers handle things across many sectors can point us to practical solutions. We can implement them to improve our lot and find simplicity on the other side of complexity. This is the purpose of my book.

I start this narrative by describing the obscure NFL "tuck rule," used to decide a playoff game in favor of Tom Brady's New England Patriots against the Oakland Raiders amidst a snowstorm in 2002. Football, alongside baseball, is one of our favorite pastimes. The rest of the world watches soccer, a much simpler game with a huge following – a billion people watch a World Cup final. But we enjoy our sports and their complicated rules; it is like a puzzle to be solved and then argued about. This is fun and harmless. Puzzles are fun if there is little at stake. However, complexity brings much more adverse consequences in other areas. If our financial security or health is at stake, complexity may end up costing us a lot. This can be exacerbated when we have to make critical decisions. In sports, officials are there for that. In health care, energy, finance, and taxes, we have significant choices to make with less than a full understanding of their consequences. This is a lot less fun, and potentially harmful. I explore the costs we all pay for the complexity in our socio-economic system in health care; energy and electricity; finance; taxation; laws and regulations; and technology throughout the chapters of the book, focusing on these sectors.

Yet complexity is not in our DNA. The greatest institutional successes in American history have been defined by their simplicity. Our Constitution is legendary in its brevity and simplicity of purpose; our early inventors and industrialists thrived in making our world simpler and easier to live in; we won World War II with simple and very effective tools, and the Cold War because our market-based approach to economics was much more effective than central planning complexity. Conversely, many of our current policy failures are due to their complicated nature. Increased political polarization has led us away from practical solutions forged out of compromises achieved by pragmatic centrists. Today laws are voted with narrow, partisan majorities, and holdouts can get amendment upon amendment added to already complex legislation in exchange for their much-needed vote. In the private sector, the increased roles of finance and globalization have led to many complex arrangements, benefiting the few at the expense of the many. And the private and public sectors cannot succeed in untangling themselves, creating collages of complex interactions.

Nowhere is this truer than in health care, where complexity is piled upon complexity, with suboptimal results for most of us. It is imperative that America seeks simple solutions to our many issues today, in health care, energy, finance, and several other areas. Otherwise we are condemned to a future of declining economic competitiveness, increased inequality, and erosion of the social fabric of our country.

I decided to write this book and tell this story for a number of reasons.

First, there are too many aspects of our lives where we put up with far too complex and ineffective processes, with poor outcomes. There are better ways to manage our education, health, finances, taxes, and social programs.

Second, we are falling behind. Why should Americans get a worse deal in education, health care, infrastructure, protection of the environment, and safety net than the citizens of other developed countries? After all, when it comes to GDP per capita, we produce more than most of them.

Third, we often forget the impact of history on what affects us today. My book looks at critical decisions taken years and decades ago that help explain where we are today. Having that perspective is fundamental to understanding how we can change things in a number of sectors fundamental to our economy and lives.

Fourth, invective and personality fights appear to have replaced exchange of ideas at the heart of our political discourse. One of my hopes in writing this book is that it will put ideas on the table that can be embraced by decision makers more interested in practical solutions than ideology.

My book also touches on a new topic. If one googles "complexity," a number of scientific publications appear about an astrophysics and mathematical theory that shares some elements with the better-known "Chaos Theory." Other books offer self-help solutions in navigating today's complex world. There are, of course, countless publications on our current socio-economic trends, the sorry state of our polarized political world, and large sectors of our economy such as energy, finance, and health care. But I have not found other books looking at complexity as one of the root causes of the main economic, political, and social issues afflicting us today. We need to re-think fundamentally whole areas of our economy, as well as the legislative apparatus regulating them. To do this, we need to devise simple and effective solutions, with clear goals in mind. These new solutions should allow us to eliminate whole chunks of business practices and government bureaucracies. In particular, the maze of intersections between the private sector and government needs to be greatly simplified. There is much clamoring today about the need both to "unleash the competitive and innovative forces of the private sector" and to "have a government that guarantees our basic health, human and social rights." A strong yet smaller government focused on our health, safety and welfare, with the private sector taking care of the rest, can achieve this double objective, unlike the ideology-driven solutions offered today.

I have written this book in a very colloquial style, with a lot of personal anecdotes to illustrate the points I make. Complex situations are deconstructed

step-by-step so as to be very understandable. External data and sources supporting my argumentation are clearly identified. I bring a lot of historical perspective so the reader sees how complex situations have developed over time. I also
provide many comparisons with our trading partners in the developed world,
countries like Japan, Germany, France, the U.K., and Canada. Relating personal
experiences and using other countries as reference points allowed me to tell
part of my story as an immigrant to America, one well travelled and versed in
the cultural, economic, and health habits of many other countries. In this way,
this book is autobiographic to a small degree, but more importantly it provides
a perspective that has not been shared widely in our country. One of the reasons
I believe this case against complexity has not yet been made is that most Americans do not have much access to how day-to-day life works in other countries.
This may explain why many in the U.S. accept a status quo that would be
viewed as intolerable by many habitants of other developed countries. In too
many cases we get subpar outcomes from our complex processes, but things do
not have to be this way. There are better solutions out there, and even if copying
them is not practical, we can do much better while still adhering to the unique
values we hold dear as Americans, values that led us to such a successful history.
In writing this book, I want to propose viable solutions to problems we all face,
prompting readers to get new ideas on aspects of their lives they believe are
settled and encouraging them to add their own contributions. Hopefully these
solutions will become part of the debate and embedded in our policy landscape.

"La semplicità è l'ultima sofisticazione."

(Leonardo Da Vinci)

Etienne Deffarges
San Francisco, California
November 2017

Etienne Deffarges welcomes your conversation, comments, and interaction about this book and its topics.
Visit his website etiennedeffarges.com to read more of his writing and share your thoughts, or email him
directly at comments@etiennedeffarges.com.

1 Sports

Can NFL refs find the rule book in a snowstorm?

It is a miserable night and a blinding snowstorm in New England. On a football field, twenty-two NFL players battle together like two opposing Siberian armies. The field is buried in snow, it is dark, and even for TV viewers it all looks like an old black and white movie. One team sports white jerseys, like a camouflage uniform, and the opposing party wears black shirts, or perhaps dark blue? The dark blue offense lines up; their quarterback tries to throw, is tackled by the quasi-invisible opponent, and . . . fumble!!! Another white shirt comes out of nowhere to recover the ball. The army in white is celebrating wildly; surely they have won the game?

But wait: suddenly all action stops; the referees gesticulate, say something on their microphones no one hears, and leave the field to huddle under a dark canvas hood . . . long minutes of freezing waiting ensue. And then, after a brief announcement, the quarterback in blue has the ball again! He throws the ball above the white tundra, again and again. Eventually he has advanced enough to give his kicker a field goal opportunity, against the gusting wind and with no visibility. The football clears the cross bar, barely, to the wild cheers of local fans. Game tied, we are going to overtime. What happened?

The application of an obscure NFL rule, that's what happened. One of a myriad of rules in the NFL Rule Book, which most spectators do not get and many official referees navigate with caution, the "tuck rule" has just taken a sure playoff win away from the Oakland Raiders and handed it instead to the New England Patriots. Most football fans may have forgotten this game, but surely once I mention the words "tuck rule" you remember, right? Particularly if you are a Raiders fan. Allow me to jog your memory further.

The Raiders had been dominating the game in these terrible winter conditions. This had continued until the Patriots stopped attempting to run the ball and placed their trust instead in the arm of a young quarterback, who earlier in the season had replaced their starter Drew Bledsoe: Tom Brady. Still, even though Brady had the ball, his team was trailing 13–10, far from field goal range, with less than two minutes left on the clock. When Brady's former teammate Charles Woodson tackled him and caused the fumble, recovered by Raider linebacker Greg Biekert, it certainly looked like the Silver and Black would run out the clock and move on. The Patriots' season was over! But then, before the Raiders stopped celebrating, an instant review was called, and referee Walt Coleman reversed the call on the field: Brady's arm movement was deemed a forward pass while he was being tackled, and therefore an incompletion! Following this application of the "tuck rule" (abolished eleven years later), Brady kept the ball and led the Patriots to a 16–13 victory in overtime.[1] The Patriots went on to defeat the Pittsburgh Steelers for the AFC Championship and win their first Super Bowl 20–17 against the St. Louis Rams. The Raiders would reach the Super Bowl the following year, to be demolished 48–21 by the Tampa Bay Buccaneers, but this January 19, 2002 divisional playoff loss against the Pats is still very much talked about in Raider Nation.

Let's pause a minute: the "Tuck Rule" stated, in NFL Rule 3, Section 22, Article 2, Note 2:

> When (an offensive) player is holding the ball to pass it forward, any intentional forward movement of his arm starts a forward pass, even if the player loses possession of the ball as he is attempting to tuck it back towards his body.[2]

Needless to say, given the speed at which quarterbacks throw the ball, the referees can only catch this in slow motion, therefore only during formal reviews of plays . . . tricky! And even in slow motion, what if the arm only moved imperceptibly forward before a tackle or a sack? And let's not forget the hapless spectators, freezing in the stands of old Foxboro Stadium, without a clue of what the final decision would be, patiently waiting long minutes until the referee delivered the verdict. This was not a game for those enjoying continuous action on the field, or for those who like simplicity and clarity.

But perhaps this was one exceptional moment: a controversial application of a single rule, now obsolete anyways, with NFL games today enjoying clear and transparent officiating through straightforward rules everyone gets?

Let's move forward in time to the fall of 2015, Monday Night Football, October 5. The game between the hosts Seattle Seahawks and visiting Detroit Lions has a nationwide audience, glued to their TV sets after a hard day's work. Everyone involved – players, refs, and team officials – knows they are on national TV, and they will put their best foot forward, right? Hmm, perhaps not this evening. The match is stingy in terms of points scored: the home team is playing poorly; with two fourth-quarter fumbles by their usually reliable quarterback Russell Wilson, Seattle is nursing a 13–10 lead, but there is a lot of nail biting in the stands. The Lions and their star receiver Calvin Johnson are on the Seattle 11-yard line, poised to deliver the winning touchdown and knockout punch. However, Seattle does not have one of the toughest defenses of the league for nothing. Kam Chancellor, fresh out of a contract dispute with the team, knocks the ball free from Johnson; the ball goes to the end zone, where it is guided back over the line by Seattle's K. J. Wright for a touchback: Seattle's ball on the 20. Wilson and the team will run out the clock and hold on to win.

Game over, and the Lions are 0–4 in what promises to be a miserable season. Everyone outside Detroit goes to bed, unenthused but impressed by the relentlessness of the Seahawks defense.

The next morning, driving to work, many of us listen to our favorite radio sports program, and surprise! All the talking heads are vilifying the "clueless" game officials: "A penalty should have been called, and the ball should have been handed back to Detroit at the Seattle 1." A penalty? Detroit ball? The NFL's very own VP of Officiating, Dean Blandino, is saying the referees erred in that game? What are they talking about? What is this non-call about? It all boils down to this: Seattle's Wright should have been called for deliberately hitting the ball out of the end zone. Well, isn't he supposed to do this? What if he had tried to catch the football, fumbled it, and allowed the Lions to recover and score the winning touchdown? Here it gets complicated. Blandino again: "the back judge was on the play and in his judgment he did not feel it was an overt act so he did not throw the flag." So the refs are supposed to be mind readers, know the player's intent? Wow. Fortunately, we have the TV replays, and there Blandino is sure: "in looking at the replays it looked like a bat so the enforcement would be basically we would go back to the spot of the fumble and Detroit would keep the football."[3]

Excuse me, but this mixture of fast-paced action – ball bouncing everywhere, players trying to save the game, and refs guessing their intent – appears to reach the pinnacle of complexity and opacity. No wonder everyone involved in this Monday night game, including the players, was confused at the time. So much so that no one in Detroit thought of a challenge . . .

Interestingly, this controversy occurred in the same Seattle stadium where, in 2012, replacement officials (the referees having staged a strike, probably thinking that their required mind reading skills were not compensated enough) credited Seattle with a disputed touchdown reception on the final play, which led the home team to beat Green Bay. So perhaps there is something in that Seattle stadium?

Well, no. Another 2015 game played a few weeks later twenty-five hundred miles away also generated its fair share of controversy. In the November 23 game between the Buffalo Bills and the New England Patriots (them again!), the home team emerged the winner, but there was plenty of complaining going around. An inadvertent whistle by one of the officials denied the Patriots a lot of potential yardage. But they won 20–13, so why complain? On the other hand, another strange interpretation of the rules certainly denied Buffalo another play before time expired. And it also invalidated a great play by the Bills' wide receiver Sammy Watkins, who fell backwards in a successful effort to get out of bounds and stop the clock. Head referee Gene Steratore, in another "mind reader" interpretation, declared that Watkins "had given himself up," i.e. gone to the ground making no effort to advance. Giving himself up, uh? What is this, a cops and robbers game?

I could go on and on, since referees, even more so than quarterbacks, are second-guessed every Monday morning after the games on Sunday. However, it is far too easy to pile on the referees: the reality is that the NFL's Rule Book is far too complex, lengthy and obtuse. Constant changes to it add further length and complexity. The league has tried to mitigate this through instant replays, both mandatory ones and coaches' challenges (although here again there is a fair amount of opacity about which plays are reviewable and challengeable), and many more actions to help the officiating of the game be as fair as possible. Alas, to no avail, and at the cost of so many interruptions to the game that we spectators are lucky if we get to see one or two plays per minute. To get maximum fairness and zero referee error, perhaps we should have replays at will, for any play – but then the games would last eight, ten hours … not the way to go.

The complexity of the game and its rules is clearly the root cause of these issues: after all, if players and referees alike often get confused about plays and their interpretations, it cannot be that they all are incompetent. Something else must be at play. This something else is the inherent complexity of the game, which confounds so frequently very smart human beings and extraordinarily accomplished athletes. To again illustrate this complexity, let's just look at a tiny portion of the 240-page plus 2017 NFL Rule Book[4] and review the rule that governs a successful completed pass, arguably the most basic and fundamental play of the game:

Rule 8, Section 1, Article 3. **Completed or Intercepted Pass**.

A player who makes a catch may advance the ball. A forward pass is complete (by the offense) or intercepted (by the defense) if a player, who is inbounds:

(a) **secures** control of the ball in his hands or arms prior to the ball touching the ground; and

(b) **touches** the ground inbounds with both feet or with any part of his body other than his hands; and

(c) **maintains** control of the ball after (a) and (b) have been fulfilled, until he has **the ball long enough to** clearly become a runner. **A player has the ball long enough to become a runner when, after his second foot is on the ground, he is capable of avoiding or warding off impending contact of an opponent, tucking the ball away, turning up field, or taking additional steps** (see 3–2–7-Item 2).

Note: If a player has control of the ball, a slight movement of the ball will not be considered a loss of possession. He must lose control of the ball in order to rule that there has been a loss of possession.

If the player loses the ball while simultaneously touching both feet or any part of his body to the ground, it is not a catch.[5]

Then follow six specific note items (445 more words!) assessing whether passes are complete or incomplete when players go to the ground, in cases of sideline and end zone catches, simultaneous catches, when the ball touches the ground, and when it is carried out of bounds.

As far as clarity is concerned, (a) and (b) just about do it. But (c) and the first note bring us into the realm of subjectivity: "long enough" or "a slight movement of the ball?" These could be interpreted in a number of ways, and unfortunately are, Sunday after Sunday, with similar actions being ruled as a completed pass in one game and an incompletion in another. This is not for lack of trying from the NFL, which is constantly tightening up rules and closing "loopholes," even at the cost of lengthy notes and increased complexity. For example, in an earlier version of the Rule Book, (c) above used to be:

> **maintains** control of the ball after (a) and (b) have been fulfilled, to enable him to perform **any act common to the game** (i.e. maintaining control long enough to pitch it, pass it, advance with it, or avoid or ward off an opponent, etc.).

"Any act common to the game?" Very subjective. And the use of "etc." indicated looseness in the rule, leading inevitably to varying interpretations, a lot of ambiguity, and a ton of post-game discussions.[6,7]

Now, a very complex game does not mean one that cannot be enjoyed, embraced, and adored by legions of fans. Even immigrants like me eventually get the bug.

I landed in Berkeley in the fall of 1979 to study for a MS in Transportation Engineering at the University of California, financed through a Fulbright-type fellowship. I was fortunate enough to find two great roommates, Bill and Steve. Steve took it upon himself to educate me about all things American, Californian, and from the Bay Area. And, of course, given our ages (Steve was studying for his PhD in economics at the time), sports loomed large. Here is Steve talking about global sports, way before "globalization" hit the world:

> In the U.S., sports are all about arms; baseball, basketball, tennis, even our American football, are all about arm speed, strength and accuracy. You come from Europe and South America, and there it is all about legs; football, bicycling, skiing.

Indeed. Steve and Bill humiliated me at tennis all fall, but on the ski slopes of Squaw Valley it was me who showed them the way home.

Steve was very keen to introduce me to football, and on a glorious day invited me to join him at the celebrated Cal–Stanford college football game. What a day! The crowds were widely cheerful. Who would not be enthusiastic about a team called the Golden Bears? Of course we rooted for Cal, and we duly won 21–14. Five touchdowns, the scoring all arms and hands. That is pretty much all I remember about the game itself. All the incessant talking on the field (the "huddles"); the lightening quick strikes impossible for me to observe and understand from the stands; the many interruptions; the ball hidden from sight (at least for me); most of the time, I just could not follow the action.

Over time, though, as I settled in San Francisco in 1985, Bill Walsh's genius; Joe Montana's cool and poise; and Jerry Rice's athleticism did what Steve's proselytism could not: get me hooked on American football and the extraordinary San Francisco 49ers. I even remember, during a late January 1995 business trip to Europe, watching their last Super Bowl victory at a bar in the wee hours in the morning: the 49ers' 49–26 demolition of the San Diego Chargers that day ended around 4am in Europe, but I was there, cheering the team with a small group of fellow American business travelers. And today I still watch pretty much all the games of the 49ers, no matter how well or poorly they play. Hearing radio hosts talking about the Sunday game on Monday is a mandatory activity. And I still need the help of the commentators! Many plays still befuddle me, but the TV and radio talking heads are all at hand to deconstruct these plays in bite-sized chunks that even I can understand. It is actually quite enjoyable hearing them all calmly (sometimes not) explain very sophisticated actions in a way that suddenly makes them appear quite clear and logical. Complexity does not deter the fan. On the contrary, it makes Monday morning quarterbacking even more enjoyable.

★   ★   ★   ★   ★

The fan base most knowledgeable in statistics

My roommate Steve did not give up. Even though I had enjoyed being at the stadium for the Cal–Stanford game, it was clear to him that this did not translate into any lasting NFL or college football interest on my part, at least then. So on to major league baseball. In a sunny day of April 1980, Steve got tickets to the Oakland Coliseum to go watch the Oakland Athletics, or simply, the A's. Steve gave me a lot of prep: the 1979 season had been terrible, with 54 wins to 108 losses, and the A's had finished dead last (7th) in the American League West. This was their worst season since moving to Oakland from Philadelphia in 1968. But things were looking up: we had a charismatic, very bright if eccentric manager, Billy Martin. The team played a fast-paced game, called "Billy Ball," full of stolen bases by a young rookie who had made his debut in that abysmal 1979 season, Rickey Henderson. Steve was confident the A's would have a winning season (they did, 83–79, finishing second in the AL West, just behind the World Series–bound Kansas City Royals). Steve also explained to me the crucial role of the starting pitchers, and ours were very good: Rick Langford, Mike Norris, Matt Keough, Steve McCatty, and Brian Kingman. We were going to play our arch nemesis of the West, the California Angels, from Anaheim in Orange County.

The game is a very pleasant experience. Very few players are on the field at a given time. The format is a bit like a sort of collective tennis, in the "serve and return" sense with, at least at the beginning of the inning, a lone batter facing the opposing team pitcher. Nine athletes, looking like normal folks except for their helmets, all neatly spaced and organized in geometric fashion in the field. The noise is remarkable, the loud crack of those amazingly narrow bats hitting the ball, the "pop" made by the huge gloves swallowing the same ball – what amazing hand–eye coordination all these players have! There is plenty of time between plays; the sun is out; we can chat about lots of things other than the game. The whole thing is a great social experience. The A's win 8–2; the crowd, which is much gentler and more family-like than the college football one, applauds regularly and sometimes even roars, but not too frequently. Steve tells me that this was a very good game, with a higher than usual number of runs, and asks me again if I understood that a run is scored when a batter/ runner gets back to the home "base" after having passed bases one, two, and three. Home runs score everyone that was on base at the time. I think I get this too. So far so good.

Things get definitely more difficult when I try the next day to read the report of the game in the newspaper delivered every morning at our door, the *San Francisco Chronicle*. The A's win is duly mentioned on the top right of the first page. I turn to the Sporting Green section: a couple of editorials, all in English. I turn to page 4 and . . . what is this? Apart from the result of the game and the headline "A's beat Angels 8–2," and a few lines of text, the page is black with numbers. It looks to me like a cross between Mendeleev's Periodical table of Chemical Elements and one of the logarithmic tables I used in high school math. Is this for real? C'mon, I am studying for my MS at Berkeley, and I vow I'll be able to understand this sports page of the newspaper! After a good hour of hard work, this is what I surmise: in the game, there are pitchers, catchers, infielders, outfielders, and batters. Catchers, infielders, and outfielders also get to go at bat. Batters are individually assessed on games played, "at bats," "batting average," "home runs," "RBIs (?)," "hits," and "on-base percentage"; fielders on "fielding percentage," "double plays (?)," "errors," "total chances," and "outfield assists"; pitchers on games pitched, innings pitched, "ERAs (?)," wins, "waves," "WHIP (?)," and "strikeouts." So, when you multiplex all these categories by the individual players in each position, with fielders getting assessed as batters as well, and you add the whole team statistics, which are almost the same categories except for runs scored, this does add up to a lot of numbers! OK, I think I got the hang of it. I proudly share my understanding with Steve, and also ask him about the RBI, ERA, and WHIP acronyms, which remind me of aviation navigation letter combos.

The answers are, respectively, runs batted in, earned run average, and walks plus hits per inning pitched; that last one is a math formula in itself. He points out that I missed two acronyms, WAR (wins above replacement) and FIP (fielding independent pitching). I am not sure these words make much more sense to me than the acronyms – in the case of the last two, they certainly do not – but I believe I have bothered Steve enough with my ignorance. Never mind, he is launched:

> In the National League, you know, the one that has the San Francisco Giants across the Bay, the pitchers get to bat as well; you forgot to mention the important stat on stolen bases, Rickey Henderson is a leader in this; you did not see a "double play" at the Oakland game, here is how it works, amazing isn't it? Perhaps they will show one on the TV highlights this evening; there are also "triple plays" which are very rare. There is a lot of strategy in determining the batting order; who gets to bat against a given pitcher; the manager (Billy Martin) thinks very hard about that. He may determine for example it is time for a pitcher deliberately to walk a batter, to prevent an RBI or worse, a home run.

Well, new questions arise. What would happen if the A's played the Giants? Would the A's pitcher have to go at bat? Does Billy Martin have to memorize all these stats, and more, to be an effective manager? And when Steve uses the word "strategy," is this a polite way to mention "things you would not understand anyways?" I think it is reasonable to leave it for another day; with a fresher mind I might get more of this complicated game. Fascinating, though, the way anyone who opens the sports section of the local newspaper is transformed into an expert in statistics. For sure, other team sports fans cannot hold a candle to the baseball fans here with their amazing analytical sophistication![8]

Over the years, baseball has managed to retain quite a bit of this statistical mystery to me. The Oakland A's were quite successful around the times the 49ers were, with three consecutive appearances in the World Series from 1988 to 1990, and one memorable win against the Giants in 1989, unfortunately shadowed by the Loma Pieta earthquake (in what other sport can we say that "when our two Bay Area teams met for the finals, the earth shook, literally!"). But I could never consider myself a fan. Many things are admirable about the game, and the A's: the talent and skills required are obviously of the highest order. I assume this is why professional major leaguers go through a much longer apprenticeship than in almost any other sport. And the players tend to look like the male crowd out of the 8 o' clock movie: compared to them, most basketball and NFL players look completely outsized, quasi extra-terrestrial. The A's obviously are amazing at growing their talent in-house, year after year, so they can compete successfully at the highest level with one of the lowest budgets in the majors. This is admirable, something that few sports teams manage to emulate.

One has to be really close to the action, first few rows of the stadium, to appreciate the insane speeds at which the plays take place. On TV, it looks like slow motion, not nearly as impressive as it should be. But the games take forever, with continuous action measured in seconds, while the interruptions take many minutes. Not to mention that with rules not allowing ties, games can go on and on beyond the regulation nine innings. I heard of a 1984 game in the majors that played on for twenty-five innings over eight hours and two days! Too much of a good thing ruins it. So, one must undertake another occupation while the game is on. If I want to "watch" a game, I prefer to listen to it on the radio, while driving for example: then the sporting event doubles up as a wonderful English lesson in what I perceive is New York–type American; and the radio announcers appear to keep impressively calm, the "here comes the pitch" having the same tone as the Oakland airport tower FAA controller saying, "Skyhawk Tango Papa, clear to land, two eight right." As I stayed longer in the Bay Area, and became a proud American citizen in 1993, I became clearly able to hold my own in football small talk, but not in baseball: I never invested enough time in the required players and team statistics.

The key question about statistics and baseball is, does one need deep and detailed statistics to really understand the game, or do many fans feel the game is too boring to watch in itself without the added complexity of statistics? In the first instance, statistics support the game and help the fan become more knowledgeable in a sport he or she already enjoys. In the second instance, a whole new generation of fans might have emerged in which the enjoyment is generated not by the game itself, but by the combination of the sport and the statistics that describe it in painstaking, step-by-step analysis. These fans might parallel those for whom the most important thing of the weekend is to win at fantasy football, never mind if achieving the win requires the team one is supporting to lose. Sports fans have left. Statisticians; gamblers trying to find strategies to "defeat the house"; and fantasy players compiling individual player scores have replaced them. Perhaps this can help explain why the average baseball fan actually going to the stadium is getting older: over 45 years of age in 2015.[9]

In essence, we started as fans of a complex sport: a baseball game unfolds in a series of discrete steps, one-on-one duels between pitcher and batter, then one-on-one races between batters who made contact with the ball and fielders. Each discrete action, or duel, leads to an outcome. Those outcomes can easily be aggregated into statistics. And then the intellectual challenge of deciphering the game through these statistics may become more stimulating, more enjoying than simply admiring the elegant motion of a pitcher throwing the ball; or the lightening quick reflex and brute strength of a batter cracking a home run; or the amazing over the fence defender catch that prevents said home run. We have come full circle. Our love of a complex sport has led to the love of complex statistics, with the game merely there to support our forecasts and analyses. The numbers have become an end in themselves. Statistics have graduated from a complement to the game to its substitute.[10]

Interestingly, it is not clear to me that this enhanced importance of statistics affects the professionals of the game as much as the fans or would be fans. The super star general manager of the A's, Billy Bean, pioneered the use of statistics in his trading of players, bringing economics to the game.[11] This is one of the key tools he used to make the small-budget A's a frequent contender. However, this took place in the late 1980s and early 1990s, and now pretty much every good general manager of a major league baseball team employs similar quantitative methods. As a result, the A's are not as competitive today (yet one more losing season!) as they used to be. The use of players stats to "buy" or "sell" professional players in and out of a team has also moved beyond baseball to all ball games: American football, basketball, cricket, ice hockey, and soccer. So, the differentiated impact of statistics on baseball in the twenty-first century, relative to other sports, is not what it was in the couple of decades that led to it.

Similarly, the coaches or managers of baseball teams appear (generally) to be proud of remaining keen observers of the specific actions on the field at a given time, and to react to game challenges based more on their experience than deep statistical analyses. Bruce Bochy, the manager of World Series 2010, 2012, and 2014 champions the San Francisco Giants, has described statistics as a usual support tool, but nothing more.[12] And the players, of course, although very aware of the statistically defined performance of the pitcher or the batter they are facing, aim always to disrupt the statistically predicted outcome through anticipation, improvisation, instinct, and reflex.

So it is us, the public at large, who appear to enjoy being so immersed in stats that the sporting action on the field plays second fiddle to our interest.[13] I do find it fascinating that baseball, the sport that dominated America's psyche in the 1950s and 1960s (after all, Marilyn Monroe married Joe Di Maggio), has now come full circle to become a pastime supporting our craving for things complex, things that demand powerful analytical tools to understand and enjoy them.

$$\star \quad \star \quad \star \quad \star \quad \star$$

The sport the rest of the world watches

It is a night match in Rio de Janeiro, and the Mário Filho "Maracanã" Stadium, the largest in the world, is full. A friend of my father's has taken me to the Maracanã to watch the game between Santos and Vasco da Gama, along with over 100,000 other spectators. The match is scheduled between 9:15 pm and 11:00 pm, and I will get back home late. Today, November 19, is Brazil's National Flag Day, and there is no school, but there will be tomorrow. Why would my (very) responsible parents accept this late night for their 12-year-old? Because tonight, Edson Arantes do Nascimento – Pelé, as he is known everywhere – might score his thousandth goal. Here, in Rio.

Pelé usually scores every game, sometimes more than once, but with his personal tally at 999 he failed to do so in a game in Salvador three days ago. Now he and his world championship club winning team of Santos have come to us to play a Rio–São Paulo tournament game against locals Vasco da Gama. Even though they are visiting, Santos is the heavily favored side, but Andrade, the Vasco Argentinean goalkeeper, is the best one playing in Brazil. A cross towards Pelé's head in front of the goal – he is about to score! No, a Vasco defender beats him to the punch and scores . . . against his own side. Anything but let Pelé achieve his landmark against the local team.

Then, a clear foul in the box – penalty! Pelé places the ball on the penalty mark, takes a few steps back. Now it is he, the ball, and Andrade. A run, a small feint, a powerful shoot to the right, Andrade in a desperate lunge; his fingers touch the ball, but destiny overwhelms, the net trembles, and gooooooooal!!!

The pitch is invaded by hundreds of journalists, players, managers, officials. Pelé is crying; he says something about the need to educate and care for poor children in Brazil, everywhere – he is clearly choking on his tears. The game is interrupted for half an hour; I arrive home past midnight but have witnessed history. I will keep the *Globo* and *Jornal do Brasil* newspapers of the next days for years. In one of them, a journalist estimated that more people in Brazil watched the event on their black-and-white TVs than watched Neil Armstrong's walk on the moon four months earlier.

Today, Pelé is 77 and still the King of Soccer. His achievements are unsurpassed: 1,281 goals scored in 1,363 matches, three World Cups with Brazil (out of five wins for the country over a 44-year span), seventy-seven goals scored for the "Seleção," the Brazilian National Team, and seven "Golden Ball" awards. He started as a poor child, shining shoes to supplement his meager income as a young professional, but achieved instant fame at 17 by winning Brazil's first World Cup in 1958 in Sweden. Not only his magic touch with the ball, but also his natural talent, leadership on the field, and athleticism have made him synonymous with football, as the rest of the world calls soccer.[14]

Pelé reached his peak form at age 30, for the 1970 World Cup in Mexico, which his Brazilian team dominated. Many say that the Brazilian starting eleven (Felix; Carlos Alberto; Brito; Piazza; Everaldo; Clodoaldo; Gerson; Jairzinho; Tostão; Pelé; and Rivelino) was the finest to ever play the game. It is good to remember that at the time, Pelé's relentless focus on exercise and conditioning was new in soccer. One of his great 1970 Brazil teammates was a chain smoker (Gerson famously quipped, "I do not have to run, the ball does"), and so were others in many squads worldwide. This athleticism allowed Pelé to score Brazil's first goal in the 4–1 final over Italy: a cross came, and 5'8" Pelé jumped a good head higher than the 6'1" Italian defender Fachetti. In another tournament, Pelé also scored a perfect "bicycle" goal, his whole body horizontal in the air, back parallel to the ground and scoring leg delivering the winning kick at a 90- degree angle. A photo of that shot and his thousandth goal were children's favorite bedroom wall posters at the time.

Pelé also has natural charm, is excellent with the media, and during the Fernando Henrique Cardoso presidency courageously took on the fight against soccer corruption in Brazil as minister of sports.

In the galaxy of soccer stars, there is only one king, but many princes. In chronological order: Ferenc Puskas (514 goals in 529 matches); Eusébio (the "Black Pearl"); Lev Yashin (the "Black Spider"); Sir Bobby Charlton; Johan Cruyff (the recently deceased and much regretted pioneer of "Total Football," with the Ajax Amsterdam, Holland, and Barcelona teams); Franz Beckenbauer (the "Kaiser"); Diego Maradona ("El Pibe de Oro," or "Golden Boy"); Romario ("O Baixinho," or "Shorty," today a popular Brazil senator leading the fight against the corruption of soccer administrators in Brazil); more recently, Zinedine Zidane, Ronaldinho; Park-Ji-Sung; Andrea Pirlo; Diego Forlan; and today Iniesta; Messi; Neymar; Ronaldo; and Suarez. These were and are magnificent players, all of them reaching at least one World Cup semi-final. Many were the best of their generation, but Pelé still reigns supreme. Wait a second, though: I just rattled off what, eighteen names, and they represent almost as many different countries! Argentina; Brazil; England; France; Germany; Holland; Hungary; Italy; Mozambique; Portugal; Russia; South Korea; Spain; and Uruguay.[15]

Soccer is truly a universal sport. Just think of the audiences: the most recent World Cup final, Germany 1–0 over Argentina, attracted one billion viewers in the summer of 2014. This is more than the 900 million people who watched the 2012 London Olympics opening ceremony. In Germany, an all-time high of forty-two million tuned in to watch their national team win their fourth World Cup, or a whopping 86% share of the national audience. An additional twelve million Germans cheered the game in public spaces. For reference, compare these figures with the 167 million people who watched the New England–Seattle Super Bowl in 2015, or with the 49.6 million people who saw the sixth and last match of the 1980 Philadelphia–Kansas City World Series, the highest viewership for a World Series game. One very negative aspect of soccer popularity is that these enormous audiences lead to gigantic TV broadcasting rights, and the billions of dollars involved attract corruption. Far too often the sport's administrators are lining their pockets at the local, regional, and global level. At the top, the Fédération Internationale de Football Association, better known as FIFA, has been engulfed in quite a few scandals. The most recent one led to the 2015 resignation of its long-serving president, Sepp Blatter (currently serving a six-year ban from FIFA activities), and the arrest of many soccer officials from around the world, including from Brazil. Many cases of alleged vote buying to secure the rights for the World Cup are still being investigated, with middlemen and senior sports figures accused of siphoning tens of millions of dollars.

Nevertheless, billions continue to watch the sport. Why is soccer so popular? Mostly because it is a game that can be played by anyone, anywhere, with rules that are simple to understand. Any group of two or more children or adults, male or female, can kick a ball on any piece of grass, dirt, or pavement at any time. If a proper grass field is not available, a street corner can do. Or a basketball court: aiming to score just by having the ball touch the vertical post holding the basket will hone your kicking precision. Or a tennis court (preferably without a net) – and so forth. Goal posts can be substituted by a pair of stones, or shoes . . .

Soccer's basic rules are as follows. Players kick the ball with their feet (this is why the sport is called football) or any part of their body except their hands and arms. Goalkeepers can use their hands and arms within an area designated as the "box." The objective is to score by having the ball clear the line between two goal posts, and a transversal bar above them connecting the two. If a player causes the ball to cross one of the sidelines, it is a hand throw by the opposing team. If the same occurs on the lines parallel to the goal posts, it is a corner kick or a goal kick. Violent play is discouraged by free kicks, penalty kicks inside the box, warnings, or expulsions (yellow and red cards). The match is played through two 45-minute halves. Continuous play is encouraged, and one of the few FIFA metrics is that the ball should be running for at least 65% of the time on the clock. The only rule that requires some practice is the "off side" rule, designed to prevent a player from standing alone in front of the opposite team's goalkeeper to take advantage of a long pass, with little possibility of defense: when a pass is made forward by the team on the offense, there should be at least one defense player between the most forward player of the offense and the goalkeeper at the time the ball is passed. This off side rule is the source of most soccer controversies around officiating. What may be clearly seen on TV with modern graphics (showing the virtual "off side line of defense") is less obvious to the three officials on the field, or even the fourth one at hand to help with challenging calls. And so, on occasion, goals are scored with a player off side, and legitimate goals can be ruled out even though no attacker was off side.

Penalty kicks can also generate issues (was it a foul? Was it not? Did it take place inside the box?). And since a penalty results in a goal scored about 75% of the time, there are constant calls for the setting up of instant replays. FIFA and most countries' soccer officials tend to be against instant replays, though, because they would rather have a fluid and uninterrupted game and a few referee errors here and there than the opposite. "Errare humanum est," and soccer is life at its most human.

Recent concessions by FIFA to modern technology are soon-to-be-installed goal sensors, to detect whether the ball has cleared the line completely, and the use of video replays to review critical plays such as penalty kicks. The line clearance technology already exists and has proven itself in tennis, in tournament after tournament. In soccer, it was piloted for the first time at the 2016 end-of-year FIFA Club World Cup in Tokyo (won 4–2 by Ronaldo and Zidane's Real Madrid against a heroic side of Kashima from Japan). The video replays, which were also available in Tokyo for the first time, taxed the patience of the worldwide soccer audience, which was not used to waiting several minutes for a verdict like in the NFL: in one such application, a penalty kick not initially signaled was awarded to Kashima in its 3–0 semi-final victory against Latin American champions National of Colombia, but there were lots of complaints about the stoppage time due to the video review. Still, in the end most agreed the penalty was fairly awarded.

Although neither mistakes in the application of the off-side rule nor awards of penalty kicks have marred a World Cup final, there have been at least a few goal line controversies. The World Cup finals represent the Holy Grail of soccer. After all, only eight countries have won the World Cup, which is played every four years by thirty-two qualified countries, the first having taken place in 1930. The English, inventors of the sport, have only one World Cup win to their credit, in the 1966 edition they organized. The final took place at the newly built Wembley stadium in London, packed with 96,000 fans and watched on TV by thirty-two million in England alone. After England and Germany were tied two apiece in regulation time, England won 4–2 in the 30-minute overtime. In overtime, players are exhausted, nerves are frayed, and scoring the first goal can determine the outcome. And most observers agree, with the "help" of 1960s' TV and camera technology, that the first English overtime goal awarded did not cross the German goal line . . . History, though, gave some payback to the German side: during the 2010 World Cup in South Africa, England faced Germany in a playoff game in the round of sixteen, and the English side had a 2–2 tying goal by Frank Lampard disallowed, even though it appeared on TV to have crossed the line by at least a foot. Germany went on to win 4–1, eliminating England from the tournament. More recently, the tying goal scored by Panama during its 2–1 victory against Costa Rica on October 10, 2017, clearly did not pass the goal line. This glaring error from the referee officiating the match had consequences. A good one for the small Central American nation of Panama, which qualified for the World Cup for the first time in its soccer history; and a disastrous one for team USA, which was knocked out of the competition and thus failed to reach the World Cup tournament for the first time since 1986. Our national squad had lost 1–2 its last qualifying game in Trinidad and Tobago against the local national team the same day, at the same time, and depended on either Honduras not beating Mexico or Panama not defeating Costa Rica to advance, neither of which occurred. Until the 88th minute of the second half of the game, two minutes before the end of regulation time, when the second Panama goal was scored, the U.S. was qualified. Lots of uncertainty and last-minute suspense in soccer! The next day, FIFA president Gianni Infantino declared that video technology had become inevitable, and that he hoped it would be used in the upcoming 2018 World Cup in Russia.

PS: Team USA is in good company. Two soccer powerhouses will not be going to Russia, either: the Netherlands, which finished third in the last World Cup in Brazil; and four-time champions Italy, eliminated for the first time since 1958.[16]

("Apocalisse!") We will not be the only national team in need of a rebuilding effort . . .

Soccer officials have elected over the years to keep the game rules almost intact, and the game continuous with as few interruptions as possible, at the potential cost of error-prone officiating. This may change the day after a World Cup is awarded on a mistaken penalty call, but thus far the "beautiful game" continues to enchant crowds worldwide. It even appears to be one of China President Xi Jinping's "strategic priorities", with a couple of soccer divisions created and lots of Argentinean, Brazilian, European, and other foreign players and coaches lured with fat contracts. Of the world's largest countries, only India has not embraced soccer in a significant way (it is cricket country), although a professional league was recently created there, and a successful under-17 World Cup was organized very well by the country in October of 2017. Zico, one of Brazil's brightest stars in the 1980s, is coaching a team in India, after having coached several Middle East teams and the Japanese national team.

In contrast, cricket (England and countries of the former British empire); rugby (New Zealand, Australia, Oceania; South Africa; parts of Europe; Argentina; Japan); ice hockey (North America; Russia; Scandinavia; Central Europe); American football (North America); and baseball (North and Central America; the Caribbean; Japan and Korea) are regional sports on the world stage. One main reason for these sports lacking a global followership is complexity. Complexity in the line-ups (three different formations, offense, defense, and special teams in American football); the non-continuing-action; the required protection equipment to play the game to its fullest; a field that has to be purpose-built; and the bewildering complexity of rules.[17]

There is one major American sport with a truly global audience, though: basketball. Like soccer, the action is non-stop – well, almost, if timeouts and a variety of scheduled interruptions (principally in the fourth quarter) are not taken into account. The game is simple and straightforward to understand. It can be played on any courtyard, the "basket" being easy to install. So, there should be no surprise that basketball has universal appeal, too. In many countries, it is the only ballgame, apart from soccer, watched by large numbers of people. Every day when I look at the websites of *Globoesporte* in Brazil and *l'Equipe* in France (a daily sports newspaper – what a cool idea. We should have one here, too), amidst an avalanche of soccer news there are always all the NBA scores from the day before. I also enjoy on these international sites many articles about current basketball greats: the 2015 and 2017 NBA champions Golden State Warriors' Stephen Curry (compared to ballet great Mikhail Baryshnikov in a November 24, 2015 front page *New York Times* article, amazing); LeBron James and his Cleveland Cavaliers defying all odds to beat the Warriors for the 2016 championship in a game seven played at the Oakland Coliseum; Kevin Durant, playing with Curry and the Warriors to win the 2017 title and bring the NBA championship back to the Bay Area; Kobe Bryant before his recent retirement; Tim Duncan; James Harden; Klay Thompson; and so many other great players. *L'Equipe* also follows with great attention the French NBA players Tony Parker, Alexis Ajinca, Nicolas Batum, Boris Diaw, Evan Fournier, Rudy Gobert, Joffrey Lauvergne, Joakim Noah, and Kevin Seraphin.

★　★　★　★　★

Sports are an inherent part of our culture, complex or not

We in America embrace complex sports like American football and baseball. Why this attraction to complexity? Let's go through a few hypotheses to try to understand.

First, do complex sports allow us to see superlative athletes? Well, yes, American football players have amazing skills, successfully marrying physical contradictions like very large body size and astonishing running and throwing speed with lethal accuracy. I use the word lethal because I have often heard American football compared to the U.S. Army in its successful 1991 Iraq invasion, both relying upon meticulous planning, followed by the application of brute force.

Baseball players possess such a high level of proficiency that the difference between a great batter and one who is merely good is only one base hit every four or five games. And pitching! Catapulting a ball at up to 100 mph about 50 feet away towards an area little larger than a pillow cover is an amazing sporting feat, repeated dozens of times every game.

But basketball and soccer players also have extraordinary talents. When teammates at powerhouse Real Madrid, soccer legends Zidane, Ronaldinho, Figo, and Roberto Carlos (the "Galacticos") used to enjoy playing volleyball ... with their feet. This finesse did not prevent Roberto Carlos from being able to hurl the ball at over 80 mph in free kicks.

Superlative athletes are not the preserve of complex games, clearly. Even outside sports, this can be confirmed by looking at chess and the Chinese game of Go: both have exceedingly simple rules, yet chess Grand Masters and Go experts define outsized brain power.

Second, do complex sports allow teams to be more efficient or effective? After all, we pride ourselves in outperforming the world in such different areas as business, the economy, and the military. Do our sports teams transcend the individual players' abilities? I turn here to the columnist David Brooks, who wrote in a *New York Times* op-ed on July 10, 2014:[18]

> Is life more like baseball, or is it more like soccer?
>
> Baseball is a team sport, but it is basically an accumulation of individual activities. Throwing a strike, hitting a line drive or fielding a grounder is primarily an individual achievement. The team that performs the most individual tasks well will probably win the game.
>
> Soccer is not like that. In soccer, almost no task, except the penalty kick and a few others, is intrinsically individual. Soccer ... is a game about occupying and controlling space. If you get the ball and your teammates have run the right formations, and structured the space around you, you'll have three or four options on where to distribute it. If the defenders have structured their formations to control the space, then you will have no options. Even the act of touching the ball is not primarily defined by the man who is touching it; it is defined by the context created by all the other players.

David Brooks makes a fascinating parallel between soccer and modern life, where the "decisions (we make) are shaped by the networks of people around us more than we dare recognize." But in doing so, he also offers an arithmetic definition of sports: baseball is the sum of its parts (players); soccer, when played by a team that knows how to create open spaces, is more than the sum of its parts. In other words, soccer teams can create more collective effectiveness than baseball teams.

Third, do we enjoy American football or baseball because we (the amateurs, not the pros) are better at it? Back to David Brooks, in a dialogue with other commenters about his July 10, 2014 column:

> I stand by my subjective judgment that soccer is a logarithmic sport while baseball is an exponential one — that is, you can take up soccer and play at

a totally fun level right away but baseball has skills that are harder to master up front.

Fourth, do we like our national sports because they define us? Can we individually relate more to an NFL or baseball pro than to a soccer player? No, and here again David Brooks, in the conclusion of his July 10 op-ed, provides an elegant response:

> Once we acknowledge that, in life, we are playing soccer, not baseball, a few things become clear. First, awareness of the landscape of reality is the highest form of wisdom. It's not raw computational power that matters most; it's having a sensitive attunement to the wildest environment, feeling where the flow of events is going. Genius is in practice perceiving more than the conscious reasoning.
>
> Second, predictive models will be less useful. Baseball is wonderful for sabermetricians. In each at bat there is a limited range of possible outcomes. Activities like soccer are not as easily renderable statistically, because the relevant spatial structures are harder to quantify ... soccer is like a 90-minute anxiety dream – one of those frustrating dreams when you're trying to get somewhere but something is always in the way. This is yet another way soccer is like life.[19,20]

If rational factors cannot explain the passion we have for our national sports very well, what does? I believe sports are part of our culture, learned and nurtured since our childhood years. Just like our tastes in food. It is just as futile to try to rationalize why we prefer to watch college football and the NFL on weekends rather than soccer matches as it is to explain why we prefer certain types of food relative to others. From a young age, Americans are immersed in these very complex sports, just as other people (Hungarian and Finnish children come to mind) have to learn a very complex language in their early years.

Complexity in sports also brings benefits, and few collateral costs: no one has ever produced a top-rated movie about soccer. *Field of Dreams*; *Jerry Maguire*; and *The Draft* are just a few of the many Hollywood productions that immortalize our sports. Our sports create good literature, too: for example, Michael Lewis is enormously gifted at explaining complicated phenomena that few people understand. And what did he write about? Modern finance (*Liar's Poker*; *The Big Short*); baseball (*Moneyball*); and American football (*The Blind Side*).

Complexity allows a myriad of television and radio commenters to entertain us all day long, any day of the week. This multiplies the impact of the actual games and prolongs it from the weekend to the whole week. Who can stand our freeway traffic jams without our favorite radio hosts telling us "like it is" about our local team quarterback; the wide receivers; tight ends; offensive linesmen; cornerbacks; and defensive players? I cheer with them after our team has won and laugh with them at stupid team management, owners, or coaches when we lose ...

And all of this is great for our economy. These activities, involving many highly compensated participants, can never be outsourced.

Costs? Not much, really. While traveling outside the U.S., unless raised abroad, we are not going to be able to indulge in small talk about sports like at home. However, small talk is a quintessential American habit. Abroad, business is conducted more formally. No great handicap here.

It used to be that when outside the country, keeping informed about the home teams was a challenge. What is the point of getting the score of a key game a day or two later, without any comment on how the action on the field unfolded? With the advent of the internet, sports websites and the like, this is no longer an issue.

Yes, as long as soccer is not a top professional sport here we are unlikely to enjoy the thrill and angst of having our national team face another country in a World Cup final watched by a billion people. So what? We cannot miss what we have never experienced. Defeating the Soviets for a gold ice hockey medal and having our basketball dream team roll over the opposition at the Olympics did give us a taste of being all united behind our national team, so we know what patriotic fervor in sports is.

Sports complexity is in our American genes. This makes us different and unique relative to the rest of the world. But we are not any worse for it. Far from it – we enjoy our sports with passion and feel sorry for the rest of the world. Who needs soccer when we have football, baseball, and basketball?

What is the bottom line from all of this? It could be that we like complexity in sports like we enjoy puzzles. Puzzles are fun when there is little at stake. Would we find it so much fun if we had to decipher such puzzles to obtain quality health care? Or pollution-free, reliable electricity? Or financial security? Read on . . .

2 Health care

Are health care costs spiraling out of control in developed economies?

Dalian, China, September 2013. This busy northeastern Chinese port, facing South Korea, exudes confidence. Dozens of sparkling glass and concrete towers populate downtown, and the 200-mph high-speed rail line from the large Manchurian towns of Harbin and Shenyang has just reached the city. There is now an airport-style futuristic bullet train station, in addition to the stately traditional one. Yet Dalian is also a very livable city, proud of its nineteenth-century heritage (Dalian used to be the Russian city Port Arthur) of large squares, tree-lined avenues, and beautiful parks. There is even a historical tramway line downtown, very popular with locals and visitors alike. The many pedestrian streets are bustling with shoppers and restaurant goers. Seafood is fabulous in Dalian, times are good, and the future looks even better.

The brand new, beautifully architected conference center is hosting the "Annual Meeting of the New Champions," the title for the September gathering of the World Economic Forum (WEF), of Davos fame. This summit, also known as "Summer Davos," alternates every year between Tianjin, the gigantic port city near Beijing, and Dalian. In the quiet of a large room inside the conference center, two dozen health care executives from all over the world exchange ideas and experiences. These are busy people, used to spending time in windowless conference rooms. Before the serious conversations start, there is small talk, covering Dalian, the beauty of its peninsula and mountainous site, and the clean air from the maritime environment. After breakfast, everyone starts working diligently on the project at hand, the findings of which will be presented next January in Davos, Switzerland, at the WEF's annual flagship event. The executives manage hospitals, health insurance groups, biotechnology, and pharmaceutical companies. There are management consultants to facilitate the proceedings, a couple of NGOs, and health care government officials from many countries.

The main objective of this WEF project is to provide advice to developing countries on their health care systems, in particular how to grow health care coverage of their populations without repeating the mistakes of developed economies. Mistakes . . . what mistakes? Aren't we talking about the United States, Japan, Germany, France, and the United Kingdom, leaders in economic development? Well, yes. But in health care, one major concern in these countries is that health care costs have far outpaced inflation over the last twenty-five years. If these trends continue, the sustainability of these developed health care systems might be in question. It is obviously in the interest of the "Brics" (Brazil, Russia, India, China, and South Africa), as well as countries like Argentina, Colombia, Egypt, Indonesia, Malaysia, Mexico, Nigeria, Thailand, Turkey, and Vietnam, to discover how to grow health care coverage for their citizens more economically.

Let's look at health care costs in developed countries. How do they stack up?

Exhibit 2.1 shows the 2015 health care costs per capita of thirty-five OECD (Organization for Economic Co-Operation and Development) economies, in descending order, using selected data from a comprehensive OECD database. It also shows for each country the health care costs as percentage of GDP, calculated from a small sample of GDP per capita and PPP (current international $) data for the same countries, from the 2015 World Bank International Comparison Program database.[1,2]

Looking at these figures, one notes that for most of these OECD countries (U.S. and tiny Luxemburg excepted), annual health care expenditures as percentage of GDP are relatively similar. They amount to between 6.9% (Israel) and 11.1% (Switzerland) of GDP for countries that spend above $2,500 per capita in annual health care expenditures, or twenty-four out of thirty-five countries listed above. This corresponds to a $2,533–$6,935 range of spending per capita, or a 2.7:1 ratio. If we focus on developed countries with populations over thirty million people, the range is even narrower, from $2,488 (South Korea) to $5,267 (Germany), or a 2.1:1 ratio. In terms of spending as a percentage of GDP, we have a 1.6:1 ratio between Israel and Switzerland, and 1.5:1 between South Korea and Germany, remarkably close.

The clear outlier is the United States: $9,451 per capita in annual health care spent, and a whopping 16.8% of GDP, 53% more than the average for Switzerland, Germany, Sweden, and the Netherlands, the four European countries with the highest health care spending as percentage of GDP. Is there some "statistical error" in these numbers? This is very unlikely. Our very own Centers for Medicare and Medicaid Services (CMS) reported in a study published in *Health Affairs* that health care spending in the U.S. in 2015 reached $3.2 trillion. This represented $9,990 per person, or 17.7% of GDP, both figures higher than the OECD and World Bank figures shown above. In 2016, the CMS official data showed total spending of $3.3 trillion – $10,348 per person or 17.9% of GDP.

Well, perhaps we reap the benefits of this much higher health care spending in better health outcomes for our population? Health outcomes are much more difficult to assess and quantify than actual expenditures, so to get a clear idea we should look at several metrics: the most straightforward one is life expectancy,

1) United States: $9,451 (health care costs represent 16.8% of GDP)
2) Luxemburg: $7,765 (7.5% of GDP)
3) Switzerland: $6,935 (11.1% of GDP)
4) Norway: $6,567 (10.6% of GDP)
5) Netherlands: $5,343 (10.8% of GDP)
6) Germany: $5,267 (11.0% of GDP)
7) Sweden: $5,228 (10.9% of GDP)
8) Ireland: $5,131 (7.5% of GDP)
9) Austria: $5,016 (10.1% of GDP)
10) Denmark: $4,943 (10.1% of GDP)
11) Belgium: $4,611 (10.1% of GDP)
12) Canada: $4,608 (10.4% of GDP)
13) Australia: $4,420 (9.5% of GDP)
14) France: $4,407 (10.7% of GDP)
15) Japan: $4,150 (10.2% of GDP)
16) Iceland: $4,012 (8.4% of GDP)
17) United Kingdom: $4,003 (9.6% of GDP)
18) Finland: $3,984 (9.4% of GDP)
19) New Zealand: $3,590 (9.5% of GDP)
20) Italy: $3,272 (8.8% of GDP)
21) Spain: $3,153 (9.1% of GDP)
22) Slovenia: $2,644 (8.3% of GDP)
23) Portugal: $2,631 (8.9% of GDP)
24) Israel: $2,533 (6.9% of GDP)
25) South Korea: $2,488 (7.2% of GDP)
26) Czech Republic: $2,464 (7.3% of GDP)
27) Greece: $2,245 (8.5% of GDP)
28) Slovak Republic: $2,064 (6.9% of GDP)
29) Hungary: $1,845 (7.0% of GDP)
30) Estonia: $1,824 (6.3% of GDP)
31) Chile: $1,728 (7.3% of GDP)
32) Poland: $1,677 (6.2% of GDP)
33) Latvia: $1,370 (5.5% of GDP)
34) Turkey: $1,064 (4.4% of GDP)
35) Mexico: $1,052 (6.1% of GDP)

Exhibit 2.1 Current total health expenditures per capita, current prices, in purchasing power parity (PPP) dollars, and percentage share of gross domestic product (GDP), for thirty-five OECD countries in 2015

Sources: Organization for Economic Co-Operation and Development; The World Bank.

right? We tend to live well in the U.S. and in OECD countries, so the longer the better.

The World Health Organization (WHO) tabulates life expectancy figures every year for 190 countries, so we have lots of data here. The WHO also produces an annual ranking of the overall effectiveness of national health care systems for the same 190 countries. This ranking includes other key data beyond life expectancy, such as infant mortality; women's deaths in childbirth; low birth weight; chronic lung disease; heart disease; obesity; diabetes; and disease-adjusted life expectancy. And for those who are suspicious of United Nations type statistics, we have very much private sector Bloomberg. According to an article by Kavitha A. Davidson in the *Huffington Post* on August 30, 2013[3] and another by Meg Bryant in *HealthcareDive* on September 30, 2016,[4] Bloomberg has been publishing an annual study ranking a number of countries by "health care efficiency" since 2009. This Bloomberg "index" describes how much "bang for your buck" countries get from their health care expenditures, looking at outcomes following a number of criteria and assessing "efficiency" by comparing the results with the amounts spent per capita on health care for the countries surveyed.

Exhibit 2.2, a small sample from a comprehensive WHO database, shows life expectancy figures in 2015 and ranking of health systems for the same thirty-five OECD countries listed in Exhibit 2.1, in descending order of life expectancy.[5]

What about the Bloomberg results? They show very similar trends in health care spending efficiency. According to the *Huffington Post* article mentioned earlier, Bloomberg researchers used data from the World Bank, International Monetary Fund, WHO, and Hong Kong Department of Health to determine their rankings. The studies considered only countries with a population of at least five million, a life expectancy of at least seventy years, and a GDP per capita of at least $5,000.

Each one of the qualifying countries' health care system was evaluated based upon 1) life expectancy, which accounted for 60% of the ranking; 2) relative per capita cost of health care (as percentage of GDP per capita), which accounted for 30%; and 3) absolute per capita cost of health care (expenditures including preventive services, family planning, nutrition, and emergency aid), which accounted for 10%. Bloomberg gave each country an "efficiency score," with a score of 100 representing a perfect system.

The top three countries in 2013 were Hong Kong; Singapore; and Japan. Four European countries – Italy, Spain, Sweden, and Switzerland – were also within the top ten in the Bloomberg Index. Leading in 2015, just like in 2013, were Hong Kong and Singapore, according to the *HealthcareDive* article mentioned earlier. They had respective life expectancies of 84 and 83 years, and efficiency scores of 89 and 84 out of 100. They were followed in the index by Spain, South Korea, Japan, Italy, and Israel, all countries that fared well in Exhibits 2.1 and 2.2. As one can see, there's not much difference in terms of trends between the Bloomberg studies and the data shown in Exhibits 2.1 and 2.2.

1) Japan: 83.7 years (10th)
2) Switzerland: 83.4 years (20th)
3) Australia: 82.8 years (32nd)
4) Spain: 82.8 years (7th)
5) Iceland: 82.7 years (15th)
6) Italy: 82.7 years (2nd)
7) Israel: 82.5 years (28th)
8) France: 82.4 years (1st)
9) Sweden: 82.4 years (23rd)
10) South Korea: 82.3 years (58th)
11) Canada: 82.2 years (30th)
12) Luxemburg: 82.0 years (16th)
13) Netherlands: 81.9 years (17th)
14) Norway: 81.8 years (11th)
15) New Zealand: 81.6 years (41st)
16) Austria: 81.5 years (9th)
17) Ireland: 81.4 years (19th)
18) United Kingdom: 81.2 years (18th)
19) Belgium: 81.1 years (21st)
20) Finland: 81.1 years (31st)
21) Portugal: 81.1years (12th)
22) Germany: 81.0 years (25th)
23) Greece: 81.0 years (14th)
24) Slovenia: 80.8 years (38th)
25) Denmark: 80.6 years (34th)
26) Chile: 80.5 years (33rd)
27) United States: 79.3 years (37th)
28) Czech Republic: 78.8 years (48th)
29) Estonia: 77.6 years (77th)
30) Poland: 77.5 years (50th)
31) Mexico: 76.7 years (61st)
32) Slovak Republic: 76.7 years (62nd)
33) Hungary: 75.9 years (66th)
34) Turkey: 75.8 years (70th)
35) Latvia: 74.6 years (105th)

Exhibit 2.2 Life expectancy data by country in 2015 and WHO's ranking of the world's
health systems (in parentheses), for thirty-five OECD countries

Source: World Health Organization, Global Health Observation data repository.

(Note that China is credited with 76.1 years in the same database.)

There is a fair amount of consistency in these countries' health care rankings, even though the criteria used in Bloomberg studies led to a somewhat different sample of countries, with a number of non-OECD countries included in their health care efficiency index.

And the United States? In 2013, Bloomberg ranked the U.S. 46th in health care efficiency out of 48 countries, with only Serbia and Brazil behind. In 2015, the U.S. was ranked 50th out of 55 countries in the Bloomberg index, behind almost all OECD countries listed in the study (Russia was last, at 55th). The results for the U.S. in the Bloomberg health care efficiency studies are very similar to the OECD and WHO figures mentioned earlier: according to the Bloomberg index in 2015, U.S. residents have a life expectancy of 78.9 years and annual health care costs of $9,403 per capita, representing 17.1% of GDP.

The OECD and WHO data, as well as the Bloomberg studies involving data from the IMF, the World Bank, and the WHO, all show that in the U.S. we spend a lot on health care for subpar aggregate health outcomes. In other words, we achieve very little "bang for our buck." The main driver for this is the tremendous amount of money we spend on health care.[6,7] Our GDP per capita is higher than pretty much all countries mentioned earlier (behind only Luxemburg, Switzerland, and Norway), yet our health care expenditures as a percentage of our very large GDP are roughly one and a half times that of the cohort of rich European countries that follow us in this regard. And a number of OECD countries with excellent health care systems and outcomes spend roughly half what we spend per capita in health care. No matter how we look at the data, we have a problem.[8] Why is this so? To understand these phenomena better, let's review the history of the various health care models that developed economies have been using in recent history.

★   ★   ★   ★   ★

Bismarck, universal health care coverage pioneer . . . in 1883

No, this is not a typo. In 1883, the "Iron Chancellor" Otto von Bismarck gave Prussians universal health care coverage and social security – a full 127 years before the U.S. Affordable Care Act of 2010, or "Obamacare."

Otto von Bismarck, one of the most influential statesmen of the nineteenth century, unified the German states into a powerful German empire under Prussian leadership. Bismarck was extraordinarily skillful at waging wars for a strategic purpose and was a consummate multilateral diplomat. After defeating in turn Denmark, Austria, and France, he succeeded in keeping a Continental European peace under German hegemony between 1870 and 1890. At home, Chancellor Bismarck was adept at managing a complex relationship with Kaiser Wilhelm I and managed to rule with an iron fist the newly formed German empire. At a time when the German parliament, the Reichstag, was elected by universal male vote, Bismarck created the first welfare state in the modern world to ensure political dominance over his socialist adversaries. His bargain with the German and Prussian working class was that he would give them social security and "disease insurance," and in turn they would let him govern as he saw fit. Thus was born the first program of universal health care coverage, administered by the state with the same Prussian precision used to operate the railways. The state, employers, and workers funded health insurance, with direct paycheck deductions for the workers. This was not socialism: the well-to-do at the time, the aristocracy, the land-owning and military officer classes could and did use the health care services of private and expensive doctors. But the German state guaranteed all its citizens a basic layer of health care services.

To this day, modern health care systems that combine universal health care coverage and a basic health care delivery infrastructure administered by the state with a thriving private sector provider of additional health care insurance and delivery services are called "Bismarck systems." Bismarck systems include those in a number of developed countries. Such countries include large economies such as Japan and the European Union (E.U.) trio of Germany, France, and Italy, as well as smaller ones such as the Netherlands, Switzerland, Austria, and Belgium. All these countries have mature health care systems, with universal social insurance combined with largely private providers and some public hospitals. To be a little more specific, let's briefly describe how health care works in Japan, Germany, and France.[9]

Japan's health care system was launched in the late 1920s, with U.S.-style employer-provided insurance plans. Just like in the U.S., employees had health insurance, with retired people and those unemployed left behind. It was only in 1961 that Japan adopted universal health insurance coverage. But this proved to be very popular, and since then all Japanese citizens have enjoyed access to health coverage, with over 95% choosing to do so. Access to medical services is very equal in Japan, with most physician fees set at very affordable levels by a government committee, after bi-annual negotiations with the National Medical Association. Most people still get health insurance through their employer, but those who do not have an employer-sponsored insurance plan can participate in national insurance programs administrated by local governments. There are eight health insurance systems in Japan (e.g. National Health Insurance for students; Municipal Insurance for long term care), with over 3,500 not-for-profit health insurers. Most of these health insurers are employer-based, with the largest companies even maintaining their own hospitals. Retirees and the self-employed can use Citizens Health Insurance plans.

The system of health providers in Japan, called the Kaihoken, has some unique features. One is the prominent role played by Primary Care Physicians (PCPs), who literally spend all day visiting patients at their homes. Japanese PCPs are not well paid but enjoy immense prestige: many patients will offer their PCP gifts in kind, for example. The medical service culture is strong, and PCPs' children routinely follow in their parents' footsteps and become doctors, too. Another feature is that hospitals by law are not-for-profit institutions and must be run by physicians. Even private clinics must be owned and managed by physicians. Physicians, however, are free to advertise their services and do so frequently. They behave in a very competitive manner, to keep as busy as possible given the low medical fees. As mentioned earlier, medical fees are strictly regulated and kept low to be affordable to all. Patients are responsible for paying different proportions of these fees, ranging from just 10% for primary insurance holders, children, the elderly and low-income people, up to 30% for high-income earners. Nevertheless, relatively low out-of-pocket thresholds for such medical expenses are set for each household (up to a maximum of about $750 for a given month and lower for low-income people, children and the elderly), and the government reimburses fees in excess of these thresholds.

Japanese people like to use their very affordable hospitals as well: they visit hospitals for minor health problems, and enjoy CT scans and MRIs without waiting periods at a fraction of U.S. costs. Among other partnerships, Japanese physicians have worked with the likes of Hitachi and Toshiba to develop low cost CT and MRI equipment: $200,000 for an MRI machine versus over $1 million in the U.S. As a result, people in Japan tend to be hospitalized three time as often as Americans, and typically for longer periods: for example, women giving birth tend to stay a week at the hospital with their baby. Even though Japan has a world-leading number of hospitals per capita (twice as many as in the U.S., with a total of about 11,000 hospitals and 1.5 million beds in Japan), this enthusiasm for hospital visits creates some capacity constraints and cost issues, principally in the largest metropolitan areas of the country. Overall, though, the Japanese system is relentless in its control of costs, from ongoing government efforts to a myriad of cost-saving initiatives by doctors and medical staff. The low medical fees, enshrined in widely available phone book–sized reference guides to medical treatments, put a lot of pressure on hospitals, physicians, and nurses. But thus far Japan achieves this successful paradox of heavy consumption of medical services for all at the lowest cost per capita among large industrial countries.

What about Germany, the birthplace of Bismarck systems? To start with, the German health system guarantees universal care to all German citizens and also non-German people working in the country. Health care benefits are very generous and medical treatment world class. There is little or no waiting for treatment, even for elective procedures. Patients can choose their physician and hospital. Coverage for about 90% of the population is provided by over 200 insurance plans called "Krankenkassen" (Sickness Funds). Prices for medical insurance are fixed, usually by local entities, with regulations by the federal and local governments to keep costs under control. Krankenkassen and hospitals are all private, but typically not-for-profit. Municipalities own most hospitals, although there are a growing number of for-profit clinics and hospital chains. Physicians are established through private practice and tend to behave as one-person businesses. German people above a certain income threshold are allowed to self-insure, and many (about 10% of the population) doing so patronize the for-profit medical facilities. Patients pay about 15% of income, evenly split between employer and employee, to their insurer. Patient pay after insurance is non-existent, beyond a small €10 ($12) fee per visit, except in the for-profit hospitals and clinics. It is important to stress that there is automatic continuation of health care coverage after loss of unemployment, no matter how long it takes for the insured person to find another job. Students, retirees and the elderly also have access to insurance plans at competitive prices.

One main difference in Germany relative to Japan is health care costs. German citizens and workers enjoy an amazing array of insurance and medical treatment options. With free access and choice of care, and insurance funds competing for patients on the basis of service, total system costs are high compared to most large developed economies, 27% higher per capita than in Japan and 20% higher than in France. This occurs even though local authorities and the federal government regulate medical fees very tightly. Pricing for medical services are negotiated between a region's hospital and local doctors' associations, and then become the norm in that region. The upward pressure on costs, driven by the choices patients enjoy and advances in modern medical technologies, is starting to strain the system. This medical cost inflation is partially met – just like in Japan, although not in such a scale – through tighter pricing regulations for physicians. The way this is administrated is as follows: the Federal Health Ministry asks the Krankenkassen to cap their reimbursements to hospitals and physicians through a global budgeting formula. Typically, they do this by setting an upward limit on the number of patients a physician can see every year, and similar types of limits in treatment volumes for hospitals. This has created recent tensions with physicians, who find they have to be very innovative in the range of services they offer to patients to maintain or increase their incomes. But overall, Bismarck would be very proud of the state of German health care today.

France sits between Germany and Japan in terms of health care costs per capita. Universal care reigns supreme in La République, with medical outcomes world class as well. Medical research in France is also extremely productive, perhaps second only to the United States. For example, who does not remember Luc Montagnier's role in finding medical solutions for AIDS, recognized by the 2008 Nobel Prize of Medicine he shared with Françoise Barré-Sinoussi and Harald zur Hausen for the discovery of the HIV virus? Compared to Japan and Germany, one key difference is how the public and private sectors are involved in health care, both for insurance purposes and hospital operations. There are many public hospitals in France, of very high quality. Many physicians work both in their private practices as well as in public hospitals. In France, the "Sécurité Sociale" provides health care insurance, with limits of spending, to all citizens. Public hospitals deliver all the basic health care services. To access the more expensive private clinics and physicians, one can either pay additional fees or more commonly use supplemental insurances called "mutuelles," which are not-for-profit private mutual insurers. They are very much sought after, even though they require additional monthly fees. Mutuelles are therefore included in many professions as part of employment packages, or benefits achieved through collective bargaining. The MAIF, the mutuelle that offers supplemental insurance for most academic teachers and professors, is very successful at getting the best possible care for its "adherents." As a result of successes like this, about 90% of French workers belong to a mutuelle.

Just like in Japan and Germany, there is total transparency in medical services in France. Patients seeing their physician will know to the euro the cost of the visit, with highly detailed lists of authorized fees clearly displayed at the doctor's office. As in Germany, there is a small out-of-pocket medical visit fee. Beyond this, the basic "Sécurité Sociale" health insurance will reimburse 70% of physician visits and hospital costs, with a cap on total patient costs. With a mutuelle, the coverage becomes virtually 100%, across the wide variety of public hospitals and private clinics patients can choose from. The insurance plans on offer in the country ("caisses d' assurance maladie") are all not-for-profit and cannot turn any patient down for pre-existing conditions, nor deny a claim. In case of unemployment, the government pays for the share of the premium paid previously by the employer. And the patients' insurance premiums are very cheap: typically about 20 euros per month, or about $24 at year-end 2017 exchange rates.

French people do not go to the hospital as often as Japanese, but they go to the doctor about 50% more often than Americans. And given the pace of health care innovation in the country, the French are leading consumers of pharmaceuticals: anyone who has ever been to any French city can attest that "pharmacies" (drugstores) are almost as ubiquitous as the local cafés. France is very proud of what its health system has achieved for all living there, but naturally, as in any developed country, there are concerns about mounting costs. To control this, the French government takes the lead in negotiating medical fees for doctors, hospitals and pharmaceutical companies on behalf of the fourteen main insurance plans, essentially acting as a single payer in that critical dimension. This helps contain costs to some degree, although most in France are well aware that their health care costs per capita are higher than in neighboring countries Italy, Spain and the United Kingdom. Doctors are also unionized for the most part and are not shy about demonstrating en masse in the streets of Paris if they are not happy about their negotiations with the government. Despite this, reforms have been implemented, notably a bill that encourages primary care physicians (PCPs) to act as "gatekeepers" for more expensive specialists' services: those are reimbursed to a lower degree if the use of the specialist has not been pre-approved by the relevant PCP. French people recognize inequalities inherent in any capitalistic economy like theirs, but also like to say, "In sickness and death we are all equal." In a country where the national motto is "Liberté, Égalité, Fraternité," equality of access to medical care remains a key feature of French society.

Overall, health care outcomes in Bismarck systems are very good: Japan ranks first in life expectancy among the thirty-five OECD countries we reviewed earlier, and France is first in the WHO's ranking of health care systems. Three of the ten most efficient systems in the 2015 Bloomberg study are Italy, Japan, and Spain. In the 2013 study another Bismarck system, Switzerland, also ranked in the top ten. And without spending hours performing statistical regression analyses on multiple data sets, one might very well award Japan the top health care prize after looking at these OECD, WHO, IMF, and World Bank data: Japan achieves top health care outcomes, for a very large population, at an annual cost of \$4,150 per capita, or only 44% of U.S. costs.

One factor that makes Bismarck systems efficient is the clear separation of activities between public services provided by the state and those provided by the private sector. In Japan and Germany, almost all insurance and hospital activities are provided by the private sector, with government regulations; in France there are significant public insurance and hospital operations, but with clear delineations relative to their private sector counterparts.

Bismarck systems also strive for national fairness, as again seen in the examples of Japan, Germany, and France. In Switzerland, the government runs a study every year comparing the average "sickness" levels, or need for care of each insurance company's members. And through a financial pool, those companies that insured "healthier" patients compensate financially those companies that had "less healthy" patients on average, through a balancing formula established in advance.

Following Otto von Bismarck's direct government style, today's governments with health care systems bearing his name can also be very assertive. To start with, there are strict price guidelines governing all services provided by the public component of the health sector. As an example, recent German chancellors have been known to intervene directly, through executive orders, if they felt physician fees were rising too fast. We have also seen that Japan's PCPs complain about their low wages.

In both France and Germany, at the beginning of the twenty-first century, the governments defined clear and mandatory IT guidelines to be followed by all in the medical professions, so that most health care transactions could be handled electronically. This led to the "Carte Vitale" and the "Gesundheitskarte," which everyone carries in their wallet, and essentially paperless physician offices. With these digitized patient records came automatic billing for most medical services. All of this helped to contain galloping health care costs in a major way.

Prevention is another area where governments mandate activities with authority in Bismarck systems: mandatory children vaccines, nutrition efforts, and physical check-ups are all part of a strong effort in preventing diseases and illness. France and Japan have prevention programs touching all their population that are the envy of the world. Needless to say, it is also more economical to prevent than to cure.

In summary, countries that deploy Bismarck types of health care systems strive to combine the best of the public and private sectors, with some regular government interventions aimed at containing costs. People get public universal coverage, supplemented by the effectiveness and performance of the private sector. The rules of engagement for the various government institutions and private companies involved are kept as simple as possible to keep costs contained within reasonable limits.

★　★　★　★　★

William Beveridge, or health care socialism in post–World War II Britain

In 1945, shortly after the end of World War II, to the world's surprise the United Kingdom (U.K.) electorate chose the Labour Party's Clement Attlee to lead the government over World War II victor and legend Winston Churchill. As soon as he was elected, Prime Minister Attlee announced he would put in place the welfare state outlined in the 1942 Beveridge Report, including the creation in 1948 of the National Health Service (NHS), providing public medical treatment for all.

William Beveridge, 1st Baron Beveridge, was an economist and noted social reformer best known for his 1942 wartime report "Social Insurance and Allied Services."

Lord Beveridge had served under Winston Churchill, but it was his Beveridge Report and its proposals that sealed his place in history: when the Attlee government established the NHS, as well as a national system of benefits to provide social security to all, the modern welfare state was born. The people of the United Kingdom – English, Scottish, Northern Irish and Welsh – were now all protected "from cradle to grave." As a footnote to recent U.S. health care history, the NHS was a bi-partisan institution agreed upon by both Labour and Conservative parties.

The NHS is the largest and oldest single-payer health care system in the world. Funded by taxpayers, the NHS provides health care to every legal resident in the U.K., with most services free at the point of use. I will always remember the day when, in vacation in northern England, I accidentally injected hydrogen peroxide in one of my eyes. This is not recommended! Half blinded and in acute pain, I rushed to the nearest hospital I could find in the small Cumbrian town I was staying in. Less than one hour later, treated by an excellent physician, my eye was on the mend and I stopped at what looked like a registration desk. I talked about "paying for the service, fee for the doctor's work," showing my credit card and my U.S. passport to the nurse in attendance. She looked bewildered. I insisted: "I am on vacation in your beautiful country, you saved my day, and I understand I should pay now." It must have been the pain I had in my eye: the locals did not appear to understand my French-accented American English. Ah, finally, a look of recognition. "Sir, this is the U.K. and the NHS. We do not need your ID, and the service is free. Have a good day, sir." From the vantage point of my U.S. world, this was truly amazing. But true!

This is repeated many, many times every day, for the NHS is by all measures a gigantic institution: $175 billion of annual spending (in 2015, using exchange rates at the end of that year) and 1.7 million employees, which in terms of public employers puts it third worldwide, after only the U.S. Department of Defense (3.2 million) and China's People Liberation Army (2.3 million). As such, the NHS represents very clearly what Americans think about when they talk about "socialized medicine." After all, the U.K. government owns the hospitals and pays all its people's medical bills as well as the NHS doctors. It has a gigantic supply chain organization, buying anything from pharmaceuticals to very complex IT systems. But before we start calling our British friends communists, let's remember that right here at home, we work in exactly the same way when we provide medical services to our military personnel and veterans. Our Department of Veterans Affairs, popularly known as the VA, is the best example of this. The NHS is also remarkably resilient. It went through the reformist eras of Prime Ministers Margaret Thatcher and Tony Blair with its essential mandate and function intact. The Thatcher government announced a review of the NHS in 1988. Would the "Iron Lady" tame this socialist relic, like she had successfully tamed the unions? Not really. What happened was more consultant-driven reorganization moves, with notions like "internal markets" and "competition through independent trusts of physicians" attempting to re-shape the NHS, than fundamental change. The private sector, in particular, remained at bay, representing less than 10% of health care expenditures in the U.K. A few years later in 1997, Tony Blair and his "New Labour" came to power, in part because of their aggressive campaigning in opposition to the Conservatives' alleged intention to privatize the NHS. This will just not do, "my dear chap" or "my lad" (depending on the social standing of the individual with whom you are talking). Tony Blair did a fair amount to modernize the NHS, however. Detailed service standards, strict financial budgeting, revised work specifications, closure of many surplus facilities, and an emphasis on better governance were all implemented. There was also the occasional debacle, such as an ill-managed multi-billion-pound IT transformation effort that achieved little. The emphasis on efficiency also led to creation of long waiting periods (counted in years) for older people needing relatively mundane operations such as a hip transplant. The NHS focus is on treating "productive" people first. The NHS budget represents about 90% of total U.K. health care spending. As a result, the country's spending on health is essentially determined by government fiat. If budgeting is tight, for political or economic reasons, then some kind of rationing must occur.

Before he resigned in the summer of 2016 after losing the "Brexit" vote, Conservative Prime Minister David Cameron tried to address this, for obvious political reasons: pensioners are increasing as a percentage of the population every year. But in 2012, yet another attempt at comprehensive NHS reform died at its inception, with Health Secretary Andrew Lansley demoted and replaced by Jeremy Hunt. The U.K. government then changed the focus of its efforts to making the services of NHS general practitioners available to all, seven days a week. Cameron, who had presided over a very large reduction of government spending between 2010 and 2015, actually made a formal pledge to "ring fence the Health Service from spending cuts," and did deliver on this promise. He also committed to keeping the NHS' universal care mission intact, once rebuking one of his deputies and telling him "not to scaremonger about privatization that is not happening." Almost seventy years old, the NHS remains what it has always been: universal care, administered by the government. It is an immensely popular institution in the country, and politicians meddle with it at their peril. One should add that a key message of the "Brexiters" in their successful 2017 campaign to take the United Kingdom out of the European Union was that E.U. dues (in billions of pounds per year for the U.K.) could be "saved" and redirected towards the NHS budget. This has now been debunked as "fake news," and Brexit negotiations will likely take years, but this simple and effective slogan confirmed the enduring popularity of the NHS in the United Kingdom. Prime Minister Theresa May's conservative government is very unlikely to tinker with it, except to ensure that it is correctly funded: despite laudable improvements in productivity, the financial squeeze imposed upon the NHS by conservative governments in recent years is taking its toll in terms of deteriorating service and increasing waiting times. This has caused a very public outcry, and the government will have to increase the NHS budget to ensure it functions well.

Overall, though, the NHS results speak for themselves. High quality universal care, at very affordable aggregate costs for a leading economy like the U.K. In terms of the WHO life expectancy and health care systems rankings reviewed earlier, the United Kingdom is 18th in both, in the middle of the pack among developed countries. There are strict spending guidelines for the NHS, so few end-of-life heroics there, and the U.K. may not be the most sought-after destination for challenging brain or cancer surgeries. On the other hand, the unique administrative and regulatory simplicity of the NHS ensures that these solid results in health care outcomes are achieved at a very reasonable $4,003 per capita or 9.6% of GDP, below the 10.2% European Union average and a mere 42% of what the U.S. spends. Given the NHS' performance, a number of countries, many with historical ties to Britain, have been quite happy to emulate the NHS and offer their citizens "Beveridge" types of health care systems. Australia, Canada, Ireland, and New Zealand are among them.[10]

Canada, our great neighbor to the north, combines national health insurance administered by the government with public and private hospitals. In Canada, everyone is covered by a taxpayer-funded health care insurance system called Medicare. Medicare was set up in 1961, following a very popular and successful program launched in 1946 in the province of Saskatchewan. This in itself is interesting, because it is the only significant example of a Beveridge system (or Bismarckian, for that matter) that had a local experiment as its genesis, as opposed to a national political decision. The main difference between Canada's government-financed health care system and the NHS is decentralization: unlike the U.K., Canada has a long tradition of decentralized political power, and thus there are really thirteen Medicare plans, one for each one of the ten Canadian provinces and three territories. There are some differences across the provinces, for example in patient co-pays and deductibles, but these are relatively small since the federal government provides most funding for Medicare and as such sets strong guidelines and rules to be followed by the local plans. This coordination orchestrated at the federal level allows all Medicare plans to have aggregate power when it comes to negotiating fees for treatment and prices for medical equipment and pharmaceuticals. The provincial health care systems are all operated on a not-for-profit basis and must provide accessibility to all, anywhere in the country. Another key difference from the U.K. is that most Canadians (above 60% of the population) also have private insurance to pay for services not covered by Medicare, i.e. dental care and hospital luxuries such as private rooms. It should be noted that these private plans cannot be used for services already covered by Medicare – a defining distinction within Bismarck health care systems. Most in Canada accept this because of fears about a "two-tier system," in which the wealthy would gain access to much superior care relative to the rest of the population. Yes, our northern friends are much more egalitarian than we are! Medicare is extremely popular with Canadians, but there are budget issues: attempts by successive federal and provincial governments to keep spending at reasonable levels by developed countries standards (around 10% of GDP, up from 8% ten years ago) have led to some "rationing" of non-critical medical services and long waiting periods for these. In 2005, the Supreme Court decision in *Chaoulli v. Quebec* appeared to open the door to broader access to private medical services, but instead it led to increased spending at the provincial level and a temporary easing of the waiting periods for routine operations. The waiting problem remains to this day, although most Canadians remain fundamentally attached to their Medicare, just like their British cousins.

Scandinavian countries have also adopted Beveridge's ideas about universal care with highly socialized insurance and delivery systems, albeit with more generous spending. All these countries achieve excellent health care outcomes, several of them among the top twenty in WHO outcomes (Australia; Sweden; Canada; Norway; New Zealand; Ireland; and the U.K., in terms of life expectancy) and in the 2015 Bloomberg health rankings (Australia; Canada; and Norway). It should therefore come as no surprise that the fundamental principles outlined by Lord Beveridge in 1942 are here to stay.

What is the key difference between Bismarck-type health care systems and the ones that followed William Beveridge's NHS? It is the role played by private clinics, hospitals and health insurance plans, even if not-for-profit, as opposed to public ones. This leads to a key trade-off between overall system costs (lower in Beveridge-type systems) and access to top end medical services without any waiting time, a key feature of Bismarck systems. This is why health care spending per capita is typically lower in countries that followed Beveridge's principles, but health outcomes are better in those descending from Otto von Bismarck's pioneering nineteenth-century health care program.

The polar opposite to systems like the NHS are to be found in countries where most health care is delivered on a cash basis: if you are wealthy, you will pay and be treated. If you are poor, well, hopefully your God is looking after your health, because in your country you are unlikely to receive much care, unless administrated by some international NGO that happens to be near you. Fortunately, this type of third-world situation has become increasingly rare in OECD countries. Many developing countries, for example Mexico, Malaysia, and South Africa, have increased health care coverage for their people. Mexico today spends a respectable 6% of GDP on health care. Most of these countries have done so through a very basic form of universal coverage mandated by the State and administered by a combination of public and private insurance companies. In Brazil, the "Bolsa Familia" living subsidy granted to the poorest citizens is contingent upon parents showing proof of vaccinations and preventive care for their children. This very successful government initiative has reduced poverty for tens of millions and also overall health care costs because of the advances in prevention achieved by the program. The country also has basic universal health coverage, as well as public hospitals in all its major cities. But access to the best private hospitals for the most part still requires cash payments or very expensive private insurance.

★   ★   ★   ★   ★

The U.S. path to a complex, costly care system

The U.S. health care system shares features with all the other systems mentioned above. It features a thriving private sector, mostly in the form of giant insurers, with also many private hospitals, just like in Germany and France. The federal government is directly involved, through Medicare; Medicaid; the State Children's Health Insurance Program (SCHIP); the Department of Health and Human Services; the National Institutes of Health; the Department of Defense Military Health System (MHS); the Veterans Health Administration (VHA); and the Indian Health Service.

Medicare, for those who are 65 years of age or older, is universal coverage administered by the government (Center for Medicare and Medicaid Services, or CMS), very similar to the universal coverage all Canadian citizens enjoy regardless of age. Cash also plays a big role in U.S. health care, and an increasing one. Insurance deductibles, payments after insurance, and co-pays at the time of visits with physicians are all growing. This means that Americans are paying higher and higher out-of-pocket medical costs. And this is for those of us who enjoy medical insurance. For the thirty or so million who still do not today (since the passage of the Affordable Care Act in 2010, over twenty million Americans have gotten health coverage for the first time), cash is obviously the only way to purchase health care services. How did we get there?

During World War II, the Franklin Roosevelt administration enacted wage controls, because the labor market was tight due to both the increased demand from the war effort and the decreased supply of workers available at home.

Employers thus were not allowed to compete for workers by raising wages. However, the War Labor Board had declared that fringe benefits did not count as wages for wage control purposes. As a result, employers started attracting workers through increasingly more generous fringe benefits, principally health care coverage. President Harry Truman proposed a system of public health insurance in November 1945, but he had to retreat in face of strong business, hospital and physician opposition.[11] Many denounced the proposed system as "socialism." Labor unions chose to campaign for employer-sponsored health coverage, a less desirable but politically attainable goal. This was how the tight relationship between employment and health insurance was created in the U.S. Between the end of World War II and 1960, the total number of people enrolled in work-related health insurance plans grew tremendously, so that by the end of the Dwight Eisenhower presidency, 75% of Americans had some form of health coverage.[12]

However, work-related health insurance left many behind (25% of the population is not a small number), including the working poor with jobs offering no benefits, the unemployed, and the elderly. In the affluent, optimistic years of the John F. Kennedy presidency, millions of Americans who had retired from work were experiencing poverty in their sunset years: this was due to lack of health coverage when they needed it the most or private health insurance premiums costing several times what they paid while working. In 1965, President Lyndon Johnson signed the Medicare and Medicaid programs into law, creating for the first time publicly run insurance for the elderly and the poor. This was one of the cornerstones of Johnson's Great Society progressive program of social reforms.

The very popular Medicare program was supplemented in 1997 by Medicare Advantage plans. Those were created during the Bill Clinton presidency under the Balanced Budget Act of 1997. The objective was twofold: offering seniors a wider choice of coverage under Medicare and reducing costs through participation of the private sector. It is fair to say that only the first objective was attained. Similarly, in 2003, George W. Bush got Medicare Part D voted into law by Congress. Part D provides a private sector option for Medicare beneficiaries to purchase subsidized coverage for the costs of prescribed drugs. With the cost of pharmaceuticals increasing much faster than inflation during the last twelve years, Part D and its popular prescribed drugs subsidy for seniors is one of the key factors of increased health care costs in the U.S. over the same period.

Medicaid was created at the outset as a social welfare program, partially funded by the federal government, and as such enrollees have always had to pass a means test. States administer Medicaid, so there are really fifty different Medicaid programs – see Exhibit 2.3 showing the state Medicaid and CHIP income eligibility standards for all fifty states, expressed in monthly income for a household size of four, from the Center for Medicare and Medicaid Services (CMS), 2015.[13] Most such programs are called Medicaid, but some are not: in California, it is called Medi-Cal; in Tennessee, TennCare. More importantly, the means tests and therefore Medicaid eligibility vary tremendously across states. For example, in Florida, Kansas, Texas, and a dozen other states, no single male can qualify, no matter how poor. In Alabama, where the local Medicaid is one of the stingiest, families with a pregnant woman need to have a monthly income (household size of four) of less than $2,802 to qualify in 2015. In contrast, in Iowa, where Medicaid is much more generous, this minimum monthly income requirement in 2015 is $7,453, or 2.7 times more. California and New York are in between, with a minimum qualifying monthly income of $4,134 and $4,383,

CMS
CENTERS FOR MEDICARE and MEDICAID SERVICES
State Medicaid and CHIP income eligibility standards
Expressed in monthly income, household size of four
(For MAGI Groups, based on state decisions as of October 1, 2014)

	Children				Pregnant women		Adults		
	Ages 0–1	Medicaid ages 1–5	Medicaid ages 6–18	Separate CHIP[3]	Medicaid	CHIP	Parents	Other adults	Medicaid expansion
Alabama	$2,802	$2,802	$2,802	$6,201	$2,802	N/A	$258	$0	N
Alaska[5]	$5,045	$5,045	$5,045	N/A	$4,970	N/A	$3,206	$0	N
Arizona	$2,922	$2,802	$2,643	$3,975 (closed)	$3,101	N/A	$2,643	$2,643	Y
Arkansas	$4,194	$4,194	$4,194	N/A	$4,154	N/A	$2,643	$2,643	Y
California	$5,187	$5,187	$5,187	N/A	$4,134	N/A	$2,643	$2,643	Y
Colorado	$2,822	$2,822	$2,822	$5,168	$3,876	$5,168	$2,643	$2,643	Y
Connecticut	$3,896	$3,896	$3,896	$6,320	$5,128	N/A	$3,896	$2,643	Y
Delaware	$4,214	$2,822	$2,643	$4,214 (1–18)	$4,214	N/A	$2,643	$2,643	Y
District of Columbia	$6,340	$6,340	$6,340	N/A	$6,340	N/A	$4,293	$4,174	Y
Florida	$4,094	$2,783	$2,643	$4,174 (1–18)	$3,796	N/A	$596	$0	N
Georgia	$4,074	$2,961	$2,643	$4,909	$4,373	N/A	$696	$0	N
Hawaii[5]	$7,040	$7,040	$7,040	N/A	$4,366	N/A	$3,040	$3,040	Y
Idaho	$2,822	$2,822	$2,643	$3,677	$2,643	N/A	$477		N
Illinois	$2,822	$2,822	$2,822	$6,221	$4,134	N/A	$2,643	$2,643	Y
Indiana	$4,134	$3,140	$3,140	$4,969	$4,134	N/A	$398		N
Iowa	$7,453	$3,319	$3,319	$6,002 (1–18)	$7,453	N/A	$2,643	$2,643	Y
Kansas	$3,299	$2,961	$2,643	$4,869	$3,299	N/A	$656	$0	N
Kentucky	$3,876	$3,160	$3,160	$4,233	$3,876	N/A	$2,643	$2,643	Y
Louisiana	$4,214	$4,214	$4,214	$4,969	$2,643	N/A	$378		N
Maine	$3,796	$3,120	$3,120	$4,134	$4,154	N/A	$1,988	1	N
Maryland	$6,300	$6,300	$6,300	N/A	$5,148	N/A	$2,643	$2,643	Y
Massachusetts	$3,975	$2,981	$2,981	$5,963	$3,975	$3,975	$2,643	$2,643	Y
Michigan	$3,876	$3,180	$3,180	$4,214	$3,876	N/A	$2,643	$2,643	Y
Minnesota	55.625	$5,466	$5,466	N/A	$5,525	N/A	$3,975	$3,975	Y
Mississippi	53,856	$2,842	$2,643	$4,154	$3,856	N/A	$437	$0	N
Missouri	$3,896	$2,981	$2,981	$5,963	$3,896	N/A	$358		N
Montana	$2,842	$2,842	$2,842	$5,187	$3,120	N/A	$934		N
Nebraska	$4,233	$4,233	$4,233	N/A	$3,856	N/A	$1,133	$0	N
Nevada	$3,180	$3,180	$2,643	$3,975	$3,180	N/A	$2,643	$2,643	Y
New Hampshire	$6,320	$6,320	$6,320	N/A	$3,896	N/A	$2,643	$2,643	Y
New Jersey	$3,856	$2,822	$2,822	$6,956	$3,856	$3,975	$2,643	$2,643	Y
New Mexico	$5,963	$5,963	$4,770	N/A	$4,969	N/A	$2,643	$2,643	Y
New York	$4,333	$2,961	$2,961	$7,950	$4,333	N/A	$2,643	$2,643	Y
North Carolina	$4,174	$4,174	$2,643	$4,194 (6–18)	$3,896	N/A	$894	$0	N

Exhibit 2.3 State Medicaid and CHIP income eligibility standards for all fifty states, expressed in monthly income for a household size of four, from the Center for Medicare and Medicaid Services (CMS), 2015

CMS
CENTERS FOR MEDICARE and MEDICAID SERVICES
State Medicaid and CHIP income eligibility standards
Expressed in monthly income, household size of four
(For MAGI Groups, based on state decisions as of October 1, 2014)

	Children				Pregnant women		Adults		
	Ages 0–1	*Medicaid ages 1–5*	*Medicaid ages 6–18*	*Separate CHIP[3]*	*Medicaid*	*CHIP*	*Parents*	*Other adults*	*Medicaid expansion*
North Dakota	$2,922	$2,922	$2,643	$3,379	$2,922	N/A	$2,643	$2,643	Y
Ohio	$4,094	$4,094	$4,094	N/A	$3,975	N/A	$2,643	$2,643	Y
Oklahoma	$4,074	$4,074	$4,074	N/A	$2,643	N/A	$835		N
Oregon	$3,677	$2,643	$2,643	$5,963	$3,677	N/A	$2,643	$2,643	Y
Pennsylvania	$4,273	$3,120	$2,643	$6,241	$4,273	N/A	$656	$0	Y(1/1/15)
Rhode Island	$5,187	$5,187	$5,187	N/A	$3,776	$5,028	$2,643	$2,643	Y
South Carolina	$4,134	$4,134	$4,134	N/A	$3,856	N/A	$1,2,32	$0	N
South Dakota	$3,617	$3,617	$3,617	$4,055	$2,643	N/A	$1,153	$0	N
Tennessee	$3,876	$2,822	$2,643	$4,969	$3,876	N/A	$2,087	$0	N
Texas	$3,935	$2,862	$2,643	$3,995	$3,935	N/A	$298	$0	N
Utah	$2,763	$2,763	$2,643	$3,975	$2,763	N/A	$1,014		N
Vermont	$6,201	$6,201	$6,201	$6,201	$4,134	N/A	$2,643	$2,643	Y
Virginia	$2,842	$2,842	$2,842	$3,975	$2,842	N/A	$974	$0	N
Washington	$4,174	$4,174	$4,174	$6,201	$3,836	N/A	$2,643	$2,643	Y
West Virginia	$3,140	$2,802	$2,643	$5,963	$3,140	N/A	$2,643	$2,643	Y
Wisconsin	$5,982	$3,697	$3,001	$5,982 (1–18)	$5,982	N/A	$1,888	$1,888	N
Wyoming	$3,061	$3,061	$2,643	$3,975	$3,061	N/A	$1,113	$0	N

Exhibit 2.3 (Continued)

respectively. As a result, the percentage of enrollees is much higher in states like Iowa, California, and New York than in those like Alabama, Idaho, and Texas.

The Affordable Care Act (ACA), which passed in the first term of the Barack Obama presidency, expanded Medicaid considerably. Everyone with income under 133% of the federal poverty level, who was not old enough to qualify for Medicare, could be enrolled in Medicaid. The benefits available in the expanded Medicaid were also essentially the same as those obtained with private insurers through the newly created state exchanges, a key feature of the ACA. This expansion of Medicaid did not cost anything to the states, at least initially: it was fully funded by the federal government until a gradual phase down starting in 2020, when it would be 90% federally funded. There was one big caveat, however: as the result of one of the Supreme Court decisions on the Affordable Care Act, this expansion of Medicaid coverage had to be accepted by the states, one by one. For political reasons, eighteen out of fifty states, all with Republican governors, have refused the Medicaid expansion offered by the ACA.

To summarize, let's list the dozen types of institutions that make up the U.S. medical landscape, focusing on the insurers (payers) and hospitals.

Public insurance, federal: Medicare ($672 billion spending in 2016, with federal outlays net of fees and premiums totaling $595 billion); Medicaid ($367 billion federal spending in 2016); Department of Health and Human Services (HHS); Department of Defense's Military Health System (benefits provided through TRICARE); Veterans Health Administration; Indian Health Service.[14]

Public insurance, administrated by states: The states spent about $200 billion on Medicaid in 2016, in addition to federal Medicaid funds. Medicaid programs were administrated state-by-state, totaling $565 billion in aggregate spending. The states also administrated the $17 billion Children's Health Insurance Program (CHIP), financed mostly with federal dollars ($15 billion in 2016).

Private insurance: 1) multi-billion-dollar groups that operate throughout the U.S., such as Aetna and United Health; 2) a myriad of state-level insurers, some quite large, some much smaller. All these insurers offer many types of plans, such as Preferred Provider Organizations (PPOs); Point of Service (POSs); Health Maintenance Organizations (HMOs); tax-deductible Health Savings Accounts (HSAs); Medicare Advantage; Medicare Part D, etc. Some are subsidized.

The Blues: The Blue Cross and Blue Shield Association (BCBSA) is a federation of thirty-eight separate private health insurance organizations. Combined, they provide health insurance to over 100 million Americans. They administrate Medicare in some states and provide coverage to federal and state government employees under the option of the Federal Employees Health Benefit Plan. The largest "Blue" is Anthem Insurance Corp, after its 2014 acquisition of WellPoint, formerly Blue Cross of California. Spending by all private health insurers exceeded $1.1 trillion in 2016, representing 34% of total U.S. health care spending, according to CMS and HHS.

Major medical centers: These are the flagships of the U.S. medical system, the envy of the whole world. Major medical centers have multiple specialized hospitals and clinics, as well as medical research centers. They are destinations of choice for patients who need specialized treatments that require a multidisciplinary approach and the latest in health care innovation and technology. Major not-for-profit medical centers enjoy very large endowments, like our top universities. They include the Cleveland Clinic; Duke University Health; Johns Hopkins; the Mayo Clinic; Massachusetts General (teaching hospital of the Harvard Medical School); New York Presbyterian; the National Institutes of Health (the primary agency of the U.S. government for health and biomedical research); the University of Pennsylvania Health System; the University of Pittsburgh Medical Center; the Texas Medical Center; the University of California San Francisco (UCSF) Medical Center; and the UCLA Medical Center.

Research and teaching hospitals, not-for-profit: There are 1,100 teaching hospitals in the U.S., 375 of which are large facilities with research capabilities belonging to the Association of American Medical Colleges' Council of Teaching Hospitals and Health Systems (COTH). Many universities in the U.S.

have an academic medical center, some of them quite prominent. For example, Dartmouth–Hitchcock in New Hampshire and Stanford Health Care in California are world famous.[15]

Private hospitals, not-for-profit: Of the 5,750 or so acute care hospitals in the U.S., 2,600 are private, not-for-profit community hospitals. Among these, about 1,500 are faith-based, including 730 Catholic hospitals, which represent about one in seven hospital admissions in the U.S. With over 130 hospitals nationwide, Ascension Health, based in St Louis, MO, is the largest not-for-profit hospital system in the U.S. Catholic Health Initiatives (105 hospitals, based in Denver, CO) and Trinity Health (91 hospitals, based in Livonia, MI) are two other large Catholic systems. In 2010, the president and CEO of the Catholic Hospital Association of the USA (CHAUSA), Sister Carol Keehan, was instrumental in the passage of the Affordable Care Act. Sister Keehan and CHAUSA, supported by 61 Catholic religious orders, voiced a very public support of Barack Obama's health care reform proposal, in the face of the U.S. Catholic bishops' opposition to it. The sisters convinced several Catholic Democratic members of Congress from Michigan to vote in favor of the ACA, securing its passage in the House.[16]

Private hospitals, for-profit: Hospital Corporation of America (HCA) is the largest hospital system in the U.S. It is based in Nashville, Tennessee, and manages 165 hospitals. Community Health System (Franklin, TN) is another very large for-profit system. Many for-profit hospital systems, some of them owned by private equity groups, are roll-ups of small community hospitals that were in need of an operational turnaround. There are about 1,050 for-profit hospitals in the U.S, and for-profit systems represent a little less than 20% of U.S. hospitals.

Public hospitals: There are slightly over a thousand state and local government community hospitals in the U.S. They represent an urban "safety net" for medical services and attend to many low or uninsured patients. Some of the largest ones in the U.S. include Jackson Memorial (Miami, FL), Cook County (Chicago, IL), Grady Memorial (Atlanta, GA), and Santa Clara Valley (San Jose, CA). The largest system of such hospitals is the New York City Health and Hospital Corp.

Public integrated systems, federal: The Veterans Health Administration (VHA) is an enormous system that implements the medical assistance program of the VA through the administration and operation of over 160 medical facilities, hospitals, clinics, and recovery homes. The Defense Military Health System is also a very large integrated system that serves our military. Within it, the Defense Health Agency is responsible for providing TRICARE, an integrated health program that provides civilian medical care to our service members and their families.

Regional integrated system: Kaiser Permanente, headquartered in Oakland, CA, is a huge integrated system, combining the Kaiser Foundation Health Plans (KFHPs) and Kaiser Foundation Hospitals. It reported $64.6 billion in 2016 annual revenue, with 209,000 employees and 21,300 physicians, dwarfing the size of the largest U.S. hospital groups such as HCA or Ascension Health. Operating in eight states, foremost in California, Kaiser offers both insurance and medical services to its 11.7 million plan members. KFHPs, offering prepaid health insurance to members, are not-for-profit and invest their members' contributions in the medical operations entities of the group, the Kaiser Foundation Hospitals and the Permanente Medical Groups, which are for-profit. Members have a Kaiser card, and with it get access to the hospitals and physicians of the group. The choice of physicians is limited compared to an employee-funded PPO plan, but most Kaiser members appear to be very happy with the service they receive. Although not directly state-funded, Kaiser can be described as the health institution in the U.S. closest to a U.K. or Canadian-style NHS, serving California and seven other states.[17]

Private integrated systems, not-for-profit: A number of prominent regional not-for-profit health systems also offer internal, integrated health plans that compete with private insurance for the patients they treat. For example, the prestigious Salt Lake City, UT-based Intermountain has a division of health plans, called Select Health, which insures patients in Utah. This integration of health plans with hospitals, even partial, helps reduce administrative complexity and tends to reduce overall costs, also providing strategic advantages in competitive regional markets.

To keep this maze of interacting institutions in perspective, the $3.3 trillion of U.S. health care costs in 2016 can be split along insurance lines, or among categories of treatment facilities (figures rounded up to the nearest $5 billion).[18]

On the payer side, federal spending accounted for 28.3% of the total ($935 billion); households, including patients' growing out-of-pocket expenses, represented 28% ($925 billion); private business 20% ($660 billion); state and local governments 17% ($560 billion); the remainder 6.7% ($220 billion) included charity care provided by numerous hospitals and private health foundations.[19]

On the provider side, hospitals (including government and public facilities) represented about 33% ($1.09 trillion); physicians not working directly at hospitals and clinical services 20% ($660 billion); other medical professionals (e.g. optometrists) and dental services 7% ($230 billion); retail prescription drugs 10% ($330 billion); nursing homes, home health care, and personal care services 13% ($430 billion); medical devices and equipment and other spending 17% ($560 billion). These numbers, built from figures from the U.S. Government Health and Human Services Department (HHS), CMS, and the Congressional Budget Office, are very high-level orders of magnitude type figures, but they give a fair idea of where the money goes to keep the people living in the U.S. healthy.[20,21]

Health care activities in America are of course heavily regulated through a number of federal and state entities. The largest of them is the Food and Drug Administration (FDA), which regulates over $1 trillion worth of products sold annually, mostly food, pharmaceuticals, and cosmetics. The FDA is responsible for all regulatory approvals to bring to market any type of drug and treatment, from the simplest painkiller to the most advanced genome-based cancer-fighting therapy. HHS is the largest U.S. government department in terms of spending, with an approved fiscal 2016 budget of $1.09 trillion. Most states also have a health department headed by a cabinet level secretary. Major federal laws regulating the insurance industry include COBRA (mandated 18 to 36 months extension of employer-sponsored coverage, varying by state, after employment has been lost) and HIPAA (which provides very strict standards to protect patient medical information and records confidentiality).

This is truly amazing complexity. And it did not happen sui generis. By the end of World War II this intricate web of not-for-profit hospitals, academic centers, for-profit hospitals, government entities, and even Kaiser (founded in 1945) already existed. Because the starting health infrastructure in the U.S. was already very complicated, every incremental change – always implemented in a good-faith effort to improve the system – added to its complexity, piece by piece. Tying health insurance to employment brought coverage to 75% of Americans. But because this left the elderly and poor behind, separate programs had to be developed to help them. Lyndon Johnson gathered enough political capital in 1965 to make Medicare a comprehensive federal program for all seniors, but the implementation of Medicaid was left to the states, which took fifty different paths to help the poor get access to health care.

As the number of uninsured started to increase by millions every year from the 1990s due to the shift from middle-class jobs with full benefits to more precarious ones, legislative attempts were launched to reform health care. They went nowhere, from the comprehensive reform sought by the Clinton administration to Republicans' ideas about privatizing Medicare, until the Affordable Care Act in 2010. Having survived a couple of Supreme Court challenges in its short history, the ACA has worked as intended, even though there were still about thirty million people without health insurance in the U.S. at the end of the Obama presidency. But the ACA added a whole new layer of complexity to the overall edifice – the state exchanges, which were actually originally a concept floated by the conservative think tank Heritage Foundation during the Clinton Administration in the 1990s. Some exchanges' websites worked from the word go, like in California. Others, including (most visibly) the federal exchange, experienced lots of problems and crashed repetitively until most problems were ironed out a few months later.

Other problems persist, beyond website crashes. In the country of IBM, Accenture, and Silicon Valley, information technology struggles to make health care work more efficiently. Despite billions of dollars spent on them, electronic health records (EHRs) and patient accounting systems cannot for the most part "talk" to each other. EHRs were supposed to save us all. I remember attending a health care conference early in 2005, full of American luminaries. Most speakers, including former Speaker of the House Newt Gingrich, agreed with great enthusiasm that EHRs, if funded properly, were going to straighten out all the problems we had had in health care up to then. Less than a year earlier, Senator Hillary Clinton had proposed a national health medical records system as part of her health care plan. Hillary and Newt: have they ever agreed on anything else during their long political careers? Over a decade later, many patients with complicated health cases who need treatments from several hospitals and physicians have medical files and records that are half electronic, half paper. Faxes and PDFs still reign supreme. If EHRs, which have been described as "digitized faxes," do not acquire the ability to integrate and share information electronically across the IT systems of different medical centers, they will prove to be a lot less useful than hoped for.

Even a simple function like accounting is unusually complex in the hospital world. In most businesses, there is a "top line" on the profit and loss statement, called "revenue," which represents simply the amount of revenue, or sales garnered by the business. Operating and net profit margins, for example, are expressed as percentage of revenue. Not so for U.S. hospitals. There the line that appears on top of their P&L statements, often called "gross revenue" or "total patient revenue," is not the "top line" from which operating margin percentages are calculated. That "top line" for hospital accounting purposes is called "net patient revenue" (sometimes supplemented by a small amount of non patient related revenue, like gift stores and cafeterias, to get to total operating revenue). And how does one get from "gross" to "net" revenue? By subtracting from the former the payer (insurance) "discounts" or "deductions." What are these? They are the result of complex contractual agreements between hospitals and payers. You see, any hospital has an average of over a hundred insurance contracts with federal, state, local, and private payers. Those contracts are typically several hundred pages long, and for each procedure (hundreds, if not thousands of them), there is a discount, which has been negotiated between the hospital and the payer. So when dealing with payer x, the hospital will list gross revenue of 100 for a given procedure. The contract with x stipulates that there is, say, a 70% discount for that operation, so the real, "net" revenue to the hospital is 100, less 70, or 30. The resulting total "net revenue" showed in the hospital P&L is thus the result of thousands of different discounts being applied to each procedure-payer combination. And for cash paying patients, there is another category of discounts, typically lower than for payers. Individual patients do not have the payers' negotiating powers, so in their case the discount is just calculated to maximize probability of payment by the patient, following marketing type formulae. No wonder patient accounting systems are challenging to hospitals, with half a dozen IT vendors doing solid business helping set them up. All of this also means that hospital revenues fluctuate with their patient mix, their payer mix and with the types of interventions they perform, which makes forecasts quite challenging.

Let's illustrate this with a simple example from a hospital in the Midwest: in Exhibit 2.4, we can see that actual 2015 revenue (split between various categories of inpatient and outpatient revenue) year-to-date is $1,102,142,479. Then come a number of deductions, the largest by far the contractual adjustments (discounts) with payers, at over $811 million. The total deductions amount to $818, 280, 204. This leads to a Net Patient Revenue of $283,862,275, or 26% of gross revenue. Simple!

All in all, with every incremental improvement, the complexity of U.S. health care increases, like entropy. It has become almost impossible even to conceive of

STATEMENT OF REVENUES AND EXPENSES

Fiscal year 2015, as of June 30, 2015

	YTD Actual FY15	YTD Budget FY15	YTD Variance
Revenues			
Inpatient revenue			
Acute care	602,243,286	583,106,594	19,136,692
Rehabilitation	16,310,923	17,603,814	(1,292,891)
Psychiatric	12,926,901	9,269,186	3,657,715
Total inpatient revenue	631,481,110	609,979,594	21,501,516
Outpatient revenue			
Outpatient clinics	417,861,718	368,885,920	48,975,798
Emergency room	52,799,651	39,942,527	12,857,124
Total outpatient revenue	470,661,369	408,828,447	61,832,922
Total patient revenue	1,102,142,479	1,018,808,041	83,334,438
Deductions			
Contractual adjustments	811,099,711	717,917,455	(93,182,256)
Charity care/Provision for doubtful accounts	16,282,181	37,186,494	20,904,313
Supplemental state programs	(7,974,167)	(6,517,294)	1,456,873
Patient care assurance	98,859	(2,000,000)	(2,098,859)
Cost report settlements	(1,226,380)	(1,200,000)	26,380
Total deductions	818,280,204	745,386,655	(72,893,549)
Net patient revenue	283,862,275	273,421,386	10,440,889
Other revenue	12,643,539	10,416,482	2,227,057
Total operating revenue	296,505,814	283,837,868	12,667,946
Expenses			
Salaries	117,677,350	113,100,496	(4,576,854)
Benefits	32,273,644	29,016,187	(3,257,457)
Supplies	55,578,123	55,496,414	(81,709)
Supplies – drugs	25,089,042	15,800,097	(9,288,945)
Travel	903,588	857,002	(46,586)
Information and communication	3,494,245	3,393,991	(100,254)
Outside purchased services	15,294,094	14,970,796	(323,298)
Physician payments	8,500,000	8,500,000	—
Miscellaneous	2,344,511	3,535,925	1,191,414
Interest expense	4,641,315	4,250,625	390,690
Depreciation	15,418,277	16,833,445	1,415,168
Total operating expenses	281,214,189	265,754,978	(14,677,831)
Operating income (loss)	15,291,625	18,082,890	(2,791,265)
Operating margin %	5.2%	6.4%	

Exhibit 2.4 Hospital in the U.S. with about $600M in annual net patient revenue

starting from scratch: re-designing a $3.3 trillion health care world with a blank sheet of paper is a chimera. The additional costs associated with this complexity are very real, though.

★   ★   ★   ★   ★

The costs of complexity

How much does this cost us? Over a trillion dollars, every year. According to the CMS 2016 data, the U.S. spends $3.3 trillion or 17.9% of GDP on health care. This is up from 13.4% of GDP in 2000. The European Union and Japan spend an average of 10.2% of GDP on health care, 7.7% less than the U.S. OECD countries spend 8.9%, or less than 50% of U.S. spending. Even if we use the OECD 2015 figures for the U.S. (16.8% of GDP), which appear understated relative to our own data, the difference from Europe and Japan is still 6.6%. A difference of 7.7% of U.S. GDP amounts to a gigantic $1.4 trillion every year, and 6.6% would still represent over $1.2 trillion. These are the very hypothetical savings we would enjoy should our health care expenditures be at E.U. and Japanese averages. Being at the OECD average would net us an additional $200 billion per year, but a comparison with the E.U. and Japan makes more sense, given that these are the economic markets we typically compare ourselves with.

As we saw earlier in this chapter, this enormous spending does not buy us better health outcomes – far from it. Not only are our health care costs extremely high, but also our outcomes are poor. What are the key factors commonly attributed to this excess health care spending in the U.S. relative to other developed countries? Which ones help create these "low bang for your buck" results? And how does the unique complexity of our health system drive these factors? Let's discuss seven key factors mentioned frequently in studies of U.S. health care costs and outcomes:

Cost factor #1: **The superior innovation**, technology, and advanced cures used at most U.S. hospitals. This is good. Our fabled major medical centers provide very expensive care, but they literally perform medical miracles. If I collapse on the San Francisco pavement with a stroke, I hope I will muster the strength to utter the words "UCSF" to the ambulance driver. At UCSF they are more likely to perform brain surgery successfully if needed than at any other hospital in California. In doing so they will extend my life, and yes, this is valuable to me. This is obviously driven by the complexity of our system. The multiplicity of academic medical research facilities, for example, creates a very healthy competition to find the best cures, but it fosters in turn a wide array of solutions using many different technologies.

Cost factor #2: A natural extension of the superlative levels of care one can get at our leading medical facilities is called **"end of life heroics."**

Also good, in my mind. However, it is worth noting that superlative care and "end of life heroics" tend to be concentrated in the U.S., with the well-to-do getting the lion's share of them. According to a study by the Agency for Health Care Research and Quality (AHRQ), the 1% of the population with the highest spending accounted for 27% of aggregate health care spending in 2009.[22] There are many avenues we might pursue to improve the health care outcomes for the "99%" without jeopardizing the excellence in high-end care our leading medical institutions are world known for. So I would not criticize this excellence. But it should also be noted that "end of life heroics" have detractors: a number of studies have shown that increased spending; more procedures; lots of fancy testing; and longer hospital stays in the last two years of life are not necessarily associated with better patient outcomes. Very hypothetically, managing innovation and "end of life" procedures more effectively might save us about $300–400 billion per year. A number of studies advocate for this, but clearly this area of diagnostics and treatments in the U.S. is of much complexity and cost compared to the rest of the developed world. This book is not the place for the serious medical, ethical, and philosophical thinking that needs to take place when discussing end of life. Still, honestly, when my turn comes, I want them to try their best to keep me going.

Cost factor #3: The U.S. has below average utilization of physicians and hospital beds compared to the OECD, E.U., and Japanese averages. A myriad of studies have covered this; most consulting firms have programs on this; many start-ups aim to tackle this utilization issue with leading-edge software-based algorithms, or with artificial intelligence. However, this issue should be treated very carefully, because it is not intuitively obvious that treating all hospitals and physicians as "units of capacity" is the road to improved health care efficiency in the U.S. Who has analyzed the trade-offs between maximum utilization and improved (or worsened) health outcomes? Clear analyses can be made on utilization, with convincing data, but the link between filling hospitals beds and using physicians at or near 100% and better health outcomes is what is missing in all this work.[23]

The best study in this area is probably the extensive research done by Harvard Business School professors Robert Kaplan and Michael Porter, described in the September 2011 *Harvard Business Review*[24] and outlined in an April 14, 2012 *New York Times* article.[25] In that latter article, the authors write:

Because health care charges and reimbursements have become disconnected from actual costs, some procedures are reimbursed very generously, while others are priced below their actual cost or not reimbursed at all. This leads many providers to expand into well-reimbursed procedures, like knee and hip replacements or high-end imaging, producing huge excess capacity for these at the same time that shortages persist in poorly reimbursed but critical services like primary and preventive care.

Applying Kaplan and Porter's recommendations would lead to an encyclopedic cost accounting exercise, which would (yet again) give us one additional layer of complexity in our health care construction. That is a certainty. Less certain is how health outcomes would improve. They probably would, given the need for more prevention and primary care in the country, but there are no hard data or analyses to predict this. This resources optimization approach also assumes that the solution to our health care woes is to apply market principles with specific prices for each individual procedure based on detailed cost analysis. Many people object to this, believing that health is a public good, not just another commodity one buys and sells.[26] Think about it: is anyone advocating treating the police, fire people, or national security this way?

Cost Factor #4: Too many specialists, too few general practitioners (GPs) or primary care physicians (PCPs). This is a common curse of many developed countries, but it is exacerbated in the U.S. for a simple reason: the astronomical costs of medical studies. Beyond a bachelor's degree, medical students must at least have four years of graduate studies, plus three years of internships. So most young doctors start practicing with hundreds of thousands of dollars of personal debt. And the average GP or PCP in the country makes about $150,000 per year. Costs of setting up even a simple practice are high, what with all the administrative costs and the onerous malpractice insurance. Specialists make twice as much on average, and if very successful can make millions. Yet, having PCPs seeing patients regularly can increase much needed prevention efforts in this country. PCPs can ensure babies, infants and adults all follow prescribed vaccinations and prevention steps identified to prevent adverse medical situations down the road. We all know that preventing an illness is much more cost effective than curing it. The lack of systematic PCP coverage, exacerbated by the situation of millions of our citizens not carrying health insurance, is one factor explaining why prevention efforts in the U.S. lag relative to those in other developed countries.

Having more PCPs or GPs treat more patients and determine the need for a specialist more selectively would cut costs. This is one of the outcomes HBS professors Kaplan and Porter want to achieve through their proposals of making the costs of procedures more explicit. The complexity of health care in the U.S. exacerbates this factor, because it is increasingly difficult for GPs to navigate the complexity of administrative issues and the dizzying array of available treatments within the confines of small practices, with little available support staff. Unlike the French and German GPs with their automated billing systems and electronic health records, our GPs have to spend hours performing complex administrative and record-keeping tasks. Even with a huge cottage industry dedicated to support them, they struggle to balance this burden and a healthy patient visit schedule.

Cost Factor #5: Administrative complexity. The fragmentation and complexity of U.S. health care is extreme. Its tangle of relationships between multiple government participants; a myriad of private payers and hospitals of all shapes; and a maze of federal and state-by-state regulations are unique. Administrative complexity is a natural corollary, with a high number of activities redundant. These administrative costs total about $210 billion per year, according to HHS, and are between twice and four times higher per capita than in the E.U. and Japan. Think about this: we spend more just in health care administration than the NHS spends in health care for the whole of the U.K. Then again, our total health care spending dwarfs the U.K.'s full GDP, and is close to Germany's, the world's fourth largest economy.

So our excess administrative costs range between $100 and $150 billion relative to our peers among OECD countries. Naturally, as we try to "automate" these legions of administrative tasks, IT costs rise in parallel.[27] Far from helping to reduce health care costs, it seems that the increased use of technology contributes to their increase. CommFor Research (CFR) estimated in 2015 that U.S. health providers spent $40 billion in IT, versus $14.6 billion in Western Europe, a geographical area with a similar population.[28] Other studies assess total U.S. health IT spending in 2016 at $65–100 billion, over 60% of it from hospitals due to heavy EHR system investments.

Cost Factor #6: Fee for service pricing. During the 1980s and 90s, in an attempt to reign in already galloping health care costs, insurers in the U.S. set up Health Maintenance Plans, or HMOs. HMOs were very successful in reducing unit costs, i.e. hourly physician fees or hospital rates. This led to a significant reduction in physicians' income. Just like airline pilots following deregulation of the U.S. skies in the late 1970s and 1980s, physicians lost their status as very wealthy professionals with lots of time for golf. However, what they lost in unit costs they made up with volume, at the cost of much longer hours. This became true for hospitals as well. Fee for service ensured that health insurers (and principally their rate payers and the government) picked up the tab pretty much systematically for this increase in physician visits, hospital in- and out-patient treatments, expensive brand-name drugs, and state of the art CAT scans. The complexity of fee for service pricing is overwhelming and makes the U.S. reimbursement system one of the most complex systems known to mankind. Words like "CPT codes"; "practice net days in accounts receivable"; and "professional services denial percentage" are common jargon used by physicians, hospitals, and payors in revenue cycle management

(RCM). RCM is a big industry in the U.S. (billions of dollars and tens of thousands of employees), whereas in France and Germany pricing and billing are so simple they have already been automated for the most part. Needless to say, fee for service, administration costs, and complexity in the U.S. are tightly interwoven and go hand in hand.

During the last five years, serious attempts have been made to wean U.S. health care away from fee for service, through the creation of Accountable Care Organizations or ACOs. ACOs are hospitals or groups of physicians that provide coordinated care to a patient population with the double objective of reducing total cost of care and improving health outcomes. The future according to ACOs is a world where health providers are paid for successful outcomes or at least a fixed fee per "life" to keep a given population of patients healthy. The CMS has made ACOs official, allowing participating ACOs to share in the savings they achieve for the Medicare program. The CMS and Medicare approved thirty-two pioneering ACOs in 2011, and there were 404 Medicare Shared Savings Program ACOs in 2015, representing 7.3 million beneficiaries. However, like most new initiatives in U.S. health care, take up is slow and savings small. These 404 MSSP ACOs achieved only a combined $338 million in savings, a paltry amount. And prominent voices in the industry are saying no. The Mayo Clinic, a pioneer in integrated care and quest for best outcomes at the lowest total cost of care, declined to participate in the ACO program in 2011. So did other advanced provider systems such as the Cleveland Clinic and Intermountain Healthcare. Reasons given were the proposed ACOs' burdensome, complex rules, shared savings, antitrust rules, and concerns about oversight boards including patients. Today, despite all the intellectual and administrative efforts directed at the ACOs, fee for service still dominates the U.S. health care landscape. Every doctor wants to do the right thing and get us to good health. At the margin, however, in those "gray zones" that exist for example at diagnostic time, physicians are incentivized to perform that additional test, even if expensive. Doctors worry patients will sue them for malpractice, and more often than not patients too will be happy with extra care, lab work, and technology-intensive treatment. Which one of us wants a doctor simply to say go home and put ice on that twisted limb?

One of the most visible effects of fee for service in the U.S. is overtreatment. In her powerful book *Overtreated: Why Too Much Medicine Is Making Us Sicker and Poorer* (2007), Shannon Brownlee advances the thesis that overtreatment is the single biggest culprit in excessive U.S. health care costs. In the introduction to her book, she states: "Wasteful bureaucratic overhead, malpractice, moral hazard and high prices . . . all contribute to the high cost of American medicine." She continues:

The most important piece of the puzzle has been consistently overlooked. There is one more factor that contributes to our medical bills, and that's unnecessary care. We spend between one fifth and one third of our health care dollars, an exorbitant amount of money, between five hundred and seven hundred billion dollars, on care that does nothing to improve our health. And while overhead and high prices hurt our pocketbooks, the vast amount of unnecessary care in the system also makes our health care worse than it ought to be. Unnecessary treatment and tests aren't just expensive, they also can harm patients.[29]

Among the many examples of unnecessary and harmful treatments administrated to patients in Shannon Brownlee's book, one stands out. In the chapter "Your Local Hospital," she tells the story of cardiologists Chae Hyun Moon and Fidel Realyvasquez, Jr., practicing surgeons at the Redding Medical Center. Redding is a small northern Californian town in the foothills of Mt. Shasta. Between June 2001 and 2002, Moon performed as many as a dozen cardiac stent or balloon angioplasties per day, and billed Medicare $4 million. The Redding Medical Center was also performing about 800 open-heart surgeries per year, many of them done by Realyvasquez. All in all, the good people of Redding were suffering from catheterizations and open-heart interventions at ten times the national average! It all ended in tears, or rather multi-million-dollar fines for the physicians and the for-profit Redding Medical Center. There were also patients and shareholders lawsuits. Moon and Realyvasquez paid $1.4 million each in fines and had their Medicare privileges revoked, but the harm was done.

Cost Factor #7: The price of drugs is increasing too fast. At 14% per year from 2012 to 2015, it was the fastest growing component of health care expenditures in the U.S. during that period, with prescription drugs spending reaching $330 billion in 2016. This has not gone unnoticed, courtesy of a few spectacular cases that have stirred public opinion. Martin Shkreli, the now disgraced CEO of Turing, acquired Daraprim, an off-patent drug treating toxoplasmosis, an anti-parasitic infection, in the fall of 2014. Turing then promptly raised its price to $750 a pill from $13.50, a 5,500% increase! An immensely more respected pharmaceuticals company, Gilead Sciences, developed a very effective new Hepatitis C drug called Sovaldi and decided to retail it at a very steep $84,000 for a 12-week treatment. This treatment is extraordinarily effective and has cost a fair amount to develop. We should be happy to have it, but its pricing contributes to the inflation of health care costs.[30]

And then there is the saga of Valeant. Throughout 2016, Valeant appeared to be run like a private equity group doing "roll-ups" of existing drugs. All the emphasis was on deal making, marketing, and sales rather than research; the whole thing was leveraged to the hilt with $31 billion in debt. How was this debt going to be repaid? Through systematic price increases, at an average of more than 66% for 81% of the drugs in Valeant's portfolio, according to a December 23, 2015 *Financial Times* article.[31] Around that time, Congress started being concerned about companies like Valeant and Turing. At a hearing of the Senate Special Committee on Aging, the committee's chairwoman, Senator Susan Collins (R–ME), said, "some of the companies that have been the focus of our investigation look more like hedge funds than traditional pharmaceutical companies." Eventually the markets realized this. The "E" word (as in Enron) was whispered, and Valeant saw about 85% of its market capitalization evaporate between the summer of 2015 and the spring of 2016. Valeant's CEO, Michael Pearson, stepped down in May of 2016, and hedge funds heavily invested in the company, like Pershing Square, suffered heavy losses on their investment.

Given that Medicare Part D does not allow Medicare to negotiate drug prices, and that private payers often follow Medicare's steps, there seems to be strong incentives for drug companies to test continuously rising prices: price gouging? Well, that is one of the oldest economic sins in the world, and one of the simplest, too. The industry is one of the largest users of paid political lobbyists, and the simple message Joe Public hears is that "without high U.S. drug prices, pharmaceuticals groups would not have the funds they need to pursue expensive research into new drugs for the benefit of the whole world." Is this why prescription drugs are 50% costlier in the U.S. than in other OECD countries? The McKinsey Global Institute (MGI) looked at this in 2009 and concluded that neither the "R&D subsidy for the rest of the world" nor higher marketing and sales spending in the U.S. could explain this difference, which MGI estimated at $98 billion per year in extra U.S. costs.[32] Martin Shkreli has been arrested and could go to jail for years, ironically for financial sins that have nothing to do with the cost of Daraprim. In the meantime, drug prices keep rising.[33] To be fair, this cost factor has much more to do with politics (Medicare Part D and CMS are prevented from negotiating drug prices, in stark contrast with, for example, the NHS and Canada's Medicare) and aggressive pricing behavior by pharma companies than with complexity. Still, it had to be mentioned.

The overall impact of the cost factors described above is brilliantly illustrated by the most comprehensive work on excess U.S. health costs and challenged medical outcomes, performed to date on medical practice variation across our fifty states. The brainchild of Dr. John Wennberg at Dartmouth–Hitchcock, practice variation looks at the differences in total cost of care across the country not dictated by illness or medical need. These variations are quite large and lead to widely varying health care costs per capita for different sets of populations and geographies in the U.S. They can be caused by shortfalls in effective care (services of proven clinical effectiveness), quality of care, patient preferences, and supply-sensitive care (services provided in the absence of medical evidence). Dr. Wennberg's work, which started in the late 1960s with Medicare, led to the assertion that most practice variation is unwarranted. With Dartmouth colleagues Jonathan Skinner and Elliott Fisher, Wennberg's research on unwarranted and geographic variation led to the *Dartmouth Atlas of Health Care*, first published in 1996. The *Dartmouth Atlas* shows a more than two-fold variation in per capita Medicare spending in different regions of the country. It compares the intensity of a myriad of procedures across all U.S. geographies and finds startling differences: for example, "why are the rates of coronary stents three times higher in Elyria, Ohio, compared with nearby Cleveland, home of the famous Cleveland Clinic?"[34]

Dartmouth research teams looked at Medicare rates per procedure; regional population income levels; sickness levels per region; higher hospital service intensity; and spending, and found that these factors offered little correlation to explain these variations. They also found a strong correlation between Medicare spending and overall spending in health care for given regions. The Dartmouth research leads to estimates that between 20% and 30% of the nation's spending on health is unnecessary. This represents $660 to $990 billion per year! But at least three other groups of analysts have reached similar estimates of unwarranted spending: the New England Healthcare Institute, the McKinsey Global Institute, and Thomson Reuters.[35,36]

Needless to say, research pointing at such dramatic findings is not without detractors. The Dartmouth Institute for Health Policy and Clinical Practice, now led by Dr. Elliott Fisher, has seen its analysis challenged by several sources. Some simply argue that the correlation between Medicare spending and total cost of care in a given region is not as tight as the Dartmouth researchers claim. Others agree there is waste, but not nearly as much as 30%, and that by eliminating unnecessary variation, the system may save some money but mostly will reach better medical outcomes (not necessarily a bad result). There is also recent economic analysis that shows that local health care markets suffer in some cases from provider or payer quasi-monopolies, leading to higher prices, independently of volumes of care.[37,38]

Are there cures for practice variation and more generally excess health costs in the U.S.? Yes, and without going into much detail at this stage, one can cite: increased roles for PCPs, with incentives for them to be very selective when recommending specialists and expensive treatments to their patients; focus from the same PCPs on the sub-set of (typically poorer and less educated) patients who need the most follow-up to ensure they follow their prescribed treatments and do not need expensive hospital readmissions; and allowing health insurers to break down state barriers and compete nationally, like for example in automobile insurance.

Overall, though, practice variation (and the ensuing high total cost of care for less than optimum medical outcomes) is a direct corollary of the complexity and state-by-state fragmentation of the U.S. health care system. The *Dartmouth Atlas* makes this link explicit:

The irony is that the level of spending on health care in a community is uncorrelated with the incidence of effective care. The

Dartmouth Atlas Project's studies of Medicare enrollees show that even in regions where Medicare spends the most money per capita on enrollees, there is no guarantee that these simple, cost-effective, proven care measures will be included in the roster of medical interventions. In fact, Atlas research shows that spending is *inversely* correlated with the likelihood of receiving recommended care, meaning that people who live in higher- spending regions (who see many more different physicians and make many more physician visits) are *less* likely to receive these services than those who live in areas where per capita spending is lower, and continuity of care might be higher. Indeed, enrollees in traditional Medicare in regions with fewer specialists and more family practice physicians (and less Medicare per capita spending) are more likely to receive effective care. Why? One explanation is that patients with chronic illnesses who live in high-spending regions (where there are also many more medical specialists per capita) tend to have many more physicians involved in their care. That can complicate the care processes to such an extent that no one physician is clearly in charge and responsible for assuring that needed care is provided.[39,40]

Conservatively, complexity in health care, with its systematic use of expensive drugs and technologies; redundant administrative and IT activities; dysfunctional pricing; and state-by-state practice variation costs us $500–600 billion per year (assuming half the estimates mentioned above). That is at least $5 trillion every ten years: think of what we could do with this, in terms of education, fixing our infrastructure, or financing our social safety net . . .

In sports, our love of complexity is cultural and a harmless pursuit.

In health care, the unbelievable complexity of our U.S. system has historical roots dating from World War II and is very political in nature. This complexity feeds on itself, each proposed remedy adding to it. But unlike in sports, this is for keeps! The resulting unnecessary costs to our nation are amazingly high and carry huge opportunity costs in terms of federal, state, local, and family budgets. Individual frustration is rampant: I was talking to my former Berkeley roommate Steve the other day, and he had just finished enrolling his family in a new health plan.

> I had to choose between two very complex health plans, one involving health savings accounts, and one with variable deductible and co-pays. Both had very different reimbursement rates and deductibles depending on whether the physician or hospital chosen were "in or out of network." In one of the plans, my GP was in network, but not my children's pediatrician. The whole process was time-consuming and nerve-wracking. I eventually decided on one of the plans, but still do not know if I made the right decision for my family.

Millions experience the very same frustrations in the U.S., year after year. And this does not take into account the millions of people still left without health insurance of any kind, a unique feature of U.S. health care among developed countries. There is no easy fix here. Even if (imagine) we woke up one day with the Japanese health system, one unintended consequence would be to have to deal with the millions (literally) of administrative, medical, and technical jobs that would have vanished. Because one key factor not mentioned thus far is that, besides the government, health care is the only sector in the country that has seen a net creation of jobs since the year 2000.

It is not difficult to understand this. Within the recent regime of the ACA and ACOs, a few incremental steps here and there; better adoption of identified best practices; and expansion of Medicaid in many states have been like adding new bricks to an already giant Lego construction. After the November 8, 2016 election, though, we have been promised, loudly, solemnly, and umpteenth times that "Obamacare is dead." Surely repealing the ACA is a simple step, and our Lego construction is going to have a few bricks fewer? Think again.

As soon as the Trump administration and the House Republicans put health care on the table as their first legislative priority for early 2017, many voices, not from Democrats but on the winning Republican side, warned that we "cannot eliminate the ACA from day one without a replacement in hand." Politicians are not suicidal, and even the most diehard nemesis of Obamacare does not want to be held responsible for over twenty million people suddenly losing health insurance. So, there was talk for a brief while of "repeal and delay." This was a surrealistic concept in which repeal of the Affordable Care Act would happen on day one of the new presidency, with the actual implementation of this repeal delayed for . . . at least two years (so that no one would suffer electorally during the 2018 mid-term elections), and perhaps more?

This did not last long, and Speaker Paul Ryan and his GOP leadership went to work drafting a new "American Health Care Act (AHCA)." When the specifics were released, what surprised most observers was how much of the basic Obamacare architecture had been retained in the AHCA. Essentially, the proposed plan would do away with the ACA taxes on high individual brackets, including on investment gains, and on medical devices; insurance companies would be able to charge people 50 years of age or older up to five times more than for young individuals, versus three times in the ACA; the Obamacare subsidies would be replaced by less generous tax credits, depending upon age as opposed to income; and the extension of Medicaid would be phased out by 2020, with fixed payments per Medicaid recipients given to the States instead of the current federal funding. The latter is a long-desired GOP recipe for decreases in Medicaid funding and coverage. Pillars of the ACA kept in the Ryan plan included insurance companies not being able to deny insurance for pre-conditions or to cap coverage; the ability of individuals up to 26 years of age to stay on their parents' health plan; and Medicaid extensions protected until 2020.

The Congressional Budget Office (CBO) then published its report, which was devastating: over the next ten years, twenty-four million Americans would lose insurance under the GOP plan; and a $800 billion tax windfall would accrue to the wealthiest Americans, essentially financed by a $1.1 trillion in Medicaid cuts. Speaker Ryan professed to liking the implied $300 billion or so budget reduction, which "could help finance tax reform (and assorted tax cuts)." Interestingly, the most conservative House Republicans, grouped under the "Freedom Caucus," did not see it at all this way. They revolted, arguing vociferously that the proposed plan was way too much like Obamacare. In the Senate, the Republicans held a narrow 52–48 majority, meaning that three Republican senators would be able to block passage of the bill, given the unanimous Democratic opposition. And three such senators, Ted Cruz (TX), Mike Lee (UT), and Rand Paul (TN) echoed House Freedom Caucus members, potentially blocking the passage of the GOP law – even if it cleared the House. A fourth, Tom Cotton, urged his House colleagues to "start all over again, and take their time to do it right." On the other hand, three moderate Republican senators (Susan Collins of Maine; Bill Cassidy of Louisiana; and Dean Heller of Nevada) also said they would vote no, but for opposite reasons: they would not countenance millions of low-income adults and children losing their health care coverage. A number of Republican governors opposed the AHCA as well, fearful of declining federal support for their Medicaid programs.

All of this is not surprising. One of the cardinal virtues of the very complex ACA was its simplicity of purpose: provide insurance to those Americans who do not enjoy it, period. But what did the Ryan law stand for? On its face value, it was something like, "cut Medicaid funding and health benefits to the poor in order to give tax cuts to the rich." But it is difficult to make this the center-selling point of a health law. So, then, what was the mission of this hodgepodge of legislation? Ending Medicaid as we know it? Removing subsidies to low-income Americans? Maintaining coverage for pre-existing conditions? It was all very diffuse, which is why the proposed GOP law had many detractors, and even for its supporters provided few catchy "sound bites" to promote it. We were far away from Trump's simple promise during his campaign that "everyone will be taken care of, coverage for everybody." On March 23, Speaker Ryan and the White House had to announce postponement of the full House vote on the proposed AHCA. But President Trump, who had spent two days negotiating with the Freedom Caucus, signaled his patience was at an end: "no more negotiations, time to vote!" All this on the seventh anniversary of the Affordable Care Act. At the end of this eventful day, Trump gambled and demanded a full House vote for the next day: "vote yes today, or Obamacare stays!" Who would Republican representatives be more afraid of, Trump or their constituents? With the AHCA polling at 56% of negative opinions to only 17% of favorable ones, there was another dilemma for these conservative congress people. Vote to pass a bad law, likely to hurt Trump-voting, rural working-class poor the most; or vote against the law and be on record for a vote to keep Obamacare after screaming "repeal" for seven years. The vote on the House was scheduled for 3:30pm on March 24. But the votes to pass the bill still weren't there, despite all the arm-twisting and presidential tweets. So President Trump asked Speaker Ryan to pull the GOP health care bill. He also said, famously, in a meeting of the nation's governors at the White House during this convoluted process: "it's an unbelievably complex subject. Nobody knew health care could be so complicated."

After one more failed attempt in April, the House approved on May 4 an amended version of the AHCA by the narrowest of margins, 217 for to 213 against. The new amendments placated the extreme voices of the "Freedom Caucus" by allowing states to "opt out" of insurance coverage for patients with pre-existing conditions and essential benefits guaranteed under Obamacare. To provide some reassurance to a couple of congressmen from Michigan and Missouri concerned about the effectiveness of "High Risk Pools" to help states cover those unfortunate patients with pre-existing conditions, $8 billion of funding was added at the last minute to the bill to secure its passage. Most experts think that these opaque and complex "High Risk Pools" need at least $25 billion per year to be effective in protecting those with pre-existing conditions, so what could $8 billion over five years achieve?

And what about CBO scoring? Not yet available for the amended law, which was thus voted on by congress people who did not have any CBO visibility on its impact on patient coverage and financial costs. Never mind the fact that several of them admitted to not having read the full text of the bill. President Trump celebrated a "great victory." Needless to say, Democrats in the both the House and Senate were defiant and unanimous in opposition. The AHCA bill then had to go to the Senate, where new provisions would be added, others removed, and things changed to such a degree that most House members might no longer recognize the bill they had passed on May 4. The Senate leadership actually stated quite clearly that they were starting their own health care bill from scratch, not using House bill. This would be no easy task, as the Senate has its own version of the House's Freedom Caucus versus the more moderate "Tuesday Group" challenging dynamics. Think Ted Cruz versus Susan Collins, for example. Before much could happen in the Senate, the CBO released on May 24 its verdict on the AHCA version passed by the House. Twenty-three million Americans would lose health insurance (instead of twenty-four million in the earlier March version); over ten years, deficits would be reduced by $120 billion – versus $300 billion in the earlier version; much touted reductions in the cost of health insurance coverage would occur very sparingly, and only in case of new, bare-bones insurance packages. Net, virtually no change: a million fewer people losing health coverage (a mere 4% difference with the earlier version), at the cost of $180 billion.

This does not sound simple, does it? To the contrary, it looks like any scenario will lead to additional increments of complexity to our health care construction. We had for example in the AHCA the favorite Republican proposal of "replacing Medicaid with state block grants." In which states? How? With what transition? We also had quasi-uniform tax credits replacing Obamacare's much more income-based subsidies. Speaker Ryan insisted on those in name of Republican orthodoxy, and they might have worked fine for those earning above $100,000 a year, but what about those near but not yet of Medicare age?

What about the working poor, already impacted by the decimation of Medicaid? There were also the negotiations between the White House and House Republicans, started on March 23 and concluded on May 3, that let states "opt out" of the ACA's "essential benefits" provision, allowing insurance companies to offer "light packages" targeted to the young, without coverage for mental health treatment, wellness visits, and maternity care. Again, in which states? How? Under which conditions? Would this lead to "basement-level" health insurance? And what about the $75 billion (over ten years) proposed to ease the burden on older, but pre-Medicare, low-income working adults, which is the Trump majority voting population that ironically would have lost the most under the GOP-proposed AHCA? How would it work? So many complex questions and so few answers . . .

I will not even attempt to discuss the potential privatization of Medicare through the "voucher care" program dear to House Speaker Paul Ryan. Some House members floated the concept again, discretely, only to be rebuffed immediately by several leading Republican senators, along the lines of: "we should not attempt to chew too much at the same time." Things were complicated enough already – the AHCA travails in the House, President Trump's own admission that health care was much more complex than he ever thought, etc. – without attempting to go after Medicare as well. As "repeal and replace Obamacare" efforts moved to the U.S. Senate, it was clear that this health care legislative effort could prove as challenging as the attempts by the George W. Bush administration to privatize Social Security during its second term.

In particular, the timing of the Senate to arrive at its own health bill was uncertain, to say the least. In the meantime, the ACA remained the law of the land. To be continued . . . more on our ongoing health care political saga in the last chapter of this book.

One thing is certain: complexity in health care will likely continue to grow inexorably. Most of us will continue to pay very high premiums for coverage and care that may reach world-class levels for some, but that on average lags behind that on offer in all other developing countries. Millions of Americans remain without health insurance, with their number likely to grow by additional millions. We will continue to watch with astonishment as many of our hospitals teeter on the verge of financial insolvency, despite their high prices. And we will remain upset at seeing outsized profits at insurance and pharmaceutical companies on the business pages of our newspapers. Even in a country happy to celebrate winners, having some of these players laugh all the way to the bank while health care faces so many challenges is not what we aspire to.

Unless we find the collective political will for a massive and radical overhaul, possible only with a bi-partisan enthusiasm impossible to imagine today, health care complexity will remain a heavy load to carry in the U.S.

3 Electricity and utilities

Thomas Edison, electricity, and the most innovative decades of history

In this cool summer of 2011, my five children and I have decided to go to the top of the Eiffel Tower. We are vacationing in Paris, and this ritual is a must-do. One can easily forget that Eiffel only got permission to build his tower for the 1889 Universal Exhibit on the condition that it be destroyed ten years later. Fortunately, local authorities saw the light, and this symbol of the City of Lights dominates the Paris skyline to this day. It did not go the way of Pennsylvania Station in New York, another steel construction masterpiece, or Paris' own beautiful steel architected central market, les Halles – both are sorely missed.

Paris is not the most visited city on earth by accident, and there are huge lines to the beautiful arched elevators that bring tourists to the first and second floors of the landmark tower. Never mind: a small sign indicates there is no line if one chooses to ascend by foot. Here we go: "it will be excellent exercise for you, Papa," the kids tell me. I am happy to comply, because a prize awaits me at the top. Not the great 360-degree view of Paris, which looks decidedly grey today with all these clouds. This will be for the children; I know the city very well already. No, the goal for me is to see the small room in which a nice, full-sized wax replica of Gustave Eiffel proudly shows his beautiful creation to a certain distinguished American guest, Thomas Edison. The brilliant architect and engineer shares his revolutionary design with the genius and foremost inventor of the late nineteenth century.

Thomas Edison! What don't we owe him?

During the first half of the nineteenth century, residences, commercial buildings, and streets were lit by manufactured coal gas. Then oil was discovered in Pennsylvania in 1859. With oil came large quantities of natural gas, which by the 1880s had been harnessed on a large scale in cities like Pittsburgh. A number of early inventors had succeeded in creating early types of arc lamps, but none of these could burn for more than a few minutes. Edison chose a new approach, raised a lot of money from leading industrialists of the time (three Morgan partners; other bankers; and the president of Western Union), and created the Edison Electric Light Company in 1878.

Edison was inventor, visionary, and shrewd businessman all in one. He had already anticipated that electricity and the wires carrying it would bring not only light, but also power to all sorts of machines, and heat to cook food and stay warm. He got his backers to give his company royalties on all electric lamps sold. Edison wanted his invention to be a big business as soon as it materialized. There were lots of skeptics, but gas company stock prices declined significantly following the incorporation of Edison Electric Light. Edison organized his research on a grand scale in Menlo Park, New Jersey, with offices, laboratories, machine shops, a glass blowing facility, and lots of the most able chemists, machinists, and scientists of the time. He had more resources at his disposal than any inventor of his era. Applying Ohm's law, Edison understood first that the electric lamp should have a high resistance filament, which would generate heat proportional to the resistance times the current intensity squared. The heat would then cause the filament to glow, producing light. In 1879, he and his team developed an electric generator with wires laid out around a drum that was much better than anything produced thus far. He understood that his high resistant filament should be inside a glass where all air had been taken out through a vacuum pump. Edison then discovered after lengthy research and a lot of trials that carbon (a carbonized cotton thread, spiraled), not platinum, as originally thought, was the material to use for the filament. In December 1879, Edison filed his patent and performed several demonstrations that showed the brightness and consistency of his incandescent lamp design. By January 1880, his lamps could burn for over three hundred hours without any failure. Edison was 33 years old.[1]

Here we need to pause and look at the last three decades of the nineteenth century and the first two of the twentieth: Edison; George Westinghouse (failsafe compressed air brakes for trains, then AC current); Alexander Bell (telephone and gramophone); and the fabulous expansion of the railroads. In 1869, the first U.S. transcontinental railroad was completed by Central Pacific and Union Pacific, the former led by the "Big Four" (Leland Stanford; Charles Crocker; Mark Hopkins; and Collis Huntington). By the turn of the century U.S. railroads had added over 220,000 miles of track throughout the country. The first years of the new century represented the advent of the automobile, with pioneers on both sides of the Atlantic and Henry Ford's chain assembly of his popular Ford T in 1908. Eventually, fourteen million Ford Ts would be built.

All the technological revolutions of the late nineteenth century transformed the world.

These inventions fundamentally changed every aspect of our ancestors' daily lives. All could see at night, both outside and in their homes; they could keep warm in the toughest of winters; they could communicate with each other over the longest of distances; clean piped water, new chemicals and pharmaceuticals ensured they stayed healthy; and back-breaking domestic chores such as carrying water, washing and cooking became a drudgery of the past. Thomas Hobbes' "solitary, poor, nasty, brutish and short" life of the people was no more. During the 1930s and the immediate post–WWII years, this progress was made available to all, even in the remotest rural areas. It is easy to take this creation of new personal comforts for granted, but let's remember that even today, in the twenty-first century, over two billion people do not have access to sanitized water; nearly as many still do not have access to clean cooking facilities; and 1.3 billion do not have electricity in their homes.[2]

The five decades between 1870 and 1920 stand as the most innovative in our history and unleashed tremendous productivity gains that lasted until 1970, or over 100 years. According to Northwestern University economics professor Robert Gordon:

> The rise in U.S. standard of living from 1870 to 1970 was a special century – and won't likely be repeated ...
>
> ... The 1920–70 expansion grew out of the second industrial revolution, when fossil fuels, the internal-combustion engine, advanced metals and factory automation came together to produce electric lighting, indoor plumbing, home appliances, motor vehicles, air travel, air conditioning, television and much longer life expectancy ...
>
> ... Many of the benefits of the second tidal wave of invention showed up in gross domestic product, output per person and output per hour. Total factor productivity (TFP) – how quickly output is growing relative to the capital and labor being used, and therefore a measure of innovation's contribution to growth – grew more rapidly from 1920 to 1970 than ever before or since ...
>
> ... From 1970–1994 it was only 0.57 percent a year, less than a third of the 1.89 percent rate of 1920–1970 (From 1994 to 2004 it was 1.02 percent; from 2004 to 2014 only 0.40 percent) ...
>
> ... Why did TFP growth accelerate rapidly after 1920? The roaring 1920s, followed by the dislocations of the Great Depression and World War II, disguised the rapid pace of innovation that began in the 1920s and took flight (figuratively and literally) in the 1930s and 1940s ...
>
> ... Although revolutionary, the Internet's effects were limited when compared with the second industrial revolution, which changed everything. The former had little effect on purchases of food, clothing, cars, furniture, fuel and appliances. A pedicure is a pedicure whether the customer is reading a magazine or surfing the web on a smartphone. Computers aren't everywhere. We don't eat, wear or drive them to work. We don't let them cut our hair. We live in dwellings that have appliances much like those in the 1950s and we drive in motor vehicles that perform the same functions as in the 1950s, albeit with more convenience and safety.[3]

★　★　★　★　★

DC or AC: early competition, duopoly, and oligopolies in electricity

The first great fight in electricity generation and distribution was between Thomas Edison (DC) and George Westinghouse (AC). Edison had developed the first electricity distribution system in 1882, but its main handicap was its short transmission range due to the losses in direct current (DC) wires over any distance superior to a mile. As a result, early DC networks had to operate within a mile or so of a central generation facility.

George Westinghouse was also a prolific inventor, who had pioneered the air braking system in trains that still carries his name. In a Westinghouse compressed air brake system, any leak will lead to the brakes slamming shut, and therefore provide automatic system safety for trains of any length. The "Westinghouse" also removed the need for brakes having to be applied separately to each wagon by brakemen, thus eliminating a very labor intensive and dangerous activity. Westinghouse also had interests in telephone switching and early gas distribution networks. Moving from gas to electricity distribution was a logical step. In 1885 Westinghouse imported transformers developed by Lucien Gaulard of France and John Gibbs of England, which allowed alternating current (AC) voltages to be increased to reduce transmission losses, and then decreased again for consumer use. In 1886, Westinghouse and physicist William Stanley developed the Gaulard–Gibbs design further to allow up to 3,000 volts for transmission, and with a Siemens AC generator installed the first multiple-voltage AC power system in Massachusetts. In 1887, Westinghouse had 68 AC power stations (versus Edison's 121 DC stations). The Westinghouse Electric Corporation, thus named in 1889, was born.[4]

Naturally, Edison fought back aggressively, in what became known as the "War of Currents." In 1888, Edison launched a media campaign claiming that high voltage AC systems were dangerous, would kill people and should be used to replace hanging as a method of execution for condemned prisoners (the first execution by electrocution did take place in August 1890). In the end, the leading financiers of the time, led by J.P. Morgan, took a position and ended the feud. Edison Electric was pushed towards AC, and Thomas Edison lost control of his own company, which was merged in 1892 with a Westinghouse AC competitor, Thomson–Houston, to form the General Electric (GE) of today. GE had all the Thomson–Houston AC patents and the Edison distribution networks, and the next thirty years would be dominated by the General Electric–Westinghouse duopoly. Westinghouse completed his integrated AC system by licensing Nikola Tesla's patents for the first AC polyphase induction motors in 1888. In 1896, GE and Westinghouse signed a patent-sharing agreement. This ended costly patent battles and cemented their duopoly, controlling the market for all power-generating equipment, transformers, electric motors, and lighting. The two companies then moved into consumer goods and domestic appliances.

In these ferociously innovative years between 1870 and 1920, a number of key arbitrages were made in the U.S. with regards to electricity. Some occurred as a direct consequence of the entrepreneurial genius of the likes of Edison and Westinghouse. Others followed from the strong involvement of the leading banks and financiers of the time. And several were the consequence of the decentralized nature of the U.S. political system. The result is worth mentioning, because it was quite different from what took place across the Atlantic in the U.K., France, and Germany. In the U.S., early electricity generation and distribution networks shared four main characteristics: development and ownership was in private enterprise hands; concentration of stock ownership, with Westinghouse and General Electric owning shareholding in many utilities, allowed for oligopolistic rate setting with large industrial customers favored over residential ones; physical decentralization led to a myriad of small generating stations; and decentralized government allowed local communities to grant concessions to private utilities.

This oligopoly of electric utilities, revolving around the powerful GE–Westinghouse duopoly, was totally dominant, and maintained by several industry associations. These linked the very active General Electric and Westinghouse research labs that had started creating all the appliances that brought to Americans modern home comforts and easier work in industrial settings, with utility executives, investors and businessmen. The largest such organization was the National Electric Light Association, or NELA, which held its first meeting in Chicago in 1885. NELA played a key role in the distribution, sales and marketing, and engineering activities of most U.S. utilities. As such, it kept the electrical industry tightly bound together.

However, leading politicians of the time started to espouse and promote different views. Not surprisingly, given his successful "trust busting" efforts, Theodore Roosevelt was the first U.S. President (and before that New York governor) to advocate strongly for some government control, at both the state and federal level. He wanted some control of at least key power generation assets such as New York's hydroelectric resources. Roosevelt felt strongly that the electrical industry oligopoly had to be disturbed by new actors in this dominant industry of that age. Al Smith and Franklin Roosevelt, both as New York governors, took the same position. Fiorello La Guardia, the legendary mayor of New York, tried to build municipal power and have New York build its own generating plants. But the powerful utility lobby succeeded in defeating all these attempts. The private utility industry, led in great part by the NELA president and Edison's former first secretary Samuel Insull, achieved a master stroke with the creation of state regulatory agencies to provide oversight of the utilities' "natural monopolies." By 1920, most U.S. states had set up regulatory bodies that provided a form of public supervision to electric utilities. This allowed utilities to keep their geographical monopolies and their private sector ownership, protecting them as well against the vagaries of popular state and federal elections. At the same time, the regulatory bodies were commissions made up of a few appointees by the local state governor, which made lobbying efforts easy and effective. This system of regulated "natural monopolies" still exists in some form to this day.

★   ★   ★   ★   ★

The New Deal disturbs the status quo: FDR, the TVA, and the REA

Like in so many areas, Franklin Roosevelt and his New Deal disrupted the comfortable status quo for the U.S. electricity industry. And in doing so, FDR also played a role in increasing the complexity of the overall system. Already the electric system had grown in a fairly complex way between 1880 and 1920. One reason was that originally, technological constraints prevented the integration of a myriad of local systems. As alternating current technology improved, transmission of electricity became possible over longer distances, and regional consolidation and integration of power generation, transmission and distribution started to take place. However, this was a slow process. Another reason was the decentralization of the U.S. political system, where federal, state and local authorities all wielded different powers. This prevented a very quickly growing industry from following any type of national energy policy. Invariably, those who had been the early advocates of some type of government oversight at both the federal and state level, like Teddy Roosevelt, would lose their public campaigns for public power against the NELA and what was already a gigantic private sector industry. And why not? After all, the increasingly consolidated and integrated electric system could deliver electricity to industrial and residential consumers alike far more cheaply than the few smaller public systems in existence.

However, several factors helped prepare the ground for changes in the electric industry as the "roaring twenties" crashed with the stock market in 1929. First, as utilities started to use water resources in an ever-increasing scale for the sole purpose of power generation, politicians, led by progressives, started to push legislation that would also take into account key environment issues as well. The Water Power Act of the 1930s allowed government supervision of utilities to ensure that dam construction had the multiple purposes of flood control, irrigation, and soil conservation in addition to power generation. Second, private utilities struggled with the electrification of rural America. Very large distances, sparse populations, and challenges in installing electric equipment in most farm equipment all contributed to a low level of rural electrification in the late 1920s. Even a well-publicized dam construction initiative planned by no less than Henry Ford and Thomas Edison around the Tennessee Valley failed to take off. Third, the 1929 financial market crash put a further damper on any expansion effort by private utilities. As a result, apart from in the Northeast and the Pacific coastal states, most of the rural areas in the U.S. had no electricity. This put the country far behind European countries in terms of percentage of people having access to electricity.[5]

Enters Franklin Delano Roosevelt in 1932: one of his first priorities as newly elected president was to help farmers. They had been devastated by utility land grabs (to build new hydroelectric plants, work on which stopped abruptly when utilities shares collapsed) and by banks that were taking over family farms as low crop prices prevented them from paying their debts. FDR acted promptly to stabilize crop prices and curtail the number of bankruptcies. But he also firmly believed that only government intervention could bring electricity to rural life and help transform it. The massive construction projects required to achieve this would also provide work to millions of unemployed Americans, a key feature of the New Deal. FDR and his administration created the Tennessee Valley Authority (TVA) in 1933, with strong support from Congress led by progressive Republican Nebraska Senator George Norris. The Rural Electrification Administration (REA), one of Roosevelt's New Deal Agencies, was established in 1935. Before the REA was established, utilities had successfully fought any government involvement in electrifying rural areas, and at the same time claimed it was unprofitable for them to extend their lines over many miles of sparsely populated lands. Private utilities charged rural rate payers as much as four times as much as city customers. As a result, in 1934 less than 11% of U.S. farms had electricity, against 90% in France and Germany. The REA made loans available to all local cooperatives that applied for them to create rural transmission and distribution networks, and by the early 1950s pretty much all farms in the country had electricity. By then REA had also moved into telephones and financed rural telephone lines in the same way.[6,7]

The TVA would revolve around a series of dams to be built along the Tennessee River, which experienced frequent floods and challenging navigation due to constantly changing water levels. The area covered by these projects was well over 100,000 square miles, spanning seven states: electrification would transform the local rural economy. Agriculture would benefit from flood control and irrigation; transport of bulk materials would benefit from new navigation routes; and millions of small farmers and village habitants would discover the magic of electricity. For the first time in U.S. history, the government would be engaged in the power business in a very large way (twenty-nine dams were eventually built), which would help it create its own set of metrics to assess the performance of private utilities. Roosevelt was no doubt well aware of several very successful public utility experiences in European countries, several of which continue to this day.

Naturally, private utilities across the nation were furiously opposed to the TVA, seeing it as a "state socialism" vehicle encroaching on their hitherto protected "natural monopolies." The utilities' fears were not unfounded, since Roosevelt and Congress viewed the TVA as a pioneering experiment in government-sponsored regional development and planning that might lead to a new social and economic order. In the end, the TVA proved to be a significant infrastructure program helping many local private companies, rather than the harbinger of rural socialism. But the debate around the TVA raged fiercely for over a decade. It went all the way to the Supreme Court, which in 1936 (*Ashwander v. Tennessee Valley Authority*) affirmed the constitutionality of the TVA. As a direct result of the creation of the TVA, most of the major U.S. hydropower systems, such as the Bonneville Power Administration around the Columbia River in the Pacific Northwest, are federally managed today. And the TVA remains extremely popular in one of the most conservative regions of the nation. Local taxpayers, by definition also local electricity ratepayers, enjoy the fact that there is a direct correlation between the TVA's financial health and their states' coffers. If the TVA is financially successful, their state budgets will benefit, potentially leading to lower state taxes or available funds for other public projects. If the TVA keeps power rates low, potentially costing it profits, then locals will enjoy electricity at low cost.

The TVA today is a gigantic power generation system that includes twenty-nine dams, six nuclear reactors (located at the Browns Ferry, Sequoyah, and Watts Bar plants), fourteen natural gas–fired plants and fifty-nine coal-powered units located at ten plants. It also has several power-purchasing agreements with wind farms from Maryland to Illinois. Emphasis on renewables is increasing as eighteen coal-fired units are to be retired by 2018, with others modernized with the latest emission scrubbing equipment. It is interesting to note that hydro represents only about 10% of total power generation for the TVA today, vs. 33% for nuclear, 28% for coal (decreasing), 20% for natural gas and 9% for renewables (both increasing).[8]

One can conclude from this brief historical overview that the TVA and the REA were necessary to correct the imbalance between electrified urban centers and an unelectrified countryside. This was an inequity the private electric industry was unable to correct profitably and as such was unwilling to address. There is no denying that both the TVA and the REA were very successful components of the New Deal. But their very success further increased the already significant complexity of the U.S. electricity system. By the end of World War II, we had essentially the same fragmented power industry that still exists today, with a dominant private sector fragmented in many local and regional integrated utilities; a few very large federally owned power producing systems; and a legion of municipal systems and local cooperatives. When utilities involved in other natural resources such as natural gas and water are added to this patchwork, our utility industry ends up a very complex one indeed.[9]

To mention the example of large utilities just in my home state of California: we have four very large publicly traded utilities: Pacific Gas and Electric (PG&E) around the San Francisco Bay Area; Southern California Edison (SoCal Edison) and Southern California Gas (SoCal Gas) around the Los Angeles basin; and San Diego Gas and Electric (SDG&E) in San Diego. All are integrated, i.e. with resource generation, transmission and distribution. PG&E and SDG&E serve both electricity and gas customers: this requires two very different types of physical networks, with for example the necessity to protect against different types of risks – think nuclear accident versus gas explosions. SoCal Edison and Gas, on the other hand, each focus on one source of energy. The LA area also boasts one of the largest (and municipally owned) water distribution companies in the U.S., the Los Angeles Department of Water and Power, or LADWP. LADWP is the largest municipal utility of the country, with over four million residential consumers, and distributes electricity as well as water. The state capital, Sacramento, is served by the Sacramento Municipal Utility

District, or SMUD. SMUD is a public agency of the state of California, and even operated a lone nuclear plant, Rancho Seco, until its ratepayers voted to decommission it in the late 1980s. Some counties (e.g. Marin County) have successfully taken electric power purchasing out of the hands of their local utility, with a goal to increase the share of renewable power generation through Community Choice Aggregation (CCA) initiatives. Wind farms, solar plants and independent cogeneration facilities together now produce 28% of the state's electricity. And so forth.

At the U.S. level, there are over 3,000 utilities of different shapes and forms. Beyond the forty federal, state and district systems, providing power generation for the most part, there were 189 publicly traded/investor-owned utilities in 2015 in the country; 2,013 publicly owned utilities, mostly municipal systems; and 877 cooperative systems serving rural communities. There were also 218 independent power marketers.[10]

American investor-owned utilities had aggregate revenues of $220 billion in 2015. They served over 100 million U.S. customers, selling 53% of the electricity used in the country. The thirty largest utilities are all multi-billion-dollar businesses, including American Electric Power; Arizona Public Service; Baltimore Gas and Electric; Commonwealth Edison; Consolidated Edison; Consumers Energy; Duke Energy Carolinas; Florida Power & Light; Georgia Power; Houston Light & Power; Northern States Power; Pennsylvania Electric Power; PG&E; Potomac Electric Power; Public Service Electric and Gas; Public Service of Colorado; SoCal Edison; SDG&E; TXU; and Virginia Electric Power.[11]

The municipal systems (munis) are much more fragmented and smaller on average. Similarly fragmented, the cooperative systems served nineteen million customers and sold 11% of the electricity used in the country in 2015, with independent power marketers selling 20% of the electricity and serving six million customers in the U.S.

Public Power, which started under FDR with the TVA (still the largest public utility in the U.S.), is more concentrated: it served thirty-one million U.S. customers and delivered 16% of the electricity used in 2015.

In terms of electric power generated in the country, investor-owned utilities accounted for 39% in 2015, a little less than the 40% produced by non-utility generators. Public utilities produced 10%, federal systems 6%, and cooperatives 5%.

When one adds natural gas and water-only utilities, plus all the other energy activities from the many holding companies owning the investor-owned utilities, this amounts to a $800 billion per year industry. The largest three utility holding companies by number of customers in the U.S. in 2015 were Duke Energy (headquartered in Charlotte, NC, with over seven million customers, $24 billion of revenue, and 58 GW of installed electricity generation capacity); Exelon (Chicago, IL, with six million customers, $29 billion of revenue, and 35 GW of installed capacity); and PG&E (San Francisco, CA, with six million customers, $17 billion in annual revenue, and 7 GW of installed capacity). Edison and his successors launched a very large sector of our economy, albeit one of the most complex ones.

*   *   *   *   *

Nuclear power: a great American invention, marred by unforeseen complications

Our country invented nuclear power. The Manhattan Project, launched in 1942, required the creation of the first nuclear reactor to produce enriched uranium and then plutonium for use in the first nuclear bombs, dropped on the cities of Hiroshima and Nagasaki at the end of World War II. Less than ten years later, electricity was produced for the first time by the EBR-1 experimental nuclear reactor in Idaho. The first nuclear-powered submarine, the USS *Nautilus*, was launched in 1955. President Dwight Eisenhower amended the Atomic Energy Act in 1954 to promote private sector development of nuclear energy for civilian uses through declassification of U.S. reactor technology. This was followed in 1957 by the first operational commercial nuclear generator in the U.S. in Shippingport, Pennsylvania. Between 1957 and 1973, twenty or so nuclear reactors for commercial use were built in the U.S., but construction really accelerated after the first oil shock of 1973. Over 250 new nuclear reactors were ordered, with private sector involvement and competition strongly encouraged.

Four nuclear reactor manufacturers competed: General Electric, which alone offered a boiling water reactor (BWR) design that proved successful not only in the U.S. but in Japan as well. Three other manufacturers offered different pressurized water reactors (PWRs). Babcock & Wilcox, the venerable industrial company, had built the reactors for the *Nautilus* submarine in 1955 and the first New York state nuclear station, Indian Point, in 1962. Unfortunately, B&W also designed the Three Mile Island reactor, which caused the worst accident in U.S. nuclear history in 1979. The B&W design was sound, but when the temperature of the core increased unexpectedly, the reactor operators did not have a lot of time to react and make the appropriate decisions. This was not an issue with the PWR design provided by Combustion Engineering, which was perhaps the most advanced of the time because of a sophisticated computerized control system. The fourth manufacturer, Westinghouse, built more PWRs in the U.S. than either B&W or CE, and also was by far the most successful U.S. nuclear reactor manufacturer on the export markets. Therefore, Westinghouse and GE remained top dogs in this market, fifty years after their duopoly era in the electric manufacturing industry.[12]

To complicate things, there were also over half a dozen engineering and construction firms (E&Cs, also called architect and engineers, or A&Es) competing to design the plant itself around the reactor; integrate the reactor with the required steam generators; and perform overall project management in these multi-billion-dollar endeavors. Bechtel (by far the most successful); Black and Veatch; CB&I; Fluor; Foster Wheeler; Sargent and Lundy; and Stone and Webster were the E&Cs involved in a significant way. To win the competitive tenders, sometimes for different nuclear units for the same utility, these E&Cs would promote "customized" designs, which would offer the best solution for the "very unique characteristics" of the utility's nuclear plant being considered. The only E&C stressing standardization as a feature to decrease construction costs was Black and Veatch, but only on their novel modular design for coal-fired power plants. Those coal plants were built very economically indeed, unlike the nuclear plants in the country.

Four reactor manufacturers; over half a dozen engineering and construction companies; and of course dozens of utilities vying for the privilege to have their "own" flagship nuclear plant, some of them munis not in the least equipped with the necessary operational experience to manage such complex projects. The result was that hardly any nuclear plant in the U.S. was designed and built like another.

Let's look at the numbers: between 1957 and 1983, 132 nuclear reactors were built in the U.S. No nuclear station site in the country had more than three reactors on it, and even those were somewhat of a rarity. What dominated the landscape were single units, or double units on the same site. Of the seven nuclear power stations where three reactors were built, sometimes over a decade or more, four (Dresden; Millstone; Peach Bottom; and San Onofre) had one unit closed, that unit being of a different design than the other two units on the same site. This was due to an inability to perform reliably or to the updated 1980s Nuclear Regulatory Commission (NRC) standards. Even after a strong wave of utility mergers in the last fifteen years, the landscape of U.S. nuclear power units remains very fragmented. At the end of 2016 there were ninety-nine nuclear reactors in operation in thirty states in the country. Sixty-five were of a PWR design and thirty-four BWRs. Three sites had three reactors running on them: Brown Ferris (operated by the TVA); Oconee (Duke Energy); and Palo Verde (Arizona Public Service - the Palo Verde station being the largest nuclear site in the country, with a capacity of 3.3 GW). No less than twenty-eight companies operated the ninety-nine reactors, in thirty states. Of these, Exelon (Chicago-based, with extensive operations in Illinois, Pennsylvania, and a number of other Midwestern and Northeastern states) had made the most significant effort at consolidation, operating seventeen nuclear reactors. Duke Energy (including its recent acquisition of Progress Energy) followed suit with twelve units. Then came Entergy (New Orleans, LA), with ten reactors. Exelon, Duke, and Entergy all had a succession of CEOs who were committed to nuclear power. At the opposite end, fourteen utilities operated only one or two nuclear reactors.[13]

Why do I go on and on about all this fragmentation, twenty-eight utilities, over half a dozen A&Es, four types of reactors, and so forth? Because nuclear power plants are extremely sophisticated, technology-intensive and costly projects. For obvious reasons, they are also subject to the most stringent regulations known to mankind. And this is not for construction only: maintenance and operations are also very closely monitored and regulated by the NRC as well as other regulatory bodies, not to mention the public and elected officials. All this means that experience is a very valuable commodity in this business. And experience grows a lot faster if one accumulates experience with many units of the same design and manufacture, as opposed to single or double units all different from each other.[14]

To illustrate this, let's look at the most successful nuclear electric power program in Europe, that of France. After the first oil shock, the French government decided to embark on a large-scale nuclear program to improve the country's energy independence. Unlike, say, the U.S., France does not have fossil resources in any large quantity, except for some natural gas in the southwest of the country. The French decided in 1974 to base their program upon a successful design already operating well – no customization here – even though at that time France had already developed its own "Force de Frappe" or hydrogen bombs with air, land silo, and submarine launching capabilities. The government instructed a team of scientists and electric operators to go on a fact-finding mission in the U.S., and "come back with the license of a nuclear reactor design that works." After a few months, this delegation came back with a license for the Westinghouse PWR reactor. Electricité de France (EDF), the country's electric operator, and Framatome, the national manufacturer of PWRs under Westinghouse license, then teamed up to build thirty-four reactors, all with a 900MW capacity and pretty much the same. All these PWRs started operation between 1979 and 1985. After this, Framatome and EDF, using all the lessons learned and experience from building and operating these thirty-four reactors, teamed up again to update the original design, increase the power capacity, and build another twenty PWRs with a 1,300MW capacity between 1986 and 1994. Four more modern PWRs with a 1,450MW capacity were then built between 1996 and 2000.[15]

These fifty-eight nuclear units provide about 80% of the country's electricity, very reliably, without any significant incident over their history, and with an available capacity of over 90%. This means that total actual nuclear electricity production, as a percentage of the French reactors full-time, full-load potential, has been 90% or more since the early years of operation. Having essentially two types of reactors of the same basic design helps a lot for maintenance, since the same problems tend to appear in repeated sequences. When issues occur, for example in heavily radioactive areas, and very expensive industrial robots need to be developed for repairs (for example when corroded steam generator tubes have to be fixed), the French only have to build two of them. If a technical issue shows up at one reactor, complex solutions can be developed with the confidence that they will likely be used at dozens of units, with reduced costs per unit. Scale, standardization and cumulative experience all matter enormously in this industry. French citizens and local industry thus benefit from low electricity prices. France's nuclear-generated electricity is also exported to pretty much all its geographic neighbors, including the U.K., making the country the largest electricity exporter in Europe.

And in the U.S.? Well, the good news is that the country's ninety-nine reactors have been operating reliably for over fifteen years, with an average available capacity of 90% since the year 2000. In recent years the industry achieved 91% in 2010; 89% in 2011; 86% in 2012; 90% in 2013; and 92% in 2014, 2015 and 2016. The industry produced 19.7% of U.S. electricity generation in 2016, and nuclear power does not contribute to greenhouse gas emissions. The bad news is that to get there the industry experienced a nightmarish thirty-year journey. There were systematic cost overruns, on average by a factor of over two, and sometimes by a factor of ten above industry estimates. Think about this for a second: a ten times cost overrun in an original budget of a billion plus dollars! This led to bankruptcies, none more dramatic than the financial collapse of the Washington Public Power Supply System (WPPSS or "Whoops"), a local public agency that undertook to build five nuclear reactors. By 1983, cost overruns and delays led to the cancellation of two of the WPPSS units and halted the construction of two others. WPPSS then defaulted on $2.25 billion of municipal bonds, the largest municipal bond default in U.S. history.

When U.S. utilities finally got their nuclear stations completed, they struggled mightily to operate them. This is not surprising given that many of these utilities were relatively small entities, some of them in the extreme (think again about the Sacramento Municipal Utility District and its single Rancho Seco reactor); most of them had only one or two units to learn from. It amounted to what strategic consultants would call a very shallow experience curve. Over one-quarter of U.S. nuclear reactors suffered outages lasting over a year. As a result, available capacity was abysmal: 54% on average for the 1970s; 57% in the 1980s; and 74% in the 1990s. This led to billions of dollars in operating losses.[16]

There were also over 100 notable incidents and accidents between 1960 and today. Think of the earlier example of industrial robots needed for repairs in high radioactivity areas: in the U.S. we would need thirty such robots, or more, given the variety of configurations encountered in our nuclear plants. Among these 100 incidents and accidents, twenty had repair costs of over $100 million in today's dollars, and four cost over a billion dollars to fix: the Three Mile Island accident in 1979 ($2.4 billion); Brown Ferris in 1985 (instrumentation systems malfunction, with these three TVA reactors having to be shut down and then re-started much later, at a cost of $1.8 billion); Boston Edison's Pilgrim Nuclear Plant in 1986 (emergency shutdown due to recurring equipment problems, at a $1 billion cost); and more recently in Florida in 2009, where opening the containment building at Crystal River nuclear unit 3 to install a new steam generator caused the building to be so severely cracked that this unit had to be closed, at a cost that will be well in excess of $1 billion. Of these, none was more dramatic than the 1979 Three Mile Island accident, where the B&W PWR reactor experienced a big loss of coolant and a partial meltdown of the core. There were no casualties, but wow, this was a very close one. The whole country woke up to the fact that a nuclear core meltdown could actually happen, with terrifying potential consequences. The Three Mile Island accident thus unfortunately cemented the fate of U.S. nuclear power for a very long time, as far as new plant construction is concerned. It took until 2012 (thirty-three years later) for the NRC to approve the construction of four new units, with work starting in 2013. Cancellations of new projects also multiplied after 1979: of the 253 new reactors ordered by the industry, 121 were cancelled, or 48% of the orders; of the 132 that were built, thirty-three were closed, more often than not prematurely due to significant reliability or safety issues.[17,18]

The San Onofre nuclear station in Southern California offers a good illustrative example of the scale and costs of problems occurring when things go wrong with nuclear units: this three-reactor facility was built from 1968 to 1984, over a sixteen-year span, with a projected capacity of 2.65 GW. Typically, the first reactor was a first generation, 450 MW Westinghouse PWR, while the next two were more modern, 1,100 MW Combustion Engineering PWRs. Being in earthquake-prone California, with the Christianitos fault less than a mile away, the units were built to withstand a 7.0 magnitude earthquake directly under the site. A 25-foot tsunami protection wall was also built. Needless to say, there were severe cost overruns for SoCal Edison, the operator, and for minority owner SDG&E. The original Westinghouse reactor was closed in 1992, no longer meeting the latest NRC regulations. Between 2001 and 2011, Edison replaced the steam generators at both CE units with improved Mitsubishi generators, at a cost of almost $700 million. Unfortunately, both reactors had to be shut down in 2012 due to premature wear found on over 3,000 tubes in these replacement steam generators. The NRC started investigating, and then U.S. Senator Barbara Boxer from California called for a "criminal investigation" for these "unsafe modifications" endangering eight million people living within fifty miles of the plant.[19,20]

In summary, building within cost budgets and operating 132 nuclear plants economically proved to be too much of a challenge for a very fragmented and complex utility industry, and its equipment and design providers. In its February 11, 1985 cover story, *Forbes* called this journey

> the largest managerial disaster in business history, a disaster on a monumental scale ... only the blind, or the biased, can now think that the money has been well spent. It is a defeat for the U.S. consumer and for the competitiveness of U.S. industry, for the utilities that undertook the program and for the private enterprise system that made it possible.[21]

Today the nuclear industry is in much better shape in the U.S. But after Three Mile Island, the Russians had Chernobyl, where the cost in lives will probably never be fully known; and just when the nuclear industry appeared to be back in favor, Fukushima occurred, again with a devastating loss of lives and at enormous cost.[22] Still, a number of new reactors with enhanced safety features are being built today, mostly in China. There are flagship projects in Europe (France; Finland; the U.K.) and in the U.S. as well, all with multi-billion-dollar cost overruns and delays of several years. Most of these are not completed yet. It is worth noting that even new reactors built recently by French companies have suffered from enormous cost overruns: with many new safety features, much increased complexity and "one-off" designs, such as in Finland, a successful nuclear history and experience has not proved sufficient to avoid problems. This is why it seems unlikely that nuclear power will increase its share of electricity generation on a global scale over time and prove to be a significant solution to the planetary emissions of greenhouse gases.

★ ★ ★ ★ ★

PURPA, independent power, and the tortuous early trails of deregulation

In the 1920s, the electric and utility industry achieved a major political victory through regulation of their businesses. This regulation enshrined many of their "natural monopolies." FDR and his New Deal opened the door for public power on a large scale, but by the 1970s regulated utilities still dominated the U.S. electricity landscape. There were many complaints, though, about stodgy performance, lack of competition, and the inability to harness new, renewable sources of power. Both conservative and liberal think tanks started talking a lot about deregulation. Interestingly, deregulation efforts in U.S. infrastructure were launched during the administration of a Democrat, President Jimmy Carter. In 1978, he and Congress passed the Airline Deregulation Act, which would profoundly transform our airlines. He also helped pass the Railroad Revitalization and Regulatory Reform Act of 1978, the prelude to the Staggers Rail Act of 1980, which deregulated Class 1 U.S. railroads. The breakup of the AT&T and Bell Labs monopoly would come a little later, in 1982, opening up the telecommunications industry. Natural gas, unlike oil an essentially regional (read: pipelines) source of energy, was also deregulated in the mid-eighties, with long lasting impact to the industry.

Deregulation efforts in the airline and railroad industries had their roots in the first global oil price shock of 1973, followed by a more serious one in 1978, and the creation of the Organization of Petroleum Exporting Countries, or OPEC. These oil shocks created energy crises that ripped through industrialized nations, in North America, Europe, and Japan. Suddenly U.S. energy independence and one of its corollaries, energy efficiency, were at the forefront of most economic and political discourse. Carter was determined to advance the U.S. as far as possible on this road, and the Public Utilities Regulatory Policy Act (PURPA) of November 9, 1978, was one of his signature achievements.

The main objective of Congress and the president in passing PURPA was to help reduce U.S. dependence on foreign oil through increased energy efficiency, diversification of the electric power industry and promotion of alternative energy sources. In essence, this new regulatory compact allowed utilities to keep their local monopolies but regulated their returns through the "allowed utility rate of return." In practice, this meant that a complicated and somewhat changing formula allowed utilities profits up to this allowed rate of return. These regulatory formulas varied state by state, and statewide Public Utility Commissions (PUCs) took a very important role. Most of these formulas were based on the total costs incurred by the utility business, which many said put a strong damper on any efficiency efforts. If your allowed rate of return is a percentage of total costs, why reduce costs given that your maximum profit depends on them being as high as possible? In practice, things were a bit different because many utilities, not that well managed in the first place, often struggled to reach this allowed rate of return.

However, one of the intended and most important aspects of PURPA was to create markets for new, non-utility power producers. Before, only utilities could operate power plants in the U.S., and therefore PURPA was the policy that launched independent power in the U.S. It did so by requiring utilities to buy power from independent producers at their "avoided costs," or what it would have cost a given utility to produce the same power. Any independent power producer that generated power at below the local utility's avoided costs could therefore keep the difference to build up profits. As such, PURPA led to the development of renewable power in the U.S., first wind and later solar. Mostly, though, new independent power came in the form of natural gas-fired cogeneration (cogen) plants, where steam is produced alongside electricity to be used for industrial purposes. None of these new independent power producers were regulated, provided they obtained a PURPA's Qualified Facility (QF) certificate. There were no size limits for renewables (which nevertheless were relatively small scale compared to hydro, nuclear and fossil-fueled power plants). Cogen plants were typically limited to 150MW in size, although most new cogen (and hydro) QFs built after 1978 were smaller than that. A few larger such plants (e.g. Bechtel built a 250MW cogen facility) were built, but they were not designated QFs. Overall, PURPA is credited with the impetus to create a significant wave of more efficient power generation in the U.S., including 12,000 MW of renewables.

Of course, there was also complexity galore: no state PUC was quite the same, and their regulations and allowed utility rate of return differed widely. The Federal Energy Regulatory Commission (FERC) allowed different states to set-up different avoided costs over different number of years. The interconnection of regional and/or statewide electricity distribution systems through very high voltage interstate transmission lines was a very complicated affair, both from the physical construction standpoint (who pays for what?) and regulatory consequences (who has access to what power?). A large state like Texas, where electricity is regulated through the surprisingly named "Texas Railroad Commission," is still today essentially an "electric island" in the country. Many utilities decided to start their own deregulated subsidiaries to get into independent power themselves. Uncertainty reigned: there was always the possibility that the main rules of the game (avoided costs, for example) could change with a change of political administration in a state, which led independent power producers to experience "boom and bust" cycles. And so forth.

Some states decided to interpret PURPA as aggressively as possible: California, in the early 1980s under the governorship of a very young Jerry Brown, figured out long-term avoided costs over 20–25-year timeframes, called "standard offers." The state then forced its local utilities to accept these standard offers, thus providing low hurdles for the new promoters of renewable and cogen power. This led to a kind of "gold rush" in all sorts of alternative power, including wind, solar and cogen, as well as small-scale hydro, biomass and waste to energy projects. When one drives from the Bay Area to the Central Valley through the Altamont pass, the forest of wind mills above the pass is a tribute to that era: they were built on standard offers and tax rebates in the 1980s. California was not alone: Washington state helped facilitate 35-year hydro projects, which appeared also in New Hampshire and Vermont. Oklahoma and Texas created 20–25-year rate formulas to help develop significant wind power capacity. However, other states, for example coal-producing states in the South, were not nearly as welcoming of independent power, with avoided costs that were very short-term in nature and discouraged new projects. New power generation, almost no matter what its shape, needs long-term contracts and tariffs so that a private developer can amortize very large up-front costs through at least twenty years of stable expected returns.

One can easily see that the physical and legal build-up of the electricity industry in the U.S. was far from a simple endeavor. And I am not even expanding on further deregulation efforts in the 1990s, with the creation of independent system operators (ISOs) in many states and rules that unfortunately led to much publicized abuse (more on this later). It is interesting to note, though, that this electric construction has proven remarkably resistant to consolidation and the creation of large scale, world-class companies. We have seen that there are at least thirty multi-billion-dollar utilities in the U.S.: contrast this with five Class 1 railroads; three enormous airlines (American, Delta, and United); and three major mobile carriers (T-Mobile, Sprint, and Verizon). Major oil companies have also re-consolidated to the point that, with one additional merger between them, Chevron and ExxonMobil could together become very close in U.S. geographic reach to the original Standard Oil trust. Of course, one can argue convincingly that consolidation in these industries has been excessive, leading to an oligopolistic behavior of poor services at high prices. But the stubborn fragmentation of the utility industry also carries significant costs. We have already seen that it was one of the main causes that prevented nuclear power, invented here, to develop smoothly and in a way that would allow it to be a realistic solution to future power challenges. There were also significant other costs, in terms of blackouts, bankruptcies, and generally poor economic performance. As we try to embrace the need to move to renewables on a much bigger scale to mitigate climate change issues, this industry complexity is also an impediment to desirable change.

★　★　★　★　★

Blackouts, brownouts, bankruptcies, and the "E" word

During the five decades of economic expansion from the 1950s to the 1990s, there were many more blackouts (and rolling blackouts, as well as brownouts, lesser but sometimes necessary evils) in the U.S. than in other industrialized countries. Let's start with the big ones: in November of 1965, New York experienced an almost complete blackout due to the failure of a circuit breaker in a high transmission line carrying power north from Niagara Falls to Canada. North, to Canada? How could that affect New York, far to the south? What happened is that the circuit breaker "thought" the line to Canada was overloaded (even if it was not), and therefore prevented electricity from going to the north. But when the electric loads were redirected to the south, these unforeseen additional electric loads overwhelmed the high voltage transmission lines to New York and caused them to shut down in a matter of seconds, affecting all the towns along the Hudson River, from Buffalo, Rochester, and Albany all the way to the Big Apple. New England was also affected. Even though Consolidated Edison had enough reserves for a normal emergency, it could not cope with a shortfall of that magnitude, and it took more than twelve hours to resolve the problem and restore electricity to New York. Hospitals without emergency power; tens of thousands of commuters stranded in powerless trains; people stuck in upper floors of office buildings and hotels; street traffic chaos; flights cancelled, and more. However, everyone behaved well during the blackout. Fortunately, it had occurred on a very mild day, but it does not stretch the imagination to imagine accidents, looting and even riots during such a large outage. And when millions are interrupted in their daily activities, there is significant economic cost, too.

New York suffered again a large outage in 1977, and this time it was on a sweltering hot July day. During the 1970s, New York suffered from significant economic reversals. The city was on the verge of bankruptcy, large companies like the Penn Central railroad had gone bankrupt, and a million jobs had disappeared. Unemployment was rampant and all the city's services were severely understaffed. During that blackout, in contrast to what had (not) happened in 1965, the city exploded with arson, looting and riots, principally in poor and marginalized areas like the Bronx. It took days for police to restore order and for fire departments to control over 10,000 fires.

The biggest blackout in the U.S. was to come later, on August 14, 2003. That day a series of transmission line problems around Akron, Ohio, and the First Energy electric network caused an enormous outage covering over 10% of the country, from Ohio, Michigan, and Ontario in Canada to the whole Northeast. Again, New Yorkers were left in the dark, but at least they had a lot of company. This blackout affected forty-five million people in the U.S., ten million in Canada, and caused economic damage estimated at $7 billion. We all remember the famous satellite image showing the U.S. at night, full of lights except in the western deserts and a giant black hole from the Northeast to the Great Lakes, as if the Northeast seaboard had become a new Gulf, going as far west as Columbus. Former Clinton administration Secretary of Energy

Bill Richardson, interviewed that evening on CNN, declared: "we are a major superpower with a Third World electric grid."[23]

Why is that? Again, the decentralized and fragmented structure of our utility system is at the heart of the problem. A North American Electric Reliability Council (NERC) had been established in 1968, and it had created voluntary guidelines for utilities to create contingency plans, principally in high voltage transmission. But the key word here is "voluntary." As our electric system grew more complex and somewhat more interconnected, utilities no longer operated in essentially self-contained local systems. But they had very weak incentives to follow these NERC guidelines, which involved both heavy investments many could not afford and working with competitors with overlapping networks. In some way, transmission investments were against the short-term interests of many utilities, since it would cost them vast amounts of capital investments . . . to let competitors enter their territory, among other things. Without any mandates, standards and enforcement mechanisms in place, utilities flouted the NERC guidelines repeatedly. Progress had occurred by the beginning of the twenty-first century in the area of power generation, but upgrading our transmission system to the capacity and quality required to avoid these blackouts would still cost over $100 billion. No one during the George W. Bush administration would back up such a program. Congress did pass the Energy Transmission Act of 2005, but the identification of transmission congestion and fixing capacity issue takes years. Even with eminent domain invoked, detailed plans have to be made; billions of dollars in investments found; approval from FERC secured; and many environmental impact assessments by federal as well as state authorities conducted and approved.

And so blackouts continued, costing about a billion dollars every year during the years 2000–2008. Outages affecting more than 50,000 people increased from forty-one between 1992 and 1995, to ninety-two between 2001 and 2005, according to research at the University of Minnesota.[24] In 2006, utilities reported thirty-six such outages, well on pace to exceed 150 over a five-year period. During hot summers, when demand is at peak levels due to air conditioning, utilities try to "protect" their customers by first enacting "brownouts" (during which the voltage available to consumers is reduced) and then "rolling blackouts." This type of planned blackout allows the utility to tell its customers in advance when their local power will be cut, so they can better prepare. Industrials can prepare to shift to back-up power (e.g. diesel generators), commercial outlets can adapt their opening hours, and residential customers will do their laundry the next day. This is not catastrophic, but certainly inconvenient, and not what one expects in the world's largest economy.[25]

Thanks to the enormous amount of new renewable capacity installed in the U.S. over the last ten years, brownouts have become much less frequent, although load balancing remains more complex here than in other industrialized countries. We still have more blackouts than other large developed countries, though: yes, our climate can be fierce, but most advanced economies have a much simpler utility industry structure, enabling centralized power dispatch systems, automatic emergency response processes, much better transparency in operations, and more stringent mandatory maintenance programs. Large-scale high voltage transmission programs are undertaken as a matter of national strategic priority, with strong government involvement. So, there is a lot less congestion and obsolete equipment. European countries also coordinate their surplus and deficits of power generation better. France uses its large nuclear capacity to export significant quantities of electricity to its neighbors, thus adding much needed base load capacity to Germany, the U.K., Italy, Spain, and Switzerland. Even in the U.S., other large infrastructure-based industries are much better coordinated at the national level. To support air transport, we have a nationwide radar network, weather reporting, and an air traffic control system administrated by the federal government. And the Federal Aviation Administration (FAA) does not issue "voluntary" guidelines on critical matters: when the FAA mandates, airlines, pilots, mechanics, and everyone involved in flying follows suit, or they are grounded. Similarly, when rail and truck transport were deregulated, the country benefited from the vast interstate highway system built under President Eisenhower, and more than enough railroad lines. And telecoms companies are large enough to be able to afford the required bandwidth investments in their business.

During the 1980s and 1990s, under presidencies as diverse as Reagan, Bush Sr., and Clinton, deregulation became the politicians' mantra to solve these U.S. utility woes. Real industry deregulation, not just PURPA's early deregulation efforts opening up power generation markets in a limited way. Real deregulation, allowing freedom of trade for electric power and letting new entrants purchase utility assets, would stimulate supply and create all the needed capacity, while competition would be much more effective at reducing end-user costs than all these regulatory bodies. This worked well in so many other industries, so why not for utilities? Why not, indeed . . . today, electricity deregulation is still fundamentally associated in our minds with one name: Enron.

California's deregulation law, voted on in 1996, was put into practice in 1998. It was strongly supported by the state's local utilities. Lobbying in favor of deregulation was also a relatively new company, Houston-based Enron. Enron had started as a natural gas pipeline company (InterNorth) but was now an active electricity trader and power generator. At that time there was plenty of generating capacity in California, and local utilities decided to take advantage of deregulation by selling off a big chunk of their electricity generation assets, 50% in PG&E's case. Everything started smoothly, until a severe drought – not uncommon in California – significantly reduced the hydropower available from dams in California and its neighboring states Oregon and Washington. Enters deregulation, with the power producers and traders' ability to set the price of an increasingly rare commodity: by 2001 the average wholesale price of electric power was ten times what it had been in 1998. This bankrupted PG&E, which had never anticipated having to pay such high prices for the electricity it no longer produced. One of the country's largest utilities sought Chapter 11 protection from its creditors on April 6, 2001.[26]

How could this happen? There were regulatory loopholes galore, the Independent System Operator (ISO) did not monitor its already high price cap effectively, and the state of California itself had mandated a 10% reduction in retail electricity prices so that local consumers could "benefit from deregulation." When power producers and traders caused prices to increase massively, utilities like PG&E were squeezed dry (no pun intended). Essentially their wholesale electricity costs became much higher than the retail prices they charged customers. And of course, Enron and other traders "gamed" the system on a massive scale: they quickly understood that it was much more advantageous financially for them to sell small amounts of power at hugely inflated prices, as opposed to large quantities at lower set prices. So, Enron and others created all sorts of scams to artificially shut down power-generating capacity when demand was at its highest – also creating over fifty days of California blackouts in 2001 alone. At one point in 2000 almost half of Californian power plants were experiencing outages. Traders overbooked transmission capacity in advance, creating artificial congestion, and sold power to out-of-state buyers, exacerbating shortages, to then sell back the same power to Californians at much higher prices. In essence, traders knew that their business profited from volatility, and they went about in a big way to increase this volatility by all sorts of artificial means. Natural gas players got in the game, too, so that natural gas prices paid by California power generators increased a lot as well. After analyzing records, computer transcripts and conversations, state investigators concluded that Enron, AES, Duke, Dynegy, and West Coast Power had overcharged Californians by $9 billion. Needless to say, after the California debacle many states put their own deregulation plans on hold. Other states, which had not suffered as much, kept their own partial deregulation programs. So, the U.S. became a patchwork of regulated and deregulated state networks, with many utilities crossing regulated and deregulated lines. Recent FERC rules have opened transmission lines to all power generators, but this patchwork of different regulatory regimes remains.[27]

Ah, Enron went bankrupt, too, in December of 2001. This was initially a Chapter 11 reorganization involving over $65 billion of assets (the largest corporate bankruptcy of U.S. history at the time, until WorldCom a year later), but in the end Enron disappeared completely. A creative, institutional and systematic pattern of accounting fraud was exposed in lengthy trials, involving bogus entities, "special purpose vehicles" or off-balance sheet accounting vehicles, and obscure LLC partnerships. Enron used complexity, in its business model and financial statements, to keep its shareholders and analysts confused. Earnings of the company were misrepresented and its balance sheet artificially inflated. Enron used "market-to-market accounting," in which the full value of a market transaction is reported as revenue, as opposed to just the trading, brokerage and risk management fees earned by the company. This "merchant model" represented a considerably more aggressive accounting practice than the traditional agent model, where only transaction fees are recorded as revenue. Former Enron

CEO Jeff Skilling is still in jail today; CFO Andrew Fastow served a ten-year sentence. Enron chairman Ken Lay died in 2006, three months before his sentencing date. In the wake of the Enron scandal, their auditors Arthur Andersen, a venerable $25 billion "big 5" global accounting firm with well over 100,000 employees, disappeared as well following another high-profile prosecution. It was politically helpful for the George W. Bush administration that some of the Enron blame be spread around, since it was perceived to have been (too) close to Enron, principally on energy policy matters. Michael Chertoff, who led prosecution in the Arthur Andersen case, subsequently became the country's second Homeland Security Secretary in 2005.[28]

Enron is not the only giant bankruptcy to have blighted the U.S. electric sector. I already mentioned the WPPSS fiasco earlier, and there is also need to mention the private equity Energy Future Holdings (formerly TXU) default, which happened much more recently. WPPSS (again, "whoops!") was a large municipal corporation organized in 1957 to combine the resources of a number of local public utilities to build power generation facilities in Washington State. Seattle City Light, as well as sixteen other public utilities in the state, signed on to this program. During the 1960s, Washington Public Power Supply System built a number of small hydro facilities, usually behind schedule and over budget. But the seeds of the disaster occurred in 1971, when WPPSS planners, anticipating a doubling of electricity demand every ten years in the area, decided to build not one, not two, but . . . five nuclear reactors on the Hanford and Satsop sites. Unfortunately, the well-meaning directors and managers of WPPSS had no experience whatsoever in either nuclear reactor construction or large-scale project management. Most board members and officials were commissioners from the local, smallish public utilities, with more legal and local politics backgrounds than engineering or scientific ones. As a result, construction work was very poorly supervised, with delays piling on top of delays. An alarmed NRC mandated new safety features after new ones, which were sometimes directly built with the design blueprints changed after the fact to show what had actually been erected on site. The WPPSS board became aware of this much too late. Seattle City Lights then started to backtrack; the Washington Environmental Council filed suit to require an environmental audit; a 27-member Citizen's Overview Committee was established to have another look on how power needs of the state should be met; Seattle City Light produced a report supporting 10% of nuclear plants 2 and 3, but voted not to support plants 4 and 5 any longer; and the Citizen's Committee opposed participation in nuclear power, recommending conservation be used instead. Uncle!

In early 1982, work was halted at plants 4 (Hanford) and 5 (Satsop), with total system costs projected by then to exceed $24 billion. Since no power (and therefore no money) was produced, WPPSS defaulted on $2.25 billion of municipal bonds. Public utility members, muni bond holders (e.g. "widows and orphans") and small-town ratepayers carried the can, to the tune of about $12,500 per utility customer. Plants 1 at Hanford and 3 at Satsop were never finished either, but the large hydro Bonneville Power Administration (BPA) backed their costs. After several years of complex lawsuits, 75,000 bondholders received about 40 cents on each dollar invested. In 1984, reactor 2 on the Hanford site was finally completed, and today is part of the BPA system, producing about 12% of its electricity.[29]

So, we have two enormous bankruptcies, the WPPSS one caused by good intentions destroyed by too much ambition relative to competence, and the Enron one caused by greed and malfeasance. During the last three decades, a new breed of mega, privately held and enormously successful organizations has emerged: private equity giants such as Bain Capital, Carlyle Group, Kohlberg Kravis Roberts (KKR), and Texas Pacific Group (TPG). Surely this type of debacle could not happen to them? Think again.

In 2007, KKR, TPG, and Goldman Sachs Partners led a consortium of private investors that bought Dallas-based utility TXU in a $45 billion transaction that was at the time the country's largest leveraged buy-out (LBO). Private equity firms increase their profits through debt leveraging (tax-deductible; this debt multiplies the financial "muscle" of equity and the returns on investment, at least when things go well). So the TXU transaction came with over $40 billion of debt. The new owners of TXU, renamed Energy Future Holdings, expected that natural gas prices in the U.S. would rise, making the company's coal-fired power plants much more competitive over time. To be fair, many energy analysts expected the same thing. Demand for natural gas was growing in the U.S.; few new supplies were being found; and new liquefied natural gas (LNG) projects would come on line to increase U.S. natural gas exports, constraining domestic supply and strengthening prices further.[30,31]

We all know what actually happened: fracking. The success of fracking glutted the market with natural gas, and prices stayed low. Far from coal displacing natural gas in electric power generation, the opposite happened, with coal being displaced by natural gas on a grand scale as the fossil fuel of choice to produce electricity. Fracking is controversial because of its enormous use of water, increasingly scarce in many places, and chemicals. The latter may cause potential pollution to aquifers, harming local populations. States where fracking is done on a large scale, such as Oklahoma, also appear to experience an increased frequency of earthquakes. But natural gas produces a lot less pollutants, principally greenhouse gases, than coal. What represented good news for the U.S. from an air pollution standpoint became terrible news for Energy Future Holdings. With prices of natural gas in the U.S. stubbornly low, electricity from natural gas–fired plants became cheaper, making it increasingly difficult for the Energy Future Holdings coal plants to be competitive. With deteriorating operating results and the weight of its large debt, the venture struggled year after year with financial losses from its coal plants. Debt grew to be at least twice the equity in the company. So eventually, on April 29, 2014, Energy Future Holdings filed for Chapter 11 bankruptcy. Equity holders KKR, TPG, and Goldman Sachs Partners together lost over $8 billion in this venture.[32,33]

In summary, integrated utilities in the U.S. are complex businesses. Their power generation component is subject to high capital costs and the price uncertainties of their primary fuels, or the intermittent nature of renewables. When saddled with too much debt, the steady operating cash flows that characterize most utilities can morph into steady losses – these are not businesses that can turn on a dime.[34] The American utility edifice has also become more and more complex over time. History; private and public power; state by state fragmentation; regulated distribution, partially deregulated transmission and ISOs; competitive power generation; new entrants versus incumbents; and a constant stream of changes in local, state and federal regulations have all played a part in making this industry much more complex in the U.S. than what is found in other industrialized countries. The consequences are three-fold:

First, the electric power and utility business in our country is one where regulatory strategies are often more important to the financial wellbeing of a utility than real business strategies. Lawyers abound in management teams, whereas an industry with such high engineering demands across many scientific disciplines would likely benefit from more engineering and science talent at the top.

Second, and more importantly, any kind of national strategy in electricity (and natural gas) is nearly impossible to conceive, let alone implement. Think about the many strategic imperatives we face in this industry: security, system reliability and transition to renewables, just to mention a few. We urgently need to beef up the physical and cyber security of our system nationwide. Thus far, all of our outages have been accidental, but we can be sure that ill-intended people are trying to cause blackouts here, and not by accident. Think of hackers tinkering with transmission switches or, even worse, nuclear plant controls. We need to ensure we have enough capacity in all segments of the electric system to continue to be a reliable electricity provider to industries and people – otherwise we will lose companies and jobs. Some states, foremost California (28% renewable) but also Oklahoma, Texas, and others in the Pacific Northwest and the Northeast, have done well at transitioning to renewables. Smaller countries like Denmark have gone further than we have, to close to 50%, but at the scale of California and its world's seventh largest GDP, only Germany plays in the same league (and German electricity is much more expensive than in California). Most people believe that climate change is a reality and that we cannot transition to renewables fast enough. Those who do not believe in climate change can think instead, "we need to reduce our dependency on Middle Eastern oil for security reasons." Despite fracking and the boom in oil and gas production in the country, we still depend, and too much, on Saudi, Iraqi, and Venezuelan oil (just to name a few OPEC countries). But with our current utility structure, any type of national planning to increase the share of renewables is basically impossible, even assuming the political will is there.

Third, this is a long-term game. Wins and losses in major programs and strategic decisions are determined over ten to twenty years: this is the exact opposite of flash trading! Sometimes we are lucky as a country. One of the strongest benefits of increased natural gas production due to extensive fracking operations has been that fewer and fewer utilities use coal-fired power plants.

Natural gas-fired ones have become cheaper to operate, principally when it comes to new plants. The result has been a significant decrease in the carbon emissions produced by the industry, with cheaper electricity to boot. But many of the strategic imperatives we face demand solutions coordinated nationally. This includes the future of utilities themselves. As many residential customers transition to solar, for example, the utilities have to spread the fixed costs of their extensive network over fewer and fewer customers, or face mounting financial losses. Issues like this need to be addressed, lest we end up with a strategic industry in deep financial trouble.

We can do better with utilities than we have historically and need to if we want to address successfully all the energy challenges we face as a nation. Our bill for complexity here is less horrendous than in health care but is still hefty. We should all long for sports, where complexity was just a fun puzzle to solve! But wait: if you liked "Enron," the movie, you will love its banking sequel, "Sub-Prime."

4   Finance

"Never was so much owed by so many to so few . . ."

"Never in the field of human conflict was so much owed by so many to so few."
Is this Winston Churchill's famous speech on August 20, 1940, after British
Royal Air Force fighter pilots defeated their German counterparts in the Battle of Britain, or should it be a line describing the 2008 U.S. bank bailout? For
years up to 2008, banks ("the few") racked-up record profits. Then the financial
crisis hit, and they had to be rescued with hundreds of billions of dollars ("the
so much") of public ("the so many") money, lest the whole economy suffer
potential collapse. Or, as some put it, "privatization of profits and socialization
of losses."

The funds involved in the 2008 bailout were indeed staggering: in March of
2008, investment bank Bear Stearns had to be bailed out by JP Morgan, with
the Feds sweetening the deal with a $30 billion guarantee. Yet, things worsened.
The Bush administration authorized the Treasury Department to spend up to
$150 billion to subsidize Fannie Mae and Freddie Mac. Lehman Brothers went
bankrupt on September 15, triggering a bout of panic in Wall Street. The Feds
then had to use $150 billion to bail out insurance giant American International
Group (AIG), saving it from collapse and also helping other financial institutions like Goldman Sachs, which were owed vast amounts by AIG.
On Sept 19, 2008, there was the beginning of a run on money market funds,
with over $140 billion moved in one day from these very safe funds to even
safer U.S. Treasury Bonds.

Treasury Secretary Henry Paulson proposed a $700 billion bailout pack-
age, to be approved by Congress. Federal Reserve Chairman Ben Bernanke,
who had built his academic career on lessons learned from the Great Depression, supported this drastic move. Congress first voted Paulson's bailout package
down, leading to the Dow Jones dropping 777 points, or 7%, on September 29.
The following week the Dow dropped another 1,874 points (18%). After this
meltdown on Wall Street, Congress approved the bailout in a second vote.[1,2,3]

Looking back, Lehman Brothers went under; Merrill Lynch, AIG, Freddie
Mac, Fannie Mae, HBSC, and Royal Bank of Scotland (rescued by the U.K.
government), as well as many other banks all around the world, came within a

whisker of going belly up and needed bailouts. Here is what Federal Reserve Chairman Bernanke said later about the 2008 financial crisis, in a document filed with the U.S. Court of Federal Claims as part of a lawsuit linked to the bailout of AIG:[4]

> September and October of 2008 was the worst financial crisis in global history, including the Great Depression. Out of the 13 most important financial institutions in the United States, 12 were at risk of failure within a period of a week or two.

Asked why he thought it was essential for the government to rescue AIG, Bernanke said:"AIG's demise would be a catastrophe"[5] and "could have resulted in a 1930s-style global financial and economic meltdown, with catastrophic implications for production, income, and jobs."[6,7]

To be specific, U.S. taxpayers were not out $700 billion: $350 billion was used in 2008 to buy bank and automotive (famously GM) stocks to inject liquidity in their ailing finances. By 2010, banks had paid back $194 billion into the Obama administration TARP fund, and the GM stock held by the government was later sold at a profit. Instead of using the other $350 billion, President Obama launched the $787 billion Economic Stimulus Package, credited with helping the economy recover from the "Great Recession." Still, even two years after the 2008 summer crisis, house prices in the U.S. were still a third below their pre-crisis value, and 9% of the working population was unemployed. The U.S. taxpayers had to be "on the hook" for the banks through the Paulson bailout, and did suffer extensive financial hardship and lasting negative economic consequences from the financial crisis. Even today, with record low unemployment at 4.1%, millions have stayed out of the work force (i.e. not counted in the unemployment statistics), and median wages have not recovered much. Millions have lost their home through foreclosure. A very steep price indeed for tens of millions of U.S. citizens . . .[8,9]

Much has been written about the complexity and opacity of the financial investment instruments, the cascading defaults of which led to the 2008 crisis and the Great Recession, foremost Collateralized Debt Obligations, or CDOs. A word on these CDOs: during the years leading up to 2006, after the economy had recovered somewhat from the dot.com boom and bust of the turn of the century, banks increased their volume of activity by extending loans to "subprime" borrowers. These were people with poor credit history who would likely struggle to pay interest and principal (if there was any principal) to the mortgage issuer. These very risky mortgages were pooled together by banks into allegedly low-risk securities by aggregating large numbers of them into one single pool. However, this aggregation ("pooling") of risky mortgages only reduces investment risk in a significant way if the risk of each individual loan is uncorrelated with that of the other loans in the same pool. The underlying idea was that property markets in different U.S. geographical areas would increase and decrease in value independently of one another. This proved wrong when property prices started to go down nationwide in 2006. The pooled mortgages were used as the collateral behind the securities (essentially interest-paying instruments), which were called CDOs. The CDOs were separated into different types, or tranches, by the perceived degree of exposure to potential defaults on the mortgages by the subprime borrowers. Most individual investors bought the tranches rated AAA by credit agencies such as Moody and Standard and Poor's, thinking that these CDOs would be relatively safe while providing higher returns than corporate bonds or treasury bills. Not understood then was that banks got both enthusiastic and sloppy in creating many slices of CDOs, leading to a level of complexity that eluded complacent credit agencies – which were also paid by the same banks they were supposed to rate.

Michael Lewis, who writes about either complex U.S. sports (*Moneyball*; *The Blind Side*) or big finance (*Liar's Poker*, more recently, *Flash Boys*), wrote a detailed analysis of mortgage-based finance instruments in his book *The Big Short*. The book deconstructs step-by-step what led to the creation of CDOs; how they became ever more complex and opaque; and how a few analytical, insightful and determined contrarians debunked the whole construction, and made themselves fortunes in the process. Essentially, they found that conventional wisdom assumed the U.S. housing market could never go down across most states simultaneously. Therefore, buying high interest securities backed by home mortgages across the country was viewed as very safe. They decided to bet against this conventional wisdom and, among other things, bought insurance against defaults on CDOs.

One of the pivotal moments in the book is when the contrarian investors discover that complacent credit agencies (paid by the volume of financial instruments they rate) gave triple-A ratings to portfolios of CDOs that were actually 80% composed of triple-B-rated subprime mortgage bonds. Bingo! Research such portfolios with the worst possible underlying collateral (e.g. mortgages in depressed areas such as Detroit or overbuilt ones like in Florida), and get cheap insurance on these triple-A bonds. These bonds are rated as very safe; hence their cost of insurance is very low. Actually, they are a pile of subprime junk and therefore likely to default, triggering payment of the insurance.

However, the market was taking its sweet time to see this evidence that had jumped to the eyes of our contrarians: yes, housing prices were down all over the country already in 2006, but CDOs still sold, investors piling on them. Pressure built up: would this large bet against the U.S. real estate market just be an expensive folly? Things became edgy and discussions tense. More analyses ensued, and the contrarians understood why the CDO markets showed such inertia. Financial firms were so eager to swallow all these CDOs and global appetite for these higher interest-paying instruments was such that this bubble would still grow a while before it burst. Not only CDOs were sold in great volumes, but credit default swaps were also used to replicate bonds backed by actual home loans, creating synthetic CDOs on a very large scale. "There weren't enough Americans with sh … credit taking out loans to satisfy investors' appetite for the end product." So "they were creating them out of whole cloth.

One hundred times over! That's why the losses in the financial system are so much greater than just the subprime loans."[10] The contrarians understood the feet of clay of the whole CDO construction and doggedly stayed the course until the first cracks appeared. When the whole construction collapsed, they laughed all the way to the bank. The book was thrilling enough to be made into a recent movie replete with A-list stars: Brad Pitt; Steve Carell; Marisa Tomei; Ryan Gosling; Christian Bale; Finn Wittrock; Jeremy Strong; and Margot Robbie.

★ ★ ★ ★ ★

Bankruptcy under the sun in Orange County

Not being a very sophisticated investor, in the early 1990s I used to like to put some of my savings in California Municipal Bonds, at least those rated AAA. That way the interest paid on these munis was free of both federal and state income taxes for me. Then came the massive Orange County Municipal Bond default, leading to the whole county going bankrupt. The Orange County Treasurer and his team had invested in financial instruments they did not understand, on a massive scale. Let's relate the story in a little more detail.

On December 6, 1994, Orange County, south of Los Angeles (its airport is named after the actor John Wayne), the fifth most populous and one of the ten richest counties in the U.S., filed for Chapter 9 bankruptcy protection against its creditors. Chapter 9 means that Orange County literally could no longer pay its bills. Yet, until that fateful day of December 6, Orange County boasted of the highest possible credit rating for a municipality by Standard and Poor's and Moody's. The Orange County Fund had also enjoyed annual returns of 10% or more over the prior decade. What happened?

What happened is that the Orange County treasurer, Robert Citron, had invested the county's largest pool, $7.5 billion, in a portfolio consisting mainly of highly leveraged interest rate–linked securities. This complex play on derivatives relied on short-term interest rates in the U.S. remaining at much lower levels relative to medium-term interest rates. This portfolio of derivatives was highly leveraged, which means that even small shifts in the value of short- versus medium-term interest rates translated into large gains (or losses) for the portfolio. During the late 1980s and early 1990s, Citron's pool rewarded Orange County fund investors (many of them retirees and unsophisticated investors attracted by a AAA-rated muni fund from a wealthy California county) with above average returns. However, when in February 1994 the Federal Reserve decided to raise interest rates, short-term interest rates spiked, and Citron's pool started to exhibit large paper losses. During the next few months Citron ignored these paper losses, hoping that a reversal in interest trends would help him ride the storm. But by the fall of 1994, demands for collateral from Wall Street counterparts and looming threats of a run on deposits proved too hard to ignore: Orange County fell into a liquidity squeeze it could not get away from. In essence, without quite understanding it, Robert Citron had made a billion-dollar gamble on interest rate movements and lost.[11,12]

Yet Citron was no novice. He had been county treasurer since 1972 and had accumulated an excellent track record over twenty-plus years. So much in fact that Orange County, happy to have Citron's returns help with local budgets, allowed a relaxation of the strict rules governing the types of investments the fund could engage in. And local cities and government authorities, attracted by the returns of Citron's fund, added their investments to Orange County's. It is also good to remember that during the 1980s and 1990s California's political environment was dead set against any type of tax increase. Therefore, better than average returns from a county's investment fund were more than welcome. Local budgetary requirements were growing, not shrinking, due to a quickly expanding population with acute service and infrastructure needs. Everything contributed to supporting Citron's actions, from the local political environment to financial institutions promoting complex derivative instruments and credit agencies that did not do their job properly.[13]

By December 1994, Wall Street investment banks, which had lent Citron $15 billion for his leveraged bet on interest rates, were tripping over themselves to sell off the Orange County collateral they were holding. This was messy. Credit Suisse First Boston managed to sell off $2.6 billion of that collateral on Dec 6, precipitating the county into bankruptcy protection; Paine Webber sold $300 million the same day. On December 7, Nomura sold $900 million; Kidder Peabody $100 million. But Smith Barney, Merrill Lynch, Morgan Stanley, and Prudential still held billions of dollars in near-worthless Orange County collateral. Then followed years of lawsuits, culminating in a June 2, 1998 $400 million settlement with Merrill Lynch, the company Orange County attorneys felt was the most responsible for steering the treasurer towards what was now deemed overly risky and unsuitable securities.[14] Merrill Lynch did not plead guilty to any type of non-professional behavior in its relationship with Orange County. Additional settlements followed with dozens of other securities firms the county held responsible for its losses. This led to the courts awarding in February 2000 around $860 million to the various local government entities that had suffered from the 1994 collapse. However, Orange County was still paying off $1.2 billion of the recovery bonds issued in 1995 and 1996, with future such payments scheduled to last several decades. Needless to say, Orange County's habitants carried the can in several ways: retirement savings went bust; years of litigation prevented any type of sustained investments; and the county suffered from a decade of deferred maintenance and cuts on essential services like water, sanitation and local transport.[15]

Today, new Orange County investment policies mandate safety of principal and liquidity as the primary objective of any county fund. These policies also prohibit leverage, i.e. borrowing for investment purposes, most kinds of structured notes and derivatives (e.g. options). County treasury officers are prohibited from receiving gifts and are mandated to disclose any potential conflicts of interest. They also have to submit monthly reports to investors that are transparent and clear enough for investors to understand the performance of their investments. And Citron? Having pleaded guilty to six felony counts and three special enhancements, he was condemned to one year of house arrest and had to pay a $100,000 fine. A relatively light sentence, but again, the political, economic and financial environments had encouraged his behavior over a couple of decades. Robert Citron passed away on January 16, 2013, aged 87.

The recycling of petro dollars into Third World debt in the 1970s; the junk bond craze (remember Michael Milken and Drexel Lambert?) of the 1980s; the Savings and Loans crisis, derivatives excesses, and the Long Term Capital Management collapse in the 1990s; and of course the 2008 financial crisis and ensuing great recession: what do all of these have in common, apart from their decade or so cyclicality? Financiers, traders and professional risk takers make fortunes through overly complex and opaque investments sold to gullible investors. The price paid by the finance community when a crisis occurs is very small compared to the outsized profits made during the years ramping up to the crisis. On the other hand, small investors, local governments and of course taxpayers end up paying over many years for their gullibility and the folly of the finance profession. Complexity in finance ends up being a vehicle through which a few enrich themselves at the expense of many. This major problem of complexity in finance has two aspects.

First, finance professionals keep creating investment vehicles with underlying risks not easily understood by the people who buy them.

Second, decision-making is separated from risk-bearing. For example, those deciding who get mortgages are not those who ultimately suffer the risk of default on the same mortgages.

In Orange County's case, finance professionals from Merrill Lynch and other investment houses had created complex packages of derivatives and interest rate–linked securities. Only they knew how these securities might fare in case of unforeseen swings in interest rates. Robert Citron and his team, who bought billions of dollars of these securities, did not understand them well. Yet, buy they did, on an enormous scale, alongside millions of investors. The issuers of these securities were astute enough to sell them at a time where their benefits were obvious, paying higher interest rates than normal bonds. This is why Citron and his team enjoyed above average returns while the underlying trends in interest rates were not changing much. But risks not understood by the buyers became painfully apparent when conditions changed with new swings in interest rates. When this occurred, it exposed the separation between those who decided (Citron and the investment banks) and those who bore the brunt of the risk when things turned sour: the millions of people and retirees in Orange County.

★ ★ ★ ★ ★

Securitization, swaps, dark pools, shadow banking: complexity meets opacity

What do securitization; swaps; dark pools; and shadow banking have in common? They represent large domains in the global world of finance where complexity and opacity reign supreme. As such, risk is also poorly understood in these domains, least of all by those who suffer the potential negative consequences.

Let's start with the mother ship. **Securitization** is the process of taking a group of illiquid assets and transforming them through financial engineering into a security, for example a fixed-income interest-bearing bond. The Collateralized Debt Obligations or CDOs reviewed earlier fall under that category. A typical example of securitization is the creation of mortgage-backed securities that are secured by a collection of mortgages. Collateralized Mortgage Obligations (CMOs) can be packaged and bundled together, then re-split into different tranches. For example, the first tranche gets principal and interest until paid off; other tranches might get interest after the first tranche is paid off. With all this packaging and slicing, investors can buy pretty much anything, e.g. 1) the interest on these CMOs for the first ten years; 2) the principal on the CMOs; 3) the interest on the same CMOs after ten years, etc.[16]

From a technical standpoint, the financial engineering process works as follows. First, a regulated financial institution originates numerous mortgages, which are secured by claims against the various properties purchased by those holding the mortgages. Then, all the individual mortgages are bundled together into a pool, which is held in trust as the collateral for the mortgage-backed security. This security can be issued by a third-party financial company, such as a large investment bank; by an aggregator like Fannie Mae or Freddie Mac; or by the same bank that originated the mortgages. The new security thus created is backed up by the claims against the mortgagors' assets. It can be sold to participants in the secondary mortgage market, which is extremely large, providing a significant amount of liquidity to the group of mortgages.

In addition, the security issuer will often choose to break the mortgage pool into a number of different tranches. These tranches can be structured in virtually any way the issuer sees fit, allowing the creation of a myriad of securities for all sorts of risk tolerances. We saw earlier how tranches could focus on different real estate markets; the interest on the mortgages; their principal, etc. Pension funds will tend to invest in high-credit–rated securities; other, less risk adverse investors in pursuit of higher returns such as hedge funds may elect lower credit–rated securities. Several hedge funds are known, for example, to invest in bonds of distressed economies, such as Argentina in the 2000s, and Greece more recently.

With all these tranches, understanding one's risk, default, prepayment, etc., is a nearly impossible proposition. Indeed, CMOs are an excellent example of the problem of complexity in finance.

Not confused yet? All right, let's move to **credit default swaps**. As seen earlier, to increase the volume of CDOs beyond what the number of actual mortgages on physical homes could support, financial engineers created "synthetic CDOs." A synthetic CDO invests in credit default swaps or other non-cash assets to gain exposure to a portfolio of fixed income assets, such as mortgages in a CDO. Synthetic CDOs are typically divided into credit tranches based on the level of credit risk assumed. All tranches will receive periodic payments based on the cash flows from the credit default swaps. If a credit event occurs in the fixed income portfolio, the synthetic CDO and its investors become responsible for the losses, starting from the lowest rated tranches, all the way up to the highest rated ones. With synthetic CDO, we are now at least three financial transactions removed from the actual mortgages. We have seen how complacent credit agencies were in even rating the basic risk of these mortgages, so is there any surprise that it is almost impossible to assess the real risk of a synthetic CDO accurately?[17,18]

Credit default swaps gained notoriety because of their heavy role in the 2008 financial crisis. But they are by no means the only swaps in the financial engineering world. More generally speaking, what are swaps? A swap is a derivative contract through which two parties exchange financial instruments. These instruments can be almost anything, but most swaps involve cash flows based on a notional principal amount that both parties agree to. Usually that principal does not change hands. One leg of the swap is typically a fixed cash flow, the other leg a variable cash flow based upon, for example, a benchmark interest rate or a floating currency rate. The most common kind of swap is an interest swap, but swaps on currencies and credit defaults are also common. Swaps do not trade on exchanges, and retail investors do not generally engage in swaps. Rather, swaps are over-the-counter contracts between businesses or financial institutions.

Let's illustrate how swaps work, using a hypothetical **interest swap** as an example. This will also shed more light on the type of derivatives that created so much trouble for Orange County in 1994. In an interest rate swap, the parties exchange cash flows based upon a notional principal amount to hedge against interest risk or to speculate. For example, say company X has just issued $1 billion in five-year bonds with a variable annual interest rate defined by the one-year U.S. T-bill, plus 1.3% or 130 basis points. Let's assume the one-year U.S. T-bill is at 1.7%, low by historical standards (recent years of Central Banks quantitative easing monetary policies notwithstanding), when this transaction is taking place. This means company X is willing to bet that U.S. short-term interest rates will soon rise. It finds another party, firm A, that is willing to pay X an annual rate of the one-year U.S. T-bill, plus 1.3% on a notional principal of $1 billion for five years. A will therefore fund X's interest payments on its latest bond issue, in exchange for which X will pay A a contractually agreed fixed annual rate of 6% on $1 billion, or $60 million per year for five years. Company X benefits from the swap if short-term U.S. interest rates rise significantly over the next five years. Firm A benefits if rates fall, stay flat, or rise only gradually.

What happens if the rate for the one-year U.S. T-bill rises 1% per year for five years?

Company X's total payments to its bondholders over the five-year period would have been $1 billion × (5 × 0.013 + 0.017 + 0.027 + 0.037 + 0.047 + 0.057) = $250 million, or $100 million more that X would have paid to its bondholders if the one-year T-bill rate had stayed flat at 1.7% (if this rate had stayed at 1.7%, X would have owed its bondholders $1 billion × (0.013 + 0.017) × 5, or $150 million). On the other hand, having engaged in the interest swap with A, X will have to pay A $300 million (6% interest on $1 billion over five years)). A will pay X's bondholders, but X is still $50 million worse off ($250 million compared to $300 million) in this transaction, a loss on this interest swap.

Let's now see what happens if the rate for the one-year T-bill goes up faster, or 2% per year for five years. Company X's total payments to its bondholders over the five-year total $1 billion × (5 × 0.013 + 0.017 + 0.037 + 0.057 + 0.077 + 0.097) = $350 million, or $200 million more that X would have paid to its bondholders if the one-year T-bill rate had stayed flat at 1.7%. On the other hand, X only owes A $300 million (6% interest on $1 billion over five years). A will pay X's bondholders, and thus company X will be $50 million better off ($350 million less $300 million) in this transaction, a gain on this interest swap. We can also note that this swap is neutral (i.e. neither gain or loss) for X if the one-year T-bill rates go up at 1.5% per year.[19]

Fortunes can be made or lost depending on the fluctuations of the underlying interest rate of a swap. Of course, these gains or losses are vastly exacerbated when there is leverage, that is, if the parties also borrow money to engage in this type of transaction – this is what happened to Orange County.

There are many other types of swaps. Relatively common arrangements include **commodity**, **currency**, **debt**, and **total return swaps**. Commodity swaps involve the exchange of a floating commodity price, such as the Brent crude oil spot price, for a set price over an agreed-upon period. Crude oil is by far the most actively traded commodity in the world, but many other traded commodities such as natural gas; iron ore; copper; and agricultural feedstock can be used in commodity swaps. In currency swaps, the parties exchange interest and principal payments on debt denominated in different currencies. Unlike in an interest swap, the principal in a currency swap is not a notional amount but is exchanged along with interest obligations. Currency swaps can take place between countries, helping one of the countries stabilize its foreign reserves. Debt-equity swaps involve the exchange of debt for equity, which for a publicly traded company means bonds for stock. It is a way for companies to refinance their debt when interest rates have gone down or their stock gone up. In a total return swap, the total return for an asset is exchanged for a fixed interest rate. This gives the party paying the fixed rate exposure to the underlying asset – a stock or a financial index, for example – without having to spend the capital to hold that asset.

The list of potential swaps is infinite . . . and so is their potential complexity and opacity, particularly when involving assets that are not remotely close to be traded on public exchanges. Opacity, by the way, is complexity's best friend.

It helps keep away from the public eye – and regulators – finance operations that are useless to most people and benefit only a few. The use of swaps is often much more akin to gambling than hedging one's risk in an operating business. The more complex swaps are, the less likely they are to correspond to a real business risk requiring hedging. In that case, they benefit from being as removed as possible from the sunlight of public exchanges. But we can still go further in our quest for complexity and opacity in the world of finance. Let's now talk about dark pools.

Dark pools are private exchanges or forums for trading securities. Unlike stock exchanges, dark pools are not accessible to the investing public and are so named for their complete lack of transparency. Dark pools were invented to facilitate block trading by institutional investors who did not wish to impact public markets with their large orders, and suffer as a result from adverse prices for their trades. Dark pools are the subjects of Michael Lewis' recent book *Flash Boys: A Wall Street Revolt*. In his book, Lewis castigates dark pools for their absence of transparency, which makes them vulnerable to conflicts of interest by their owners and to predatory trading practices by high-frequency traders. Defenders of dark pools use that most convenient and self-serving argument, often used in defense of the excesses of the financial world: they increase liquidity in the markets. As if markets suffered from lack of liquidity before "flash-trading" existed! Figures are difficult to confirm, but industry insiders estimate that 15% of U.S. trading volume in 2015 took place off-exchange, in dark pools.[20]

Why are dark pools growing in volume? The lack of transparency works in the institutional investor's favor, since it may result in a better-realized price than if the sale was executed on a public exchange. It is important to note that since dark pool participants do not disclose their trading intentions to the exchange prior to execution, there is no order book visible to the public. Trade execution details are only released to the consolidated tape after a delay. The institutional seller also has a better chance of getting a buyer for the full share block in a dark pool, since it is a forum dedicated to large investors. In 2015 it is estimated that there were forty-five dark pools in the U.S., consisting of three types: 1) broker–dealer owned (most of them large investment banks such as Goldman Sachs), set up for clients or proprietary trading; 2) agency broker or exchange-owned, pools acting as agents, not principals, such as Liquidnet and NYSE Euronext; 3) electronic market makers, dark pools offered by independent operators like Getco and Knight, operating as principals for their own account.[21]

Although dark pools offer institutional investors the advantages of lower transaction costs, reduced market impact and a reduction in adverse prices during large trades, they have significant drawbacks. The main one is that if the amount of trading taking place on dark pools continues to grow, exchange prices quoted to Joe Public may no longer reflect the actual market. For example, if a mutual fund owns 20% of company X's stock and sells it off in a dark pool transaction, the fund may get a higher price than it would have achieved selling that stake on a public exchange. But individual investors who have just bought shares in X will have paid too high a price for it, since the stock could very well collapse once the mutual fund's large sale becomes public knowledge. Michael Lewis also points out in *Flash Boys* that the dark pools' opaqueness can give rise to conflicts of interest if a broker–dealer's proprietary traders trade against pool clients, or if the broker–dealer sells special access to the dark pool to high-frequency-trading firms. Lewis further stresses that dark pool client orders are ideal fodder for predatory trading practices by some high-frequency-trading firms, which employ tactics such as "pinging" dark pools to unearth large hidden orders, and then engage in front running or latency arbitrage.

Needless to say, both advantages offered to institutional investors in dark pools and corresponding adverse effects for individual investors (and in some cases for institutions as well) are impossible to quantify in a remotely accurate way. Conflicts of interests and predatory behaviors have been observed and documented, but remain unpredictable events. Risks inherent to dark pools therefore exist, but are about as well understood as dark pools are transparent. The only certainty is that, in most cases, institutional investors benefit from them, and individual investors may suffer as a result.

Shadow banking is a term used to describe the financial intermediaries involved in providing credit across the global financial system, but whose members are not subject to regulatory oversight. Examples of such intermediaries and activities not subject to regulation include hedge funds, unlisted derivatives and other unlisted instruments. The shadow banking system also refers to unregulated financial activities by regulated institutions. Examples of unregulated activities by regulated institutions include credit default swaps. Private equity funds, payday lenders, and certain activities performed by investment banks and insurance companies are part of shadow banking as well. The shadow banking system is not regulated, primarily because it does not accept traditional bank deposits. As a result, many of the institutions involved in shadow banking do not have capital requirements commensurate with the higher market, credit and liquidity risks they face. Absent these higher capital requirements, their returns can be significantly higher.[22]

Despite the higher level of scrutiny of participants in shadow banking since the 2008 financial meltdown, the sector has grown tremendously, and it is estimated that over $25 trillion in funds flowed through it in 2015. Much of the activity centers on the creation of collateralized loans and repurchase agreements with broker-dealers. Nonbank lenders, such as Quicken Loans, account for an increasing share of mortgages in the United States. There is a constant stream of new entrants in the sector: one of the fastest growing segments of the shadow banking industry has been peer-to-peer lending (P2P), with over $1.7 billion of loans initiated in 2015. Sector leader LendingClub enjoyed a very successful $1 billion IPO in the NYSE in December of 2014, valuing the company at $9 billion. Since then, however, LendingClub founder and CEO Renaud Laplanche has had to resign in 2016, due to his origination of loans that did not follow the process established by the company. LendingClub's stock price is now well below its IPO level of $15 a share, but this setback does not mean that P2P, or CrowdLending, has stopped growing. The sector is rebounding, with many "fintech" entrepreneurs starting new platforms using big data technology.

There are obvious concerns about the financial risks posed to the overall financial system by shadow banking operations. The 2010 Dodd–Frank legislation focused primarily on the banking industry, leaving the shadow banking sector largely immune from regulation. The Federal Reserve Board has proposed that nonbanks, such as broker–dealers and peer-to-peer lenders, operate under similar margin requirements as banks, but this is far from enacted. The overall size of shadow banking and the risks it poses to the global financial system are quasi-impossible to determine, and the wide variety of shadow banking participants can only increase its complexity.

Securitization, swaps and dark pools all played a role in the recent financial crises, notably that of 2008. Exuberant financiers bragged in the years leading up to 2008 that they had found a way to eliminate risk, when in fact they had simply lost track of it amidst all these derivatives, swaps, etc. sliced and diced in a multitude of tranches. Regulators, credit rating agencies and even Central Banks were asleep at the wheel, believing for the most part that the modern finance-driven economy had found a permanent solution of stable growth and low inflation. Ever increasing levels of household and institutional debt were ignored; after all, irresponsible mortgage lending in great volume was the fuel that fired the whole financial engine. In the U.S., low interest rates (driven by a global surplus of savings, principally in China, seeking safety in U.S. bonds) and the tax deductibility of borrowing made it profitable for many to borrow to invest in instruments paying higher levels of interest than regular treasury or corporate bonds. This leverage, used to buy much riskier securities, compounded the aggregate level of risk to a degree no one anticipated. And it was not just U.S. banks fueling the fire. European banks were just as happy to borrow heavily in American markets to buy risky securities they did not understand in the least. And, of course, when the U.S. housing market went south, pooling, derivatives, swaps and complex financial engineering did not give investors the promised protection. The investors, principally retail ones, ended up being hurt by risky investment schemes designed by others, i.e. these financial engineers who had long before collected vast amounts of fees and bonuses. Banks had to be rescued in part because they had to engage in fire sales to pay collaterals they owed, which dented their capital; and in part because of "market-to-market" accounting rules that forced them to recognize enormous paper losses. Short-term credit became difficult to get, and the institutions most reliant on wholesale credit floundered one after another.

The whole global financial system was interconnected, and complex chains of debt between counterparties were vulnerable to just one link breaking. In particular, credit-default swaps that were meant to spread risk actually concentrated it. This is what caused AIG to start failing within days of the Lehman Brothers bankruptcy, because of the enormous weight of all the credit-risk protection it had sold. And if AIG had been allowed to fail, other institutions, foremost Goldman Sachs (for a similar reason: it had a ton of loans to AIG on its books), may very well have been in mortal danger too. Lax capital ratios, with banks defeating early central banks' efforts to set a minimum of equity capital banks had to hold relative to their assets, provided little or no safeguards. Banks had a strong incentive to keep capital ratios very low, since low equity on their books allowed them to show higher returns on equity to Wall Street investors. And so total assets ballooned with very little equity capital to dampen shocks in the system. It looks like financial institutions had bet on themselves with borrowed money; this worked wonderfully during the good times but proved catastrophic when the music stopped. As for the average Joes, they had maintained their living standards through heavy borrowing as well. The illusion that debt could provide lasting prosperity for all crashed and burned with a vengeance in 2008, affecting hundreds of millions worldwide who had scant knowledge of modern finance.

After this cursory review of the ever-increasing complexity of the global financial industry, noted *Financial Times* columnist John Kay provides us with a very relevant summary. In his April 13, 2016 *FT* column titled "Complexity, Not Size, Is the Real Danger in Banking," Kay wrote:

> The central problem is not so much "too big to fail" but "too complex to fail": Lehman was a systemically important financial institution but not an important financial institution. Nor was it a big one; it had fewer employees than Citigroup today has compliance staff. Lehman's collapse created major problems for the global financial system because of the extent of its interactions, with more than 1m outstanding contracts at the time of its bankruptcy. Similarly, Long Term Capital Management was insignificant in size when it failed but capable of massive impact by virtue of the exposure of other institutions to its activities ...
>
> ... Ahead of the global financial crisis, it was argued that the growth of securitisation and other complex instruments similarly contributed to financial resilience. The reverse proved to be the case; trade between institutions represented concentration and multiplication of risks rather than diversification.
>
> Complexity is the enemy of stability. Financial conglomerates have become too diverse and sprawling for their chief executives or boards to understand what they do. The same complexity creates endemic conflicts of interest and is associated with cross subsidy between activities. There are fundamental differences in the cultures required to trade derivatives, to give private financial advice to big corporations, to manage assets on behalf of savers and to provide an efficient retail banking services ...
>
> ... These issues are compounded by the regulatory complexity that follows from attempts to monitor behaviour in impossible detail. As the size of the Dodd–Frank legislation shows, we have locked ourselves into a spiral in which regulatory complexity gives rise to further organisational complexity and the construction of yet more esoteric instruments ...

... They (legislators) cannot hope to have more than a basic knowledge of the rules they promulgate or the workings of the regulatory institutions they have created.[23]

Kay concludes his column by lamenting the regulatory complexity that follows the complexity of the financial world. Can regulatory frameworks that do not themselves contribute to a doomed loop of ever increasing complexity mitigate the risks inherent to global finance?

★　★　★　★　★

Regulating the financial world: complicated legislative solutions

After the 2008 global financial crisis, one of the top priorities of the newly installed Obama Administration was legislation that would prevent such financial calamity in the future. After lengthy legislative battles, the bi-partisan "Dodd–Frank" set of laws was born, named after the Democratic Massachusetts Congressman Barney Frank and Connecticut Senator Christopher Dodd. The complexity of this legislative solution governing a myriad of institutions was remarkably in tune with the complexity of the modern finance world.

The **Dodd–Frank Wall Street Reform and Consumer Protection Act** was passed by Congress and signed by President Obama on July 21, 2010. The Act's many provisions were spelled out over 2,300 pages or so, and were to be implemented over a period of several years. The act also established a number of new government agencies tasked with oversight of the various components of the act. The Financial Stability Oversight Council and Orderly Liquidation Authority monitor the financial stability of the largest U.S. financial institutions, like banking giants JP Morgan or Wells Fargo, which are deemed "too big to fail." The Council has the authority (not used yet) to break up banks that are so large as to pose a systemic risk to our financial system if they become dangerously unstable. The Council can also force these "too big to fail" banks to increase their reserve requirements, something it has done on a few occasions already. Increasing reserve requirements means banks must hold a higher percentage of their assets in cash, which decreases the amounts they can hold in marketable securities and their market-making power. In the potential case of break-up, restructuring or liquidation, the Orderly Liquidation Fund would provide money to assist with the dismantling of the affected financial companies, to prevent taxpayer dollars to be used to prop up such entities.[24,25]

For "too big to fail" insurance companies, a new Federal Insurance Office was created to monitor the risks posed by such institutions. A controversy arose early in March of 2016 when a federal judge struck down MetLife's designation as a systematically important financial institution. In essence, MetLife won its case against the Financial Stability Oversight Council that it was not "too big to fail." The insurer hailed the verdict as a significant victory, saying that its business model did not pose any threat to the financial stability of the U.S. – unlike, say, AIG in 2008. A month later the Federal Reserve said that it would soon take up the rules impacting the insurance companies deemed "too big to fail," illustrating that the complex set of laws under Dodd–Frank would take years to be written. The Feds would also propose the capital requirements for large insurance companies across the industry, six years after Dodd–Frank was passed into law. As legislation, Dodd–Frank was like the celebrated Sagrada Familia basilica by Gaudi in Barcelona, Spain: ambitious, striking, but far from a completed work.[26,27,28]

The Consumer Financial Protection Bureau (CFPB) was established as part of Dodd–Frank to protect consumers, principally in the area of "predatory" mortgage lending. As such, it reflected the widespread sentiment that the sub-prime market and its reliance on shaky mortgages were the main cause of the 2008 disaster. Among other things, the CFPB prevented mortgage originators from steering potential borrowers to the loan that would result in the highest payment for the originator. The CFPB also set new rules in consumer lending, credit and debit cards, as well as for financial brokers. It required lenders to disclose information in a form that was easy for all consumers to understand, even for auto loans. Credit card applications were made simpler as a result. Setting up the CFPB met with fierce financial industry and political opposition. One result of this opposition was that the Obama administration was unable to name as head of the CFPB its most enthusiastic proponent and early architect, Massachusetts Senator Elizabeth Warren. In September of 2016, the CFPB attained national recognition with consumers in the wake of the Wells Fargo fake banking and credit card account scandal. Thousands of the bank's retail banking employees had created one and a half million new accounts since 2011, under the bank's much-hailed strategy of "cross-selling." This strategy was one of the reasons the Wells stock had gone up faster than its peers during the aftermath of the financial crisis. The problem, as explained by the CFPB in its report, was that most of these new accounts had been created without their owners knowing about it. These phantom accounts allowed thousands of Wells Fargo employees to meet their sales quotas, but led to lots of additional account fees for the bank's retail customers, who knew nothing about this. Wells Fargo, a company employing about 300,000 people, was fined $185 million, a relatively minor sum in today's banking world.[29]

The bank initially fired 5,300 employees, most of them at the bottom of the totem pole, with no senior executive affected whatsoever – not even the head of the retail banking division, Carrie Tolstedt, who had retired in the summer with an eight-figure package. However, given that thousands of small retail consumers of the bank were defrauded, the scandal was enormous. Wells lost $18 billion in market capitalization in a matter of days. CEO John Stumpf was hauled in front of Congress for a bi-partisan grilling, with Elizabeth Warren demanding that he should be "criminally investigated."[30] What got Stumpf in most trouble with Congress was his refusal to offer a view on whether the Wells Fargo board should claw back pay from him or Ms. Tolstedt; Stumpf himself was also the bank's board chairman . . . A week later, though, Wells Fargo announced that it would indeed claw back compensation from Mr. Stumpf. He would forfeit $41 million in stock awards, with Ms. Tolstedt forfeiting $19 million of her own stock awards, both also giving up any bonuses for 2016.[31,32] On October 12, to no one's surprise, Stumpf's resignation as chairman and CEO was announced. He still retired with an estimated $130 million, even after the claw back. His replacement as CEO? Timothy Sloan, Wells' COO, with lead director Stephen Sanger named as non-executive chairman of the board. So, the board voted to replace the bank's outgoing chairman and CEO with insiders. Customers also voted, with their feet: over the two months following the scandal, the bank lost 14% of its customers, with many more predicted to leave. Things became even worse when, on August 30, 2017, Wells admitted it had found up to 3.5 million potentially fake bank and credit card accounts in total, significantly more than the 2016 tally.[33] Congress, Wall Street, everyone expressed shock, and the bank suffered a credit downgrade from ratings agency DBRS. The bank's stock fell 3%, on top of an underperforming trend in 2017. No heads rolled this time, but most analysts stressed that Well Fargo's reputation would be tough to repair. Legendary investor Warren Buffett, while expressing his long-term commitment to the bank and his confidence that these "very bad things" would be corrected, also said in an interview with *CNBC* on the same day that when one puts the spotlight on a large financial institution, one is likely to find something: "what you find is there's never just one cockroach in the kitchen when you start looking around."[34] This story is not over.

Another key component of Dodd–Frank was the Volcker rule, named after former Federal Reserve Chairman Paul Volcker. This federal regulation prohibited banks from conducting certain investment activities within their own accounts, and limited their ownership of and relationships with private equity and hedge funds. The Volcker rule thus curtailed a financial institution's ability to engage in speculative trading strategies with retail clients' government-insured deposits. The idea was to eliminate conflicts of interest by not allowing banks to engage in vast amounts of proprietary trading, i.e. for their own account, unless they used their own equity or had enough "skin in the game." No less than five federal agencies (the Federal Reserve System; the Federal Deposit Insurance Corporation, or FDIC; the Office of the Comptroller of the Currency; the Commodity Futures Trading Commission; and the Security and Exchange Commission, or SEC) approved the final version of the Volcker rule in 2014. Some original provisions of the rule were somewhat diluted, allowing banks more leeway in their investment and trading activities. But clearly the Volcker rule was an attempt within Dodd–Frank to emulate the Great Depression Glass–Steagall Act, recognizing the financial risks of financial institutions engaging in commercial and investment banking at the same time.

Dodd–Frank regulated the financial institutions' use of derivatives as well, such as the credit default swaps that contributed so much to the 2008 financial crisis. It did so through the set-up of centralized exchanges for swaps trading.

This reduced the possibility of counterparty default and provided greater disclosure of swaps trading information to increase transparency in those markets. Again, this aspect of the Act led to much recrimination from financial institutions and their lobbyists. An additional feature of Dodd–Frank was the creation of the SEC Office of Credit Ratings, which was tasked with ensuring that agencies improved their accuracy in rating financial instruments, businesses, municipalities and other entities evaluated by them. The reliability of this rating activity had been much criticized after 2008, credit rating agencies being accused of giving far too many misleadingly favorable investment ratings. Dodd–Frank also strengthened the "whistleblower" program and executive pay claw back provisions enacted by the earlier Sarbanes–Oxley Act.

Overall, Dodd–Frank's complexity (over two hundred rules overseen by a dozen federal agencies) was the reflection of a complex mess that took years in the making, culminating in the 2008 financial meltdown. As a financial channel television commentator once said, "it is hard to unscramble the eggs." Such is the complexity of modern finance.

★   ★   ★   ★   ★

Simple but effective: Glass–Steagall and Basel

It is interesting to contrast Dodd–Frank with the **Glass–Steagall Act**, passed by Congress and signed by Franklin Roosevelt in 1933. Glass–Steagall, a mere 37 pages long, was enacted into law after the 1929 financial crash and the Great Depression that followed it. After the crash, commercial banks were accused of engaging in too many speculative transactions, not only investing their assets but also buying new issues for resale to the public. Risky loans were issued to companies in which banks had invested; clients of the banks were encouraged to invest in the same companies; add a good dose of leverage, and this behavior led to disaster. Glass–Steagall set up a regulatory wall between commercial and investment banking; banks were given a year to choose between commercial or investment banking activities. Only 10% of commercial banks' total income could be from securities, with an exception allowing them to underwrite government-issued bonds. The main idea was to prevent the banks' use of commercial retail deposits to invest in stocks or other securities. Giant banks like JP Morgan became as a result much smaller institutions, but also far less risky ones. The authors of this landmark law were Senator Carter Glass, former Treasury Secretary and founder of the U.S. Federal Reserve System; and Henry Steagall, Chairman of the House Banking and Currency Committee. Steagall insisted on adding to the legislation bank deposit insurance for retail customers, a first at the time. In a nutshell, Glass–Steagall told banks they had to choose between serving Main Street or Wall Street. The law was repealed in 1999 during the Bill Clinton presidency, which created a debate on financial regulation that lasts to this day.

Glass–Steagall separated traditional banking from investment banking very cleanly. This prevented banks from making speculative financial plays with government, i.e. taxpayer-backed deposits. For sixty-six years, Glass–Steagall performed its intended mission. In particular, there was very little proprietary trading by large investment banks for their personal account. Institutional proprietary trading really took off after Glass–Steagall was abolished in 1999, investment banks' trading desks taking huge bets not on behalf of clients but for their own firms, and becoming the fulcrum of profits and power. Take Goldman Sachs, for example; for decades a venerable and very lucrative partnership where investment banking represented the golden track, it evolved into an immense publicly traded firm; Lloyd Blankfein, Goldman Sachs' CEO since 2006, and Gary Cohn, the Goldman COO (also since 2006), who left the firm to serve as Chief Economic Advisor in the Trump White House, both came from the commodities trading side of the business.

It could be argued that Glass–Steagall did a much better job at keeping our U.S. banking system safe than the much more complex Dodd–Frank legislation. There are also many people who disagree with this premise. It is often said, for example, that Glass–Steagall could not mitigate the potential risks of shadow banking. That the "Volcker Rule" can achieve more or less the same result. *New York Times* columnist and author Andrew Ross Sorkin (*Too Big to Fail: The Inside Story of How Wall Street and Washington Fought to Save the Financial System – and Themselves*)[35] stresses that Glass–Steagall could not have prevented the Bear Stearns or Lehman Brothers failures, since these firms only served Wall Street, with no commercial banking activities. He is right, but only as far as Lehman. And the fall of Lehman was followed by the bailout of AIG; that bailout was quite possibly motivated by the fact that Goldman Sachs was the next domino to fall, since it was owed a lot of money by AIG . . . Glass–Steagall would have prevented Goldman from becoming such an integrated banking giant, with its overexposure on AIG and CMOs. Let's look at it another way. Wouldn't reining in the excesses of Wall Street be simpler with Glass–Steagall in place, and the addition of narrower, more specific legislation addressing the systemic risks created by the growth of shadow banking? One can certainly make the case that this could be a credible alternative to Dodd–Frank, and politicians from both sides of the aisle have supported this position: President Donald Trump (reinstating Glass–Steagall was included in the official GOP platform for the 2016 convention that nominated him), and Senators Elizabeth Warren and Bernie Sanders are among them. Sanders, Trump, and Warren have all argued at some point over the last two years that the largest U.S. banks are so big they present a systemic risk no one can control. Therefore, they should be broken up, and the simplest way to do this is to bring back Glass–Steagall.[36,37,38]

Let's go further; the fact that Dodd–Frank is huge and very complex also makes it very evadable, unlike the very short and clear Glass–Steagall Act. Under Dodd–Frank, thousands of new staff had to be hired to carry on the new regulations; thousands of lawyers found additional work in helping financial firms find new loopholes and ways around regulations. Complex rulebooks always lead to opportunities to subvert their original intent, whereas the simpler a rule, the simpler it is to enforce it. Clarity makes distortion very difficult. In addition, regulation complexity advantages the largest companies, which are the ones that can afford the armies of accountants and lawyers needed to find the relevant loopholes. This means that complexity in regulations is costly but also ineffective. After November 8 election and the inauguration of President Donald Trump on January 20, 2017, many Republican and business voices started clamoring for the full repeal of Dodd–Frank. Not joining this chorus: some of the leading U.S. bank CEOs, who would like a loosening of regulations, but to a point. Better the devil you know . . . The CEOs of the largest banks, even though they feel their industry is now over-regulated, have a clear preference for Dodd–Frank over Glass–Steagall or equivalent.[39,40,41]

In all fairness, Dodd–Frank, despite a length and complexity that allowed bankers and their political allies to engage in many efforts to weaken it, appears to have been successful at controlling some of Wall Street's excesses. In the end, though, banks are simply highly leveraged plays on economies. Even in 2016, their leverage (expressed by the ratio of their total assets to their equity capital) was above 20, despite the efforts of global regulators to decrease it. The Basel III efforts in mandating increases in equity capital for the world's largest banks receive much less attention in the U.S. than Dodd–Frank, but they may represent a much simpler and effective formula for addressing systemic banking risk to the global economy.

In 1974, the G-10 countries plus Spain and Luxembourg formed a standing committee under the Bank for International Settlements (BIS), called the **Basel Committee on Banking Supervision (BCBS)**, in Basel, Switzerland. In 1988, the BCBS published a set of minimum capital requirements for banks, known as Basel I. Basel I focused on default risk and defined capital requirements and structure of risk weights for banks. Basel I did not attempt to address other risks banks may face, such as market, liquidity and operational risks. In 2004, Basel II laid down guidelines for adequate capital levels for banks, with use of external ratings to set the risk weights for corporate, bank and sovereign claims. But Basel II did not offer any regulation on the amount of debt banks could take on their books and ignored systemic risk for the whole industry. So, after the global financial crisis, the Basel III Norms were proposed in 2010, to be implemented within the following few years.[42]

Basel III focuses on four key banking parameters: capital, funding, liquidity and leverage. The requirements for common equity for banks are 4.5%, i.e. equity capital has to be at least 4.5% of total capital (essentially debt plus equity). Tier 1 capital, which is the first to absorb losses, before debt holders for example, has to be 6% of total capital (Tier 1 capital for a bank includes the value of its common stock, retained earnings, accumulated other comprehensive income, and non-cumulative perpetual preferred stock). The liquidity coverage ratio requires banks to hold a "buffer" of high quality liquid assets sufficient to deal with the cash outflows a given bank could face in an acute short-term stress scenario as specified by industry supervisors. This liquidity coverage ratio will have to reach 100% by January 2019 to prevent potential bank runs in future financial crises. The bank leverage ratio, calculated by dividing Tier 1 capital by total consolidated assets, has to be above 3%. As one can see, Basel III requirements are easy to describe and explain: this simplicity will likely make Basel III easy to monitor, and the associated transparency will render evasion of these requirements difficult. The type of regulation offered by the BCBS had a strong proponent in Hillary Clinton, who was opposed to reinstating Glass–Steagall (she favored instead Dodd–Frank and strengthening the Volcker Rule by closing the derivative loophole for banks). In a December 7, 2015 *New York Times* op-ed, Hillary Clinton proposed BCBS type rules for the whole financial sector, not just banks:

> My plan would strengthen oversight of the ("shadow banking") activities, too – increasing leverage and liquidity requirements for broker-dealers and imposing strict margin requirements on the kinds of short-term borrowing that also played a major role in spurring the financial crisis. We need to tackle excessive risk wherever it lurks, not just in the banks.[43,44]

Do Dodd–Frank and similar bank resolutions in the U.K. and the E.U. offer enough protection against potential financial meltdowns to allow banks to hold less equity capital as a percentage of risk-weighted assets than recommended by Basel III? This debate is akin to the "prevention versus cure" set of issues facing the health care industry. In both cases, prevention is much cheaper for economies and societies in the long run. Prevention – in the cases of banks, higher levels of equity capital – is also much simpler than a very complex set of "living wills for banks," equity substitutes like risk-weighted equity, balance sheets few if any can understand, and ineffective talk about breaking-up "too big to fail" institutions. Even the many multi-billion-dollar fines and settlements paid by many financial institutions since 2008 do not seem to work as a deterrent. Enormous fines were paid by several banks following the exchange rates and LIBOR scandals (over $12 billion); and by others for engaging in money laundering on a large scale with corrupt dictators, drug lords, etc. Even larger amounts were paid by pretty much all "too big to fail" U.S.-based banks and European ones for their role in selling CDOs, leading to the 2008 crisis. The most recent agreed upon fine is the $7.2 billion to be paid by a leading European bank, after a protracted legal battle involving a "too big to fail" institution not in the best of financial health. According to a global banking study by the Boston Consulting Group in 2017, banks around the world have paid over $320 billion in fines since the financial crisis. In another study, Reuters estimated at $235 billion the amounts paid by the world's twenty largest banks since 2009 for breaching a variety of financial regulations. These fines, as enormous as they may be, only punish the shareholders of the institution at fault and do not much affect the executives who make the decisions. Wouldn't jail sentences for the same senior executives be a much more effective and simpler deterrent?

But there lies the rub . . . bankers and their lobbyists will always argue for complexity, both in terms of the services they offer and the regulations that are imposed upon them. Complexity is one of the keys to profitability in financial services, inasmuch as bankers can charge large fees for financial instruments only they understand, while leaving their customers to bear the brunt of their inherent risk. On the regulatory side, banks do not like higher levels of equity in their balance sheets: it reduces their return on equity (ROE), a key measure performance analysts use to rate banking stocks. The average ROE for the MSCI index of world banks was halved from 16% in 2007 to 8% in 2016, following Dodd–Frank, Basel and other regulatory efforts aiming to make the global financial system safer. Higher required levels of equity capital following the Basel efforts after 2008 is one reason both bank stocks and financial sector indices lagged behind the performance of broader markets up to late 2016. For the same reason, bank stocks have rallied more than 40% a year after the November 8, 2016 election, outperforming the broader market: investors assume that with the Republicans controlling all the levers of power in the U.S., regulations governing Wall Street will be diluted to a significant degree, if not repealed altogether.

Bankers will argue endlessly (and in a very self-serving fashion) that lending costs will go up with increased equity capital, and that as a result fewer businesses and individuals will receive the loans they need. Beyond equity capital, any effort to regulate, even in the smallest way, shadow financing, dark pools, etc., will trigger the same argument about liquidity and lending costs. Yet, trust in bankers is still at an all-time low, and focusing on simpler solutions like increased requirements for equity capital, as opposed to complex corrective legislative fixes (typically post-financial catastrophes), is likely the best recipe for financial stability. Complexity in finance did not benefit societies as a whole, and simplicity in regulating excesses in the sector may be the best answer we have. Many voices supporting a clear separation between commercial banking involving government-insured retail deposits and riskier investment banking and trading activities have expressed a desire for the largest banks to be broken up. The idea here is to return the commercial and retail operations of large banks to the days of "boring, utility like banking."[45,46]

In conclusion, complexity in the finance world does not just represent a large cost to the U.S. economy, as we saw in health care and for utilities. Rather, it is more like a zero-sum game, where complexity helps bankers and financiers reap substantial gains at the expense of taxpayers and society as a whole. And when the financial system breaks down, losses by many may help a select few avoid a large share of these losses as well. To quote former U.K. Financial Services Authority head Adair Turner, in 2009:

"Most financial world activities are of dubious social value."[47,48]

Our own Paul Volcker, in a December 2009 speech, said:

The most important financial innovation that I have seen in the past 20 years is the automatic teller machine. How many other innovations can you tell me of that have been as important as the automatic teller machine, which is more of a mechanical innovation than a financial one? I have found very little evidence that vast amounts of innovation in financial markets in recent years has had a visible effect on the productivity of the economy . . .

. . . All I know is that the economy was rising very nicely in the 1950s and 1960s without all these innovations. Indeed it was quite good in the 1980s without CDOs. I do not know if something happened that suddenly made these innovations essential for growth. In fact, we had greater speed of growth in the 1960s, and more importantly it did not put the whole economy at the risk of collapse.[49]

We should listen to Paul Volcker and bring simplicity back into our banking system, including in the way we regulate it. In the newspaper opinion page of the February 16, 2016 issue of the *Financial Times*, an editorial titled "Simplicity Is the Key to a Resilient Banking Regime" stated:

The best way to inspire confidence in the banking system . . . is to ensure that lenders have clear capacity, primarily in the form of equity capital, to absorb large losses if a crisis hits . . .

. . . Given the fragile state of confidence in the financial sector, it would be preferable to err on the side of simplicity, even if this entails a slightly higher cost of lending.[50]

We may also want to set our horizons beyond the discussions about modern finance and how to make it safer. Perhaps our global competitiveness could increase if more of our brightest university graduates would eschew trading with each other on Wall Street in favor of endeavors that would add more value, i.e. designing and building products and services other countries would love to buy? Paul Volcker, again:

What about the effect on our economies (of taking) all our best young talent? In Britain, I was just talking to a high-tech company about the immense attraction to go into finance when both Britain and the United States are suffering from a basic inability to produce things competitively.[51]

Image 1.1 Pelé, 75, shows his much celebrated 1965 bicycle kick, New York, 2015

Image 1.2 Pelé celebrates scoring his goal number 1,000 at Rio de Janeiro's Maracanã stadium, on November 19, 1969

Image 2.1 Otto Von Bismarck addressing the Reichstag in 1888. Bismarck tried to end socialism's grip by offering government health care.

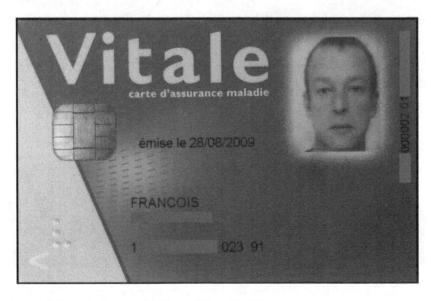

Image 2.2 France's electronic health care "Carte Vitale"

Image 2.3 President Lyndon Johnson signing the Medicare Act on July 30, 1965, with his wife Lady Bird, former president Harry Truman and his wife Bess looking on

Image 3.1 Thomas Edison and Gustave Eiffel, wax figures at the top floor of the Eiffel Tower

Image 3.2 Early auto race near Los Angeles, with the referee Glenn Martin in an ... airplane. From: "Popular electricity magazine in plain English," photo circa 1912. Credit: Architect of the Capitol.

Image 3.3 TVA's Ocoee Dam No. 3 on the Ocoee River in Polk County, Tennessee

Photo taken circa 1945. Source: Tennessee Valley Authority, *Hiwassee Valley Projects Volume 2: The Apalachia, Ocoee No. 3, Nottely, and Chatuge Projects*, Technical Report No. 5, p. 12 (Washington, D.C.: U.S. Government Printing Office, 1948).

Image 4.1 Franklin D. Roosevelt signs Glass–Steagall, the Banking Act of 1933

Image 4.2 President Barack Obama delivers remarks and signs the Dodd–Frank Wall Street Reform and Consumer Protection Act at the Ronald Reagan Building in Washington, July 21, 2010

(Official White House Photo by Lawrence Jackson) Speaker Nancy Pelosi is to the president's right, Senator Chris Dodd and Representative Barney Frank to his left. Credit: Architect of the Capitol.

How High Are Income Tax Rates in Your State?

Top State Marginal Individual Income Tax Rates, 2016

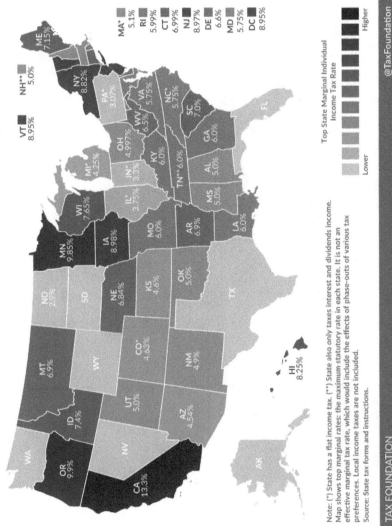

Note: (*) State has a flat income tax. (**) State also only taxes interest and dividends income. Map shows top marginal rates: the maximum statutory rate in each state. It is not an effective marginal tax rate, which would include the effects of phase-outs of various tax preferences. Local income taxes are not included.
Source: State tax forms and instructions.

TAX FOUNDATION

@TaxFoundation

Image 5.1 Top state marginal individual income tax rates, 2016

Source and credit: The Tax Foundation, Washington DC.

How High Are Property Taxes in Your State?

Mean Effective Property Tax Rates on Owner-Occupied Housing

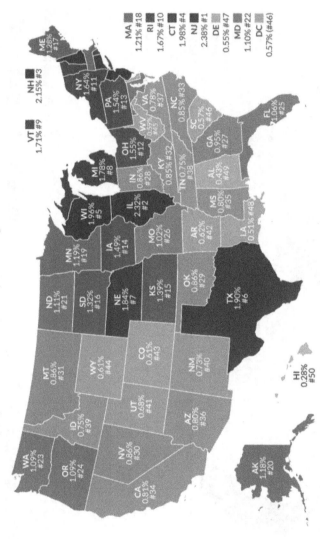

Notes: The figures in this table are mean effective property tax rates on owner-occupied housing (total real taxes paid divided by total home value). As a result, the data exclude property taxes paid by businesses, renters, and others. D.C.'s rank does not affect other states' rankings, but the figure in parentheses indicates where it would rank if included.

Source: U.S. Census Bureau; Tax Foundation.

TAX FOUNDATION   @TaxFoundation

Image 5.2 Mean effective property tax rates on owner occupied housing by state, 2016

Source and credit: The Tax Foundation, Washington DC.

5   Taxation

Taxation complexity, effectiveness, and fairness . . . or lack thereof

"Taxes are what we pay for civilized society," wrote U.S. Supreme Court Justice Oliver Wendell Holmes in 1927. In 1938, in a book about Holmes, U.S. Supreme Court Justice Felix Frankfurter added this:

> He [Holmes] did not have a curmudgeon's feelings about his own taxes. A secretary who exclaimed "Don't you hate to pay taxes!" was rebuked with the hot response, "No, young feller. I like to pay taxes. With them I buy civilization."[1,2]

Perhaps taxes were simpler then? Today pretty much everyone agrees that our tax code is incredibly complex – 74,608 pages long! – and as such, ineffective. This complexity also enables and masks a very unfair system. Warren Buffett, one the world's richest men, chastised this unfairness in 2013 after marginal federal income tax rates had been raised to 39.6% for the top bracket: "The differential between me and the rest of the office, not just my secretary, but the rest of the office . . . will be closer, but I'll probably be the lowest paying taxpayer in the office." Buffett has been advocating for a minimum tax on top earners – those like himself who benefit from the fact that capital gains are taxed at a much lower rate than regular earnings. His proposal, popularly known as the Buffett rule, had the support of the Obama administration but was strongly opposed by Republicans in Congress. After the November 8 election it is very unlikely we will see the Buffett rule become law. The opposite – lower tax rates for the richest taxpayers – has happened instead.[3,4]

Buffett is not the only voice to promote changes in our tax system and to want it simplified. But U.S. taxation complexity has endured for decades. It enables an unfair system by creating a maze of rules that only the richest Americans and large corporations have the resources to navigate, exploiting a myriad of loopholes to lower their effective rate of taxation significantly. We all remember that 2012 Republican presidential nominee Mitt Romney, a very wealthy man, disclosed paying only 14% in income taxes in 2011 – with tax filings hundreds of pages long. Famously, Mitt Romney also complained that only 47% of people in the U.S. paid income taxes: true, but everyone in the country is subjected to other taxes such as payroll taxes (by definition taxes on wage income) and sales taxes, which are very "regressive," i.e. their percentage is the same for everyone regardless of income levels. In addition, the way we collect whatever taxes are owed at the federal, state and local level is massively inefficient. There is the cost of the Internal Revenue Service, the IRS, which is a huge bureaucracy. Some of the largest states' taxes collecting agencies, for example the California Franchise Tax Board (FTB), are not small either. More than this, however, is the cost of all the lawyers and accountants who are employed to meet, and often exploit, this complexity. Also, what about the cumulative cost of individual taxpayers' time, and so forth?

In theory at least, our **income tax system** aims to be "progressive," ensuring that the highest earners pay more in percentage of income than low earners. What is the history of progressive taxation?[5]

Taxation on owned property and wealth already existed in the early days of the Roman Republic, and could be increased to finance wars. After many such wars led to increased wealth but also higher government and military spending for the new empire, Caesar Augustus (63 BC – 14 AD) introduced the first flat poll tax, which affected all adults, on top of a 1% wealth tax. In 1798, Britain's Prime Minister William Pitt the Younger created the first progressive income tax to finance the war against revolutionary France. Taxation also proved useful in fighting the wars against Napoléon. Pitt's tax started at a rate of 2% and increased up to 10% on incomes over $30,000 in today's terms. Income taxes were levied, then abolished a few times, and became a fixture of the British taxation system after Robert Peel's Income Tax Act of 1842. Those who paid it only accepted progressive taxation grudgingly, but it was too effective a tool for financing the frequent wars of the nineteenth century for British Prime Ministers and Chancellors of the Exchequer to abandon it.[6,7]

In the U.S., the Revenue Act of 1862, signed by President Abraham Lincoln, established the first progressive income tax. This law was repealed in 1872. Congress passed another – small – income tax in 1894, but the Supreme Court declared it unconstitutional in 1895, in the case of *Pollock v. Farmers' Loan and Trust Company*. Justice Stephen J. Field echoed in his 1895 opinion an argument that has been used ever since by opponents of progressive taxation as a tool to reduce inequality: "a small progressive tax will be but the stepping stone to others, larger and more sweeping, till our political contests will become a war of the poor against the rich."[8] In 1913, after twenty years of efforts by the Progressives, Congress ratified the 16th Constitutional Amendment, permitting a progressive income tax. The top rate was a mere 7%, on income over $4,000 (about $80,000 today). Tax rates went up significantly after the end of the "Gilded Age" of the 1920s: Herbert Hoover raised the top income tax rate to 63% to fight the Depression; Franklin Roosevelt hiked it to 79%, then to 90% to help finance the World War II effort.[9]

Income tax rates stayed very high during the Truman and Eisenhower presidencies. President John Kennedy lowered them a bit, but it took the advent of the modern conservative movement to put lower taxes at the top of the Republican Party's agenda. This agenda, first espoused by Barry Goldwater in his failed 1964 presidential bid, triumphed with Ronald Reagan in 1980 and 1984, then with George W. Bush in 2000, and again with Donald Trump in 2017. Lowering taxes remains at the top of the agenda of most Republican candidates for elective office, from the presidency to state houses and congressional offices. And pretty much all these candidates mention Ronald Reagan, who did lower federal income taxes substantially, but raised taxes through other means in five of his eight years as president. President Reagan also kept long-term capital gains at the same level as the top income tax bracket, which would be heresy to today's Republicans. While Republicans base their constant advocacy for ever lower taxes on the economic successes of the Reagan years, Democrats counteract with the even higher prosperity attained during Bill Clinton's presidency, when the top federal income tax bracket was raised to 39.6%. Democrats also point out the economic failure of George W. Bush's second term (he cut taxes for all brackets in his first term) and the sustained economic recovery achieved during the Obama presidency, when the top individual rate went back to 39.6%. They quip, "Mitt Romney promised us 6% unemployment in his 2012 campaign through lower taxes for the wealthy, and we have achieved 4.7% unemployment under Barack Obama with increased taxes for the top bracket." With Republicans controlling Congress and Donald Trump as president, 2017 marks the return of the GOP's agenda of lower taxes.

The political debate goes on, but how progressive is U.S. taxation today?[10]

In nominal terms, before the Trump administration's late 2017 tax cuts, which focused more on corporations and business "pass through" entities than individuals, the seven federal income tax brackets ranged from 10% to 39.6%. (With the new tax cuts, there will still be seven individual tax brackets, ranging from 10% to 37%, the lower rates being scheduled to expire in 2026.) In the tax code prevailing until 2017, there were also deductions for state and local taxes for lower income levels. Deductions for such taxes and certain types of credits started phasing out above $261,500 of income for single filers, and $313,800 for married couples filing jointly. Taxpayers enjoying higher incomes were subject to the Alternative Minimum Tax, which limited deductions and set a flat tax rate of 26% up to $187,800 of annual income, and 28% above that amount.

Investment gains are for the most part taxed at a lower rate than income. Since the George W. Bush administration, a top rate of 15% applies to qualified dividends, and gains on the sale of securities or most other types of assets held more than one year. This rate of 15% was raised by the Barack Obama administration to 20% for those who fall into the top income tax bracket; to this was added the ACA's 3.8% "Medicare surtax." These lower rates on investment gains advantage investors over wage earners, a major contributing factor to social inequality according to French economist Thomas Piketty. Still, from this short description, our federal income tax system would appear fairly progressive, at least in theory. But this is just the start, and a very small tip of this iceberg of complexity.[11]

Detracting from this progressivity, there are taxes borne by anyone working in the U.S. that are regressive, since they are levied on everyone at the same percentage rates. **Payroll taxes** are the first example of this. Employers withhold payroll taxes on behalf of their employees, based upon their salaries. Revenues from payroll taxes are used to fund a variety of social programs, such as Social Security and Medicare at the federal level. By law, employers take 6.2% of their employees' earnings for payroll taxes, and also need to match the amount withheld from their employees' wages. So, the IRS will collect 12.4% of the employees' gross earnings. There is also an additional 2.9% Medicare tax, which employers do not need to match. Every employee in the country pays payroll taxes, even if they happen to be undocumented or are documented non-citizens. The self-employed, contractors and small business owners are also subject to payroll taxes, the IRS collecting from them the same 12.4% rate, plus the 2.9% on Medicare. Mitt Romney's 2012 claim that 47% of Americans do not pay taxes is therefore totally inaccurate. Furthermore, that 6.2% rate is the same for everyone, with employers only needing to withhold payroll taxes at that rate on the first $118,500 of income. Payroll taxes thus constitute a flat tax for everyone up to that earnings threshold. Beyond it, only 0.9% of earnings must be withheld, for employees and self-employed alike. As such, large incomes pay a much smaller percentage of payroll taxes relative to their total earnings than those making $118,500 a year or less – the majority of the population. This is why payroll taxes are very regressive.[12]

State income taxes vary state by state, and on average have nominal rates that are much less progressive than federal income taxes. To start with, seven states do not levy any income tax: Alaska, Florida, Nevada, South Dakota, Texas, Washington, and Wyoming – Texas is the Union's second most populous state, and Florida the third. Then two states, New Hampshire and Tennessee, only tax dividend and interest income. The other forty-one states tax wage income. Among those, eight have a single-rate tax structure, applying to all taxable income. Interestingly, the flat rates of income tax for these eight states are fairly similar: 3.07% for Pennsylvania; 3.3% for Indiana; 3.75% for Illinois; 4.25% for Michigan; 4.63% for Colorado; 5% for Utah; 5.10% for Massachusetts; and 5.75% for North Carolina. One can note that "business friendly" Utah has basically the same level of income tax as "Taxachusetts." This leaves thirty-three states that have nominal progressive income taxation. California has the highest top bracket rate, with its 13.3% "millionaire tax surcharge" applied to incomes above a million dollars. California also has the highest number of tax brackets, ten, ranging from 1% to 13.3%. After California, the states with the highest top tax brackets are Oregon (9.9%); Minnesota (9.85%); Iowa (8.98%); New Jersey (8.97%); Vermont (8.95%); the District of Columbia (DC – 8.95%); and New

York (8.82%). In the other states with progressive income tax, the top rates range from 8.25% (Hawaii) down to 2.9% (North Dakota). There are many other differences across states. For example, some index tax brackets, exemptions and deductions for inflation; others do not. Certain states tie their standard deductions and personal exemptions to the federal tax code; others have their own rules or offer no deduction and exemption at all.[13,14]

In 2014, aggregate income taxes collected by the fifty states represented $357 billion, or 41% of aggregate state revenues. **Sales and gross receipt taxes** represented 48% of the total at $411 billion. Sales taxes in the U.S. are taxes placed on sales of products and services. These sales taxes are collected by businesses on behalf of the states, since no national general sales tax exists in the country – although the federal government levies selective sales taxes on the sale of particular goods and services. Forty-five states, plus DC, Puerto Rico, and Guam impose these general sales taxes, at a variety of rates. Purchasers of goods and services pay these taxes on top of the indicated sales prices, unlike, say, in most European countries where a government value-added tax (VAT) is already included in the sticker price. Five states – Alaska; Delaware; Montana; New Hampshire; and Oregon – do not levy any sales tax. The highest sales tax rate, at 7.25% (lowered in 2017 from 7.5%) is in California, although Puerto Rico has started collecting a VAT of 10.5% since early 2016 to try to alleviate its significant fiscal issues. At the other end of the spectrum, Guam, Georgia, South Dakota, and Wyoming only charge 4%. In some states, counties and cities may impose additional sales taxes, increasing the total rate up to 11%. Unlike VATs, sales taxes are imposed only at the retail level. When products such as used cars are sold more than once, sales taxes may be charged on the same item at every resale, indefinitely. Definitions of what goods and services are taxable vary across the fifty states, as do the applicable rates. Every state also has its list of categories of goods and services exempt from sales tax or taxed at reduced rates – most commonly food sold at grocery stores or prescription medications.[15]

Even with food and medication exemptions, sales taxes, just like VATs, are very regressive, since poor and middle-class people spend a much higher percentage of their income than wealthy ones. When added to payroll taxes, this can have a dramatic impact. Consider a simple example. A solidly middle-class household earns $100,000 per year and spends $50,000 on products and services other than food and medication. They live in a state with a 6% sales tax, with no additional city or county sales tax. Payroll taxes, including Medicare, will consume $9,100 (6.2% plus 2.9%); sales taxes (assuming none is levied on groceries and medications) will take another $3,000. Payroll and sales taxes will total $12,100, or over 12% of their pre-tax income. Let's turn now to a much wealthier household, earning ten times more or $1 million per year. This household also spends much more, but probably not ten times as much: let's assume they spend $350,000 on non-food and medication items, or seven times more than our middle-class household. How much will the wealthy household spend on payroll taxes? 9.1% of $118,500, or $10,783, and then 0.9% on $881,500, or $7,934, for a total of $18,717. Their sales tax will total $21,000. Their payroll and sales taxes will thus amount to $39,717, or less than 4% of their pre-tax income. So, when it comes to payroll and sales taxes, the household earning $1 million per year will end up taxed less than a third in percentage terms relative to the middle-class household earning ten times less. And when comparing with poor households who spend virtually every dollar they earn, the effect of this regressive taxation is even more dramatic. Most developed countries experience this, which is why progressive income taxation is so important to controlling social inequality.[16]

Moving to an entirely different taxation area, every state and territory charges **property taxes**. The rates are low, but these taxes are levied on property that may have value in eight figures for personal homes, and much more for commercial real estate. At the bottom, Hawaii charges 0.28%, but the average home there is very expensive. At the top, New Jersey (2.38%), Illinois (2.32%), and New Hampshire (2.15%) are the only three states above 2%. The four most populous states, representing together a third of the country's population, have very different rates, with California at 0.81%; Florida at 1.06%; New York at 1.64%; and Texas at 1.90%.[17] According to the Census Bureau, in 2015 the average American household spent $2,100 on property taxes for their home, with about $12 billion in property taxes unpaid, due to debt, personal bankruptcies and other issues. Of course, these taxes only directly impact the 68% of people who own their homes. Property taxes represent only 5% of the aggregate state revenues in the country, but because they may represent a large item for owners of large homes in areas where property prices have increased a lot, their political impact transcends their financial weight. For an illustration of this, there is California and its (anti) taxation "cause célèbre," Proposition 13.

The "People's Initiative to Limit Property Taxation," or **Proposition 13**, is an amendment of the Constitution of California that limits real estate tax in the state to 1% of the full cash value of the relevant property as assessed in 1975. For the purpose of this real estate tax, increases of the assessed value of the property are restricted to an annual inflation factor, not to exceed 2% per year. Reassessments of property values are prohibited except in cases of change of ownership or completion of new construction on the property. Proposition 13 was approved by California voters at a 65% majority on June 6, 1978. Proposition 13 survived legal challenges and was declared constitutional by the Supreme Court in the 1992 case of *Nordlinger v. Hahn*. Two key factors in the success of Proposition 13 were high inflation during the 1970s and large increases in the state's population at the time, which combined to increase nominal prices of California homes to a very high degree. Since taxes were levied as a percentage of the nominal value of real estate properties, they grew dramatically in that decade. Many seniors with fixed retirement incomes had to pay so much in property taxes they could no longer afford to remain in homes they had purchased long before. California had also experienced sustained increases in government size during the previous decades, with correspondingly higher taxation weight and increasing voter fatigue. Several anti-tax ballot measures also passed in 1978, such as Proposition 8, which allowed decreases in property taxes following real estate price slumps.[18]

At the national level, passage of Proposition 13 in California is often viewed by historians as presaging a "taxpayer revolt" throughout the country, which contributed to the election of Ronald Reagan in 1980. In addition to decreasing property taxes, Proposition 13 also contained language requiring a two-thirds majority in both California legislative houses for any future increase in state income and sales tax rates.[19] This had a lot of sustaining power – thirty-four years, in fact. It took the third election of Jerry Brown as governor in 2011 and gains by Democrats in both houses to muster the two-thirds majorities required to pass a series of tax increases (and spending cuts) to balance the state's budget. This happened in November of 2012, and these sensible fiscal actions quickly took the state budget out of the "hole" years of increased spending and too low taxation had created.[20] For example, Proposition 8 had been duly used by the California State Board of Equalization to reduce significantly property taxes for millions of Californians after the 2008 financial crisis. Property values had decreased a lot because of the crisis, but the state had not benefited from the tremendous ramp-up in home values between 1980 and 2007. Remember when California was compared to Greece, an economic "basket case?" No longer, by any means. Today the state boasts the world's seventh largest economy and enjoys a large budget surplus, with a special fund for "rainy days." Thank you, Jerry Brown![21] Amidst this success and recent tax increases, though, Proposition 13 sails on majestically, like an untouchable "third rail" of California politics . . . no politician will touch it with a barge pole.[22]

This cursory review of U.S. federal and state income, payroll, sales and property taxes does not show a huge amount of complexity thus far, just the wide variety of rates one would expect from a federalized country with fifty states and legislatures possessing taxation power. To get into true tax complexity in the U.S., one has to start looking at the taxation of profits generated outside the U.S. for corporations and individuals; and at the many instruments, often based offshore, that are used by wealthy taxpayers and corporations to lower actual taxes paid to well below the nominal tax rates applying to them.

★　★　★　★　★

$2.1 trillion of corporate profits parked offshore!

The offshore cash holdings of U.S. corporations doubled between 2008 and 2016. This huge amount held abroad is the direct result of the way the U.S. corporate income tax rules treated the earnings of foreign subsidiaries of U.S. multinationals during that period. We are unique among developed countries with respect to taxation, because taxes on American entities and citizens are collected on income earned both domestically and abroad. However, corporations have been able to defer paying taxes on foreign income until they repatriate foreign profits, i.e. when they pay them to the U.S. parent company as dividends. The tax code also provides a foreign tax credit on any taxes paid to foreign governments. This deferral of taxes on foreign income has created a strong incentive for U.S. multinationals to increase the share of earnings they book abroad.

Accounting features like transfer prices for goods manufactured domestically or abroad can be "adjusted" to increase profits declared abroad at the expense of those declared in America. Adding to the incentive was the nominal rate of taxation of corporations in the U.S. until 2017: at 35%, it was higher than in most other developed countries. For example, this rate is only 12.5% in Ireland; 20% in the U.K.; 25% in Spain; 30% in Germany; and, of course, there are "tax havens," where corporations pay little to nothing in taxes. So, in 2016 Apple held $215 billion offshore;[23] Goldman Sachs $29 billion; Nike $11 billion, and there were hundreds of other companies with significant amounts stashed offshore as well. Authors of a recent report from the U.S. PIRG Education Fund and Citizens for Tax Justice and other researchers have reported that 73% of Fortune 500 companies maintained subsidiaries in offshore tax havens in 2015. Tax havens allowed these companies avoid an estimated $212 billion in federal taxes that year.[24]

There are over a dozen well-known tax havens: the Bahamas; Bermuda; the British Virgin Islands; the Cayman Islands; the Channel Islands such as Jersey; the Netherland Antilles; Panama; the Seychelles, etc. Companies including Apple; Facebook; General Electric; Goldman Sachs; Google; McDonald's; Nike; Pfizer; and Starbucks are reported to have directed billions of dollars of profits to a variety of tax havens using the "Irish tax loophole." This permitted multinationals to be registered in Ireland but not be deemed resident in the country for tax purposes. The "Irish loophole" allowed companies to book vast amounts of revenue in Ireland and then pay equivalent amounts as royalties to a separate affiliate, headquartered for tax purposes in a tax heaven. Amid much international criticism, Ireland's finance minister, Michael Noonan, signaled his intention to close this loophole in October 2014. Three years later, however, Ireland was still one of about forty countries that had not adopted the new 2015 OECD rules changing where multinational companies pay their taxes. In particular, Ireland had not ratified article 12 of these OECD reforms, the article preventing so-called commissionaire arrangements that allow multinationals to avoid significant taxation in countries where they operate. This was the result of much lobbying throughout 2017 by a number of U.S. multinationals, notably large software companies.[25] As a result, many U.S. corporations with significant international activities ended up paying a fraction of the official 35% corporate tax rate. In his October 18, 2016 *New York Times* column, David Leonhardt mentioned a study he asked analysts at S&P Global Market Intelligence to perform to calculate the combined amount a number of multinational corporations had paid in federal, state, local, and foreign taxes since 2007. Between 2007 and 2015, according to this study, Facebook paid an average of just 4% of its profits in taxes; Boeing 8%; Amazon 13%; Alphabet (Google's parent) 16%; Apple, Coca Cola, and IBM 17%; and AT&T and General Electric 18%. Interestingly, retailers with a large U.S.-based physical presence, which cannot easily claim that a lot of their operations are based, for example in Ireland, paid a lot more in taxes. The same S&P Global Market Intelligence data showed that over the same period, CVS, Home Depot,

Target, and Wal-Mart paid over 30% in taxes, about twice the rate of the companies previously mentioned.[26,27]

Perhaps the most famous company in the world, and today the most valuable in terms of market capitalization, Apple got tangled in a foreign taxation mess in August of 2016. The European Union (E.U.) announced a huge fine, up to $14.5 billion, against Apple for having benefited from "illegal state aid" from Ireland over a 24-year period. The key evidence, according to the E.U., was that the deal with Ireland allowed Apple to pay a maximum tax rate of only 1%, and that in 2014 the technology firm had paid taxes in Ireland at just a 0.005% rate. The E.U. claimed that tens of billions of dollars in profits Apple enjoyed quasi tax-free in Ireland had been generated mostly outside of Ireland, in other European countries that were hence deprived of tax revenue. E.U. Competition Policy Commissioner Margrethe Vestager said, "Member States cannot give tax benefits to selected companies. This is illegal under European Union state aid rules." The Commission also said that Ireland's tax arrangements with Apple between 1991 and 2015 had allowed the company to attribute sales to a "head office" that only existed on paper. Rulings were "reversed engineered" to ensure Apple had a minimum Irish tax bill. Minutes of meetings between Apple representatives and Irish tax officials showed the company's tax treatment had been motivated by "employment considerations."[28,29] Apple and the U.S. government were furious. Apple said it had complied with all existing laws, in Ireland and elsewhere. Furthermore, the company does pay taxes: in a recent filing it reported paying $13 billion in taxes on $53 billion of profits – just not much of it in Ireland. The U.S. Treasury and lawmakers criticized the E.U. approach of challenging taxation using rulings through its competition law, saying that this approach targeted U.S. companies unfairly and threatened the investment climate in Europe. And the Irish government? It decided to side with Apple, defended its low tax policy (which brought many jobs to the country), and appealed the E.U. decision. This was very controversial, since in doing so the Irish government was rejecting a significant windfall. In a country of 4.6 million, where people suffered from tough austerity programs after 2008 to pay the debts of overextended Irish banks, refusing an amount equivalent of up to $3,150 per habitant was naturally not a popular decision.[30,31]

Before the late 2017 Republican corporate tax cuts, there was bi-partisan support in Congress for new legislation that would solve this thorny issue through a "repatriation holiday." Under such a proposal, corporations could repatriate their foreign earnings for a limited time, at a sharply reduced tax rate. This would allow the government to collect at least some taxes on part of the $2.1 trillion held abroad. A variant of this proposal was a "deemed repatriation," which would treat accumulated foreign profits as repatriated, whether that was the case or not, and tax them at a lower rate than the 35% corporate tax. One key issue was incentive. Yes, these proposals would bring short-term tax revenues, but wouldn't they also encourage corporations to continue to move lots of earnings offshore in anticipation of benefiting in the future from a lower "repatriation" rate? A precedent seemed to validate these fears. In 2004,

Congress allowed such a tax holiday, enabling multinationals to repatriate profits to the U.S. at a very low 5.25% tax rate. This brought $362 billion into the American economy, but critics complained that in addition to that tax rate being too low, corporations used these funds primarily to pay dividends to investors and repurchase their own stock. As a result, Senate Democrats defeated another repatriation tax holiday in 2009, and none was approved until now: with Republicans enjoying control of the White House and both Houses of Congress, repatriation is a key component of their November 2017 tax reform. One-time repatriation tax rates are proposed at 14% for liquid assets and 7% on illiquid assets. The next few years will reveal whether this repatriation tax will lead to more investments in the U.S., or just further stock buybacks and dividends by the corporations holding assets abroad. But there is a fair argument to be made that such legislation was timely, given that time was not on the U.S. Treasury's side. In the case of Apple, it appears that the E.U. was sending this message to Uncle Sam: "if you do not tax this pile of cash, we will."[32]

Despite all this, Apple has been paying taxes at about 25% of its profits. This is well below the recent 35% U.S. corporate tax rate, but far from insignificant. So how did Mitt Romney only pay 14% in 2011 – in absolute legality – as an individual theoretically submitting to the top federal income tax bracket (then 35%), not to mention state taxes? He declared no wage income in 2011. Rather, his earnings came mostly from interest income, and capital gains that we saw are taxed at much lower rates than ordinary income. And he gave a lot to charitable causes, with his generosity (justifiably) rewarded by significant tax deductions. Leaving Romney's case aside, though, a number of complex transactions can produce enormous tax avoidance benefits to those at the very top of the economic pyramid.[33]

There is a myriad of **tax avoidance vehicles**, all best handled by finance and legal professionals: do not try this at home! To start with a simple one, let's mention the lower taxation on carried interest for private equity partners – before he entered politics, Mitt Romney made his fortune as a private equity pioneer with Bain Capital. Carried interest, earned by the general partners of privately held funds in exchange for their investment management services, is taxed at long-term capital gain rates, substantially lower than income tax rates. One of the original rationales for this was the venture capitalist (VC) investment community of the 1980s and 1990s: VCs helped launch a lot of start-ups, and their general partners' earnings from investing in entrepreneurial ventures were deemed more equivalent to long-term capital gains than to regular corporate profits. But does this rationale apply when a private equity group is turning over Burger King for the umpteenth time? What may have made sense in the case of VCs no longer does when private equity firms buy very established companies, leverage them through debt, cut costs, and sell them at a profit a few years later. There appeared to be bi-partisan support in 2016 to eliminate the "carried interest loophole," at least among the presidential candidates. But thanks to intense lobbying, nothing with taxes is simple politically. The elimination of the favorable tax treatment of carried interest does not appear anywhere in the 2017 Republican tax reform, apart from the need to hold on invested companies for three years, a minor constraint in an industry where funds last seven years or more. Private equity partners need not to be concerned; this change is not around the corner. If anything, the Republican tax changes bring further advantages to the investing class relative to wage earning professionals. Back to complexity, and Mitt Romney, his tax returns also showed the use of a vast array of financial transactions. Two hundred and sixty-six pages listed foreign investments in complex financial derivatives such as CDOs, made through hedge funds managed by Goldman Sachs and a credit arm of Bain Capital. Such investments included securities with obscure names and based abroad in places like Dublin, Ireland or the Grand Cayman. There were also lots of investments in foreign corporations and partnerships. With all of this, and also significant charity giving (one-third of declared income: a lot of well-meaning philanthropy), the 14% actual tax rate paid by Romney could have been as low as 10.6% if he had used all his charity deductions. If he had used none, his taxes would have been 18.8%. It is said that he did not use all his charity deductions in 2011 because of a comment he had made on the campaign trail that he had always paid more than 13.6% in taxes.[34,35]

There can also be domestic entities that allow tax avoidance. Limited liability companies or LLCs, favored by real estate developers, allow them to deduct the cost of interest they pay on loans and depreciation on their properties to such extent that in many cases these LLCs can generate significant paper losses. These losses can then be used to offset taxes from other income. When Ronald Reagan, Tip O'Neill, and Congress agreed to a complete tax overhaul in 1986, they addressed LLCs and paper losses, at least partially. After 1986, the ability for real estate projects to generate tax write-offs used to offset other taxes was closed for outside investors (then mostly lawyers, doctors and other wealthy investors seeking tax shelters), but not to the real estate developers themselves. So huge tax losses can still be generated by real estate projects, if only for developers themselves, who may invest in certain types of real estate ventures just to collect a share of these losses for tax loss carry forward purposes.

Returning to offshore corporations, these are not just for large companies. They can also be set up with few or no tangible assets, with the single objective of allowing wealthy individuals to escape taxation from their home country. These offshore corporations, a lot of them in Caribbean tax havens, received a lot of publicity with the exposed "Panama Papers" in 2016. These were 11.5 million documents that detailed financial and attorney–client information for over 214,000 offshore entities. Amazing numbers! The leaked documents were from the Panama-based law firm Mossack Fonseca, which since the 1970s has helped wealthy individuals, celebrities, dictators, and outlaws around the world evade taxes. At the heart of Mossack Fonseca's activities was the setting up of accounts in tax havens, offering very low taxation and requiring little or no disclosure of information from the account holders. Furthermore, the use of shell companies allowed the identity of the true owners of these offshore accounts to be disguised. This is fundamental, because while federal law allows U.S. citizens to hold money overseas, they must declare these foreign holdings to the U.S. Treasury, and taxes on them must be paid as for any domestic investment. It is hard to gauge how much taxation is evaded in the U.S. through activities by entities like Mossack Fonseca, but estimates range between $100 and $200 billion per year lost to the IRS.[36,37] There was an "encore" to the Panama Papers with the "Paradise Papers," 13.4 million confidential offshore investment documents that were leaked electronically to the *Süddeutsche Zeitung*, a leading German newspaper, on November 5, 2017. More of the same, with new names including royalty; oligarchs; democratically elected presidents; cabinet members; and sports franchises owners. Clearly, there are a lot of billionaires, celebrities and powerful people who are not terribly interested in paying the type of taxes ordinary people face. Hotel magnate Leona Helmsley, who was convicted in 1989 to spend sixteen years in prison (four years after appeal) for a wide variety of tax offenses, was revealed in the course of her trial to have said: "we don't pay taxes; only the little people pay taxes."[38]

Setting up such offshore corporations or entities (they can be LLCs, too) is not simple, and requires a significant amount of experience in the matter. This is why there is a whole cottage industry of firms specializing in this, including divisions of very large banks. They are legal and discrete, although in some cases the same vehicles are used illegally, essentially for money laundering purposes. In setting up these offshore vehicles, corporations and rich individuals take advantage of both the complexity and opacity in our tax system. For example, the reporting requirements of the Securities and Exchange Commission and the Federal Reserve are very different. In the report mentioned earlier about Fortune 500 companies, a startling finding was that "27 companies reported 16,389 total subsidiaries [!] and 2,836 tax haven subsidiaries to the Federal Reserve, while reporting only 2,279 total subsidiaries and 40 tax haven subsidiaries to the SEC." A basic reporting error? No, the explanation is simply that the SEC requirements are much more vague than those of the Federal Reserve, meaning that companies reported a lot fewer offshore companies to the SEC. Complexity can be helpful to some, indeed.

★   ★   ★   ★   ★

Making the tax code simpler, but also retaining a modicum of fairness

Is there a solution to this? Advocates of a much-simplified tax code can be found in all sorts of think tanks and political movements in the U.S. Given the complexity and costs of our current taxation system, its inefficiencies and unfairness, the benefits of simplification are obvious. Such proposals advocate the elimination of most deductions and "loopholes" in exchange for lower tax brackets across the board. On the far-right side of the political spectrum, a few even advocate a flat income tax system, like 2016 Republican presidential candidate Ben Carson. Ted Cruz, another 2016 Republican presidential candidate, went further, advocating the total abolition of the IRS and income taxes, to be replaced with a VAT-based system on top of existing payroll and sales taxes. A truly regressive proposal . . . Proponents of a flat tax system, or one with lower rates, argue that even though the nominal rates will fall for everyone, the federal government will not experience a huge revenue shortfall, because they would also eliminate most of the tax deductions and loopholes. One should note that a flat income tax rate for everyone would spell the end of progressive taxation, leading to dollar gains that would be massively skewed in favor of the highest 1%, or even 0.1% of earners. But back to the government budget issue: the problem is that when asked to produce a formal list of the deductions that should be candidates for elimination, the flat or lower tax advocates can never produce concrete proposals. The answer is always along the lines of "mañana" [tomorrow]. Is this because the largest deductions are highly popular ones, such as the home mortgage deduction? Or is it because of ferocious lobbying by specific industries to keep favored deductions – think of the tens of billions of dollars in tax incentives to oil and gas companies, even when oil prices were above $100 per barrel. These, for example, are essentially untouched in the 2017 Republican tax plan, apart from the elimination of the enhanced oil recovery tax credit (dwarfed by the elimination of most green energy production tax credits). This reluctance to produce concrete proposals on which deductions should be phased out to pay for a lower rate of taxation may have another explanation: that the main intent behind such programs is the "starving" of government and the dismantling of the country's social safety net.

Proposals to "pay" for lower tax rates included an attempt by the George W. Bush administration in 2005 to privatize Social Security. Despite Wall Street's enthusiasm for the idea (think of the bonanza in investment fees!), even Republicans in the Senate and the House balked at this. This proposed legislation went nowhere, and voters reacted by giving Democrats back the control of the House in 2006. Imagine what would have happened to retirees depending on their Social Security paycheck for their livelihood in 2008 if the system had been privatized and the seniors' retirements subject to the financial meltdown that year . . . Speaker of the House Paul Ryan achieved a lot of notoriety with his 2011 budget proposal, the most notable feature of which was the replacement of Medicare as we know it by a "voucher" program, modeled around current health savings accounts. Instead of Medicare, which will take care of you no matter how seriously ill you are, Ryan's program would have provided Medicare-eligible citizens with a fixed amount to purchase private health insurance. If someone could not afford the policy necessary to cover her or his medical needs with that fixed amount, then too bad – "voucher care" could not help.[39] Privatizing Medicare was very unpopular and appears to be dead: Ryan and his House Republican colleagues did not attempt another go at "voucher care" in 2017, focusing their efforts on trying to repeal Obamacare instead.

Attempts to privatize very popular programs like Social Security and Medicare are challenging for their proponents, given the voting power of our senior citizens and the fact that their ranks are swelling as the baby boomer generation reaches retirement age. One wonders at how elected officials such as Paul Ryan can hope to win popular backing for proposals that essentially offer the following deal: the top 1% of the population will receive an enormous windfall in economic terms that will be financed by all the population through the disappearance of cherished social programs. In a democracy, how can such "Robin Hood in reverse" programs be expected to win at the ballot box? It is interesting here to mention one country that has implemented one such program, and it was not a democracy. In Chile, under the brutal military dictatorship of General Augusto Pinochet between 1973 and 1990, taxes were reduced, social programs slashed, and pensions privatized. These policies had to be reversed after the end of the dictatorship because of their huge social costs. The results of the privatization program completely failed to match its goals, which were that pensions would provide 70% of a worker's final wages at work. The real figure was 38%. Worse, the World Bank determined that the fees charged by the favored investment firms appointed by the Pinochet government to manage pensions consumed half the pension contributions of the average worker retiring in 2000. In 2016, Chile's president Michelle Bachelet ordered changes that included requiring employers to contribute to the system for the first time, saying: "we need to build a solidarity system that doesn't leave all responsibilities to the individual and that abandons them when they're left behind."[40,41]

Back to our country: we need to simplify our hugely complex tax code. The Trump administration said it understood that, but the late 2017 GOP tax legislation will likely not achieve any simplification. Instead, it will lead to large increases in both inequality and the budget deficit, the latter estimated initially at $1.7 trillion over ten years by the nonpartisan CBO and Joint Committee on Taxation on November 8.[42,43] So much for fiscal responsibility . . .

The successful reconciliation of somewhat different House and Senate tax plans appeared to confirm that tax cuts are the single issue that unifies all Republicans today. It all started with the plan passed by the House, which included wealthy Republican donors' favorites such as the elimination of the inheritance tax, the repeal of the alternative minimum tax, and the reduction of the corporate tax rate from 35% to 20%. All very regressive socially, despite insistent messaging that this tax package was "focused on the middle-class." In particular, given the existing exemption of $10.9 million on the inheritance tax for a married couple, its removal would only benefit the richest 0.2% taxpayers of the land. The lowering of the rate for "pass-through" businesses from regular income levels to 25% provided large potential windfalls to such companies: some hedge funds, private equity and real estate partnerships would gain a lot from this provision (more loopholes!) unless restrictions were to limit its applicability – a very complex thing to do. In a very candid moment, Gary Cohn, President Trump's chief economic advisor, said to CNBC's John Harwood on November 9, 2017: "The most excited group out there are big CEOs, about our tax plan."[44] Five days later, Cohn had an awkward moment when CEO supporters of the GOP tax plan appeared to undermine its basic premise: at a meeting of the *Wall Street Journal*'s CEO Council, CEOs were asked whether they would increase investment with the new tax cuts, and only a few raised their hands. Cohn asked, uneasily: "why aren't the other hands up?"[45]

Overall, then, very large and well-defined tax cuts for corporations and top earners.

The middle class? Determining winners and losers will require time, given the complexity of assessing the various moving parts of the new tax legislation impacting regular wage earners. A confusing brew of enhanced exemptions, shifting rates, and lost deductions makes benefits uncertain and hard to quantify. The relatively minor lowering of individual tax rates is also scheduled to expire in 2026 to comply with budget rules in the Senate - in contrast to the tax cuts for corporations, which are permanent. The elimination of the Obamacare "mandate," saving about $300 billion over ten years, will likely come at the cost of a big increase in the number of people without health insurance. The new $10,000 limit on state and local taxes deductions could hit a lot of middle class people in populated and high state tax states like California, New Jersey, and New York. Interestingly, this may also cause people in higher brackets, with earnings solidly in the six figures, to pay more tax. The Republican tax cuts will thus create new political dimensions in our tax environment, adding twists to the traditional "regressive vs. progressive" equation: "billionaires" will win, whereas some "merely wealthy" people living on the coasts might lose. Tax policy could thus become blatantly partisan, with many middle-class and relatively well-off people from large "blue" states losing in the new legislation. Heavily populated areas with expensive infrastructure needs and correspondingly high levels of state and local taxation, traditionally voting Democrat, may face new fiscal challenges. George W. Bush's 2001 tax cuts had the merit of being very simple to explain and lowered taxes for everybody. In the 2017 Republican tax cuts, priorities are crystal clear. Simplicity and clarity of benefits are only for corporations, large investors, and wealthy heirs. For the rest, opacity and uncertainty are on offer.

Overall, most analysts believe our tax code will become more complex, principally because of the new loopholes to be found in the treatment of "pass-through" businesses. This plan, dear to "big CEOs," will also increase our debt in a major way, to the tune of $1.5 trillion over the next 10 years after reconciliation of the House and Senate plans. So much that on November 12, 2017, more than 400 patriotic millionaires signed a letter prepared by a progressive group called Responsible Wealth, asking Congress not to pass any tax legislation that would exacerbate inequality and grow our debt. The letter signatories asked for Congress to raise their taxes instead.[46]

In summary, we have a tax "reform" that is complex, regressive, and unfunded. There has to be a better way. To achieve this elusive fiscal responsibility in a simple and equitable manner, I would suggest proceeding as follows. First, achieve political consensus on which deductions should be eliminated or gradually phased out; experiment with this for one or two years to measure precisely the financial impact on government revenues; and then, and only then, set up new lower tax rates that would balance the gains achieved by the elimination of deductions. Depending on which party is in power, this can help achieve fiscal priorities such as a flat, even lower government budget; or an increased one to pay for new infrastructure spending and social programs. If one's objective were to simplify our taxation process, isn't this a more fiscally conservative way to proceed? The same logic can be applied to the thorny issue of profits generated abroad by American companies. Rather than to start with nominal rates, perhaps we should look at the amount of taxes actually paid by U.S. corporations, eliminate the many deductions and loopholes that no longer make sense, and then determine the appropriate nominal tax rates. Lots of benefits would accrue from such an approach. Nominal tax rates would certainly be lower for the same actual revenue from business taxes; the perverted incentive for companies to "stash money" abroad could be eliminated; and taxation would be a lot simpler, providing a life line to millions of small businesses that cannot afford armies of tax accountants.

To be able to move to fiscally conservative approaches like this one, we also need to move away from the quasi-religious dogma espoused by self-interested parties that "tax cuts pay for themselves." Always! In booming economies in danger of overheating as well as during downturns. Would that be true. Because then we should bring all our tax rates to zero ... taxation problem solved! On a more serious note, there is indeed evidence that "confiscatory" tax rates hamper economic growth, even though the country experienced decent growth during the Eisenhower era, when such "confiscatory" rates were in effect. Today, with the marginal federal tax rate below 40%, we are far from such a case, and have been so for several decades. In an August 29, 2017 *New York Times* article by Patricia Cohen titled "Trump Tax Plan May Free Up Corporate Dollars, but Then What?" Nobel Prize winning economist Joseph E. Stiglitz says:

> There is no evidence that cutting the tax rates stimulates more investment ...
> ... Growth is low because labor force growth is slow ... and we're not investing in education and research, which is why productivity is slow. The notion that changing taxes is going to lead to a growth spurt is pure non-sense.[47,48]

U.S. corporations have never had as much cash as they have today. With demand relatively low because of stagnant wages in a country where 70% of the GDP is consumer spending, it is likely that most of the benefits of their reduced tax rates will go into share repurchase programs and dividends as in 2004, instead of new investments and higher wages. This is what CEOs were telling Gary Cohn on November 14, 2017, when they did not raise their hands after being asked if they would increase investment.

Simplifying the tax code and eliminating loopholes that favor mostly large corporations and high net worth individuals are not incompatible with progressive income taxation. This should be a bi-partisan objective, since very few U.S. politicians are openly advocating a return to the "Gilded Age." There was nothing too complex about the Gilded Age. It just demonstrated that concentration of economic and political power created enormous wealth for those who wielded that power. Today, complexity and opacity in finance and taxes help the very few get very rich, at the expense of hundreds of millions – a zero-sum game with the "99%" holding the can. This game is rigged, and is not compatible with a meritocratic society.

6   Laws and regulations

"Dura Lex sed Lex" or "Complecta Lex sed Lex?"

"Dura Lex sed Lex," or "The Law is tough, but it is the Law," says the old Latin adage. But perhaps we should replace "dura," or tough, with complex ("complecta")?

There will be no argument in this country that "The Law" is an enormously complex animal. And that our approach to regulations governing a range of activities, industries, and even behaviors is also extraordinarily complicated. Rather than write a full treatise on our legal system, let's review a few cases showing that simpler approaches could often help us obtain better results. As in earlier chapters, complexity gets in the way of effectiveness.

One should first note that complexity can be privately generated as well as created by regulation. For example, much of the complexity in today's finance industry, such as the creation of complex investment instruments, is generated by the industry itself. Much of the complexity in health care also comes from private industry with the plethora of insurance companies and their myriad of plans. The same can be said about utilities following many different strategies involving assets across power generation, transmission and distribution.

There is also much government-generated complexity, created through a maze of complex laws and regulations. Many of these are poorly thought-out, and their implementation is fraught with unintended consequences. It is therefore not surprising that the Republican Party has long railed against regulatory complexity, with the "natural" solution being to get rid of regulations wholesale. However, this would not solve the problem of privately generated complexity. Getting rid of regulations would not make the health care, utility or finance industries simpler and more effective. In the case of finance, it is a safe bet that, to the contrary, in the absence of regulations new complex and obtuse instruments would mushroom, leading to ever more complexity.

The challenge is therefore to produce simple regulations that will solve the problem of privately generated complexity, without creating in the process new, government-mandated complexity. Exactly the same can be said about regulations that aim to moderate certain activities or behaviors. Unfortunately, we are far from meeting this challenge in the U.S. today. Nowhere is this truer than in the protection of our environment, an area where economics, energy, health care, and national security converge. No modern challenge can impact so many strategic priorities.

How to protect the planet, grow the economy, and increase national security ... all at the same time

In a wonderful old hotel in Lisbon's exclusive neighborhood of Lapa, with nice views of the town, the Tagus River and the majestic suspended bridge crossing it, twenty-five industry CEOs, consultants and economists engage in a lively debate. After a good lunch and easy banter about how much Portugal's capital looks like San Francisco with its hills; cable cars; charming old homes; and suspended bridge over large expanse of water, the conversation turns serious. We are discussing how the U.S. can "wean itself off Middle Eastern oil." This meeting of the Energy Advisory Board of a very large global IT Services company takes place in 2004, long before the rise of Daesh and the civil wars in Syria, Yemen, and Libya.

Our chair, a very distinguished and respected former Secretary of State, and a Nobel Prize–winning economist address the group.[1]

They are describing a white paper written by the economist, arguing that a simple, across-the-board $1 per gallon tax on gasoline in the U.S. would cure a lot of ills. It would, they argue:

1) Create a strong incentive for consumers to buy more fuel-efficient cars (this is before the Tesla) at the expense of gas-guzzling pick-up trucks and SUVs.
2) Help shrink U.S. budget deficits in a significant way.
3) Reduce U.S. imports of crude oil.

This simple tax would provide a solution to the triple challenge of foreign oil dependence (think Middle East; Russia; Venezuela), environmental protection, and growing government budget deficits. What's not to like in this? Neither the former Secretary of State nor the Nobel Prize winner is a "tax and spend" liberal – much to the contrary. The brilliant economist actually adds that this is the first time in his long career that he is advocating for a tax increase. He is not a pillar of the Chicago school of economists for nothing. In the audience, the non-U.S. executives argue that since most of the developed world taxes gasoline to a similar or higher extent, the absence of such a gasoline tax in the U.S. amounts to a hidden economic subsidy relative to other developed countries. The U.S. executives moan and groan about political gridlock (this is not a new phenomenon!), and also applaud the free-market economist's courage in expressing such a contrarian opinion. Discussions progress, both amiable and very intellectually stimulating. These are powerful and influential people, yet in this small group setting interactions are direct and not devoid of humor.

The CEO of a very large U.S. utility that uses mostly coal-fired power plants, talking to the CEO of an equally large European utility with the world's largest installed wind power capacity:

"I did not realize you had so many windmills, where are they located?"
"Why, in the province of La Mancha, of course. You have not read Don Quijote?"[2]

Reflecting back on the twice a year meetings of this Energy Advisory Board, which I founded on behalf of my former employer, I cannot help thinking that so many roads lead to Rome . . . Twelve years later, the U.S. has significantly reduced its dependency on foreign and Middle Eastern oil, enhancing our supply security. Coal-fired plants represent a much-reduced proportion of our electricity production, leading to environmental gains in air quality. In 2016, wind power represented 25% of the electricity produced in Oklahoma and over 12% in Texas, which is the second largest U.S. state in terms of electricity production. In California, 28% of all electricity produced in 2016 came from renewables.[3,4,5] As is the case in Germany (34% renewables), the state is phasing out nuclear power to rely increasingly on wind and solar power.[6,7]

Yet, beyond renewables, one of the largest factors behind this success, fracking, was completely unforeseen in 2004. Fracking led to an explosion of domestic natural gas production, displacing coal as the dominant feedstock for electric power plants. In 2006, coal-fired power plants represented 49% of electricity production in the U.S., with natural gas at 20% and renewables at 9%. Ten years later, natural gas represented 34% and coal only 30% – nuclear and renewables were at 20% and 16% respectively in 2016.[8] Success in conservation efforts also meant that electricity demand in 2016 was basically equal to that of 2006, even though economic output was significantly higher. With many coal-fired plants closing and a number of new natural gas ones brought online, natural gas has become the largest primary source of electricity produced in the country.

Fracking also led to large increases in domestic oil production that directly reduced our reliance on foreign imported crude oil. Our domestic crude oil production rebounded from a low of about five million barrels per day (bpd) in 2006 to 9.4 million bpd in 2015. Even with a drop of about 50% in crude prices, U.S. oil production exceeded 8.8 million bpd in 2016, and is expected to top 10 million bpd in 2017.[9] U.S. imports of oil were above 10 million bpd during the 2004–2007 period and fell to a low of about 7.4 million bpd in 2015. According to the U.S. Energy Information Administration, U.S. imports of oil and petroleum products from OPEC (which includes all Middle Eastern countries and Venezuela, among others) fell to a 28-year low in 2015.[10,11] The U.S. is pumping more of its oil and relying less on OPEC imports than at any time since 1987.

Back to regulatory incentives to achieve national economic and political goals, and our Nobel Prize winner's gasoline tax. Most of the time, simple tools like a carbon tax or a gasoline tax are the most effective. In a March 2015 op-ed in the *Washington Post*, former Secretary of State George Shultz proposed that the United States take out an "insurance policy" against global warming by increasing government R&D and enacting a carbon tax, lest we get "mugged by reality" later on. However, thus far we have preferred more complex regulatory routes in the U.S., using CAFE standards to regulate gasoline consumption and cap-and-trade to attempt to reduce industrial and power plant emissions of pollutants. But what are "CAFE standards" and "cap-and-trade?"

The Corporate Average Fuel Economy (CAFE) standards are regulations put in place by Congress in 1975 to improve the average fuel economy of cars, SUVs and light trucks produced for sale in the United States, in reaction to the first oil shock and the 1973-1974 Arab Oil Embargo. The CAFE standards in a given year define the fuel economy levels that manufacturers' fleets are required to meet that year. These specific levels of fuel economy, expressed in miles per U.S. gallon (mpg), vary with the characteristics and mix of vehicles produced by each manufacturer. If a domestic manufacturer fails to meet its specific CAFE mpg target, then it must pay a penalty of $5.50 per 0.1 mpg under the standard, multiplied by the manufacturer's total production for the U.S. domestic market. Since production of vehicles for large manufacturers are typically counted in millions, this is a strong incentive for manufacturers to abide by these fuel economy standards. In addition, a "Gas Guzzler Tax" is levied on passenger car models that get less than 22.5 mpg. But there is a glaring loophole here: trucks, vans, minivans, and SUVs are exempted from the Gas Guzzler Tax. This helps explain why the Ford 150 pick-up truck, a fairly large contraption, is by far the most sold vehicle in the country, and why SUVs are so popular as well. SUVs, or "Sport Utility Vehicles," are anything but: these large four-wheel drive vehicles are more often than not used in metropolitan areas where all roads are paved, even if there are lots of potholes. In its often-sold four-wheel drive configuration, the Ford 150 is both a light truck and an SUV. In Europe, the most-sold vehicles are small cars like the Volkswagen Golf; in Japan, Toyota Corollas or modern equivalents. Larger vehicles in the U.S. also benefit from the fact that within CAFE standards, a vehicle with a larger footprint has a lower fuel economy target than a vehicle with a smaller footprint. Therefore, a manufacturer of small cars will have an even higher fuel economy average to meet, whereas Ford in 2012 only had to meet a target of 17 mpg published for its ubiquitous F-150. Some other loopholes have been closed, though. In the U.S., many very large vehicles, such as pick-up trucks weighting more than 8,500lbs, used to be exempt from the CAFE calculations affecting their manufacturers. Not anymore: since 2012, these "medium-duty trucks" have been added to the CAFE regulations. After 2014, so were heavy-duty commercial trucks.[12,13]

This top-down (can we think of a less market-oriented regulation than CAFE standards?) approach to regulation has led to some progress. Under the Obama administration, a new national fuel economy program was created to adopt uniform federal standards regulating fuel economy and greenhouse gas emissions. This program already required fuel economy to jump from 26 mpg for all vehicles in 2008 to 39 mpg for cars and 30 mpg for light trucks and SUVs in 2016. This meant an average fuel economy standard of 35 mpg for all new vehicles, at least on the tests used to measure this fuel efficiency. In reality, in actual road driving conditions, the results are not as good, sometimes dramatically so. Still, the Obama administration pushed forward with strict new fuel economy standards: by 2025, passenger vehicles sold in the U.S. would have to get an average of 54.5mpg.[14] The Obama program faced several legal challenges, likely to be reviewed and arbitrated by the Supreme Court. After the November 8, 2016 election and Neil Gorsuch's confirmation to the Supreme Court, the Court's new "conservative" majority is likely to rule against this Obama legacy. How will the decision affect the program and the leeway it left the Environmental Protection Agency (EPA) or leading state emission regulations like the ones put in place in California? This is very difficult to predict, and there could very well be some slippage in the constant but slow progress achieved in vehicle fuel economy in the U.S. over the last decade. What could happen is that states would be "freed" from several federal mandates. The result would then be a patchwork of local regulations, with ongoing stringent fuel economy standards in "blue" states like California and much more relaxed ones in "red" states like Texas.

As far as motor vehicle fuel economy is concerned, our choice in the U.S. has been to regulate top-down, with mandates coming from the federal government, its Department of Transportation (DOT), the EPA, and individual state governments. A state like California, for example, has long prided itself in always being ahead of the federal mandates regarding fuel economy. This multiple jurisdiction complexity in the U.S. stands in contrast to high gasoline taxes, with few or no top-down regulations, for all other developed countries. In Europe and Japan, gasoline taxes are such that the cost per gallon at the pump is between two and three times what we pay in our country. The European Union also has targets for manufacturers and has asked individual countries to put higher taxes on low fuel economy vehicles, but the main driver for fuel economy is what local drivers demand in terms of low gas bills. Who wins the outcomes game? That's easy. Average personal vehicle fuel economy in Europe has been above 41 mpg since 2010, with Japan slightly higher. And both the European Union and Japan have higher targets for 2020 as well: 57 and 55 mpg, respectively. In addition, our top-down approach to regulation is by definition subject to the prevailing political winds of the moment. Fuel economy standards, EPA regulations and their enforcement can easily be changed from one administration to the next, as we are abundantly seeing during the first year of the Trump administration. On the other hand, it is very unlikely that a new government in Europe or Japan, left or right, would lower gasoline taxes to a significant degree. It would create holes in the budget, generate howls from all environmentally sensitive citizens, and even trigger protests from the automobile industry, which would see its production strategy upended by the new changes. Europe and Japan are doing exactly what was advocated at our Lisbon meeting: tax gasoline so its price is high for everyone, and then let the consumer choose. Simplicity trumps complexity.[15,16]

Now, if you thought CAFE standards were complex, you have seen nothing yet: cap-and-trade is much more complicated . . . A carbon tax is as simple to implement as a gasoline tax: the only issue is, basically, what its level should be. Cap-and-trade, on the other hand, has several variables to play with. A cap-and-trade system essentially sets a maximum level of pollution (the "cap") and distributes emissions permits among companies that produce emissions: coal-fired power plants, steel furnaces, manufacturing plants, etc. Companies need to have a permit to cover each unit of pollution they produce. These permits are obtained either through an initial allocation, determined by the regulatory entity at hand, or through trading with other companies. Trading takes place because some companies will find it easier or cheaper to reduce pollution than others, and therefore can sell the permits they no longer need on a marketplace. As in any marketplace, the trading price of pollution permits fluctuates. Prices can go up when demand is high relative to supply, for example when the industrial economy is growing. Cap-and-trade helps create a price on pollution through trading of permits, as result of setting a ceiling on the total quantity of emissions. Therefore, for cap-and-trade to just function, one needs 1) a ceiling on total pollution (not the easiest thing to determine, physically but also politically); 2) an initial allocation of pollution permits; 3) a marketplace in which to trade those permits; and 4) a thorough list of companies eligible both for an initial allocation and the trading of pollution permits. Simple! No wonder such a sophisticated system is well liked by professional auditors, consultants, financial advisors, and traders. They will all find plenty of fees in this process and bless cap-and-trade with a "market friendly" seal of approval. But perhaps the results achieved justify the inherent complexity and set-up costs of a cap-and-trade system?[17]

Unfortunately, the recent history of cap-and-trade systems established in Europe and then in California at the beginning of this century does not confirm this – much to the contrary. In Europe, to help promote a cap-and-trade system launched in 2005 (the Emission Trading System, or ETS), free emission permits were given out initially. This meant much cheaper compliance for industry in the early stages of the scheme, because companies only paid for the additional permits they bought from others. The initial tranche of emission trading permits covering pollution under current operating conditions was free: this explained cap-and-trade's popularity with heavy industries, which were originally very reluctant to embrace any system attempting to put a cost on pollution. In addition to the generous initial dose of free permits, companies could earn clean development mechanism offsets (CDMs) by funding green projects in the developing world. These CDMs led to much more creative accounting than actual emissions reductions. Trading reached about $50 billion in the initial years after 2005, but it did not last. Under the weight of far too many free emission permits and CDM allowances, both the trading of permits and their price collapsed. This was exacerbated by the 2008 global financial crisis, which depressed industrial output. In 2013, the European Parliament voted against a plan aimed to boost the low price of carbon as determined by the

ETS. This price had fallen from about €30 per ton in 2008 to fewer than €3 per ton, when most environmental experts believed that €30 per ton was the strict minimum required to achieve any type of positive environmental impact. The European Parliament thus essentially buried cap-and-trade, after the collapse of the market for emission permits had demonstrated that the process adopted in 2005 had completely failed to work. Adding insult to injury, several coal-fired power plants, benefiting from the overly generous initial allocation of permits, ended up making money from the scheme while continuing production – and CO_2 emissions. Wouldn't a simple carbon tax have been a better solution for Europe? Most European Union policy makers believed this at the outset of the program in 2005, but in the E.U. such a tax would have required the agreement from all twenty-eight member states, which was not at hand at the time. Political expediency thus ended up in failure.[18,19,20]

Could California do better than Europe? Governor Arnold Schwarzenegger, a Republican concerned about climate change, had paved the way in 2006. Schwarzenegger signed California's Global Warming Solutions Act that year, with a stated goal of lowering California's greenhouse gases to the 1990 level by 2020, a potential cut of 28%. This law was subject to furious political and legal battles, reaching a climax when Proposition 23 to repeal it was put on the ballot for the 2010 elections in the state. Record levels of advertisement were spent in that campaign. On one hand, opposing the law and therefore supporting Proposition 23, were Oklahoma billionaire industrialists Charles and David Koch, and oil companies. On the opposite side, supporting the law and against Proposition 23, were former Secretary of State and long-time Stanford resident George Shultz, and San Francisco billionaire hedge fund founder and environmental activist Tom Steyer. In the end, Shultz and Steyer won big, with 62% of Californians voting against Proposition 23. The law required more fuel-efficient cars, renewable power, and included other clean energy mandates, but at its center was a provision capping emissions from industry, setting-up a cap-and-trade system in the state for the first time.[21]

After three years spent developing regulations, California launched its cap-and-trade system in 2013, right after the collapse of the European scheme, and under the administration of Democratic governor Jerry Brown. Just like in Europe, though, California gave away many of the required carbon permits for free to help companies ease into the system. California also allowed "offset projects," not in the developing world but in the U.S., for example in forestry, to create "emission credits" in its trading system. And carbon prices were initially set fairly low as well. But California did take some measures to prevent the issues seen in Europe. To prevent wild fluctuations of prices, the state spent years analyzing emissions data, establishing floor and ceiling prices for the permits, which traded in a $11–14 per ton range at the outset. It should be noted that one of the fears at the launch of the program was that the price of emission credits would soar, causing many industrial companies to go bankrupt or leave the state. Nothing of the sort happened. However, the California experiment still looks like a repeat of the experience in Europe, with an excess of credits and insufficient demand. In May of 2016, the state cap-and-trade market experienced its worst quarterly auction to date, with hundreds of millions of dollars' worth of unsold carbon credits left over. Only 11% of the credits on sale in the auction were actually sold, representing a shortfall of more than $500 million. This did not help Jerry Brown, who had been counting on emission credits auction revenue to fund a variety of green and infrastructure programs in the state, foremost his signature high-speed rail project. Ironically, the California emission-trading program experienced sputtering in part because of the success of many other environmental initiatives in the state. For example, California's "renewable portfolio standard" forced utilities to reduce carbon emissions directly. Other successful regulatory efforts to reduce pollution in the state also led to reduced demand for carbon allowances in the auctions. The program thus suffered under the double weight of surplus allowances and too low a demand for new credits. The California Air Resources Board running it put a brave face on these setbacks, saying that the state was on course to meet its goal of reducing greenhouse gas emissions to their 1990 level by 2020. The state regulators were also confident that refineries, power plants and other industrial units would meet the goal of reducing their emissions by 15% in 2020 relative to today's levels. Air Resources Board Chairman Mary Nichols reported that 2015 emissions from covered industries came in at 9% below mandated limits for that year. Yes . . . but again, lots of anti-pollution programs in California could have claimed credit for these achievements.[22]

What is not in doubt is that the program moved from having a lot more bids than credits at its inception in 2013 to a systematic excess of supply over demand since 2014, leading to the May 2016 auction in which only 11% of the permits auctioned were bought.[23] As incentive to get the industry to cap carbon emissions, the California cap-and-trade program thus appeared to be less successful than other emissions control initiatives in the state, more of the "command and control" variety. At an average price of $12.7 per ton in 2016, the price of carbon was not high enough to encourage most industries to invest heavily in anti-pollution equipment or in entirely new technologies that rely less on carbon. Adding to this negative picture was the February 9, 2016 Supreme Court ruling that suspended the Obama administration's federal "clean power plan" mandating cuts in emissions from fossil-fueled electric power plants until further judicial review. With the balance of power on the Supreme Court having shifted in early 2017 towards a majority likely opposed to clean power legislation, this suspension is likely to hold. In any case, the Trump administration and its EPA administrator Scott Pruitt started the process of rolling back the Obama-era clean power rules in October of 2017, not wasting any time in their agenda to favor coal.

Creative contrarian views were voiced, saying that California industry had been so proficient at cutting emissions that business no longer needed the permits put on auction . . . That argument was undercut when cap-and-trade proponents stated that the key to the program's success was its continuation beyond

2020. In the end, in a noteworthy vote on July 17, 2017, the California State Legislature voted by a two-thirds majority and in a bi-partisan way to extend the state's cap-and-trade program all the way to 2030. The extension was voted alongside a companion bill to reduce local air pollution, with a stated goal for California to contribute strongly to worldwide efforts to reduce planet-warming emissions in 2030 by 40% relative to 1990 levels. Politics did play a role. California legislators and Governor Jerry Brown were proud to highlight the extension of the emission-pricing program as an ambitious commitment to environmentally friendly policy-making. They touted their efforts, contrasting them with the Trump administration's reluctance to acknowledge the perils of climate change and its announced departure from the Paris Climate Agreement. There were opponents to the extension of the cap-and-trade program in California, notably from the Sierra Club, which along with many environmental voices complained that the program did not put a high enough price on carbon. But what may have appeared as a timid step during the Obama presidency was acclaimed by many in the national media as California taking an exemplary leadership stand against the anti-environmental actions of the Trump administration. Cap-and-trade became a political symbol, never mind its actual effectiveness.

Despite its renewed embrace by California, cap-and-trade suffers from both its complexity and the fact that (at least thus far) governments that have implemented it on a large scale have felt compelled to give industry large initial quantities of free allowances to launch their programs smoothly. Contrast this with a simple carbon tax: under this straightforward tax, the price of emitting a unit of pollution is set very clearly. This gives everyone a very transparent price signal, regardless of the actual quantity of emissions, something that is exceedingly hard to set in cap-and-trade systems. Another challenge for cap-and-trade, this time philosophical, is that it assumes, principally with an abundance of free allowances to kick-start the process, that current levels of pollution are acceptable. Cap-and-trade aims to price increments in pollution, whereas a carbon tax gives everyone a clear incentive to cut emissions. The main issue for the carbon tax, of course, is at what level should it be set. Here we can find a very interesting experiment, proposed recently to voters about 1,000 miles north of California, in our fellow Pacific State of Washington.

In the November 8, 2016 election, voters in Washington State rejected a proposal, called Initiative 732, which would have set a straight carbon tax in the state, a first in the country. The tax was to be gradual, starting at $15 per ton in 2017, increasing to $25 per ton in 2018, and then rising gradually over a few decades to a maximum of $100 per ton in 2016 dollars. The money raised by the tax would have gone to lowering the state sales tax, boosting the economy, and giving up to $1,500 in tax credits to low-income residents. This carbon tax was designed to be revenue neutral, at least in theory. It would have also made taxation in the state less regressive, through the lower sales taxes resulting from its implementation. Translated in gasoline and electricity terms, the Washington state carbon tax at $25 a ton would have increased the price of local gasoline by about 25 cents a gallon, and the cost of fossil fueled power by 2.5 cents per kilowatt-hour. A similar plan has been in place since 2008 in the neighboring western Canadian province of British Columbia, with the carbon tax currently set there at Canadian $30 a ton, or about U.S. $24. On Election Day, Initiative 732 garnered just 42% of votes. The only county in Washington State that supported the measure was King County, or Seattle, the largest city in the whole northwest. The main reason the initiative failed is that not only did it have the expected opposition from the fossil fuel and utility industries, but also from the Sierra Club, the Washington Conservation Voters, and Democratic Governor Jay Inslee. There were concerns that I-732 would actually lead to a shortfall of about $800 million over six years; and that the initiative revenue should be used to fund environmental friendly programs such as clean energy and mass transit instead of a reduction in sales tax. Supporters of the campaign expressed disappointment but nonetheless described the measure as a template for future similar efforts in the U.S. After all, we know plenty of causes that started by failing at the state polling level and eventually gained national acceptance. Think about gay marriage, for example. Perhaps this proposed initiative is a good template because of its efforts to strike the right compromise between environmentalists and advocates of balanced government budgets.[24,25]

More generally, can simpler but also stronger regulations send the right signals to the U.S. economy – for example, to continue all the progress made over the last decade on energy and environmental issues? Are we ready for a strong price signal like a carbon or gasoline tax? These can be made "revenue accretive" to help finance much-needed infrastructure revitalization in the country, the one area both 2016 presidential candidates agreed upon; or to reduce budget deficits; or they can be made "revenue neutral" for taxpayers with the help of tax credits and other fiscal rebates. Politically, the potential exists here to please both sides of the aisle. In addition, the power of simplicity in such direct price signals would also allow us to phase out a legion of complex and cumbersome "top-down" regulations, at both the federal and state level. This would be popular as well. This is why most other developed countries prefer direct price signals such as end-user taxes to complex regulations, these price signals having a direct impact on what people decide to buy ... In the U.S., we have had a historical tendency to prefer legislating and regulating rather than sending price signals. This has bred complexity everywhere. We have already reviewed this "in extenso" in health care, with the needed and well-meaning Affordable Care Act; in clean energy and electricity with the maze of federal and state regulations impacting publicly traded utilities as well as solar and wind ventures; and in banking with the enacting of Dodd–Frank and associated rules. Just like Obamacare, which gave health insurance to twenty million Americans for the first time, Dodd–Frank represented progress from the former status quo and made us safer from a potential future financial meltdown. However, can any set of complex regulations and regulatory bodies achieve more in terms of desired compliance than the formal threat of jail time for top executives responsible for economic catastrophes? "Too big to fail" and complex "living legacy trusts" for very large banks versus "no one too big to jail" – which one is more effective?[26,27]

Under the new Trump administration, there is certainly an effort to simplify regulations. Rules governing potential industrial abuses are being eliminated left and right, in finance, mining, electricity generation, and emission of greenhouse gases. But this is also a wholesale attempt at turning back the clock on protective regulations and reversing progress achieved during the Obama administration, notably in making Wall Street safer for Main Street and protecting our environment. We are in danger of moving from a regulatory culture to one of impunity. In terms of achieving better laws and regulations through simplicity, this is akin to throwing out the baby with the bath water. On June 1, 2017, the U.S. government thus decided to withdraw from the Paris Climate Agreement, much to the chagrin of the whole rest of the world. Now Europe and China will have to take the lead on global environmental protection efforts – what an abdication by America! One should not despair, though. In the U.S., the states – led by California – can mitigate much of this potential damage with their own regulations and legislative initiatives. And market forces look poised to defeat many attempts by climate change deniers to weaken anti-pollution rules. In particular, the Trump administration efforts to eliminate environmental rules that constrained the coal industry are unlike to have much impact, given overwhelming price dynamics favoring natural gas at the expense of coal. That market train has already left the station. Removing rules governing power plant emissions and the leaching of coal ash into ground water are unlikely to reverse the current trends away from coal as a source of primary energy in the country.

★　★　★　★　★

Trading pacts, outsourcing, and rebellion in the Heartland

One consequence of this complexity is the increasing abyss between our Congress, its legislators, and we the people: the public; the voters. Let's take another example, trading pacts. During the 2016 presidential campaign, the "Trans Pacific Partnership," or TPP, loomed very large. The complexity of TPP was truly mind-boggling: at least 5,600 pages; most congress people and senators could not talk about it in an articulate fashion. And Joe Public, ill-informed, confused by poor explanations from our legislators, and subject to the 30-second sound bites of the presidential campaign, thought TPP was a tool that would help China achieve dominance of our economic sphere. Now, there were several valid arguments to be made against ratification of TPP, but China was not even part of this trade deal! Actually, the main objective of TPP was to help us trade with Asian nations other than China, to keep China's potential regional economic dominance in check. One can excuse our allies in the region, the Australians, Japanese, Koreans, and Southeast Asians, for being confused by our behavior. Of course, with the election of Donald Trump to the presidency, TPP is dead and buried. But it is still worth looking at it as another illustration of how complexity and opacity can be self-defeating.[28,29]

The TPP was a trade agreement among twelve countries bordering the Pacific Ocean, which very openly did not include China. The finalized proposal was signed on February 4, 2016, after seven years of negotiations. The twelve countries signing the proposal included Australia, Brunei, Canada, Chile, Japan, Malaysia, Mexico, New Zealand, Peru, Singapore, the United States, and Vietnam. The agreement had thirty chapters and stated lofty goals such as promoting economic growth; supporting the creation and retention of jobs; enhancing innovation, productivity and competitiveness; raising living standards; reducing poverty; and promoting transparency, good governance, and enhanced labor and environmental protections. The TPP also had measures to lower barriers to trade, foremost tariffs, and a mechanism to settle potential investor–state disputes. This ambitious trade agreement had been a cornerstone of the Obama administration trade policy, with President Obama himself, Japan Prime Minister Shinzō Abe, and successive Canadian Prime Ministers Stephen Harper and Justin Trudeau being tireless advocates of TPP.[30,31]

The advocates of the Pacific trade pact stressed lower tariffs and quotas; rigorous environmental, labor and intellectual property standards, leveling the playing field between developed and developing countries in the Pacific Rim; and enhanced opportunities for services industries to trade across borders. The latter was a key objective for the U.S., given our country's strong competitive advantage in the areas of finance, education, engineering, legal, software, and information technology. Unblocked internet and data flows were key benefits TPP would bring to more than three-quarters of a billion people. Proponents of TPP hoped that ratification of the pact would help compensate for the failure and slow death of the global "Doha" trading agreements, enhancing trade in an area representing about 40% of the world's GDP. TPP should also have paved the way for a similarly ambitious Transatlantic Trade and Investment Partnership (TTIP) between the European Union and the United States.

Opponents of the TPP focused on two key areas of the pact. The one that attracted the most attention and opposition was the provision that extended intellectual property (IP) laws across the Pacific Rim and provided for new international rules of enforcement. TPP was strongly criticized, notably in Australia, Canada, and the United State, for new international digital policies that seemed to favor corporations at the expense of the public's freedom of expression and right to privacy. There was a lot of concern that TPP would allow personal data to be sent across borders with limited protection, and would also allow companies to sue countries for laws promoting the public interest in areas like privacy. TPP opponents believed the pact would further entrench controversial aspects of U.S. copyright law, and restrict the ability of Congress and individual citizens to engage in reform to meet the evolving needs of Americans within the ever-changing technology sector. In particular, there was scathing criticism that TPP provisions that recognized the rights of the public were non-binding, whereas almost all areas that benefited corporations were binding. There was fear among heavy internet users that file sharing across borders without commercial motivation could lead to heavy fines and even jail time. These TPP opponents complained that the trade pact did not take advantage of the U.S. experience and mistakes with the internet, copyrights and IP over the last sixteen years. Positive aspects of the U.S. copyright regime that have enhanced freedom of expression and individual technological innovation in our country, like fair use, were indeed absent from TPP.

The other heavily criticized area of TPP was the "Investor–State Dispute Settlement," or ISDS. A similar provision had also enflamed European opponents of the TTIP, the TPP sister pact between the E.U. and the United States. TPP critics complained that ISDS would allow foreign companies to challenge U.S. law and potentially win large settlements from American taxpayers without any court of law being involved. Essentially, ISDS allowed foreign companies from Pacific Rim countries involved in a dispute about U.S. laws and regulations (governing pollution levels, for example) to by-pass U.S. courts and present their cases in front of a panel of international arbitrators. And if a given company won its case in such arbitration, the ruling could not be challenged in domestic courts. These international panels would not employ independent judges, but rather business lawyers. One can indeed express concern at corporate lawyers going back and forth between representing corporations one day and providing judgment in an international panel of arbitration the next. Could lawyers who depend on lucrative corporate work for their law practices really be impartial in rendering arbitration in cases involving the same corporations they depend on against the U.S. government or concerned citizens?

Adding fuel to the fire was the fact that only international investors and corporations could use these arbitration panels. So, a Southeast Asian company with U.S. operations wanting to challenge, say, an increase in a local U.S. minimum wage could use ISDS. But a U.S. labor union or state government believing a Pacific Rim country was allowing its companies to use "starvation wages" in violation of TPP commitments could not use ISDS: they would have to make their case in the courts of that country. The rationale for ISDS was to encourage foreign investments in countries with weak legal systems, but the solution it offered might have been worse than the cure. TPP opponents were concerned that corporations from Asian countries would use the pact to circumvent U.S. laws, and damage employment and regulation protections in our country. The opposition to TTIP, on the other hand, came from many continental European countries, which were concerned that the TTIP would weaken local European regulations against U.S.-based multinationals. These concerns were particularly acute in the area of food and health. One common refrain among French and Germans opposed to the TTIP was that "the health of our citizens is more important to us than the profits of U.S. corporations." In Europe as well, there was widespread opposition to the use of non-accountable international arbitrators to settle international legal disputes. Most countries in continental Europe did not want current anti-competition, privacy and taxation litigation brought by the E.U. against a number of U.S. technology giants to be settled outside the legal court process.[32,33]

But what mostly played against the TPP and TTIP, when U.S. and European politicians rallied against these trade pacts, was their complexity and opacity. Very few people could speak fluently about the details of the TPP international arbitration panels; how they would work; in which cases; and with what types of lawyers. Fewer people yet understood the maze of new regulations and processes contained in the thirty chapters and 5,600 pages of the TPP. And opposition to the TPP could be summed up in a Twitter-length slogan, like "it will suck away jobs from the U.S., like NAFTA did"; "it will cement China's domination of the international economy"; or "it will contribute to the erosion of workers' rights in our country." This made for very effective politics on both the left and right sides of the political spectrum.

TPP, TTIP and other trade deal advocates, among the most educated and affluent professionals in our society, were left fuming against the dangers of populism and how the benefits of global trade were not understood at all by Joe Public. Perhaps, but who is to blame if the benefits of global trade can only be served by agreements that are gigantic in their complexity and completely incomprehensible to the vast majority of electors in our democratic societies? Trade advocates have also completely failed to make the case for those "left behind" economically by thirty years of globalization. Globalization has reduced the wealth gap between developed and developing countries, but within developed ones has increased the gap between the haves and the have-nots, increasing U.S. inequality to levels not seen since the 1920s. Just like in finance, those left behind see massive complexity being used against their economic interest. Going backwards financially and having a strong feeling of intellectual inadequacy amidst changes difficult to understand can lead to the angriest reactions. Two perceptive men understood this during the 2016 U.S. presidential election journey, united in their opposition to trade deals like TPP: Bernie Sanders and Donald Trump. The first lost the primaries to his party's economic establishment; the second vanquished both Republican and Democratic establishments all the way to the White House.[34,35]

Whatever reservations one may have, the political discourse coming from Donald Trump as a presidential candidate was neither opaque nor complex. Some of the ideas promoted during his campaign were very powerful in their directness. For example, creating a strong economic and jobs stimulus through spending a trillion dollars in revitalizing our creaking infrastructure makes sense to most Americans. After all, our bridges are falling, our roads full of pot-holes, our airports feel like they're in the Third World, and we have little rail transportation or mass transit of any kind. Fixing and developing all of this will by definition create lots of local jobs, pretty much everywhere in the country. Infrastructure spending, like FDR's New Deal massive public works projects and Eisenhower's interstate highway program, the largest infrastructure expenditure in our history, created millions of American jobs. There is strong and widespread enthusiasm for economic stimulus through infrastructure work in the country. What about the Sanders and Trump proposed antidote to large-scale outsourcing of jobs out of the country, tariffs?

When I was a child, in the mid- to late sixties, my father would often regale us at the family dinner table with descriptions of America's might: he would talk endlessly about the industrial capitals of the world, Detroit, Cleveland, and Pittsburgh; and also about smaller but still powerful cities like Erie, Pennsylvania, the "locomotive factory for the world"; Akron, Ohio, the "tire capital of the world"; or even Flint in Michigan, where "so many great General Motors cars are made." My father was a professor of "Lettres Classiques" – i.e. French literature, Latin, and ancient Greek – who ended up working for the French "Quai d'Orsay," or Foreign Service. But like all children of World War II, he had a fascination with (and gratitude for) U.S. industrial power. After all, American industrial production had saved the world from both German Nazism and Japanese militaristic imperialism. In doing so it created unheard of prosperity for all Americans, industrialists and workers alike, the envy of the world. Despite the very generous and effective Marshall Plan, it is hard for most Americans to fathom the enormous differences in standards of living that prevailed between the U.S. and Europe then. When my parents got married in 1956, both of them worked as professors. Yet, the only mode of transportation they could afford then was a 125cc motorcycle. In the U.S., they would have had a large automobile, if not two . . . Working for the Foreign Service helped the family economically, though. In the late sixties, when we lived in Denmark, my father had a nice Citroen ID (like "idea") station wagon, a technically advanced and fast car. My friends, the children of English and German diplomats, enjoyed their parents' Jaguars and Mercedes. But we all wanted to ride with the Ambassador of Greece's son: since Greece does not make cars, his father could choose any car he wished, and he drove a Chevrolet Impala. The size! The silent yet powerful purr of the V8 engine! Those six lights at the back! For us, this symbol of American strength was what we dreamt about in terms of automobiles. I often asked my father, "why can't you have a Chevrolet, too?" He would respond, "because the French government will allow me to buy a duty free car only if that car happens to be French." In Denmark, cars were subject to a 300% import duty. When we moved to Rio de Janeiro in Brazil in 1969, new imported cars were also subjected to a 300% tariff. For us, never mind, we took the Citroen as a used car with us. For Brazilians, though, it meant that if they wanted a car and were not extremely wealthy, the car better be a domestically manufactured one. Brazil built its nascent industries during the 1970s and 1980s behind a wall of protecting tariffs. This succeeded beyond the Brazilians' wildest dreams. Today the country is not only one of the largest exporters of steel, but also manufactures over 3.5 million cars per year, more than France and the U.K.; and its local aeronautical company, Embraer, is the third largest manufacturer of commercial airplanes after Airbus and Boeing. Whenever we fly a commuter jet in this country, 60% of the time it happens to be an Embraer one.

In the U.S., tariffs to protect domestic industries from cheap imported goods were a standard feature of trade policy throughout the nineteenth century and the first half of the twentieth century. These tariffs generated much revenue for the U.S. Treasury. After World War II, though, U.S. companies did not have much to fear from anyone, and the country led a movement towards freer trade and little or no tariffs. Then other manufacturing powerhouses emerged, first Germany in the 1970s and then Japan in the 1980s; South Korea and its fellow Southeast Asia "Tigers"; Brazil and Mexico followed suit, leading of course to the emergence of China as the world's largest manufacturer. Today most of the developed world has few tariffs of consequence, although some are enduring: Japan protects its agriculture, mostly through tariffs on rice, beef and dairy; the E.U. has a well-known set of policies protecting its indigenous agriculture; the U.S. protects its domestic corn-based sugar market from lower-priced global suppliers, such as Brazil and its huge local sugar cane production, and imposes tariffs of 15% or more on beverages, dairy products, clothing, and tobacco.[36]

Most manufactured imports, as well as minerals and steel, enter the U.S. essentially tariff-free (less than 3%). As a result, the United States, principally in the Midwest around the Great Lakes, has been ravaged by outsourcing, first to Mexico, then to China and Southeast Asia. Once-prosperous cities like Detroit, Flint, Erie, Akron, Youngstown, Fort Wayne, and South Bend are shells of their former selves, testifying to the grave decline of manufacturing in this country. What has more or less saved Pittsburgh and Cleveland from similar decline has not been industry, but health care – the University of Pittsburgh Medical Center and the Cleveland Clinic systems, respectively. Who makes these industrial outsourcing decisions? Mostly, chief executive officers of large corporations and their direct reports. These outsourcing transactions are extremely complex, a plus for many specialized consultants advising companies and promoting such moves in exchange of large professional fees. Over the long-term, the financial results may not be as good as promised, once large transition costs and the complexity of the sophisticated supply chain arrangements are taken into factor. Plus, the gap between U.S. workers' salaries and their counterparts in Mexico and China goes down over time, diminishing the returns of outsourcing. But in the short-term, financial markets applaud such moves, quarterly results shine, and the CEOs and their well-paid teams and advisors reap out enormous gains. For the local communities in the Midwest, unfortunately the devastation is very real. Many families have suffered from a one-two punch. Fathers (and mothers) lost their well-paid factory work when manufacturing jobs went to Mexico through NAFTA in the 1990s. They were told, "do not despair: your children, if they train appropriately, will have a bright future in the information age." The children duly trained in information technology, just in time to see a massive outsourcing of such work to India at the beginning of the twenty-first century. Today, yes, we have unemployment at 4.1% in the U.S., a great performance considering where we were in the aftermath of the 2008 financial crisis. However, we also have a smaller percentage of adult males aged between 25 and 60 in the workforce than France and its 9.2% unemployment rate. Many people have just stopped looking for employment, taking themselves out of the workforce - and unemployment statistics. Idleness and opioid addiction are rampant, and for the first time in eons life expectancy for whites (but not for minorities) went down in the U.S. in 2015. No wonder people in the "rust belt" are boiling with anger![37]

It did not necessarily have to be like this. In the U.S., short-term incentives in the stock market and CEO compensation motivated many business decision makers to seek cost reduction moves as opposed to growth-oriented investments, which pay over longer periods of time. Germany and Japan remain manufacturing powerhouses to this day. In Germany, there was much more consensus between business management, workers representatives and local communities on what needed to be done to keep manufacturing local. The famed German "Mittelstand" tissue of mid-sized industrial companies invested massively in local apprenticeship programs and educated their workforces about what they expected from them in return for keeping jobs at home. Disparity between CEO compensation and workers' wages is also much less pronounced in Germany and Japan than in the U.S., and so it is easier for CEOs to focus on the long-term as opposed to responding to Wall Street pressure about quarterly earnings. Japan and Germany have thus preserved their manufacturing successes and have even enhanced them for the new age, since both countries also specialize in making the very machines, industrial robots and the like, that the world needs to build things.

In Japan and Germany, solidarity is also a very strong tenet of top-level political choices and popular support. Solidarity? Allow me to explain this concept through a personal example. When I helped co-found my company, our first hospital clients in 2004 were in Michigan: Detroit, but also Flint, Kalamazoo, and Saginaw. Then, over the next few years, we added other hospital clients all over the Great Lakes, including in Erie, Western Pennsylvania. Having been a global management consultant before for twenty years or so, I had never been to such cities. My exposure to U.S. business life "between the coasts" had been limited to mega towns like Atlanta, Chicago, Dallas, Denver, and Houston, with a few stops in Cleveland, Cincinnati, Kansas City, Minneapolis, and Pittsburgh. In Flint, Kalamazoo, Saginaw, and Erie, I was amazed by the number of boarded-up houses, outright burned-out ones, and the dereliction of many streets. Even in Cleveland, between the shiny buildings of the Cleveland Clinic, there were many empty blocks. I heard that in Detroit, the city had to cut back on essential municipal services in whole neighborhoods. I scratched my head; had I seen anything like this in the developed world?

Actually, I had. I was privileged to get to visit the former East Germany right after the 1989 fall of the Berlin Wall, in 1990. And these Midwestern towns reminded me of Dresden and Leipzig then. Dresden and Leipzig, both with about half a million people in population, epitomized urban neglect after forty-five years of communist rule: derelict apartment buildings, abandoned urban lots, and roads in desperate need of repair. But all Western Germans decided to share in the sacrifice to help rebuild the former East Germany. Financed by a hefty surtax on all incomes, reconstruction went full speed ahead, costing well over a trillion Deutsche Marks. In 2007, when I visited again, Dresden and Leipzig had become urban jewels, rebuilt stone by stone in painstaking detail and architectural attention. Leipzig, J. S. Bach's birth place, had its historical old Renaissance age city center resplendent, every home and building rebuilt to its historical blueprints. New airports, autobahns, high-speed trains . . . wow! This is solidarity at the national level. Have you ever heard at a cocktail party in New York or San Francisco that we need as a country to invest $1 trillion to rebuild the urban areas around the Great Lakes? I haven't, and believe it is a pity: we need a twenty-first-century Marshall Plan for ourselves, and it should start in many areas of the Midwest.

Can new tariffs be part of the equation? Can 25+% tariffs applied to goods purchased from China and Mexico help bring back long-lost manufacturing jobs to this country? Should we start by applying tariffs on Chinese imports? If one does not believe in more solidarity "à la Germany," tariffs may represent the strong and simple signals that our CEOs need to reverse decisions made during the last two decades and rebuild our manufacturing base. After all, our manufacturing skills are far from dead: much is still built in the U.S., and some of our manufacturing (think satellites; commercial aircrafts; stealth military bomber and fighter airplanes) is the most advanced in the world. So, if Brazil, Mexico, and China could build their manufacturing base in a relative short time, why couldn't we rebuild ours within a decade or so? They used combinations of tariffs, quotas and low wages, and perhaps we can use tariffs to achieve similar results as well. In the 1980s and early 1990s, the widely perceived economic threat to the U.S. came from Japan, not China (remember the popular Michael Crichton novel *Rising Sun*?). And many people have forgot that Ronald Reagan and his economic team used the threat of tariffs to compel Japan to agree to export limits, such as quotas of automobiles sold to the country. This eventually led all major Japanese car manufacturers to open new plants in states like Alabama; Indiana; Kentucky; Mississippi; and Tennessee. German automakers followed suit (BMW has its largest plant worldwide in South Carolina), and millions of new jobs were created in the South.

I can already hear howls from many "globalists": "tariffs would break the complex global supply-chain arrangements so many companies depend upon! Consumers would have to pay hundreds of dollars more for their iPhones! Global trade would shrink!" Well, private sector companies are notorious for their adaptability. They would re-arrange their supply-chains. Consumers might have to pay more for certain goods, but how enticing are lower-priced products when you have no job and no earning power? And yes, significant economic changes always produce winners and losers, but fairness may dictate that we vary a little bit who those are from time to time. We should also remember that tariffs in quite a few areas already exist today, without the world economy coming to an end. Midwest farmers, as we saw above, are protected against low cost sugar from countries like Brazil. Offering similar protection to manufacturing workers around the Great Lakes will not end global trade, principally if tariffs are specific enough. Above all, those who argue that the way to solve the predicament of millions who have lost well-paying manufacturing jobs in the West is more global trade offer absolutely nothing in terms of solutions. Apart from the usual bromides on "people need to retrain," no serious idea is ever proposed to make capital work more productively for those in abandoned places. The retraining ideas always focus on college education and "skills for the information age." Yet, we know that low and middle-level IT jobs are even easier to outsource than manufacturing ones. After all, getting a large Wall Street bank to rely on a giant outsourced IT center in Bangalore, India for its back-office operations is much easier to set up than outsourcing manufacturing of key components for the Boeing 777. The hard truth is most CEOs today have no incentive whatsoever to think about the communities their companies originated from. Employers, principally in the U.S. and the U.K., enthralled with the "maximizing shareholder value is our only responsibility" mantra, no longer view generating and keeping productive work in our former manufacturing heartlands as their role. Hence Brexit. Hence Donald Trump.

Tariffs may be a crude tool to reverse what three decades of industrial neglect have imposed on millions of our fellow citizens. But in the absence of any practical solution coming out of corporate suites and their financial backers, and the strong cultural challenges for us to emulate the long-term, consensus-driven German and Japanese type efforts, they may very well be a solution we can use in the short-term. As seen above, the mere threat of tariffs motivated pretty much all German and Japanese automakers to build new plants in the U.S., mostly in the South. Couldn't we try the same thing for steel, to help revive Gary and South Bend in Indiana, as well as several other towns in Ohio and Pennsylvania? And should we accept passively that China requires our most innovative companies, such as Apple, to engage in arrangements with dubious IP protection in which, for example, they must have Chinese partners and their data stored in Chinese servers?

There are other types of direct tools that can help the country and its companies rediscover their industrial roots. One such tool is the destination-based concept, also called border adjustment tax (BAT). BAT is popular in conservative economic circles, notably among House Republicans such as Texas Congressman Kevin Brady. The idea is to tax goods at the consumption stage as opposed to production. Hence, exports by companies based in the U.S. would not be taxed, but all imports would. Another way to implement this concept is to rule that, within a framework of significant lower U.S. corporate tax rates, costs of foreign origin (e.g. parts manufactured in Mexico) would not get deducted from revenues for tax purposes; on the other hand, all domestic costs would be fully deductible. This would encourage domestic production significantly. In tweets targeting large automakers like GM and Ford in the spring of 2017, Donald Trump was emphasizing BAT: "make in the USA or pay border tax!"

Just like tariffs, border taxation is very controversial: retailers, which import a lot of what they sell, may be unfairly penalized; complex supply chain arrangements, such as in automotive manufacturing, may end up with higher costs; U.S. consumers might have to pay more for their cars and imported products; and a border tax would be extremely complicated to set up and collect. Indeed, this BAT concept was not part of the late 2017 GOP tax reform: a more modest switch to a territorial system already used by most developed countries replaced it. In such a territorial system, U.S. companies will only pay taxes on profits earned at home, excluding most profits earned abroad. In the future, there could also be tax-avoidance measures targeting multinationals, such as a special excise tax on cross-border payments.[38,39,40,41]

On balance, I am not an advocate of strong tariffs and border taxation, because they do carry economic costs, and countries like Germany show us manufacturing excellence is not necessarily achieved behind tariff walls. However, I mention them because they are tools other countries have used successfully to develop their manufacturing sectors. And, for us in the U.S., they may represent a viable short-term alternative to an undesirable status quo. Globalization has produced untold benefits for the top "1%" in developed countries and for millions of people in the developing world. Non-elite workers in the West have paid the price and are rioting at the ballot box. If capitalism as we know it in developed countries is to continue thriving, it is time to ditch our long-accepted paradigms ("la pensée unique," as they say in France) and change direction. Longer term, if we are serious about restoring our decreased – but by no means dead – manufacturing capabilities, we should give a hard look at countries that have been successful in that sector, and at what characterizes their societies. Solidarity at the national level; responsibility from those at the top towards their communities; sustained investments in vocational training and industrial apprenticeships; focus on long-term company strategies as opposed to short-term shareholder value; reduced levels of income inequality from today's grotesque levels of disparity; solidarity, again, within companies – sometimes jobs have to be cut to enable survival, but perhaps that should not go hand in hand with record executive compensation. None of this can happen immediately, and it will require a sustained long-term effort involving profound cultural changes in how business is conducted in our country. But these changes are worthy objectives for the next decade or so, and will prove more effective to take us out of our current predicament than crude tools like tariffs and border taxation.

★   ★   ★   ★   ★

Expensive regulatory bodies and over a million lawyers

Instead of a direct approach via price signals, direct taxes, and tariffs in some cases, we espouse in the U.S. a regulatory philosophy that uses indirect levers. Many of our regulations governing businesses and the economy are so indirect that they have to be interpreted at length through our court system by armies of lawyers and a full history of case law. Just writing these regulations and enforcement mechanisms takes tens of thousands of highly qualified professionals, and this is only looking at the federal level. If we add all state and municipal levels, we are in the hundreds of thousands. Of course, federal regulators often undo or redo the work of their predecessors, depending on the winds of political change in Washington. This keeps the regulatory machine very busy and fully employed, even during administrations promoting "smaller government."

There are dozens of U.S. federal regulatory agencies, some of them like the DEA and the FAA with major operational responsibilities in addition to their regulatory role. The major federal regulatory bodies are the Bureau of Alcohol, Tobacco, Firearms, and Explosives (ATF); the Commodity Futures Trading Commission (CFTC); the Consumer Product Safety Commission (CPSC); the Drug Enforcement Administration (DEA); the Environmental Protection Agency (EPA); the Equal Employment Opportunity Commission (EEOC); the Federal Aviation Administration (FAA); the Federal Communications Commission (FCC); the Food and Drug Administration (FDA); the Federal Deposit Insurance Corporation (FDIC); the Federal Election Commission (FEC); the Federal Energy Regulatory Commission (FERC); the Federal Highway Administration (FHWA); the Federal Maritime Commission (FMC); the Federal Railroad Administration (FRA); the Federal Reserve System (FRC, more commonly known as the Feds); the Federal Trade Commission (FTC); the Interstate Commerce Commission (ICC); the National Highway Traffic Safety Administration (NHTSA); the National Labor Relations Board (NLRB); the National Transportation Safety Board (NTSB); the Nuclear Regulatory Commission (NRC); the Occupational Safety and Health Administration (OSHA); and the Securities and Exchange Commission (SEC).[42] Most of these federal agencies employ thousands. Looking at eight agencies we have mentioned earlier in this book, we have the following approximate headcounts: 15,000 at the EPA; 1,700 at the FCC; 15,000 at the FDA; 8,700 at the FDIC; 1,500 at the FERC; 1,300 at the FTC; 3,800 at the NRC; and 4,300 at the SEC.[43,44,45] This already amounts to over 51,000 federal employees.[46,47]

There are also issues that are more critical than headcounts, such as conflicts of interest at the senior levels of these regulatory agencies. When one looks at the FCC; FTC; FERC; and most prominently the SEC, are these regulatory commissions really independent from the industries they regulate? This question has often been asked because of the "revolving door" between these commissions and the industries they regulate. Former senior regulators often become senior legal staff at major corporations and are very well compensated for their government regulatory expertise. And regulators are often selected from senior industry ranks. It has been argued that this is the only way to have regulators who possess deep knowledge of the industries they are supposed to regulate. However, this line of reasoning seems self-serving, at least as long as there are no legal limits on these "revolving doors."

A case in point is the 31st Chair of the SEC, Mary Jo White, who announced her resignation as of January 2017, following the November 8 presidential election. Ms. White was nominated to be the Chair of the SEC on January 24, 2013 and was confirmed by the Senate in April of the same year. Mary Jo White had a very distinguished career as a prosecutor, notably as the U.S. Attorney for the Southern District of New York from 1993 to 2002. Among other feats, she led the prosecution of Mafia boss John Gotti and oversaw the prosecution of the terrorists responsible for the 1993 World Trade Center bombing. The main perception of "revolving door" issue with Ms. White is that, prior to being named head of the SEC, she was for ten years the chair of the litigation department at law firm Debevoise & Plimpton. This law firm essentially serves Wall Street financial firms. And so, a senior partner at a law firm helping Wall Street firms defend themselves against litigation, much of it initiated by federal or state authorities, became the Chair of the SEC just a few years after the 2008 financial disaster. As a result, during her tenure at the SEC, Ms. White had to recuse herself from over fifty significant SEC enforcement cases because of her work at Debevoise & Plimpton. This created many deadlocked situations within the SEC, potentially compromising the effectiveness of the commission she led.

Above all, this question will always linger: can the head of a major federal regulatory commission be as effective as possible given her or his prior industry work and, perhaps more importantly, the prospects of lucrative earnings in future employment for law firms defending the same companies he or she is regulating? Not surprisingly, this type of tenure does not lead to universal applause. The conservative editorial pages of the *Wall Street Journal* gave Mary Jo White a complimentary review of her term as SEC Chair upon her announced resignation. The Republican-led Congress also praised her tenure. Meanwhile, Democratic Senator Elizabeth Warren has been a strong critic since 2015, accusing Ms. White of failing to finalize certain Dodd–Frank rules, not curbing the use of waivers for companies violating securities laws, and allowing settlements with financial firms without admission of guilt.[48,49,50]

In all fairness, this criticism directed at Ms. White comes from a view that institutions like the SEC should protect everyone, small investors and large corporations alike, and have a regulatory and prosecutorial bias. This view is being put upside down by the new Trump administration, in favor of encouraging industry growth over any other concern. Just to take one example, the nomination of law firm Sullivan & Cromwell's Jay Clayton to lead the SEC reinforces this point. Mr. Clayton's career in advising Wall Street firms in financial transactions and settlements related to the 2008 financial crisis is a strong signal that the new SEC emphasis will be on loosening regulations, to help companies raise money more easily. The "revolving door" has never been so active.

Again and again, this complexity in our regulatory process fuels the perception that this is a very expensive way to regulate, and that this complexity helps the powerful, large corporations and very wealthy individuals with armies of lawyers at their beckoning. If some of these attorneys end up being at the head of regulatory bodies, so much the better. Given all this, is it a wonder that we need lawyers in our country for the simplest of business or personal transaction? Too many complex regulations and too few simple rules? We are the most law-intensive country on earth, with one lawyer for every 250 of our 321 million habitants. Obviously, Washington DC leads the charge, with a whopping one lawyer for every thirteen people there. But very large states like New York (a lawyer for every 115 habitants), Illinois (one for 204), and California (one for

238) are also very fertile grounds for all sorts of legal activities. Our complex web of business regulations and legislative apparatus means that we are fully entangled in the legal profession's tentacles. We may have become a country of lawyers, where everything is done by lawyers and for lawyers![51]

Most of our congress people and senators are lawyers; so are most state governors; our presidents too come from the legal profession: from Theodore Roosevelt onwards in the twentieth and twenty-first centuries, twelve of our twenty presidents, from the 26th to the 45th, attended law school or practiced law before moving into politics. The eight who did not are Herbert Hoover (mining engineering); Dwight Eisenhower (the military); John F. Kennedy (government and international affairs); Jimmy Carter (nuclear engineering); Ronald Reagan (liberal arts, acting); George H. W. Bush (economics); George W. Bush (business administration); and Donald Trump (real estate). Our main industrial competitors, China, Germany, and Japan, prefer to be led by engineers or scientists ... Four-term Chancellor Angela Merkel trained as a physicist in the former East Germany; in China, most members of the Communist Party's Politburo are engineers; the top government body of the Chinese State, the Standing Committee, with seven members under President Xi-Jiping (nine before him), has only had one non-engineer during the last twelve years. Japan's Shinzō Abe graduated in public administration and political science, and even studied public policy in the U.S. at the University of Southern California. But his first employer was not a law firm, or even a government agency, but Kobe Steel, a large industrial group.[52]

In the land of "free markets," piling on regulations and legislations by the tens of thousands of pages is the norm. Everyone complains about this, even attorneys turned politicians. But our legal system is more immune to change than any business, economic or political feature of our country. We will cut our health care costs in half before we reduce our fundamental dependency on the legal profession for all aspects of our daily lives. This, of course, does not help our overall economic competitiveness. In the words of Commerce Secretary and billionaire investor Wilbur Ross, a few years ago: "you can't have much of an economy if people are just flipping hamburgers, trading stocks and suing each other!"[53]

★　★　★　★　★

One citizen, one vote?

One cannot write about our laws and regulations, and how they are more complicated than those in most other democracies, without also talking about our electoral system. Mostly for historical reasons, foremost the admirable sustaining power of our Constitution – unique among established democracies – we have an electoral process in which complexity trumps (no pun intended) simple rules like "one citizen, one vote" in several elections. No, I am not talking here about the Electoral College, even though we have had two elections in this still nascent twenty-first century in which the winner of the national popular vote did not become president. We are the United States of America and the rules governing the Electoral College during a presidential election are actually quite simple. Without being a constitutional scholar, one can understand that our Founding Fathers intended all fifty states to have their say, so that "the tyranny of the majority" could not be imposed upon Middle America and its vast agricultural and mineral resources. In 1789, the "majority" referred to the large population centers of the Northeast, New York, Philadelphia, Boston etc. Today this would be a bi-coastal phenomenon. It is quite clear in the Constitution that we do not have a "one citizen, one vote" election at the level of the whole country, but rather one such election for each one of the fifty states. No, when I refer to the complexity of our electoral system, I am talking about the process of our presidential primaries.

For both the Democratic and Republican Parties, the primaries in a presidential campaign take place in all fifty states over a period of over six months. Although many such state primaries are based upon a "one registered person, one vote" rule, many others are not. Precinct caucuses, for example, involve groups of citizens gathering in locales where they can make speeches for their favored candidates, attempt to influence others present at the gathering, and eventually be counted as voters for one of the candidates competing for the nomination of their party. The percentage of the registered population voting in states that hold caucuses is typically much smaller than in states where the primary is based upon a popular vote count. The first contest in both the Democratic and Republican parties' nomination process has been the Iowa caucuses for a while. The first votes for the nomination of either party are cast in Iowa. There, a very small percentage of the state population will award the first win of the season for both parties' nomination race, and thus have an outsized influence on the national outcome because of the media attention surrounding the Iowa caucuses.

In the Democratic Party, beyond the caucuses and the disproportionate impact they allow a small number of electors to have, the "super delegates" represent the other major complexity in the primary process. Super delegates are delegates to the Democratic National Convention who are not pledged to any candidate competing in the party's nominating process. These super delegates made up almost 15% of all convention delegates in Philadelphia in August of 2016 (almost 20% in the 2008 Democratic National Convention). This means that, at least in theory, the super delegates could skew the Democratic nomination towards a candidate that would have significantly less than 50% of the pledged delegates awarded state-by-state by the voters in Democratic primaries and caucuses. Who are those super delegates? They fall into four categories:

1) Elected members of the Democratic National Committee (DNC). These in 2016 were the chairs and vice-chairs of each state and territorial Democratic Party; 212 national committee people elected to represent their states; top officials of the DNC and several auxiliary groups; and 75 at-large

members chosen by the DNC. In total, there were 437 DNC members who were super delegates at the Philadelphia Convention in 2016.

2) Democratic governors (21 at the Democratic Convention in 2016).
3) Democratic members of Congress (238 super delegates in 2016).
4) Distinguished party leaders, consisting of former presidents, vice presidents, congressional leaders, and DNC chairs (20 super delegates in 2016)

Complex, and not very democratic. So much so that during the hard-fought 2016 primary race between Hillary Clinton and Bernie Sanders, the Sanders camp vociferously argued that the DNC had encouraged the vast majority of super delegates to declare early for Ms. Clinton, making the Sanders campaign look like a long shot and discouraging potential voters. Even though in the end Hillary Clinton also won a majority of the pledged delegates (representing 85% of the total), both campaigns agreed to changes: the 2016 DNC Rules Committee adopted a super delegate reform package ahead of the 2016 Democratic Convention. Under the new rules, in future Democratic National Conventions roughly two-thirds of the super delegates will become bound to the results of the state-by-state caucuses and primaries, like pledged delegates. But a remaining one-third (members of Congress, governors, and distinguished party leaders) will remain unpledged and free to support the candidate of their choice.[54]

In the Republican Party, the 2016 nomination race was one for the ages. Candidate Trump transformed the contest into six months of extraordinary media entertainment. Who will forget the "Low energy Jeb"; "Little Marco"; and "Lying Ted?" However, Donald Trump also showed a unique political talent for enthusing Republican primary voters. He ran a brilliant and winning campaign, during which he never shied away from exposing arcane rules that "rigged the system." Thanks to the Trump megaphone, all the complexities and intricacies of quite a few Republican caucuses and primaries were explained. Rarely has the adage "sausage making is not pretty" depicted so well a political process long on complicated rules and short on democratic fairness.

In North Dakota, the Republican primary rules state that delegates selected to represent the state are allowed to vote for the candidate they prefer at the National Republican Convention, regardless of the results of the party's state convention. At that convention, taking place in Fargo, Republicans voted for twenty-five national delegates out of seventy-four nominated. The various campaigns tried to "spin" the vote in the most favorable way for them, even though no one really knew how the North Dakota Republican delegates would eventually vote at the National Convention. The Trump campaign had the backing of North Dakota's sole congressman, Kevin Cramer. Cramer lobbied the delegates as strongly as he could for Donald Trump and said his candidate would win the majority of the state delegates. On the other hand, Ted Cruz's campaign enjoyed a very strong on-the-ground presence in the state and used this presence to influence potential delegates. His campaign therefore boasted that eighteen of the twenty-five selected delegates were on a list of preferred candidates that the campaign had circulated, and Ted Cruz claimed the win as well. The John Kasich campaign also tweeted that in the end South Dakota delegates would vote for the Ohio governor at the National Republican Convention in Cleveland, Ohio. In the end, all three campaigns claimed to be winning in South Dakota, a tribute to the opacity of the delegate selection process in the state. Oh, I forgot: sixteen of the twenty-five delegates nominated were chosen from a list put together by Republican Party leaders in the state. So much for popular representation.[55]

But there was still some plurality in the Republican state contest in North Dakota. This was better than in Colorado, where one candidate took all the delegates. In Colorado, the Republican Party local leaders decided to scrap the caucuses and select delegates through congressional district meetings and a state convention instead. Ted Cruz worked the state party leadership thoroughly and ended up winning all the state's thirty-four delegates to the National Convention, at a series of seven congressional district meetings and at the state party convention in Colorado Springs one month later. Voting? There was none. Needless to stay, candidate Trump was not amused, and tweeted furiously: "How is it possible that the people of the great State of Colorado never got to vote in the Republican Primary? Great anger – totally unfair!" and "The people of Colorado had their vote taken away from them by phony politicians. Biggest story in politics. This will not be allowed!"[56,57]

In truth, these new rules that put the election of national delegates in the hands of party insiders and activists had been in place since February, several months before the state convention in Colorado Springs. But this favored the candidate with the strongest local organizational skills, Ted Cruz, as opposed to the best vote getter. The *Denver Post* had already protested, to no avail, back in February when the decision was made to select delegates by convention as opposed to caucuses:

> GOP leaders have never provided a satisfactory reason for foregoing a presidential preference poll, although party chairman Steve House suggested on radio at one point that too many Republicans would otherwise flock to their local caucus.
>
> Imagine that: party officials fearing that an interesting race might propel thousands of additional citizens to participate. But of course that might dilute the influence of elite and insiders. You can see why that could upset the faint-hearted.[58]

But Louisiana went one better: it awarded the most delegates to the candidate who had lost the popular vote in the state. Donald Trump beat Ted Cruz fair and square in the Louisiana primary, gathering almost 125,000 votes or 41.4%, versus Ted Cruz's 114,000 votes and 37.8%. In the hard fought Republican primary campaign, a win by 3.6 percentage points was a solid one. But did Trump really win? Not according to the number of delegates awarded to him. Apparently, when it came to pledged delegates, a 3.6% difference was not enough in Louisiana, and both Cruz and Trump got awarded ten delegates each. However,

Cruz's supporters were more active on the ground, and they scooped up five of the six Louisiana delegates representing the state on key committees intended to write the Republican National Convention's rules and platform, as written in the *Wall Street Journal* on March 24, 2016. Through a few more tweaks, the *Journal* estimated that Cruz could end up winning ten more Louisiana delegates than Trump. So the candidate losing the popular vote ended up with significantly more delegates . . . those are the rules, claimed the Cruz campaign. Rules that were obviously too opaque for even a top-flight candidate like Donald Trump to understand and act upon. Rules that also made a mockery of democracy.[59]

In what turned out to be one of the many firsts in the 2016 presidential campaign, a leading candidate, Donald Trump, used his formidable communications skills to lambast caucuses and the very voting process in his own party's primary. He experienced winning the popular vote and coming second or worse in number of delegates in several states and counties, and was not shy about protesting this. He was not shy either about protesting the unfairness of the primary he did not participate in, often saying publicly that the Democratic Party process was rigged against Bernie Sanders by the DNC and Hillary Clinton supporters.

Somehow, even though a vote in Wyoming counts statistically in terms of the Electoral College 3.6 times as much as the same vote in California, our creaky old system still works. Several states have twice as many Senators as their lone Representative to the House, but at least the Supreme Court did not have to decide the 2016 presidential election like in 2000. Our electoral rules manage to allow citizens to believe that their vote count . . . as long as the differences in actual votes counted are not smaller than the margin of error, or the built-in imprecision of our electoral process. Hillary Clinton won the 2016 popular vote by more than 2.8 million votes – she got 65.76 million votes vs. 62.92 million for her opponent. But the differences of over 100,000 votes in Florida and close to 50,000 votes in Pennsylvania, both in favor of Donald Trump, were clear and decisive enough to ensure that the Trump victory was not contestable – a far better outcome than in 2000, with Florida, "hanging chads" and the very divisive outcome they produced.

Our electoral process, despite its complexity and many imperfections, has stood the test of time vigorously. And it is likely to continue doing so for quite a while yet. Eventually, though, the simple appeal of the universal vote may erode its longevity. Which aspect of it is likely to succumb first to the sirens of change? The Republican primary process, and its fragmented, opaque state-by-state rules? It certainly came under fierce media attack during the first half of 2016, by no less than the winning candidate Donald Trump. But winners rarely initiate game rules changes. The Democratic primary process, and its super delegates? One close race, and the super delegates could indeed be consigned to the dustbin of history. The Electoral College? Given that the current polarization of the electorate makes any type of landslide very unlikely, any change there is hard to conceive in the short-term. The simplest way to abolish the impact of the Electoral College would be for states representing 270 or more electoral votes (at least half the total plus one) to commit to vote for the candidate having won the popular vote. This would be infinitely easier than creating a new amendment to the Constitution. But for this commitment to happen, all these states would have to have state legislatures and governors from the same party, quite a challenge. Just looking at the governor side of the equation, after the November 7, 2017 partial elections the fourteen most populous states of the union (CA, TX, FL, NY, IL, PA, OH, GA, NC, MI, NJ, VA, WA, and AZ, representing 64% of our population) have seven Democratic and seven Republican governors between them, a perfect split. It is a fair bet that our grandchildren will still be arguing about the faults and merits of our electoral system while marveling at its longevity.

★ ★ ★ ★ ★

Simple regulations, understandable by all

This very brief overview of our legal and regulatory system shows how much we have embraced complexity in devising the rules that govern us every day. One could say, in a tongue in cheek manner, that maximizing legal billing hours takes full precedence over any quest for simplicity. The pervasiveness of a complicated web of laws and regulations has completely taken over our society. But amidst this overabundance of legal activities, are they areas of our country that are actually under regulated? Areas where the public good might actually benefit from stricter legal rules? That would seem nearly impossible. Yet, the legal world that embraces us with so many rules may also be faulted for its absence in one important area: business concentration, or lack of effective competition in certain industries.

When I attended business school, one of the landmark cases discussed in the classroom was the break-up of the Bell System and AT&T following the 1982 judgment by Federal Judge Harold Greene. Greene's settlement-based decree split the former AT&T Bell System telephone monopoly into seven independent Regional Bell Operating Companies (RBOCs, also popularly known as "Baby Bells"), with AT&T continuing to be a provider of long distance telephone service. The RBOCs got also Yellow Pages and half of Bell Labs. Over time, things became challenging for AT&T: its attempt to enter the computer market failed, and it had to divest its equipment manufacturer Western Electric as well. In 2005, AT&T was absorbed by one of the Baby Bells, SBC Communications in the Southwest, which then took the name AT&T to form the present-day company. Over time, the Baby Bells consolidated rapidly. SBC itself had acquired Pacific Telesis in 1997; Southern New England Telecommunications in 1998; and Ameritech in 1999, becoming the largest telephone company in the country. The new AT&T also acquired BellSouth in 2007. Bell Atlantic merged with NYNEX in 1997 and then acquired GTE, a non-Bell company, in 2000 to create Verizon Communications. There were many other acquisitions in the sector in the 1990s and 2000s, creating ever-increasing levels of market concentration, principally at the local and regional level.[60]

Fast-forward to today; we have the oligopoly of Verizon (143 million subscribers); AT&T (133 million); T-Mobile U.S. (parent Deutsche Telekom, 69 million subscribers); and Sprint (60 million) controlling the all-important cell phone market. I use the word "oligopoly" because these players all have significant areas of regional dominance. In effect, the average user typically has to choose between two of these four carriers. Furthermore, these players are integrating vertically into content, for which there are many IP and copyright barriers to competition. Recently, AT&T entered into an $85 billion deal to acquire Time Warner. This deal is being challenged by the Justice Department on anti-trust grounds – too little, too late, and are there political motivations in this move as well? After all, we have already seen such a merger of a major communications distributor with a big content provider, when Comcast, the largest cable company in the country, acquired NBC Universal. Thirty-five years after the break-up of the AT&T Bell System, we are back to very similar levels of concentration that prevailed before Judge Greene's decree.[61]

This is by no means limited to telecommunications and programming content industries. Right at the beginning of the twentieth century, Presidents Teddy Roosevelt and Howard Taft used the 1890 Sherman Antitrust Act to break up monopolies in industries as diverse as chemicals; natural resources; railroads; and tobacco. In 1911, during the Taft presidency, the U.S. Supreme Court ruled in favor of the U.S. government and dissolved John D. Rockefeller's gigantic Standard Oil trust into thirty-four companies. The largest of them still carried on the name "Standard," such as Jersey Standard (which eventually became Exxon), and the Standard Oil companies of New York (Mobil), California (Chevron), Indiana (Amoco) and Ohio (both acquired by British Petroleum), etc. Today, after a series of mergers spanning decades, only two of these exist, Exxon Mobil and Chevron.

In a totally different industry, following a wave of mergers during the 1990s and 2000s, we essentially have three major national airlines, each one with huge dominance of key national airports. Try to book a non-American flight to or from Dallas–Fort Worth; or a non-Delta flight in Atlanta (the largest airport in the country); or a non-United one in Newark near New York. Not easy, right? And obviously any large airport dominance by a given airline leads to increased fares and reduced service levels. As a result, hundreds of small airports no longer have regular airline service; complaints about poor service and on-time performance abound; and fares keep going north, principally for any type of "captive" customer, i.e. one without much competing alternative. Each one of the mega mergers that helped create these three giant carriers also provided much customer inconvenience during the post-merger transition periods, with reservation systems malfunctions and other issues.

In health care, there have also been many mergers of insurance companies. The effect, combined with the lack of competition across state borders, is that most Americans, and the companies who provide them with health insurance, rarely have a meaningful choice between insurers. Some large states have one health insurer covering up to 80% of patients, and very few offer choices between more than two insurers. In agro-business, Monsanto dominates the market for genetically modified seeds and has increased its prices much faster than the rate of inflation. And there are many more examples of industries with quasi-monopolies, with adverse consequences on prices and service quality for customers.

In the relatively new technology world, many new companies are ipso facto monopolies through a combination of engineering and marketing genius, complex global supply chains, and very strong patent protection. Many leading voices in "tech" are also putting in check the long-held market philosophy that competition is the mother of all that is good. Their argument is essentially that monopolies can grow faster and bring a lot of innovation advantages to their customers if they do not have to worry about competition. U.S. authorities appear to be going along. Even though Microsoft was sued on anti-trust grounds by the U.S. government in the 1990s for bundling its Windows operating system with its Internet Explorer browser, since then the federal government has not sued any technology giant about excessive market power. New ideas and regulatory initiatives need to emerge in the face of the anti-trust challenges posed by the dominant giants of the technology world. Instead, legal actions against anti-competitive behavior appear to have been reduced to transatlantic power games. What do I mean by that? I mean that Google and Apple are being sued by the European Union, which also prevented the GE–Honeywell merger on anti-competition grounds. The E.U. may pursue similar cases against Amazon and Facebook. It is also planning to tax U.S. technology companies on the revenues they make in the various E.U. countries where they sell their products and services, as opposed to profits in their regional headquarters, like Luxembourg and Ireland. In turn, the U.S. government sues European companies. Not new technology giants, since there are none from Europe with the required reach, but for example Volkswagen on its emission tests cheating diesel engines. VW sold over ten million cars with these engines in Europe, versus about 500,000 here, but we were the ones to find the problem. Apparently, no one in Europe realized that these engines were equipped with software that would only activate the required anti-emissions systems when the engines were being tested for pollution control purposes. Such VW engines produced pollution way beyond legal norms for years before a West Virginia University testing lab discovered the cheating software. Some of the biggest fines leveled against banks in the U.S. were also against European banks, one each for the U.K., France, and Germany. The above cases involve fines well above $10 billion. We are no longer ruling on anti-competitive grounds; rather, we are attacking each other's national champions. The longest running example of this is the Airbus–Boeing duopoly: when the U.S. is not complaining about illegal Airbus government subsidies, the E.U. is suing Boeing for illegally benefiting from U.S. armed forces military contracts at inflated prices.

Throughout most of the twentieth century, a number of legal and regulatory processes were put in place to protect U.S. consumers against the power certain large companies had to raise prices excessively and curtail service levels. Ironically, this is one area where regulations have atrophied, and where the law is put into practice much less frequently today than it used to be. In many industries, there just does not appear to be a strong rationale for this – apart from the political power of the companies involved. After all, airlines, telecommunication, and chemical companies are not markedly different in terms of structure and networks than their railroads and oil company forebears. In technology, things are newer and in some ways more complex, principally in the area of intellectual property protection, as we saw when looking at proposed international trade deals. Innovation also tends to lead to new industry standards that can dominate competition for a while, but is this so different than the General Electric versus Westinghouse battles over 100 years ago? What appears to be the new norm today is that regional blocks have become much more relaxed about market power, as long as it emanates from their national champions. Anti-competitive behavior is still fought through legal actions, as long as the companies sued are from a country an ocean away. Laws and regulations have added one new twist of complexity in market concentration cases, becoming a pawn of global competition between regional blocks, such as the U.S. and the European market.

Our laws and regulations are extraordinarily complex. This complexity often gets in the way of effectiveness in curtailing undesirable individual or business behavior. Most rules in business have become so complicated that only sophisticated and expensive legal teams can understand them. Large corporations and wealthy individuals can take advantage of this to use the law to their advantage and profit. Many loopholes also exist, hidden or in plain sight, to be taken advantage of by those who have invested deeply in the understanding of the intricacies of our laws and regulations. The evolution over time of our economy, away from tangible, visible assets to intangibles such as intellectual property, opaque financial instruments, and complex business models has also made regulation much more of a challenge. For example, employment contracts, which used to be a page or two and a handshake for most people, are now dozens of pages long, with an abundance of IP and arbitration clauses even for low-paid employees.

The best illustration of this is the difficulties many cities around the world experience in regulating a myriad of companies exploiting similar business models in the "gig" or "sharing" economy. For instance, is Uber just a smart transportation company that has defined its drivers as "individual contractors" to avoid paying them regular health care and other benefits available to most employees, thus defining an ultra-low-cost business model associated with responsive service? Or does it represent the way of the future, where jobs are available in every shape or form and in an infinite variety of time increments? At the outset, Uber and similar "disrupters" like Airbnb offered the attractive premise of allowing individuals to monetize unused assets, such as their car (used only a fraction of the time for personal purposes) or house. In times of stagnating middle-class incomes, why not make a little additional money renting Junior's room, now that he is in college? Or drive the family car for a few more dollars in our spare time? At the margin this created mutually beneficial value and excellent services for plenty of new customers. It also allowed these unused assets to be more productive, arguably enhancing sustainability.

But when a phenomenon taking place "at the margin" becomes the new norm and starts affecting millions of working people, things suddenly look very different. Instead of incremental gains, we discover that millions are holding precarious jobs with neither long-term benefits nor social protection: this looks more like a return to a Dickensian society than a prosperous future for all. And how are cities, local governments and regulators supposed to respond? As of date, there are lots of lawsuits, some verdicts, immediately followed by appeals, but a clearer regulatory picture has yet to emerge in the "new" economy. It could very well be that by the time Berlin, London, New York, Paris, São Paulo, Shanghai, and Tokyo have some type of framework regulating employment conditions for Uber drivers, it will be a moot point because the drivers will have been replaced by driverless cars. New challenges will then emerge in the "brave new world" of robots.

However, when it comes to laws and regulations, we should not "throw the baby out with the bath water." Regulations are complicated because the underlying economy is much more complex as well, with much of what exchanges hands much less tangible than a few decades ago. The trading of derivatives represents a much larger share of "commerce" today than the sales of, say, locomotives. But regulations are still needed to prevent an explosion of business activities profitable to the few and carrying big risks for the many, as we saw in Chapter 4 on finance. Regulations are still needed to prevent lead poisoning, dangerously polluted air and water, or price gauging by monopolies. And in many areas, existing legislation and regulations, even if complex, have still managed to achieve their objectives: CAFE standards; Dodd–Frank; and the Affordable Care Act have all had a positive impact despite their complexity and travails.

What, then? The overarching objectives for our legislators should be to produce regulations that are both simple and understandable by all, and effective in solving issues created by all the complexities inherent to modern business. I would like to conclude this chapter by providing an example of such legislation, proposed by two men of extraordinary experience and wisdom: the Honorable George P. Shultz, former Secretary of Labor, Treasury, and State; and the late and much regretted Gary S. Becker, Professor at the University of Chicago and Economics Nobel Prize winner.

In his book, *Issues on My Mind: Strategies for the Future* (Hoover Institution Press, 2013), George Shultz reproduced in Appendix section 4 (pages 204–206) an article he had written with Gary Becker titled, "Why We Support a Revenue-Neutral Carbon Tax," which had first appeared on the April 7, 2013 edition of the *Wall Street Journal*. In this op-ed, written more than three years before a carbon tax first appeared on an election ballot in the U.S., Becker and Shultz stressed that "Americans like to compete on a level playing field . . . We think this idea should be applied to energy producers. They all should bear the full costs of the use of the energy they provide."

The authors went on to explain that full energy costs include not only exploration and production costs, but also the impact of pollution on human health. After recommending that energy subsidies should be eliminated, the academic and the statesman offered their solution:

> We propose a measure that could go a long way toward leveling the playing field: a revenue-neutral tax on carbon, a major pollutant. A carbon tax would encourage producers and consumers to shift toward energy sources that emit less carbon – such as toward gas-fired plants and away from coal-fired plants – and generate greater demand for electric and flex-fuel cars and less demand for conventional gasoline-powered cars.

Let's read about this proposed carbon tax and its underlying policies in more detail. In the same book, *Issues on My Mind: Strategies for the Future*, Shultz shared his views on the "Strategy for the Long Run" in energy policy (Chapter Four, "A Better Energy Future," pages 50 and 51):

> Here are my ideas for the policies that will capitalize on present opportunities for a better energy future – a future that bolsters our national security, helps our economy to flourish, and improves our environment.
>
> First, let's put in place sensible, clear standards and appropriate regulations so that fracking technology can proceed confidently. We will gain handsomely in terms of greater security of supply, lower and more stable prices, and movement toward greater reliance on natural gas, the most benign of fossil fuels. The United States will also attract manufacturing activity and jobs as use of this technology increases.
>
> Second, the roller-coaster history of energy policy suggests that greater availability of oil and natural gas will divert funding from the innovative activities now under way to seek cleaner alternatives to fossil fuels. The result would be a serious setback for the development of alternative forms of energy that can operate at scale and have a beneficial effect on our environment. It is imperative that we engage in a major political effort to produce substantial and sustained funding for energy research and development. I am confident that such support will be greater if the government leaves funding for commercial enterprises to the marketplace.
>
> Third, we should rearrange the policy mix so that different forms of energy can compete on a level playing field. For example, we should mandate that new cars with internal combustion engines have a flex-fuel feature so that alternative fuels can compete effectively for use in these vehicles.

Fourth, the cost of capital required to deploy an energy technology ought to be structured on the basis of a level playing field. Currently, coal, oil, and gas have access to low-cost private capital through master limited partnerships (MLPs). All forms of energy should have access in these financing developments.

Fifth, the playing field will be leveled only if each source of energy bears the full cost of its use, including its effect on the environment. The solution I advocate is a revenue-neutral carbon tax, and the most efficient way to impose this tax would be to collect it at the point of production. Revenue neutrality comes from distribution of the proceeds, which, of course, could be done in a great variety of ways. On the grounds of ease of visibility and application, I advocate for having the tax collection and distribution administered by the IRS or the Social Security Administration. The principle of transparency should be observed. Money collected should go into an identified fund and the amounts flowing in and out should be clearly visible. The Social Security Administration could make payments, identified as "Your carbon dividend," in equal amounts to each current recipient of Social Security or to everyone either paying in to the system or receiving benefits from it.

I have been conducting an energy experiment of my own since having solar panels installed on my house on the Stanford University campus several years ago. By now the savings from my lower electricity bills have exceeded the cost of those solar panels. And as I commute to work in my electric car, I am driving on sunshine that is plentiful – and free – in California.

In summary, the massive energy industry is entering a period of radical change and great opportunity. We need to think strategically about these potential changes and develop policies, research, and investments in order to take full advantage of the vast and promising prospects for a better energy future.[62]

7 A winning history of simple tools

A winning history of simple tools . . . starting with our Constitution

As amply described in the preceding chapters of this book, complexity reigns supreme in the U.S. today. However, this was not always so: well over two hundred years old (a record among democracies), our American Constitution is uniquely effective in its elegant simplicity, among other qualities. Because it did not attempt to spell out at great length every legal possibility and relied instead of the future wisdom of those who would interpret it, it has stood the test of times much better than all others. For instance, the French – who launched their first republic in 1789, almost two years after we proclaimed our Constitution – are on their fifth republic and have had no fewer than fifteen constitutions since the fall of the Bastille.[1] Our Constitution still stands proud and uncontested today because its authors wrote it in a clear and concise enough manner so that every citizen ("We the People") would understand it directly, without any need of help from constitutional scholars; because our brilliant founding fathers created well-balanced solutions to very complex issues such as separation of power between the executive, legislative, and judicial branches of government; and because it left a lot of details of day-to-day government to the states of the Union, focusing on the strong but limited powers of the federal government.

When our Constitution was written, we were a land and people full of promise, but the great powers of the time were still in Europe, foremost England and France. A little more than a century later, we started claiming our place as the leading nation of the world, a claim that was undisputed by the end of World War II. And the tools of this winning history throughout the nineteenth and twentieth centuries were all brutally effective in their simplicity of purpose. We did not invent the railway: but American railroads, a towering achievement of the nineteenth century, were helped by scale and a single-minded focus on keeping things simple to conquer as many miles of track and carry as many goods and people as possible. Thus, we pioneered universal automatic coupling to simplify train formation; freight cars were standardized and mounted on swiveling trucks to absorb tight curves and rugged terrain; boxcars were the same on the East Coast, the Midwest, the Rockies, or the Pacific Coast; and railroad companies used lengthy convoys to carry more freight on fewer traffic patterns. Our inventors, such as Alexander Bell, never lost sight of the need to develop their inventions at the scale of our country to be truly successful, and therefore had to create hardware that was simple enough to be reproduced thousands of times by thousands of different people. Many legendary U.S. inventors and early industrialists replaced cumbersome systems with beautiful new ones. Sometimes simplicity (even at the cost of lack of choice for consumers) allied itself to massive scale to bring new inventions to millions: this is why Henry Ford said about its popular Ford T and its buyers, "they can have it in any color, as long as it is black."

In many other instances, simplicity was what brought us necessary reliability. It was a German, Rudolf Diesel, who invented the diesel engine at the turn of the century. But it was General Motors, its Electro-Motive Division (EMD), and its two-stroke diesel prime mover model 567 that demonstrated it could be used in trains on a large scale to replace the then prevalent and well-performing steam locomotives. EMD engines started winning U.S. railroads in the late 1930s with their simplicity of use, reliability, limited maintenance, and ability to travel across large deserts without needing water every few hundred miles. By the late 1950s, there were hardly any steam locomotives left in the U.S., whereas they only disappeared from Germany and Europe in the mid-1970s.

In a much more dramatic theater, with life and death imperatives, the U.S. won WWII with a lot of relatively simple and rugged hardware: the M1 Garand service rifle; the Jeep; the GM truck, with its reliable 4.4 liter GMC 270 gasoline engine; the Bazooka; the Sherman M-4 tank; the Landing Craft; the Nylon Parachute; the DC3 and its military version C-47 "Skytrain" transport airplane; the Flying Fortress; and the Liberty ship. All were designed for mass production and were not over-engineered. There was no doubt that a German "Tiger" tank in perfect working order could defeat a U.S. Sherman tank, if it were only for its much superior cannon. But many Tigers were afflicted by mechanical problems and lay disabled in the fields of battle, whereas the Shermans would never quit and thus proved to be quite effective.

We also won the Cold War with the simple premise that free markets could provide superior outcomes to economies relying on cumbersome and eventually futile central plans.

Civil Rights, too, benefited from simple solutions such as busing. Busing students of color to schools that would become racially integrated changed the path of our own history.

And today, in many daily activities, most of us bring a straightforward and friendly ("What can I do to help you?") can-do attitude to service, something that the world still envies us for.

* * * * *

The elegant simplicity of our Constitution

Our Constitution articulates how the federal institutions of our national government, the executive, legislative, and judicial branches, should work. As such, it is the foundation that binds our country together. Without it, we would be only an aggregation of territories, a "Commonwealth of States," to borrow a term from our former colonial masters. Most constitutions in other democracies are several hundred pages long: ours, including all signatures and twenty-seven amendments, is less than twenty pages long in standard letterhead type. Without the amendments, it is half that; many amendments take only a single sentence. This is nothing short of miraculous and a tribute to the genius of its framers and our founding fathers. Contrast this with pieces of recent legislation, including some described earlier in this book, often addressing a single industry but taking hundreds if not thousands of pages, and even the most accomplished legislators of our age should feel embarrassed.[2,3]

Successful ventures have many fathers, and so does our Constitution, born on September 17, 1787 in Philadelphia. By most accounts, drafting credits go to John Adams, Thomas Jefferson, James Madison, and Thomas Paine, the first three of whom were, respectively, our second, third, and fourth presidents. Our first, George Washington, oversaw the Constitutional Convention that took place between May 5 and September 17, 1787 in Philadelphia. An ageing Benjamin Franklin participated in the drafting of the Constitution, and helped broker the compromises needed to ensure its promulgation. Our first Secretary of the Treasury, Alexander Hamilton, as a Federalist Party member and New York representative, is also mentioned as a strong contributor, mostly because of his authorship between 1787 and 1788 – with James Madison and John Jay – of the influential Federalist Papers.[4,5]

Who influenced the framers and had an impact on their ideas? Ancient Greece and Rome, the 1215 Magna Carta, the late seventeenth-century English Bill of Rights, and the Mayflower Compact all had influence. But it is the Age of Enlightenment of seventeenth-century England and France and its "Philosophes du Siècle des Lumières" that had the most impact on the authors of our Constitution.[6] This is not surprising, since most of our founding fathers had crossed the Atlantic several times and many of the early ideas underpinning the ideals of democracy had come from English and French writers. Most of our early settlers came from England, and France had been an essential ally in the War of Independence. A short list (our founding fathers were exceptionally well read) of these influential English and French thinkers would include René Descartes; Thomas Hobbes; John Locke; Montesquieu; Voltaire; the founder and editor of the "Encyclopédie" Denis Diderot; and Jean-Jacques Rousseau.

René Descartes ("Cogito, ergo sum" – "I think therefore I am") is the father of rationalism, or the use of reason, in seventeenth-century philosophy and natural sciences, best extoled in his *Discours de la Méthode*. Thomas Hobbes, in his famous book *Leviathan*, argued that because humans are so self-interested and self-centered, they need a strong leader and cannot rule themselves.

Montesquieu, Voltaire, and Rousseau promoted democracy, their ideas questioning the absolute monarchs reigning then in France and raising the revolutionary concept that only the People can have the right to be sovereign.[7]

Charles Secondat, Baron de Montesquieu, used subterfuges such as a couple of visitors from far away Persia (*Les Lettres Persanes*) to demonstrate the absurdity of absolute monarchy as a ruling system. He was the first to write – in his *De l'Esprit des Lois* – about separation of powers between the branches of government, one of the key features of the U.S. Constitution. Montesquieu's theory of the separation of powers between the executive, legislative, and judicial branches was based on the republican governments of ancient Rome and seventeenth-century British parliamentary monarchy. He further wrote that checks and balances should limit the power of each branch of government, so that no one dominates the others. This is an idea profoundly embedded in our Constitution – think of presidential vetoes; impeachments of a president by Congress; and the naming of Supreme Court Justices by the president, to be approved by the Senate.[8,9]

François-Marie Arouet, Voltaire, was famous for his intelligence, sarcasm, lack of scruples, and attacks on the powers in seventeenth-century France, the Catholic Church and the Bourbon absolute kings. In *Candide*, Voltaire used satire and a naïve hero to ridicule the "optimists," theologians, armies, and governments of his time. Rousseau's more transparent ideas about democracy (e.g. in *Du Contrat Social, ou Principes du Droit Politique*) had early applications in Switzerland – Rousseau lived in Geneva for much of his life. The opening line of Rousseau's *Social Contract* deserves to be quoted, even today: "Man is born free, and everywhere he is in chains." One fundamental belief Rousseau shared with Locke is that no individual should be forced to give up his natural rights to a king. John Locke may have been the strongest influencer of our founding fathers, with his writings on the use of reason to avoid tyranny, the rights of citizens to have their natural rights protected by the government, and how rulers derive their authority from the consent of those they govern. Locke's *Second Treatise of Government* and *Life, Liberty, and Property* had a strong influence on Thomas Jefferson, starting with his writing of the Declaration of Independence. Locke advocated freedom of thought, speech, and religion, but also for property to be the most important natural right. Government had to protect property and encourage commerce but otherwise tread "lightly." This was novel thinking at the time and is reflected in what we call today the "rule of law" prevalent in most democracies but not necessarily in other political regimes.[10,11,12]

Our Constitution does not articulate the specifics of agriculture, finance, manufacture, or commerce policy (the critical components of a seventeenth-century economy). It leaves this to the members of government, Congress, and the courts. Its beautiful simplicity is effective because it articulates fundamental principles without getting in undue transactional detail. It also derives force from its deliberate ambiguity. This ambiguity, resulting from the conciseness of its writing, makes our Constitution stronger because its principles are all-encompassing, not diluted by addressing narrow specifics.[13,14]

*   *   *   *   *

Local citizens' power as living cell of a democratic society – simple and effective

The heart of our Constitution is the premise, revolutionary for the eighteenth century, that local citizens grant both the federal and state governments their authority. These have no other legitimacy than that conferred by the People during democratic elections. The governments therefore work directly for the People, as opposed to being responsible for institutions, such as magistrates enforcing the law and police responsible for order. In the existing regimes of the eighteenth century, governments controlled the institutions that kept societies together, and through a series of cascading effects hopefully created some good for those at the bottom of the hierarchy, the "People." The novel and simple concept that governments worked for the citizens and were accountable to them was a direct application of Rousseau's and Locke's thinking, which at their time in the seventeenth century was considered quite utopian. The U.S. Constitution was the first application on a large scale of this concept in the eighteenth century. At the time, over a hundred years after Rousseau and Locke had written, the idea of local citizen's power was still considered to be workable only in tiny, homogeneous counties such as those found in Switzerland, where Rousseau helped his ideas take hold. To place citizens at the heart of any political regime was viewed as too "simple" and "naïve" to reflect the complexities of "modern" societies, with their territorial size, large populations, incessant wars, vast agricultural lands, and nascent industries. Any country of significance needed strong, pre-ordained hierarchies and centralized governments to be administrated effectively.

When in the early nineteenth century the U.S. democracy started to take hold and demonstrate lasting power as the country prospered and expanded dramatically in geographic reach as well as in population, many European voices still argued that America was unique. Therefore, its ideas on democracy were not applicable elsewhere. Unlike European countries, the U.S. enjoyed stable borders, with a turbulent but weak and poor southern neighbor in Mexico and a large, peaceful but quasi-unpopulated Canada in the north; the U.S. had been developed by a homogeneous immigrant population, which shared the same ideals for the most part; it benefited from the unique influence of the immigrant Puritan communities having settled in New England, with their formative experiences in self-government; and its gentry of large land owners in the southern provinces was used to lead and engage actively in the young nation's government.[15] Of course, the nineteenth century would prove this to be wrong, and as the U.S. prospered to become one of the world's great powers, our Constitution and government model proved adept to support the quick expansion of the country, with the number of states and territories growing continuously. Even the wars the U.S. engaged in, both foreign and civil, which were viewed as so unlikely by Europeans, did not derail our republic; the possibility of new amendments had given our Constitution the flexibility and adaptability it needed to withstand any turbulence of history.

In the meantime, in Europe, the local established political regimes experienced diverse fortunes. England and its constitutional monarchy prospered. Under the long reign of Queen Victoria, the country led the Industrial Revolution, acquired the world's largest empire, and became the undisputed hegemon, or "superpower," of the time. Across the channel, its neighbor and rival France experienced a wild political roller coaster throughout the nineteenth century: three republics; three constitutional kings; two emperors; and two revolutions. The first and second republics lasted only a few years and were followed by the first and second empires, respectively. Those two Napoleonic empires both started with coups. The first one, in 1804, led to the reign of larger than life Napoléon Bonaparte, in which France first conquered most of Europe and then ended up defeated at Waterloo in 1815. The second one, after the three-year-long second republic, put Louis Napoléon III on the throne in 1851. In 1870 the country suffered ignominious defeat in the 1870–1871 Franco–Prussian War and the loss of the Alsace–Lorraine eastern region. In between, there were two experiments with constitutional monarchies, interrupted respectively by the 1830 and 1848 revolutions. On the throne were two Bourbons – Louis XVIII from 1815 to his death in 1824, and Charles X from 1824 to 1830 – and one scion of the ancient d' Orleans royal family, Louis-Philippe, between 1830 and 1848. At last all this turmoil made way for the successful third republic, which lasted seventy years and well into the twentieth century. It won back Alsace–Lorraine after World War I, but not until General Pershing ("Lafayette, nous voila!") gave a decisive hand to the Franco–British armies. The third republic statesmen created most of the institutions of the modern French state, building upon many of Bonaparte's far-sighted administrative institutions and establishing the country as a pioneer of secular societies with complete separation of Church and State. Interestingly for such an effective regime, few of its leaders were well known. In 1920, the "President du Conseil," Paul Deschanel, fell out of his presidential train sleeping car through a large open window after falling asleep at night. He collected himself, found his way to the house of a railroad-crossing keeper, and told the guard on duty he was the president. The guard did not recognize him at all and called the police, leading to an incongruous incident that took hours to get resolved.

Back to the early nineteenth century and the young U.S. democracy. One of the European voices that described most coherently the genesis, characteristics, and successes of the American republic belonged to a French nobleman, Alexis de Tocqueville. Alexis Charles Henri Clérel, Vicomte de Tocqueville, born into a noble family with good connections in the Louis XVIII administration, was a magistrate in a courthouse in Versailles in his early 20s. He was bored with his job and disillusioned by the failed 1830 revolution as well as the ascension of Louis-Philippe to the throne. When offered a leave of absence and the possibility to travel to the U.S. to study American prisons, he jumped on the opportunity. He and his friend Gustave de Beaumont spent nine months in the U.S. between 1831 and 1832, and traveled extensively. They attended formal and well-informed dinners in New York, Boston, and Washington DC, visiting a few prisons as well. They reached Saginaw, then a frontier settlement in the Northern Territory of Michigan, and went down the Mississippi all the way to the formerly French city of New Orleans.[16,17] Thus was born the social and political two-tome book *De la démocratie en Amérique*, the first of which was completed and published by de Tocqueville in 1835.

★   ★   ★   ★   ★

De Tocqueville struck by the "equality of conditions" in America

The opening two sentences of the introduction to de Tocqueville's *De la démocratie en Amérique* read as follows (translation into English by the author of this book):

> Among the new aspects that caught my attention during my stay in the United States, none struck me more than the equality of conditions. I discovered with ease the prodigious influence this original state of things has on the advancement of society: it gives a determined direction to the public spirit, and shapes the laws; it gives new precepts to the governing class, and specific habits to those governed.[18]

The book starts with seven chapters dedicated respectively to a quick geographic description of North America; the origins or "starting point" of its Anglo-American population and its importance for the future; the "essentially democratic" social nature of the Anglo-Americans; the principle of the sovereignty of the People in America; the local state governments; the power of the judiciary in the United States and its political importance; and the judicial power of the legislative branch in America, compared to France and England. De Tocqueville then writes in chapter VIII about our federal Constitution, one of the salient parts of his first tome, and well worth some excerpts here.

First, de Tocqueville summarizes the Constitution and sets out the main challenge the framers faced: how to share federal power with the states so these could continue to address all their local government needs without undue interference from the Union – "an issue both complex and difficult to solve." De Tocqueville also writes that solving this problem allowed the federal government to be limited in scope and the Constitution to be concise:

> The attributes of the federal government were defined carefully, and it was said that everything that was not mentioned in these definitions belonged to the local State governments. This way the common rule was that of the State governments; the federal government was the exception . . . .
> . . . But since it was anticipated that, in practice, questions might arise about the specific limits of this government by exception, and because it would have been risky to leave the resolution of these questions to the

local courts controlled by the States themselves, a high federal court was created. This unique court had the responsibility to maintain the separation of powers established by the Constitution between the two (State and federal) rival governments.

In footnotes, de Tocqueville quotes the Federal Papers, reiterating that the powers delegated by the Constitution to the federal government are defined explicitly and are limited in number. The French visitor to the United States is clearly full of admiration for how the Constitution framed the separation of powers between the states and the federal government. This is highly understandable, since even today, we applaud our framers for creating a construction in which one could describe in very simple terms the role and responsibilities of our federal government. This very clear federal mission established a very strong yet lean central government for the Union, since it only had to focus on a few, well-delineated sets of activities.

De Tocqueville then describes how the Constitution defines a legislative body divided into two chambers, different not only in their elective representation, but also in the type of election, duration of terms, and prerogatives. This too was novel for an observer used to seeing the role of parliament through his knowledge of English constitutional monarchy. The way the executive branch of government was organized was also a source of wonder. Executive power in the Union was both dependent on the majority and strong enough to carry its constitutional responsibilities with a lot of freedom. Even though he personally was probably more inclined towards constitutional monarchies, de Tocqueville salutes the young republic in the section "Du Pouvoir Exécutif":

> Maintaining a republic created the demand that the executive power representative be submitted to the national will. The president is an elected magistrate. His honor, his assets, his freedom, his life depend constantly on how well the exercise of his power answers to the People. He is also not completely independent in exercising this power: the Senate monitors him in his relationships with foreign powers, as well as in his nomination of positions; so that he cannot corrupt nor be corrupted.

Following this description, the French nobleman writes at length, still in the chapter dedicated to the federal government, about the differences between a president in the Union and a constitutional king in France. The most important such difference is that a United States president can lead his country without his party having a majority in the chambers, something not possible in France:

> In America the president cannot prevent laws from being formulated; he cannot escape the obligation of upholding them. His sincere and zealous cooperation is no doubt useful, but not necessary to the good working of

the government. Everything he does that is essential is submitted directly or indirectly to the legislative branch; (in situations) where he is independent from it, he cannot do much. Therefore it is his weakness, and not his strength, that allows him to function when in opposition to the legislative power.

In Europe there must be agreement between the king and the Chambers, because there can be serious fights between the two (with damaging consequences). In America, agreement is not necessary because such fight is impossible.

With a lot of foresight, de Tocqueville believed that elective types of governments could become dangerous, in proportion to the extent of the prerogatives of the executive power. As such, the popular election of American presidents was free of such risks because of the clear limits to the executive power established by the Constitution. In the section "De l' Election du Président," he wrote:

> In America the president enjoys a relatively large influence on the activities of the State, but he does not direct them; the power lies primarily within the integrality of the national representation. Therefore to change political direction, it is the whole People who would have to change, and not just the president. Thus, in America, the principle that the head of the executive branch is elected does not create much harm to the stability of the government.

De Tocqueville also marveled at the presidential election process, the "two-step election" with popular vote combined with the state-by-state Electoral College, and how in some cases of deadlock the House of Representatives could be called upon to choose the president. In his book he went on to mention that after forty-four years of Constitution, twelve presidential elections had taken place peacefully in America, from George Washington to Andrew Jackson, including the two decided by the House: "the first time in 1801 during the election of Mr. Jefferson; and the second time in 1825, when Mr. Quincy Adams was appointed." From the perspective of late eighteenth- and early nineteenth-century France, this was quite admirable.

The next sections of this chapter on the United States Constitution describe the federal court system and extol the creation of the Supreme Court:

> When one considers the extension of the prerogatives of the Supreme Court, after having examined in detail its organization, one discovers that never was such immense judicial power established within any country (people). The Supreme Court is placed higher than any other known court, because of both the *nature* of its rights and *to whom* it can render justice.

De Tocqueville then contrasts favorably (again praising the framers) the federal Constitution with the State constitutions in existence:

> Two main dangers can become existential threats to democracies:
> The complete submission of the legislative power to the volitions of the electoral body.
> The concentration of all the other government powers within the legislative branch.
> The State legislators helped these dangers develop. The legislators of the Union (authors of the Constitution) did what they could to mitigate them.

But what makes de Tocqueville's review of our Constitution unique is the praise he lavishes on the American people. He writes several detailed sections on how the role of the People is what distinguishes our federal Constitution from all other federal constitutions. He goes on, writing that most people could not make such a federal system of government work, and describes what allowed the "Anglo-Americans" to adopt this system very successfully.[19] He concludes this lengthy chapter by describing the dangers European people would face if they adopted the American federal system of government and how in America, the Union is naturally protected by the nature of its borders from the main risk federated systems face, that of war.

> In America the Union governs not the States, but mere citizens. When it wants to levy a new tax, it does not reach out to the government of Massachusetts, but to every habitant of Massachusetts. Old federal governments faced populations; the one of the Union faces individuals. It does not borrow strength, because it has its own. It has its own administrators, tribunals, judges, lawyers and army . . .
> . . .When one analyses the United States Constitution, the most perfect of all known federal constitutions, one can be weary of the amount of knowledge and judgment it presumes for those it is supposed to rule . . . [But] I have almost never met anyone in America who could not discern with surprising ease the obligations borne out of laws passed by Congress, versus those coming from the laws of his State, and, after distinguishing between the general prerogatives of the Union and those addressed by the local legislature, could not indicate the point where the jurisdiction of federal courts started, and where that of State courts stopped.
> The United States Constitution looks like these beautiful creations of human industry that enrich and cover with glory those who invent them, but prove to be sterile in other hands . . .
> . . . We saw in this review of the United States Constitution, how Americans with great artistry brought the Union within the exclusive circle of federal governments, while at the same time giving it the appearance and to some extent the strength of a national government.

Concluding the first part of his first book (the last two lines), the French visitor salutes America: "This new world has an admirable position, which ensures that man has no other enemies than himself! All it takes to be happy and free is to want it."

De Tocqueville gushes with admiration for the United States Constitution and the system of federal and state governments, but above all for the American people. The clear thesis of the first tome of *De la Démocratie en Amérique* is that the People, these "Anglo-Americans," have, uniquely, made possible this wonderfully balanced and democratic system of government. He writes with a detachment that is admirable, never advocating that Europeans, and the French in particular, adopt an American style Constitution. To the contrary, he argues that this would likely result in grave failure – "do not try this at home," we would say today, as when seeing spectacular feats that cannot be emulated.[20]

The second tome of *De la Démocratie en Amérique* was only published in 1840, after a five-year hiatus. Unlike the first one, which met with resounding success, the second book was much criticized, and was understood only many decades later. One of the main reasons is that de Tocqueville focuses on a "mirror" image of his first tome, or how the American system of government and democracy affects the local citizens. Even though de Tocqueville duly condemned slavery and the plight of Native Americans in the second part of his first tome, writing about racial inequality in the long and concluding chapter X ("The three races in the United States"), the second book is much more pessimistic. The author is afraid that, coddled by the wonderful institutions created in the New World, citizens will live a narrow life within work, family and friends, and progressively stop participating in the necessary civic duties of the citizens of democracy. This concern is quite visionary, sadly validated by today's typical 55-60% voting participation of eligible voters in a U.S. presidential election, and much less in non-presidential elections. De Tocqueville had also visited England in between the writing of the two volumes and had been appalled by the conditions of the workforce during the Industrial Revolution. He wrote about the lack of humanity of the division of labor and the miserable proletariat, totally subjugated to a narrow and rich class of industrialists. He feared that this could evolve into the "toughest feudal regime the world ever had known." De Tocqueville was no Marxist; he was actually quite conservative, in a landed gentry kind of way. But clearly, he was shocked by the abuses of the Dickensian world, and this might have affected the happy optimism he brought back from America in 1832. This optimism is pervasive in his first tome and almost absent in the second. Today, though, his observations in the second book about the modern relationship between citizens and political power, necessarily more ambiguous than his praise of our Constitution, are widely recognized for their foresight.

★ ★ ★ ★ ★

The genius of our inventors and early industrialists

Leo Baekeland (father of the plastics industry); Alexander Graham Bell (inventor of the telephone); Edwin Binney (inventor of the crayon with Harold Smith); William Boeing (aviation pioneer and industrialist); Luther Burbank (pioneer of plant breeding); Robert Bunsen (practical laboratory burners); Andrew Carnegie (steel industrialist); Willis Carrier (inventor of the electric air conditioning); Chester Carlson (inventor of the xerographic process); Earle Dickenson (inventor of Band-Aids); Charles Drew (blood bank pioneer); Richard Drew (inventor of the adhesive tape); George Eastman (industrialist of photography, Eastman Kodak founder); Thomas Edison (inventor and electricity industrialist); Philo Farnsworth (inventor of the electronic television); Henry Ford (automobile industrialist and developer of the mass produced car); John Froelich (inventor of the tractor); Leo Gerstenzang (inventor of Q-tips); Robert Goddard (creator of the first liquid fuel rocket); Joel Houghton (inventor of the dishwasher); Ida Hyde (inventor of the intracellular microelectrode); Edwin Land (inventor of the Polaroid camera); Garrett Morgan (inventor of the gas mask); Samuel Morse (single-wire telegraph and Morse code); Ransom Olds (founder of Oldsmobile and automobile assembly line pioneer); Elisha Otis (industrialist and founder of the Otis Elevator Company); George Pullman (industrialist, railroad sleeping cars); James Ritty (inventor of the cash register); John D. Rockefeller (petroleum industry magnate and founder of Standard Oil); Henry Seeley (inventor of the electric iron); Christopher Sholes (modern keyboard and first typewriter); Leland Stanford (railroad industrialist and founder of Stanford University); Levi Strauss (industrialist and founder of Levi Strauss and Co.); Nikola Tesla (alternating current pioneer and inventor of the radio); John Thurman (inventor of the vacuum cleaner); Lewis Waterman (inventor of the fountain pen); George Westinghouse (inventor and electricity industrialist); Judson Whitcomb (inventor of the zipper); Orville and Wilbur Wright (inventors of the airplane): forty American pioneers, many of them immigrants, who made our daily lives so much easier. They led the most profound transformation the world has ever known. This transformation took place in a roughly fifty-year period spanning the late nineteenth and early twentieth centuries and allowed millions to escape the "solitary, poor, nasty, brutish, and short" life of man outside society described by Hobbes in *Leviathan*.[21,22]

The genius of our inventors and industrialists in that time was to bring comforts to the masses that before had only been available to those at the very top of society. No more back-breaking household chores: instead, dishwashers, vacuum cleaners and electric irons, as well as air conditioning; well-lit cities and homes for night comfort and safety; individual mobility through cars, with Ford selling 16.5 million "Tin-Lizzie" Model Ts to legions of middle-class buyers; cheaper materials (the invention of Bakelite in 1907, a cheap, easy to use and nonflammable plastic, led to the modern plastics industry); modern energy and transportation systems bringing new products to everyone everywhere; instant communications, first telegraph, then telephone, radio, and eventually television – all in most homes throughout the country; powerful industries such as steel, automobiles and railroads dominating working lives; production advancements helping workers escape the Dickensian conditions of the English Industrial Revolution. Even work in the fields became mechanized, tractors allowing farmers to plough vast acreages much more productively and in vastly improved comfort; basic health care reached homes, too, with hospitals benefiting from blood banks and new vaccines: yes, Alexander Fleming and Louis Pasteur were from Europe, but their inventions spread around the world very quickly; everyone wore jeans and ate Russet Burbank potatoes, which across the Atlantic helped Ireland deal with its famines; distances in our huge continent of a country mattered less and less: in the 1920s, a million and a half people per year traveled overnight in the comfort of their Pullman sleeping car; and air travel was not far away. Overall, middle-class life in mid-1920s America had improved faster in fifty years than in the previous three centuries – a true economic revolution that remains unmatched thus far.

While our inventors often led directly to the creation of huge new industries, such as Edison, Tesla, Westinghouse and many others in electricity, our early industrialists had a huge impact by making inventions from others scalable to an amazing degree. In doing so, they often had to make original fabrication and manufacturing processes simpler and more standardized, a frequent pre-cursor to mass production.

Steel became a lot cheaper in 1856 when Englishman Henry Bessemer invented the process named after him, in which molten iron is converted to steel by blowing air through it. Bessemer steel helped railroads replace their old rails made of iron with steel rails that were much stronger and thus allowed heavier and more powerful locomotives. Andrew Carnegie's innovation was to see early that in the Midwest all the elements existed to produce steel at a prodigious scale and low cost with the Bessemer process: iron ore (in Minnesota near Lake Superior); coal (in Appalachia); lakes and rivers to transport raw materials; and manpower. He centralized his industry around Pittsburgh, which became the steel capital of the planet. Carnegie decided to be the provider of steel to the massively growing railroad industry, and with him in the lead, U.S. steel production easily surpassed Britain's by the late 1880s, and grew to 60 million tons per year in 1920. By then U.S. railroads had reached a phenomenal 250,000 miles of track, much of it made of steel produced by Carnegie's steelworks, now using the open-hearth steelmaking process that had been developed in France and Germany.[23,24]

Similarly, even though Germany's Karl Benz is credited with the invention of the first practical automobile in 1885, it took first Ransom Olds (credited with the first assembly line for cars), then Henry Ford and his mass-produced Ford T to bring the automobile to millions of middle-class Americans. By 1927, Ford saw the fifteen millionth Model T roll out of his Highland Park assembly line in Michigan, and his dream of building a simple, standardized and very affordable car for the masses had become reality. Ford and his descendants became business "royalty," up to 1973, when the first oil shock destroyed the supremacy of American automakers.[25,26]

What do royals do? They joust with other royals. In the early 1960s, Henry Ford II, Ford's eldest grandson, responded with interest to approaches that Ferrari was for sale. However, it is likely that the canny Enzo Ferrari, the "Commendatore" from Modena, only wanted to obtain the funding he needed for his

racing teams. Promoting rumors of a sale of this national jewel to foreign inter-
ests would prompt intervention from the Italian government and its industrial
allies. This is exactly what happened, with Fiat taking a stake in Ferrari. Henry
Ford II was not amused, and he decided to challenge Ferrari on his turf: the
World Sportscars Championship and its flagship event, the 24 hours of Le Mans
in France. Even though an American, Phil Hill, had been crowned Formula 1
World Champion for the first time in 1961 (driving a Ferrari, of course), no
U.S. car manufacturer had yet competed seriously at the top level of auto racing. Ford put together a great team, headed by Carroll Shelby, with some of the
finest F1 and sportscars drivers of the time. He gave them a very large budget
and a mandate: defeat Ferrari at Le Mans.[27]

Ford got ready to compete in 1964. But Ferrari had not won eight Le Mans
victories between 1951 and 1963 by accident. So, in 1964 it won a hat trick at
the 8.4 miles track, its winning car driven by the Italo–French team of Nino
Vaccarella and Jean Guichet. The first Ford was fourth. The 1965 edition saw
the two factory teams annihilate themselves: limping to the finish line came
a private team's Ferrari, driven by Jochen Rindt of Austria and the American
Masten Gregory. Ironically, it was the U.S.-based North American Racing Team
that had entered the winning car. Two other privateer Ferraris followed, with
the first Shelby Ford only 8th.

For Ford, 1966 was "win or bust": he redoubled budget and efforts, using
the racing regulations to full effect with a new, 427-cubic-inch or 7-liter V8
engine, while Ferrari retained its 4.4-liter V12. This time it was a triumph,
with three Ford cars crossing the finish line in a 1–2–3 finish, headed by
New Zealanders and F1 racers Bruce McLaren and Chris Amon. Ford also
duly won the World Sportscars Championship that year. Ford and Ferrari
met one more time at Le Mans the following year, and for the first time it
was a real race. After 24 hours and 3270 miles, Dan Gurney and A.J. Foyt
took the checkered flag for their winning Ford MK IV, four laps or 34 miles
ahead of two Ferraris. They won at an amazing 136 mph average speed over
the 24 hours – the "circuit de la Sarthe" has a long straight where the Fords
reached 215mph, but also many curves and even a hairpin. With regulations
changing and the very large engines no longer allowed, Ferrari took a hiatus,
and Ford left its racing in the hands of the John Wyer Gulf team with 5-liter
Ford GT 40s. As underdogs against Porsche, the Ford cars still won in 1968
(Pedro Rodriguez and Lucien Bianchi) and 1969. That year, the Belgian F1
ace Jacky Ickx started last, as a protest against the unsafe but traditional "race
to your cars" start, and finished first by pipping Hans Herman's Porsche 908 at
the last corner, winning by about a football field's length, the shortest margin
in the history of the race.[28]

Trains, steel, and the automobile: none of them invented in America. In particular, the railway was the proudest achievement of Victorian England. But it
was in America that it reached its full potential under the forceful leadership of
railroad tycoons, helped by some very simple yet effective innovations.

"Their fathers' magic carpets made of steel"

On May 10, 1969, the Central Pacific (CP) and Union Pacific (UP) railroads met at Promontory Summit, Utah Territory, completing America's first transcontinental railway. Standing near Union Pacific's Vice-President Thomas Durant, Central Pacific's President Leland Stanford drove the golden spike to mark the landmark East–West connection. As soon as they were done, the telegraph operator signaled "Done!" and celebrations erupted all across the country, from San Francisco to Philadelphia; Salt Lake City to New Orleans; and Atlanta to Chicago, where a massive parade took place.[29]

The Central Pacific had been created in 1860, under the direction of the "Big Four": Leland Stanford (who became governor of California, and also founded Stanford University); Charles Crocker (an investor, then banker who had control of Wells Fargo at the time); Collis Huntington (in charge of the gigantic supply efforts needed, and who also helped develop other railroads such as Southern Pacific and Chesapeake & Ohio); and Mark Hopkins (Huntington's partner in a hardware and iron business, and treasurer of the CP). They had hired the brilliant engineer Theodore Judah – who died in 1863, long before the completion of his masterpiece – to design the challenging route that would cross the Sierra Nevada. It reached 7,200 ft. of elevation at Donner Pass, and Judah also had to convince the U.S. Congress of its feasibility. The Central Pacific was managed ruthlessly but very effectively, and made the Big Four among the richest men of the nineteenth century.

In contrast, the Union Pacific was founded in 1862 by a more anonymous set of businessmen, bankers, and politicians. But the UP was very close to Abraham Lincoln and Ulysses Grant, both fervent advocates of railroads as the main tool for the development of the U.S. and its vast undeveloped territorial riches. Lots of generals were involved with the Union Pacific: their first president was General John Dix. He was very respected but also already 65 by the creation of the UP. So, in the effort of going west as fast as possible, two men led the company's efforts: Durant and Union Pacific's well-known chief engineer, General Grenville Dodge. Dodge had resigned from the army in 1866 after a brilliant conduct in the Civil War that had brought him very close to Generals Sherman and Grant. Ulysses Grant had been elected president of the U.S. in 1868, so the UP had top-level political backing.

Which company would outrace the other, the CP going eastwards from Sacramento in California, or the UP westwards from Grinnell, Iowa? This was not exactly a mile-by-mile race, since the federal government had taken into account the more challenging mountainous terrain faced by the Central Pacific immediately west of Sacramento, in contrast to flatter terrain in Iowa and Nebraska. In his magnificent book *Nothing Like It in the World: The Men Who Built the Transcontinental Railroad: 1863–1869*, Stephen Ambrose writes that "Next to winning the Civil War and abolishing slavery, building the first transcontinental railroad, from Omaha, Nebraska, to Sacramento, California, was the greatest achievement of the American people in the nineteenth century." Ambrose does not take sides, although he mentions how the CP crews laid out over 10 miles of new track on April 28, 1869: "Never before done, never matched." He also writes about the UP's ongoing financial challenges. He attributes the success of the Big Four to their cohesion as a management team and the brilliance of their engineers, but also to their use of thousands of California-based Chinese laborers. The Chinese work ethic was very impressive, considering that they had been systematically discriminated against in California. They would work very hard and courageously – deaths were common in blasting rocks with dynamite to get through the Sierras – and would never get rowdy, unlike their Irish counterparts. The CP, its well-organized management, Irish labor supervision and Chinese labor, and the more political UP, its Irish supervisors and Irish workers, created the first modern transcontinental link, a full thirty-five years before the Trans-Siberian railroad was completed.

Compared to their European counterparts, U.S. railroads built in the mid-to late-nineteenth century had to face much more arduous terrain: for example, Tennessee Pass in Colorado is above 10,000 ft., and this for a (former) Class 1 railway, whereas no major railroad in Europe rises above 4,000 ft. European railroads, financed by governments as often as by private companies, used an abundance of bridges and tunnels to make routes as straight and as level as possible: for example, the St Petersburg to Moscow line was essentially a straight line over 400 miles long. U.S. railroads had narrower curves and often steep gradients as well, but they quickly carried more freight than their European counterparts. How so? Because they made systematic use of bogies, automatic coupling and standardized cars, which allowed them to run long convoys over enormous distances very efficiently.[30]

Four-wheel swivel trucks, or bogies, allowed railroad cars to ride more smoothly and tolerate tighter curves, while offering less traction resistance at equal weight. Therefore cars could be heavier and carry more freight or passengers for the same locomotive power. Bogies were nearly universal in U.S. railroads from 1840 onwards, whereas in Europe they only became common in the 1880s, and then for passenger cars only. Even today much of the freight carried in Europe is on two-axel freight cars. With heavier cars came the issue of coupling. Original couplings were of the link-and-pin variety, which required a railway worker to stand between two cars as they came together to manually connect the link with the coupler and insert the pin into the right position. This was – and is – dangerous work, and by 1870 over 11,000 railroad injuries had occurred in the U.S. because of coupling accidents. Then came the first automatic coupling, invented by the American Eli Janey in 1873 and known as the knuckle coupler. Janey's invention, alongside the compressed air brake invented by George Westinghouse in 1868, did more for railroad safety and economics than any other innovation of the time. Long trains of heavy cars could be coupled automatically and safely, and when in motion could be brought to a standstill automatically, without an army of brakemen on freight car rooftops. By 1900, coupling accidents in the country had declined by over 80%, and they are virtually non-existent today. The economics of U.S. railroads also improved dramatically with automatic coupling and air braking: tens of thousands of manual and dangerous railway jobs could be converted into much more productive ones.

Janey's and Westinghouse's inventions had a determinant impact in helping railroads grow in North America as fast as they did around the turn of the century.

These two inventions were also a tribute to simplicity and efficacy of design: Janey's automatic coupling is still used universally in North America today, as well as in many countries where a lot of freight is carried by rail, such as Australia, Brazil, China, India, and South Africa. In Europe, though, the emphasis of most railroads is on passenger transport; many freight cars there are still coupled by hand with buffer and chain couplings, barely changed from the original manual couplings of the early days of the railways. The Westinghouse compressed air brake, while more complicated in design, is the first significant application of "by default" safety: in other words, the system is designed so that as soon as a fault occurs, typically a leak in the air system, the drop in air pressure causes brakes to be applied automatically. This inherent automatic safety feature is why Westinghouse air brakes are still widely used in railroading today.

Standardized cars also allowed railways to grow and prosper in America. Most freight, for decades, was carried in four types of standard cars: box cars; flat cars; hoppers; and tank cars; all of course riding on bogies with Janey couplers and Westinghouse brakes. On the passenger front, one man did more than anyone else to improve comfort during very long journeys: George Pullman. After all, even after the first transcontinental was completed, it still took about a week to travel from San Francisco to New York. The Mason Manufacturing Company designed the first purpose design sleeping car in 1857, but George Pullman generalized its use. Pullman began in 1865 with its first luxurious sleeping car, named Pioneer. Then Pullman started offering railroads a variety of his sleeping car designs, most of which allowed the conversion of two facing seats for day travel into twin sleeping berths for the night, one above the other. In this ingenious system, the upper berth was stored inside a panel during day travel. Privacy was obtained through heavy curtains. The popular Pullman sleeping "open section," later supplemented by enclosed bedrooms, compartments, and even suites (called drawing rooms), allowed much of the traveling population to sleep in great comfort at night. Pullman grew in size enormously, becoming the largest "hotel" in the country, with over 40,000 guests per night by 1920. Pullman Inc.'s activities were divided into the Pullman Company, which owned and operated the sleeping cars leased by the railroads; and Pullman Standard Manufacturing, which built the cars. Pullman's monopoly was broken up in 1947, after an anti-trust verdict forced the company to sell the Pullman Company to a consortium of railroads. Pullman Standard operated until 1982, its last large order being for the double decker Superliner cars still used over long distances by Amtrak today.[31,32]

Buoyed by inventions and standardization that allowed simple and economic operation of very long trains over continental distances, how much did the U.S. railway industry grow in its first century of existence? Enormously: from 40 miles in 1830 to 254,000 miles in 1916; up to a record 2.1 million employees in 1920; up to fifty-nine billion passenger-miles in intercity travel in 1946, before the beginning of a long decline due to Americans' increased preference for air and automobile travel; and up to 746 billion ton-miles of freight at the height of the World War II effort in 1944. But unlike in passenger travel, U.S. railroads more than maintained their competitive position in freight, and by 1970 reached wartime levels of activity again, to then double and more within the next forty years.[33]

If large European countries, and leading Asian ones like Japan, China, and South Korea, all enjoy great train passenger travel with "bullet trains" reaching 200mph for millions of passengers every day, the U.S. is the land of freight railroading. North America's Class 1 railroad companies, including Burlington Northern Santa Fe (BNSF, owned by Warren Buffett); Canadian National; Canadian Pacific; CSX Transportation; Kansas City Southern; Norfolk Southern; and Union Pacific are by most measures the best railroad enterprises in the world, running record levels of freight over a still enormous 140,000 miles of track. These companies took full advantage of the 1980 Staggers Rail Act, a landmark and very successful deregulation effort, to expand their reach and share of U.S. transportation. Unlike in the airline and telecommunication industries, consolidation among railroads has not led to the attrition of competition, shippers having enough options to put market forces to work. In this post-1980 competitive environment, most of the historical advantages of railroads in North America listed above were put to contribution, with a couple of new, decisive moves.

First, an agreement with unions allowed railroads to eliminate the venerable end-of-train car named "caboose" and its operator. Having only two operators per train, the engineer and another one in the locomotive cab, led to significant labor savings. Second, the decision to re-gauge tunnels everywhere in the west and the Rockies to allow "double stacking" of standardized maritime containers changed the competitive game in favor of railroads. With state-of-the-art diesel locomotives bringing efficient power in distributed fashion all along the train length to keep coupler effort optimal, double-stacked container trains can bring trans-Pacific containers landing in West Coast ports to the Midwest and the Northeast within three to four days of travel. North American railroads have thus conquered a lot of Atlantic and Pacific Oceans' maritime traffic that used to transit via the Panama Canal, and have become an integral part of the elaborate supply-chain arrangements established by most of the U.S. industry.[34]

Statistics are superlative: U.S. railroads carried 1.85 trillion ton-miles in 2014, more than double the 1970 total. Even with the accelerated decline of the coal industry – without replacement for the railroads, since the substitute for coal, natural gas, can only be carried across land via pipelines – traffic in 2016 was still around 1.7 trillion ton-miles. Our Class 1 railroads are in rude financial and operating health, and provide plenty of highly skilled and well-paid industrial jobs that by definition cannot be outsourced. The U.S. is the only large developed economy where railroads carry about as high a share of freight as trucks. This is remarkable given the abundance of economical alternatives such as the world's largest domestic pipeline network, the interstate highway system, and great natural waterways like the Great Lakes and the Mississippi–Missouri river system. Railroads carried over 33% of all ton-miles transport in the U.S. in 2015 (35% in 2014).[35] In the twenty-eight European Union countries, the equivalent percentage was only 18% – 250 billion ton-miles, or a mere 14% of the American total.[36,37] In several large European countries, like Italy, the U.K., and Spain, the percentage of goods carried by train is in low single digits; even in raw materials hungry, heavy industry and manufacturing powerhouse China, which essentially only has highways as inland alternative to rail, railroads carried 1.7 trillion ton-miles in 2014, less than in the U.S. Roughly 50% of Chinese traffic is coal, which will probably not grow much further because of the massive environmental issue created by coal burning.[38,39,40]

The pioneers and early industrial giants of U.S. railroading built us a magnificent tool that is still the envy of the world today: where else can hundreds of ten-thousand ton trains travel reliably over 3,000 miles in as little as 72 hours, every day, across steep mountain ranges, in blizzard winter conditions, and through sweltering hot deserts?

This historical industrial triumph can also boast of a unique feature, its romantic appeal. A number of books, popular movies (*Some Like It Hot*; *North by Northwest*; *The Sting*), and songs have the railroad as a major theme. Even as their dominance in passenger transportation faded away with the advent of interstate highways and airplanes, railroads could still stir emotions, as in the folk song written by Steve Goodman: "City of New Orleans" became a major hit when recorded by Arlo Guthrie in 1972, and then by Willie Nelson in 1985.[41]

> Good morning America, how are you? . . .
> 	. . . I'm the train they call the City of New Orleans . . .
> 	. . . And the sons of Pullman porters and the sons of engineers
>
> 	Ride their fathers' magic carpets made of steel . . .

★ ★ ★ ★ ★

"The Greatest Generation" and the effective tools it used to win World War II

The U.S. led the Allied forces in defeating the Axis powers with the abnegation of its citizen soldiers and workers; its brilliant political and military leadership; and the relentless power of its war effort hardware.

Even though my purpose here is to write about the effectiveness of the brilliantly simple hardware that helped our military forces win World War II, it is impossible to talk about WWII without first mentioning our people. And even ahead of America's exceptional leaders during this existential period of the world's history, this time belongs to "the Greatest Generation." This is the term NBC's famed *Nightly News* 1982–2004 anchorman Tom Brokaw used to portray the generation of Americans who grew up during the deprivations of the Great Depression and then rose to the challenge of a global war of unprecedented ferocity. It is also the title of Mr. Brokaw's bestselling book, published in 1998. "It is, I believe, the greatest generation any society has ever produced," he wrote.[42]

Born in 1930, my father spent the WWII years in a small village in the "Massif Central," France's central mountains, and he would certainly agree. Very early in my childhood he would always tell me, in the context of his own childhood in the war: "As soon as we heard on the BBC that Pearl Harbor had occurred, we knew the U.S. would enter the war, and our nightmare would eventually end."

Tom Brokaw's main theme in *The Greatest Generation* is that the sacrifices made by our military and workers engaged in the war effort back home; their perseverance; and their resourcefulness all came from a childhood that saw the country's 1920s prosperity evaporate in the banking crash and the Great Depression that followed. During these times of misery for millions, American men and women acquired strong values and a keen sense of "personal responsibility, duty, honor and faith." They served across two oceans against fanatical foes; toiled in factories all over our land to make sure our soldiers always had the best equipment; and survived separation from family and friends for four long years because "it was the right thing to do." Many of these brave young people fighting on land, sea and air or working long shifts rose to the pinnacle of society, such as our 35th and 41st presidents John F. Kennedy and George H.W. Bush; long time senator and presidential candidate Bob Dole; or acclaimed chef and television personality Julia Child. But at the outset of America's entry to the war, they first responded to duty. Brokaw argues that this took precedence over any quest for fame or recognition.

Let's quote here the beautiful opening lines of his book:

THE TIME OF THEIR LIVES

"This generation of Americans has a rendezvous with destiny."
                                                    – Franklin Delano Roosevelt –

The year of my birth, 1940, was the fulcrum of America in the twentieth century, when the nation was balanced precariously between the darkness of the Great Depression on one side and the storms of war in Europe and the Pacific on the other. It was a critical time in the shaping of this nation and the world, equal to the revolution of 1776 and the perils of the Civil War. Once again the American people understood the magnitude of the challenge, the importance of an unparalleled national commitment, and, most of all, the certainty that only one resolution was acceptable. The nation turned to its young to carry the heaviest burden, to fight in enemy territory and to keep the home front secure and productive. These young men and women were eager for the assignment. They understood what was required of them, and they willingly volunteered for their duty.

The influence of America's young men and women of the WWII generation extended far in time beyond the war. Brokaw also builds a powerful case that this generation allowed subsequent generations, foremost the "Baby Boomer" generation starting in the 1950s, to enjoy untold material comfort and riches. The G.I. Bill allowed many servicemen and women to go to college, often for the first time in their families. In turn, they transmitted the value of higher education to their children. All working people had access to health care, a first in our history. The egalitarian ethos of war conditions lasted decades, throughout the Truman, Eisenhower, Kennedy, and Johnson presidencies. America helped war-devastated Europe rebuild itself with the far-sighted Marshall Plan, and also saw that Japan would be reconstructed as well. The U.S. also faced with determination frequent world crises, such as the emergence of communist USSR as the next major enemy; Mao Tse Tung's takeover of China; the Korean War; and the Berlin blockade, then wall. All these events contributed to a sense that we had to lead with both force and selflessness. During the next few decades, America would be the sole dominant economic power in the world, and also its moral compass.

One of my favorite movies of that era is *The Best Years of Our Lives*. In 1946, the film depicts the return to civilian life of three servicemen, in a fictional large Midwestern city. The equality of conditions and solidarity experienced during the war effort is illustrated by the three heroes' wartime rank, which stands opposite to their status in civilian society. Thus, the former drugstore soda fountain attendant became a decorated Air Force bomber captain, whereas the affluent bank loan officer was an Army sergeant; and the former high school quarterback spent the war enlisted on an aircraft carrier. Return to civilian life is at first easiest for the sergeant, who goes back to his loving wife and family in a comfortable apartment, and a well-respected senior job at the bank. It is much, much tougher for the other two: no matter how glorious a war they had, soda fountain attendants do not enjoy the same respect as Air Force officers; as for the former high school quarterback, he has a loving family and girlfriend, but came back from the war a cripple, with two mechanical hooks for hands. In the end, solidarity, friendship, and love all prevail: the girlfriend's love will not be stopped by hooks; the banker becomes an advocate for loans to former servicemen; and the captain finds a tough middle-class job with advancement prospects, managing a junkyard. He marries the banker's daughter, and together they will build a family strong on hard work and respect for life's most important values. *The Best Years of Our Lives* is thus a tribute to Americans rising to the challenges of the war and, victory achieved, using their resources and values to build a much better future for their families.

Just like during the war of independence, our leaders served us well during WWII. Our founding fathers Washington; Jefferson; Adams; Madison; Franklin; Hamilton; Jay; and so many others provided incomparably better leadership than mediocre English kings with their tired political aides and military officers. And our WWII success was in no small part due to an exceptional generation of leaders.

At the top, our only four-time elected president, and to many the greatest we ever had: Franklin Delano Roosevelt. Born of New York wealth and power, nephew of the already great Theodore Roosevelt, he was also crippled by polio even before being elected president for the first time in 1932. He faced the most terrifying challenges of our time, both at home and abroad, and to say he succeeded in tackling them is a massive understatement. To this day there is recognition around the world that if it weren't for FDR, many of us might have lived in a vastly different world, and not for the better. There is hardly any French town that does not have an "Avenue Franklin Roosevelt." My mother's family home in Sceaux, a suburb south of Paris, stands on Avenue Roosevelt. One of her brothers' family lives in Avenue Franklin Roosevelt, just off the Champs Elysees in the heart of Paris. Obviously, there is also a Metro station with the same name.

To this day, one can feel reassured just looking at photos and listening to radio transcripts of FDR's speeches. Confident, intelligent and charismatic leadership, all together. And his choice of lieutenants! Superlative also. In his great book about Roosevelt and his wartime commanders, Eric Larrabee writes about all the extraordinary men our president relied upon during WW II.[43]

Commander in Chief: Franklin Delano Roosevelt, His Lieutenants, and Their War is easily read, because it is a succession of very well captured mini-biographies of the wartime commanders who led Americans into combat on land, across oceans, and in the air. The book has ten chapters, one each for Roosevelt, the Commander in Chief; General George Marshall, Chief of Staff of the Army; Admiral Ernest King, Commander in Chief, U.S. Fleet, and Chief of Naval Operations; General Hap Arnold, Chief of the Air Corps; General Archer Vandergrift, Commander of the Marine Corps; General Douglas MacArthur, Commander of the Allied Forces in the Pacific; Admiral Chester Nimitz, Commander in Chief, U.S. Pacific Fleet; General Dwight Eisenhower, Supreme Commander of the Allied Forces in Europe; General Joseph Stilwell, Commander of U.S. Forces in Burma and China; and General Curtis LeMay, Commander of the Third Air Division and architect of the strategic bombing of Japan.

Larrabee argues that FDR lavished untold attention on his wartime commanders. The master politician, who changed vice-presidents frequently and left cabinet members in the dark on many topics, was not above intrigue and deception when dealing with government. But he treated his key military subordinates very differently. With them he listened carefully and made key personnel moves very deliberately. When he made decisions about the theater of war, he did not come back on them. He chose Marshall, MacArthur, and Nimitz personally; let King, Arnold, and principally Eisenhower grow on him;

and handed Vandergrift and LeMay critical missions tailored for their abilities. All had the president's full attention, and he played little or no politics with them, nor they with him. The only exception was Stilwell, whom Roosevelt sacrificed to appease Chinese Nationalist President Chiang Kai-shek, who was needed in the war against Japan.

Here are a few sentences on Roosevelt from *Commander in Chief*:

> President Roosevelt's style of national leadership was both warm and lofty, both intimate and distant. It has often been noted that by his voice alone, through the medium of radio, he was able to convince people in the millions that he was speaking directly to them (whether he would have done better or worse with television, the more mercilessly demanding medium, is a subject for reflection). For many of the young men and women in the armed services he was *the* President, the only one they had ever been consciously aware of. He was quite simply *there*, a part of their lives, and he exuded confidence, a sense of being on top of the world; the idea of anyone else being President did not naturally come to mind. That – and the buoyancy, the hat brim turned up in front, the cigarette holder at a jaunty angle – made him an unbeatable politician and a reassuring Commander in Chief. It contributed to the widespread sense of deprivation and emptiness when he died.

Roosevelt was an excellent judge of character, and the extraordinary quality of those who led WW II under him is unquestionable. Several of FDR's top lieutenants went on to continuing success and fame after he passed away. Marshall became Secretary of State and Secretary of Defense under President Harry Truman, and oversaw the famous aid plan to reconstruct post-war Europe that bears his name; Eisenhower became our 34th president, twice elected; and MacArthur a figure larger than life, first promoted to Supreme Allied Commander in the Pacific by the newly inaugurated Truman in 1945, then fired in disgrace during the Korean War in 1953 after he advocated using nuclear bombing against China.

On George Marshall, Larrabee writes about the excruciating choice Roosevelt had to make in denying Marshall the honor of leading the D-Day or "Overlord" 1944 Normandy landing:

> Various attempts were made to enlarge the European command sufficiently so that Marshall could suitably occupy it. The rationale of them was that he should command *all* of the war against Germany, including North Africa, the Middle East, and the advance up the Italian peninsula. But this was quite unacceptable to the British . . .
>
> . . . the ultimate choice was Roosevelt's, "one of the most difficult and one of the loneliest decisions he ever had to make," in Robert Sherwood's opinion, "against the almost impassioned advice of Hopkins and Stimson, against the known preferences of both Stalin and Churchill, against his own

proclaimed inclination to give George Marshall the historic opportunity which he so greatly desired and so amply deserved." It would be Eisenhower instead. Roosevelt's extenuating aside to Marshall has become part of the legend of them both:"I didn't feel I could sleep at ease with you out of Washington."

(Note: Robert Sherwood wrote a Pulitzer-winning portrait of Roosevelt and his longtime advisor Harry Hopkins; Henry Stimson, a Republican, was Roosevelt's Secretary of War.)

About King and Arnold:

The admiral's relationship with the President was one that King built, on the basis of blunt speech and demonstrated fitness for the job to be done ...

... [When] asked why he kept King in Washington, rather to let him go "up front" to take command, Roosevelt answered: "The President has to have close to him the shrewdest of strategists. Most critical decisions must be made here."

HAP ARNOLD WAS TAUGHT TO FLY by the Wright brothers ...

... He was a pioneer among pilots. He was the first to fly the U.S. mail. He piloted the first plane from which a rifle was fired ...

... Hap Arnold was unusual among the Allied leaders in his absolute open-ended attitude toward the future ...

... Unlike many air officers, even today, he was not wedded to the idea of manned flight as the *sine qua non* of air power.

About MacArthur and Nimitz:

MacArthur would sacrifice a great deal to ego, and Roosevelt saw to it that MacArthur's ego was gratified, that he was offered a number of roles pleasing to him even when they were those of an *enfant terrible*, not on the face of it pleasing to the President. MacArthur's endless teeterings on the edge of insubordination I suspect bothered Roosevelt not in the slightest. There was nothing in the general's character patterns that did not suit the President's need for an idol his enemies could worship at without damage to him, so long as MacArthur was fighting a war within the Roosevelt consensus.

TELL NIMITZ TO GET THE HELL OUT TO PEARL, and stay there til the war is won. Thus the President to the secretary of the Navy on December 16, 1941, with that war nine days old ...

...Admiral Nimitz stood high in the President's estimation. Earlier that year, Roosevelt had offered him the second-highest post in the Navy, that of Commander in Chief, U.S. Fleet, but Nimitz had asked to be excused, pleading that such an advance by a junior officer over so many officers his senior would generate ill will.

The chapter on Eisenhower is the longest of the book, and why not: one of history's most acclaimed military commanders, "Ike" was also the consummate diplomat and politician. Here is how Larrabee opens the chapter:

> DWIGHT DAVID EISENHOWER GRAVITATED UPWARD as naturally as a sunflower seeks the sun. Partly it was a matter of personality, of an open and transparent fairness that immediately impressed itself upon the observer, and of a disarming grin that alone – said his colleague Lieutenant General Sir Frederick Morgan – was "worth an army corps in any campaign." Partly it was a matter of prior preparation, of study and self-discipline over many a superficially empty year. But mostly it was a quality that Eisenhower himself went to some lengths to conceal from the public: intelligence, an intelligence as icy as has ever risen to the higher reaches of American Life.

Larrabee closes with one of Eisenhower's most famous messages. After the Germany surrender ceremony, senior American officers from the "Supreme Headquarters Allied Expeditionary Force" (SHAEF) gathered at their head-quarters in the city of Reims, France. This group, including the Supreme Allied Commander, had to compose a message of victory to send to the Combined Chiefs of Staff. This was history time! All participants proposed phrases more pompous and sonorous than the other. In vain. Nothing sounded right. Until the Supreme Commander himself thanked everyone and decided to send this simple text:

> The mission of this Allied force was fulfilled at 0241 local time, May 7th, 1945.

Now, about our WWII military hardware. There is a very questionable wartime joke that has Franklin Roosevelt and "Uncle Joe" Joseph Stalin comparing notes on how to clear a mine field: Roosevelt suggests sending a dozen of tanks remotely activated, whereas Stalin would clear the mines with 1,000 of his Red Army soldiers. Each man looks at each other, horrified at the waste implied by the other's method . . .

The war statistics did claim that the Soviet Union lost, heroically, over twenty million people during the war; and that the U.S. war production machine, once into full gear, all but guaranteed victory. Simply said, America produced a lot more military hardware during WWII than Japan and Germany combined, and then some.

A tremendous amount of planning and thinking went into the war production effort, a rare example of successful collaboration between private enterprise and the U.S. federal government's direct demands. The wartime procurement machine would determine how many units of any item would be needed, tender to private industry, and then assign the runs to one or more winners. One cardinal rule was that military hardware had to be effective, but also as simple to use and maintain as possible, with bulletproof reliability. And so, millions of rifles; hundreds of thousands of trucks; tens of thousands of airplanes; and thousands of ships came out of factories all over the land. Let's have a look at this hardware that won the war, brilliantly simple and effective. Each history buff will put forward a different list, but here are ten well known such "tools," mentioned in decreasing order of numbers produced: the M1 Garand rifle; the Jeep; the GM truck; the Bazooka; the Sherman tank; the Landing Craft; the Nylon Parachute; the C-47 "Skytrain" or "Dakota"; the Flying Fortress; and the Liberty Ship.

Eisenhower said after D-Day: "the Jeep, the Dakota, and the Landing Craft were the three tools that won the war." And General George Patton called the M1 "the greatest implement of battle ever devised."[44]

World War II was not a war of trenches, like World War I. Many of its most famous battles were heavily mechanized: the Battle of England (Spitfires against Messerschmitts and Focke Wulfs); Midway (aircraft carriers and their planes); El Alamein and Kursk (tanks). But the pivotal engagements of Stalingrad on the Russian front; Monte Cassino in Italy; and above all D-Day involved hundreds of thousands of soldiers having the determinant role, even if supported by thousands of aircrafts, artillery, and ships. Close city quarters involved fierce man-to-man combat; hills had to be taken; the cliffs overlooking Normandy beaches conquered; and so individual soldier equipment mattered. In this aspect the American GIs had a fundamental advantage, their **M1 semi-automatic Garand rifle**.[45]

After a decade of experiments, tests, re-designs, and more tests, the U.S. Army had selected in 1936 the M1 Garand, a semi-automatic rifle designed by a French-Canadian firearms expert, John Garand. Other armies around the world were still relying upon bolt-action rifles, such as the Lee-Enfield used by the British. These were inferior to Garand's M1, because a soldier had to take his hands off the trigger and get them all over the rifle to reload for a second shot, disrupting his firing position. In contrast, the M1 allowed eight straight shots of .30 caliber bullets with the soldier completely steady except for his trigger finger, and then an easy change of clip would allow another eight shots, and so forth. It is estimated that a typical GI could shoot 40–50 bullets per minute, almost one per second, far more than any bolt-action rifle could allow. In addition to this superior firepower, the M1 also gave rugged reliability and excellent accuracy – its sight line with a range knob allowed a simple bullet drop calibration for distance, and even a lateral one for wind. Above all, the M1 was simple enough that a GI could assemble and disassemble one in the field in less than a minute.

Easy to manufacture, easy to maintain, easy to clean and strip if dirty, the M1 worked extremely well in all sort of weather conditions, cold and humid in Europe; hot and dry in deserts; hot and humid in Pacific theaters. It was the

GI's best friend in battle, no matter how inclement the weather was, and again gave him an advantage over enemy infantrymen. It allowed most of our soldiers to shoot very accurately up to about 500 yards, and significantly beyond when adapted with a telescopic sight. Snipers also used it, in slightly modified configurations, and it would prove effective at up to 1,200 yards. The M1 Garand was used by GIs through the Korean War and was replaced in the U.S. Army by the M14 selective-fire rifle only in 1957. About six million M1s were produced between 1936 and 1957, the bulk during WWII by arsenals such as Springfield Armory, Winchester, Harrington and Richardson, International Harvester, and Rock Island.

Glorified by Eisenhower, the **Jeep** remains the iconic emblem of U.S. ground forces, from World War II to Korea and Vietnam. I cannot recall seeing any war movie involving the U.S. armed forces without Jeeps in the picture. They carry with nonchalant ease generals to the battlefront; hurried communication staff to field headquarters; resting officers to a country retreat; airmen off their bombers; sailors on permission with their girlfriends; and many civilians as well.[46]

In 1940 the U.S. Army and the War Procurement Effort asked American automotive manufacturers to submit designs to replace its existing light vehicles, which were getting quite old. The (tough) specifications were roughly to make an extremely reliable open vehicle lighter than 1,300 pounds (!); with a short, 75-inch wheelbase; four-wheel drive; a simple four-cylinder engine with more than 85 ft-lb of torque; and a payload of 660 pounds, corresponding to three GIs and their equipment. Out of over one hundred automotive manufacturers, only the American Bantam Car Company, Willys-Overland Motors, and Ford Motor Company bid. Bantam won the bid and delivered its first such model to the Army in September 1940. But Bantam did not have the production capacity required, so the War Department forwarded the company's blueprints to the much larger Ford and Willys, asking them to submit prototypes as well. By the end of 1940, the Army had prototypes from each manufacturer, all fairly similar to each other – not surprisingly. The specs were met, except for the unrealistic 1,300 pounds, with all three cars weighting a shade below a ton, or 2,160 pounds. Each company received an order for 1,500 units.

In early 1941, the War Department decided to standardize and Willys-Overland won a new contract for another 16,000 vehicles. But by the end of the year it became apparent that a single company could not keep up with the pace of demand, and so Ford was given a production contract as well, with the requirement that both it and Willys produce units with interchangeable parts. During WWII a total of 660,000 Jeeps were produced, with Willys – the company that ended up with the famous name and brand – accounting for 55% of the total, or about 360,000 units. Jeeps were exported to England and Russia under the Lend–Lease program, and after the war gradually became ubiquitous everywhere in the world. There were many versions, including amphibious ones; armed assault vehicles; artillery platforms; messenger services; field ambulances; VIP carriers; and more.

One possible origin for the word "Jeep," at least phonetically, is the designation for the Ford entries: "GP," "G" being for "Government," and "P" Ford's code for cars with an 80-inch wheelbase – their wheelbase a little longer than the original 75 inches. Another variant on the "GP" phonetics came from the military designation for "Government Purpose" or "General Purpose." In 1940, the Willys test driver Red Hausmann had heard soldiers calling his new vehicle a "Jeep." When asked about the Willys prototype during a demonstration at a 1941 press event in Washington DC that included a climb over the steps of the Capitol, he answered: "It's a Jeep." The name stuck and remains one of the most valuable automobile brands to this day.

Not to be out-quoted by Ike, Enzo Ferrari called the Jeep "America's only real sports car." Through twists of fate, both Ferrari and Jeep share the same corporate owner today, the Italian automotive giant Fiat. Fiat acquired Chrysler a few years ago, Chrysler having acquired Jeep earlier.

Often not far from the Jeeps were the ubiquitous **GM trucks**. Over 560,000 of the 2½-ton 6x6 (six-wheel drive) trucks were made during WWII, almost as many as Jeeps. Powering them was a very strong, simple and reliable gasoline engine, the 4.4-liter inline six-cylinder (i.e. naturally balanced, with few vibrations) 92-horsepower and 216 ft-lb of torque GMC 270. GM trucks, officially designated as GMC model CCKW350, came in an amazing number of variants, including a successful amphibious one, the most common being a troop or cargo carrier type. They were inexpensive and easy to build in very large numbers. Throughout the war, GM trucks ferried supplies, materials, gasoline, and all sorts of equipment to the front. If they ran out of gasoline because supply lines were stretched too thin, then troops stopped advancing, as the fast-moving Patton experienced with his army rushing to reach Germany only a few months after D-Day. With their bullet-proof reliability, off-road and all-weather capabilities, GM trucks played key roles in the North Africa, Italy, and Normandy landings and subsequent invasions. A lot of CCKW350s stayed in Europe to help with the reconstruction effort there; and they also made most of the U.S. trucks used in the Korean War.[47,48,49]

Which powerful U.S. infantry tool could be found equally frequently on a Jeep or a GM truck? The deadly effective bazooka. Some **bazooka** historians claim that Eisenhower actually listed four "tools of victory": the "Dakota" C-47 cargo plane and the Jeep, as we saw earlier; but also the simple bazooka, and for good measure the atomic bomb as well – the Landing Craft being omitted in this version of Ike's quote after D-Day.

The bazooka was simple and light enough to be used by a couple of soldiers, and its destructive power was awesome: it could destroy or at least disable an enemy tank; demolish a bunker; and open a large hole in any building or fortification. Rocket launchers were nothing new in 1941 when the U.S. went to war. The thirteenth-century Chinese could fire rockets; and Robert Goddard, the American inventor of the liquid-fuel rocket, had developed a workable prototype for the U.S. Army in 1918, at the end of WW I. No further progress had occurred in this area after that. But in 1941 U.S. military leaders had seen how the German Wehrmacht had used their panzer divisions to great impact during their invasions of France and Russia, and they knew they needed a weapon to counteract them.[50,51]

The bazooka came out of two innovations. First, two U.S. Army ordnance officers, Captain Leslie Skinner and Lieutenant Edward Uhl, helped develop shaped-charge grenades that could pierce tank armor. But these very powerful grenades were too heavy for the regular GI Joes. Then Uhl had the idea of using a small tube to launch the grenade, with a rocket added to it for propulsion. The result, in early 1942, was the most effective anti-tank weapon to date: the bazooka, officially called "Launcher, Rocket, 2.36 inch, Anti-Tank, M-1." It was a simple and lethal weapon that could be used by a couple of GIs acting as a team, one holding the tube, the other loading the shaped-charge and igniting it for launch. The M-1 weighed only about thirteen pounds, compared for example to the nine pounds of a M1 Garand rifle.

Early models could be unreliable, though, with significant risks for the GIs using them: charges could get stuck in the tube, exploding at the GIs instead of the intended target; the battery-powered ignition system could be problematic in humid conditions, leading to premature firings; and casualties were common. But improvements were made in a heavily modified M-9 version, including smaller but more powerful charges. These would not get stuck in the tube and could pierce five-inch armor, enough to destroy tanks at up to 300 yards. In reality, to hit a tank at its most vulnerable spot, the turret, a bazooka would need to be held at much closer range, 30 to 50 yards. This is why Patton described the weapon as a defensive tool, the last resort protection for the GI against advancing enemy tanks. About 480,000 bazookas were manufactured during the war, and they continued to be used through the Vietnam War, over thirty years later. Today the American soldier has a much more sophisticated light anti-tank rocket weapon, the M-72, but simple rocket-propelled grenades (originally the Russian "cousin" of the bazooka) are widely in use, often and most unfortunately in the hands of Jihadists in the Middle East.

Just like for the Jeep, there is some uncertainty about the origin of the term bazooka. One story says that this unusual looking weapon – what device can appear more innocent than a tube? – appeared to military personnel more like a music instrument than a tool of war. Popular comedian Bob Burns was famous at the time for blowing a tubular noisemaker, which his audience took to call "bazooka," Dutch slang for "loudmouth." And the name for Burns' noise making contraption stuck.

What about our tanks? Well, we had the Sherman. **The Sherman M-4 tank**, designed throughout 1941 and mass-produced from 1942 onward (over 49,000 made), turned out to be pretty much what the Allied forces needed around the globe. Before it, all the U.S. had to offer to the British on the Lend-Lease program was a very imperfect M-3 Lee/Grant tank, with a gun-turret assembly that was inferior to both German and Russian designs, and limited armor protection. The Sherman M-4, with its three-inch armor, a powerful engine and a well-functioning rotating turret with a 75mm gun, arrived in time to help Montgomery defeat Rommel at El Alamein. Shermans spearheaded Allied efforts in North Africa and most of Europe, but also throughout the theaters of the Pacific war. They evolved through countless derivatives, with evolving armor, engines, and guns. The M-4 started production early in 1942, with a powerful air-cooled, nine-cylinder radial aircraft engine made by Continental. But it then also used engines made by GM (a diesel version); Ford; Chrysler; and Caterpillar, all developing between 400 and 500 horsepower, giving Shermans a very good 30 mph top speed.

Later in the war, a more powerful 105mm cannon replaced the outclassed 75mm gun. With excellent machine guns as well, the Sherman was very versatile, easy to maneuver around enemy tanks, and compact enough that it could engage in urban warfare through narrow streets. The crew of five could also be trained in its operation very quickly, since attention had been given to ease of operation as well. All of this made Shermans long-lasting. After confronting German Panzer and Tiger tanks in WWII, they faced Russian T-34s (also mass-produced, with over 50,000 made) in the 1950–1953 Korean War. The latest Sherman derivative, called the "Easy Eight," saw action in Korea, Vietnam, and even in the Israeli–Arab Wars of 1967 and 1973.[52]

Above all, the Sherman M-4 was successful because it was designed from the get go to be a mass-produced tool of war. And mass production demanded simplicity. So, the M-4 was simple to build; easy to maintain; simple to operate; and very sturdy and reliable. Fast and well armed, it could serve everywhere: just like the M1 rifle, the Jeep and the GM truck, the Sherman's simplicity made it an all-round armored weapon, the nearest thing to a universal tank. Even when compared to the Russian T-34, its great Cold War rival, the Sherman had a much simpler and more reliable engine, was more maneuverable, and possibly easier to use. This does not mean the Sherman was perfect – far from it. It suffered from the number of compromises that had to be made to achieve its simplicity of production. For example, against the German Tigers late in the war, the Sherman suffered from its lighter armor and less powerful gun. So a Tiger, one on one and in ideal conditions, would always defeat a Sherman. But ideal conditions are rare in the battlefield. Slower, difficult to operate and maneuver, and above all difficult to maintain, Tigers were often disabled by mechanical issues. Most of the time, they would stand, a bit like a non-movable fortress, and eventually be defeated by a swarm of more agile Shermans. Numbers helped here, too, since Shermans always outnumbered their enemy tanks. Patton remarked that it was the ease of maintenance and reliability of the M-4 that made it the superior tank in combat. And it is also said that Eisenhower got the idea of his U.S. Interstate Highway program by watching Shermans barrel down the German autobahns at 30 mph.[53,54,55]

But before Eisenhower could enjoy the sight of Patton or Bradley's Shermans racing through Germany, his Allied troops had to land. Even before D-Day, amphibious landings had proven crucial to Allied victories in North Africa, Italy, and many Pacific islands. This is why the **landing craft, vehicle, personnel (LCVP)** or Higgins boat was one of Ike's favorite tools of war. Higgins boats were based upon barge-like boats used in swamps and shallow waters, and could carry a platoon or thirty-six men to shore. During WWII, 20,000 such LCVPs were built. Simple and sturdy, they did the job well, and their bow ramp allowed easy exit of the troops they ferried, so they could start charging under heavy enemy fire to gain beach toeholds.

Moving to the air, the **nylon parachute** also played an important role in WWII. It provided some measure of safety for Air Force pilots and crews but was also very effectively used as an offensive tool. For example, many parachutists were deployed in advance of D-Day and landed in Normandy just before the invasion from the sea. Parachutes were also widely used in procuring weapons and supplies for friendly partisan forces fighting in enemy-occupied territory.

The Americans did not invent the parachute – far from it. Historians give the paternity of the first design for a parachute to Leonardo da Vinci, in 1495. In the late eighteenth century, two Frenchmen, Louis-Sebastien Lenormand and J.P. Blanchard tested parachutes made out of silk instead of a rigid frame. André Jacques Garnerin made several parachute jumps from hot air balloons starting in 1797. Parachuting continued to evolve during the nineteenth century and the beginning of the twentieth, but the basic design, using expensive silk – produced mostly in Japan – had been settled before WWII. Just before the war, an American inventor introduced a design to improve steering ability in the air, helping landings to be more accurate. But what made the difference in WWII was the landmark American invention of a revolutionary material, nylon.[56]

A Harvard-trained scientist, Wallace Carothers, who had helped invent synthetic rubber in the 1920s, became world known for his work heading a secret DuPont de Nemours program that led to the invention of a chemical fiber code named "Fiber 66," which the world discovered under the name "nylon." Nylon, introduced by DuPont at the 1939 New York World's Fair, transformed the company into one of the largest chemical groups in the world. Nylon was marketed by DuPont as a silk substitute and gained wide acceptance at the outset of WWII when Japan suspended its silk exports to the U.S. Initially, nylon was used in clothes and apparel such as stockings. With the focus of production turning to the War Effort, nylon use moved to military applications, such as parachutes for the seven Allied airborne divisions and their 60,000 men. Nylon being much cheaper than silk, and more straightforward to use, it made mass production of the much-needed parachutes a much easier proposition.[57]

And who carried the airborne parachutists for their jumps? Another one of Ike's favorite tools of war, the military version of the popular DC-3, the **C-47 twin engine airplane**, nicknamed **"Dakota"** by the British and **"Skytrain"** by our troops. The C-47 owed its success in WWII to its simplicity of design, solidity of construction, and ease of operation and maintenance. Two 1,200 horsepower 14-cylinder radial piston Pratt and Whitney engines, a very sturdy fuselage, 1,600 miles of range, with a maximum speed of 200 knots at 24,000 ft. And the fundamental ability to land on very short fields. This was perfect for the needs of the U.S. and its allies during WWII. As a result, 10,174 C-47s were made, a record for a transport airplane that still holds today – even Boeing 737s have not been made in such numbers. The "Skytrain" owed its origin to the popular DC-3, which ironically had started its career in 1936 with American and United Airlines as the luxurious "Skysleeper." In coast-to-coast flights, fourteen pampered passengers would sit on plush seats that could be folded in pairs to form seven berths for the night, with seven more folded down from the cabin ceiling, Pullman sleeping car style. In photos of the time one can spot, above the regular windows, the very small skylights bringing light to the upper berths, again just like in the open section of a streamlined sleeping car of the era.[58,59]

"Skytrains" typically ferried twenty-seven people in spartan war conditions, everywhere. Their exploits became the stuff of legend, whether they were landing in muddy fields in the jungles of Guadalcanal, New Guinea, or Burma; flying the dangerous India to China route; or transporting officers across the Pacific or North Atlantic. Most of them flew for the U.S. Armed Forces, but 2,000 of them went to the British Royal Air Force (where they were called "Dakotas") through the Lend–Lease program. Later, others were sold to the Soviet Air Force and to Japan as well after the war had ended. During the Cold War, C-47s played a vital role transporting cargo in the 1948–1949 Berlin Airlift, ensuring supplies reached West Berlin amidst Soviet opposition. Skytrains also participated in the Vietnam War between 1955 and 1975, in some cases being used as "gunships" with large caliber machine guns firing from their rear doors. C-47s flew forever! I remember flying in one during the early 80s to reach oil fields in the middle of Colombia. Lateral benches, handles to hang on to during turbulences, and a rough landing on a very short field indeed.[60]

Built in even larger numbers than the C-47s, **Flying Fortresses** played a very different role, that of the U.S. Air Force strategic bomber of choice in Europe. Just like the C-47, though, the B-17 "Flying Fortress" was almost indestructible. "Almost" is the operative word, though, because unlike the unarmed Skytrains, B-17s flew into danger every time they took off. The combination of German fighter airplanes and the "flak," powerful ground anti-airplane guns, took a heavy toll. One of my neighbors in San Francisco, H. Michael Chase, was a U.S. Air Force Colonel who had flown B-17s during WWII. He contrasted the recruitment of Air Force crews for the bombers to that of pilots of fighter airplanes:

> The fighter pilots were daredevils: brilliant, brave and individualistic. For us, the main quality had to be steadiness: we flew in "boxes" of literally 100 bombers, 10 by 10 in a giant "square" in the sky. And so when we were shot at, which was pretty much a constant thing as soon as we reached Germany, we had to take it, could not evade anything. Because if we yanked the airplane from its position to evade fire, most likely we would hit another bomber of ours, so close we flew together.

Nerves of steel, indeed. Michael also said that after twenty-five missions, a bomber crew's "statistic odds of survival" essentially dropped to zero. This despite the B-17's legendary ability to continue to fly and land back in England after taking brutal poundings over the Continent. It was common for them to arrive back home with one or two engines dead, or on fire; casualties among the crew; and an assortment of holes in the fuselage caused by flak or enemy fighters.[61,62]

The first four-engine B-17 flew in 1935, taking off from Boeing Field in Seattle. It had so many .30 caliber machine guns – nine – that it was promptly called "Flying Fortress," a name trademarked by Boeing. The B-17 was a modern, low wing airplane with a real flight deck, navigator and crew quarters, but above all carried a very respectable 4,000-pound bomb load. It was designed to fly at high elevations from the start, with the distinctive large tail for stability during high-altitude bombing raids. This enabled the U.S. Air Force crews to conduct relatively precise daylight bombing raids over Germany, in contrast with the preferred Royal Air Force strategy of flying its Lancaster bombers at low elevation, but during the night. During WWII 12,730 B-17s were built, and they dropped nearly a million tons of bombs over Europe. They also flew missions over North Africa, the Middle East, and all over the Pacific.

In the war against Japan, the U.S. Air Force soon deployed an even more formidable aircraft, the B-29, to fly over the vast expanse of the Pacific and carry heavier bomb loads. The Boeing B-29 "Super fortress" met an amazing set of specs issued by the Air Corps, capable of delivering 20,000 pounds of bombs to a distance of up to 2,700 miles, with a cruising speed of 400 mph. The 4,000 B-29 program became the most expensive one of the war, costlier even than the Manhattan Project. The B-29s were extremely effective and pretty much halted Japan's industrial production, bringing the country to its knees even before Hiroshima and Nagasaki – which involved B-29s as well. Dominant in the Pacific, without peer during WWII, the B-29 went on to fight in the Korean War before being supplanted by jet engine bombers.

Not everything could be carried by air, though. After FDR got his Lend–Lease policy with Britain approved by Congress in March of 1941, he needed lots of cargo ships to ferry millions of tons of food, oil, military equipment, and other supplies to England, the Soviet Union, China, and other Allied countries. This is where **Liberty ships** came into play. Like so many industrial age inventions, the Liberty ship was initially a British concept, but it was in the U.S. that its design got adapted for simple and low-cost construction, enabling masspro-duction. One of the key innovative features in the construction of Liberty ships was the use of welding instead of rivets, the prior standard shipbuilding technique. The 14,000-ton ships were constructed of sections welded together, allowing the eighteen American shipyards involved to deliver them in record time. Between 1941 and 1945, 2,710 Liberty ships were built . . . that is a lot of ships! More than any other type of maritime boat in history. This was necessary, since over 50 million tons of various materials and supplies were delivered to England alone during WWII; 17.5 million to the Soviet Union; and nearly as much to other Allied countries. This despite marauding German U-boats that sank a lot of ships before the English broke their codes with "Enigma" and crippled the Axis submarine effort. Liberty ships were not devoid of faults. Some of them were built so quickly that they managed to sink without any German help – three of them at least broke in half without warning. This was due to cracked hulls and decks, most likely caused by inexperienced workers using the new welding process to build ships in great hurry. However, there is a reason that so many of them are preserved today, including near my home, at the Alameda port in Oakland and also in the Sacramento River delta. The Liberty ship came to represent what Roosevelt called the "Arsenal of Democracy," the enormous U.S. industrial wartime production that eventually won the war.[63]

What is truly amazing in this winning U.S. WWII production effort is how so many brilliant minds from all sectors of society – business; government; military; academia; research; civil – all got together with the overarching goal of producing as much of the right equipment as quickly as possible. This unique collaboration led to extraordinary designs and fabulous industrial outputs. Simplicity; ease of production, operation and maintenance; and effectiveness in the battlefield were not only pursued, but always achieved. No sector of society or group of individuals sought to take advantage of the urgent and dangerous situation at hand to pull in massive profits for themselves. Tell that to some of today's yahoos in the drug industry we saw earlier in this book . . . No, pretty much everyone in America took to heart Benjamin Franklin's Independence War saying that "we must all hang together . . ." This was indeed their finest hour.[64]

★ ★ ★ ★ ★

How we won the Cold War

No rest for the brave. As soon as the fight against the Axis powers ended, the U.S. got into another existential struggle, this time against the Soviet Union. Existential, because as early as 1949, only four years after Hiroshima and Nagasaki, the USSR detonated its own nuclear bomb. Early conflicts included the 1948 Berlin Blockade and Airlift; the 1950–1953 Korean War (most of Mao's China armament then came from Russia); and the beginning of the Vietnam War. In 1957 the Soviet Union beat us into space, launching the first artificial earth satellite, Sputnik 1; and in 1961 Russian cosmonaut Yuri Gagarin became the first man to reach outer space and fly in orbit around our planet. The Cold War was on, and we were not necessarily winning.

The Cold War lasted over forty years and was fought through a race of armament, economics, and ideas. There were plenty of armed conflicts, but those involved mostly proxies of the U.S. and the Soviet Union. Very few shots and mercifully no bombs were exchanged between Americans and Russians. War Games performed at the Pentagon involving massive first nuclear strikes, retaliation and wholesale destruction remained theoretical exercises. Deterrence kept us away from a nuclear holocaust, although we came very close in October of 1962, during the Cuban Missile Crisis. Without the courage, fortitude, and forceful diplomatic skills shown by President Kennedy and his cabinet, what could have happened?

The Cold War also involved science and extraordinary achievements of mankind, foremost in space. There, we started behind, but with a strong push by

NASA surged forward to achieve JFK's 1961 stated national goal of "landing a man on the moon and returning him safely to the earth." The race to the moon involved popular heroes like John Glenn and his tiny Gemini space capsule; Neil Armstrong; Buzz Aldrin; and Michael Collins of the Apollo 11 mission, Armstrong and Aldrin becoming the first and second humans to walk on the surface of the moon on July 20, 1969. Five subsequent Apollo missions landed another ten astronauts on the moon; the last mission was Apollo 17, with Eugene Cernan and Harrison Schmitt spending three days on the moon between December 11 and 14, 1972. They even had a motorized vehicle, the Lunar Roving Vehicle, and collected over 300 lbs of lunar rocks. Upon climbing the steps of the Lunar Module to return to Earth, Cernan said:[65,66]

> As I take man's last step from the surface, back home for some time to come – but we believe not too long into the future – I'd like to just say what I believe history will record. That America's challenge of today has forged man's destiny of tomorrow. And, as we leave the Moon at Taurus-Littrow, we leave as we came and, God willing, as we shall return, with peace and hope for all mankind. Godspeed the crew of Apollo 17.
>
> Eugene Cernan passed away on January 16, 2017, at age 82.
> No one has gone back to the moon since his 1972 mission.

As an engineer, one of the many things I find astonishing in the achievements of NASA and the U.S. space program in the 1960s and early 1970s is that everything was done with analog electronics. Imagine the navigation challenges; in space de-assemblies and re-assemblies; launching of a 3,000-ton, 363-foot high liquid-fueled Saturn V rocket; all with transistors and electro-mechanical devices, decades before the digital age! This is certainly why several Silicon Valley VCs I know proudly collect instrument panels from Mercury, Gemini, and Apollo Modules. Hopefully the efforts of the likes of Elon Musk and Richard Branson will ensure that the digital age will also see other humans land on our satellite, not to mention Mars, the stated goal of Mr. Musk and a whole new generation of bright, PhD-equipped Millennials.

The peaceful space program triumph America enjoyed in the end over the Soviet Union, and the absence of nuclear armageddon, did not mean that lives were not lost. Below is a list of the armed conflicts that took place during the Cold War, involving many "proxy" wars between the U.S. and the USSR and also many intra-country conflicts. No statistics exist to add up the resulting casualties, but it is safe to say they exceeded a million deaths.[67,68]

1947 – March: communist takeover in Poland.
1947 – March: President Harry Truman declares an active U.S. role in the Greek Civil War.
1948 – February: communist takeover in Czechoslovakia.
1948 – June: Berlin Blockade and Airlift, ending in May 1949 with West Berlin successfully confirmed as a Western enclave within East Germany.

1949 – Mao Zedong and his Chinese Communist Party defeat the Kuomintang-led Republic of China in the Chinese Civil War. Mao establishes the People's Republic of China; and Chiang Kai-shek creates the Nationalist government in Formosa (Taiwan).

1950 – Start of the Korean War, with Soviet-equipped North Korea invading South Korea. The war ends in 1953. Communist North Korea remains under the long-lasting dictatorship of the Kim family, with U.S. troops still protecting democratic South Korea today.

1953 – A U.S.-sponsored coup overthrows the Iranian government and installs the Reza Pahlavi's dictatorship, ended by the Ayatollah Khomeini's Muslim 1979 revolution.

1954 – Military coup in Guatemala, actively supported by the CIA.

1956 – Hungarian Revolution, crushed by the Soviet Red Army tanks and troops.

1958 – Communist revolution in Cuba, with overthrow of dictator Fulgencio Batista and ascension of Fidel Castro in 1959 as head of the communist party and government.

1961 – April: failed Bay of Pigs invasion of Cuba.

1961 – May: military coup in South Korea led by General Park Chung-hee, who rules until his assassination in 1979, followed by General Chun Doo-hwan after another coup.

1961 – August: communist East Germany closes border with West and erects Berlin Wall.

1962 – October: Cuban Missile Crisis.

1964 – March: a military Coup in Brazil installs a dictatorship that will last until 1985.

1964 – August: Gulf of Tonkin incident in Vietnam.

1965 – March: 3,500 U.S. Marines land at China Beach to defend the American Da Nang Air Base, becoming the first combat troops to join the 23,000 American military advisors already in the country – the first U.S. advisors had been sent in 1950 to assist the French in their failed colonial Indochina War; in April comes the announcement that 200,000 U.S. troops will be deployed in Vietnam.

1965 – April: U.S. troops land in the Dominican Republic to intervene in the country's civil war, leading to occupation of the country by the Organization of American States, and the 1966 democratic election of President Joaquin Balaguer.

1967 – April: military coup in Greece, the "regime of the colonels" lasting until July of 1974.

1968 – The "Spring of Prague" Czech uprising is crushed by the Soviet Union.

1970 – President Nixon extends the Vietnam War to Cambodia.

1972 – Nixon visits Mao in China, a first of a kind summit prepared by Henry Kissinger and Zhou Enlai during secretive negotiations in 1971.

1973 – September: a CIA-supported military coup in Chile overthrows democratically elected socialist Salvador Allende and installs the dictatorship of General Augusto Pinochet, which will last until the democratic 1989 parliamentary elections.

1973 – October: Yom Kippur War. Egypt and Syria attack Israel, with Egypt briefly overcoming Israeli defenses in the Sinai Peninsula. Israel then counterattacks and threatens Damascus from the Golan Heights. General Sharon encircles a million of Egyptian troops and their Soviet built tanks in the Sinai desert. The USSR sends a lot of airlifted military equipment to the Egyptian and Syrians, while Israel gets some more limited support from the U.S., which helps negotiate the cease-fire.

1975 – Saigon and South Vietnam fall to communists forces.

1976 – February: Angola Civil War, ending in 2002; Soviet-supported Cuban forces help the MPLA (Mbundu people, led by Agostinho Neto and later Jose Eduardo dos Santos) defeat the U.S.-supported UNITA (Ovimbundu people, led by Jonas Savimbi).

1976 – March: an Argentinean military junta overthrows President Isabel Peron, leading to a brutal seven-year dictatorship. The military regime will collapse in 1983, after the defeat of the Argentinean armed forces at the hand of the British during the 1982 Falklands War.

1979 – The Soviet Red Army invades Afghanistan. The U.S. provides arms to Mujahedeen resistance fighters, with Soviet troops eventually leaving the country in 1989, in compliance with the Geneva Accords of 1988 involving Afghanistan, Pakistan, the United States, and the USSR.

1980 – Solidarity union and Lech Walesa organize the Polish shipyard workers' strike.

1983 – September: a Soviet Su-15 fighter plane shoots down Korean Airlines flight 007 over the Sea of Japan.

1983 – October: the U.S. invades the island of Grenada to overthrow the local Stalinist leader.

1987 – October: democracy is restored in South Korea, with free presidential elections held on December 16 of that year.

1989 – June: Tiananmen Square massacre of protesting university students in Beijing.

1989 – August: end of communist regime in Poland, with Solidarity forming the first non-communist, democratic government in a former Soviet satellite in Europe.

1989 – October: Hungary elects a non-communist government.

1989 – November: East Germany allows unrestricted migration of its citizens to the West. Thousands take trains to West Germany. The Berlin Wall is opened on November 9.

1989 – December: communist governments fall in Czechoslovakia after the peaceful "Velvet Revolution" led by Vaclav Havel; in Bulgaria; and in Romania, where riots culminate in the overthrow and execution of dictator Ceausescu and his wife.

1990 – May: George H.W. Bush and Mikhail Gorbachev agree to the reunification of Germany, achieved in October of that year under Chancellor Helmut Kohl.

1991 – July: the Warsaw Pact military alliance, formed in 1955, is dissolved.

1991 – August: unsuccessful coup staged against Gorbachev by hard-line Soviet communists supported by elements of Red Army; Boris Yeltsin helps fold the coup, riding a tank in Moscow.

1991 – September: Estonia, then Latvia, and Lithuania declare independence from the Soviet Union, with Russian troops staying in the Baltic countries until 1994.

1991 – December: Gorbachev resigns. The Soviet Union is dismantled, and Boris Yeltsin becomes the first elected president of the Russian Federation.

At the outset of the Cold War, America had a number of significant victories … on the economic and political front. The April 8, 1948 European Recovery Program, better known as the Marshall Plan, brought a number of war-devastated European countries solidly into the U.S. political orbit under the "Pax Americana." The three largest recipients of the plan were the United Kingdom, France, and Germany. Fifteen other European countries received significant aid as well. Eastern European countries and the Soviet Union were also offered aid, but they refused, for clear political reasons. On April 4, 1949, the Marshall Plan was followed by a military alliance, the North Atlantic Treaty Organization, or NATO. It included the United States, Canada, the United Kingdom, France, Italy, the Netherlands, Belgium, Luxembourg, Portugal, Denmark, Norway, and Iceland. Greece and Turkey would be added in 1952. The Federal Republic of Germany joined NATO in 1955. Initially, though, it was the Marshall Plan that was by far the more important of the two.

There was a real risk at the end of WWII that communist parties might take over several European countries, even through democratic elections. France, Italy, and Portugal had strong communist parties, whereas in the U.K. the Labour party harbored a large number of communist sympathizers. Right after the end of the war, the French government of national union headed by Charles De Gaulle included the communist party. In England, the "Cambridge Five," Anthony Blunt, Guy Burgess, John Cairncross, Donald Maclean, and Kim Philby all spied for the Soviet Union at least until the early 1950s before defecting to the USSR. They had been recruited during their education at Cambridge University during the 1930s, a decade during which most intellectuals in Western Europe sympathized with the communists because of the 1936–1939 Spanish Civil War, eventually won by the fascist dictator Francisco Franco. Thus, George Orwell served in the International Brigades trying to help the disorganized and underarmed Spanish Republic; so did the French writer Andre Malraux; and many others, from all over Europe; our own Ernest Hemingway did the same – remember *For Whom the Bell Tolls*? This meant that a number of very influential Western Europeans had come to adulthood in a world where communists often represented the first line of defense against fascism. Stalin – affectionately called "Uncle Joe" in America before the start of the Cold War – and the Soviet Union had resisted with utmost gallantry and sacrifice against Hitler's armies. Eventually, the Red Army, at the cost of a horrible loss of lives, bled the Nazis to death on the Eastern Front. So, even though it was Eisenhower, Bradley, and Patton who had liberated all the Western European countries, the U.S. having a monopoly on European hearts was not necessarily a foregone conclusion.

The Marshall Plan cemented admiration, affection and gratitude for America, and helped Western European economies rebuild quickly from the utter devastation wrought by WWII. Within a dozen years, all had already achieved a significant level of economic wealth. The Treaty of Rome, signed on March 25, 1957, further accelerated economic development on the continent. Signed by Belgium, France, Italy, Luxembourg, the Netherlands, and West Germany, it established the European Economic Community. The largest two founding powers of the EEC treaty, France and Germany, made significant compromises to achieve union, not unlike southern states like Virginia and northeastern ones like New York in 1787: Germany accepted the strong agricultural policy, and the pooling of coal and steel production desired by the French. The French, in turn, accepted both decentralized policy decision-making and free trade, which ran against their "dirigiste" instincts at home.

Even though France under the 1958–1969 Charles De Gaulle presidency left NATO, Continental Europe and the U.K. were solidly attached to the American camp during the Cold War. During the Cuban Missile Crisis, John Kennedy asked former Secretary of State Dean Acheson to show the U.S. surveillance photos of the Cuban missiles to De Gaulle, who replied: "I do not need to see the pictures . . . The word of the president of the United States is good enough for me."[69] In 1983, during the SS-20–Pershing missile crisis in Germany between the U.S. and the USSR, French president Francois Mitterrand quipped, during a nationwide TV presentation: "The East has developed missiles and the West has developed pacifists."[70]

With the U.K., EEC countries, Spain and Portugal, as well as Scandinavian countries and Switzerland, firmly allied to the U.S., others in Europe joined their sphere of economic influence. Two countries that had been in the wrong camp during WWII, Austria and Finland, successfully managed the high-wire act to stay within the western economic world while adhering to their mandated military neutrality vis-à-vis the communist bloc.

All of this, plus the reconstruction of Japan and Southeast Asia, were major victories for America during the Cold War, achieved through the foresight of the U.S. political decision makers of the time. What could have happened to Germany, for example, if it had been treated like after WWI and the Treaty of Versailles? Fortunately, Truman, Marshall, and Acheson, among others, had learned their history well. They espoused the simple but very effective idea that the best defense against communism in Europe was a very prosperous West Germany, even though it had been thoroughly defeated during the war. With less able and visionary leaders, a number of Continental European countries might have ended up in the Soviet orbit – typically a one-way ticket at the time.

While America maintained Western European cohesion through solid economic, political and military planning, and Stalin kept most of Eastern Europe under communism through a series of takeovers and military interventions, the developing world was much more in play. And there, while the Soviet Union continued to fight with its typical tools of forced installation of communism and oppression, the U.S. was not above fighting dirty, either. During the 1960s and 1970s, our leaders were fixated on how to fight the "Brezhnev doctrine." Leonid Brezhnev was the long-serving General Secretary of the Communist Party of the Soviet Union, presiding from 1964 to 1982, and his doctrine of expansion of communist rule in developing countries was summarized as: "what is mine, is mine; what is yours, could be mine."

In fighting potential communism expansion in Africa, Asia, and Latin America, a lot of local abuses were tolerated. The U.S. supported many violent dictatorships, which were called "authoritarian" regimes in contrast to the "totalitarian" communist regimes. These differences of semantics were a bit subtle for those who had to endure brutal dictatorships, in as many places as Guatemala, Bolivia, Paraguay, Brazil, Uruguay, Chile, and Argentina in Latin America alone. Emulating the McCarthyism paranoia that had engulfed the U.S. for a decade in the 1950s, Latin American oligarchic landowners and business interests supported long-time dictators or helped foment military coups whenever progressive regimes threatened their financial interests. They would claim to be under threat from communism and ask for U.S. support, which came in a variety of forms, from reassurances that "we are behind you" to active support.

In the most active such effort, the CIA helped plan and supported the 1973 Chilean military in their violent coup against Salvador Allende, democratically elected in 1970 and killed in his bombarded presidential palace during the coup. Allende was an avowed socialist, but most likely he would have been replaced by a conservative president, like his predecessor Eduardo Frei, during the following elections scheduled to take place in 1976. Looking back, there was no more likelihood of Chile becoming a communist Soviet satellite than France becoming one under president Francois Mitterrand at the beginning of his first term in 1981. As Allende had done in Chile, the first Mitterrand government, which included French communist party members, nationalized a number of industries. After two years of economic reversals, Mitterrand made a 180-degree economic turn, fired the communists from his government, and went on to govern for another twelve years in a very capitalistic fashion. The same could have happened in Chile. So, with the exception of the three "Bolivarian" countries of Venezuela; Colombia; and Ecuador (all getting their independence from Spain through Simon Bolivar), all of South America was under military dictatorships during the 1970s and the first half of the 1980s. I experienced a couple of these dictatorships first hand.[71]

After a few years of happy childhood in Copenhagen in Denmark, an idyllic country for the very young and old alike (isn't this the key metric of advanced civilization?), my father was transferred by the French Foreign Service in 1969 to Rio de Janeiro, in Brazil. The "cidade maravilhosa" is one of the most beautiful cities on earth with its amazing location, between volcanic peaks, tropical forests, bay, and ocean. It is also full of contrasts, between suntanned wealth and dire poverty, peaceful beaches and violent crime. Brazil was then in its fifth year of military dictatorship. I have always been a train fan, and on a Sunday in 1970, all of 12 years old, I was in the main train station of the city. The "Dom Pedro II" rail terminal is named after the son of the Portuguese emperor who achieved Brazil's independence through these simple words "Eu fico," or "I stay." I was happily taking pictures with my small Kodak Instamatic of beautiful vintage GE electric locomotives and Budd stainless steel cars, when I heard someone screaming, "Stop!" I looked around, and there was this military soldier pointing his machine gun at me. I smiled, saying to the soldier, "I am not doing anything wrong." He asked me to follow him, and we entered an unmarked door at the side of the station, and then a room, where I was told to stay. After a couple of hours, an old officer showed up, all smiles. In an avuncular way, he took me to his office, and then explained to me, "we all together have to be very careful, since the Soviets and communists would love to have train photos from Brazil, so that they could attack us and cripple the country. Understood, my boy?" I was free to go, and no one took my film. I still have the pictures and enjoy looking at them, although I also remember my parents being distinctively unimpressed by my encounter with the Brazilian military.[72]

Ten years later, I joined the oil field services company Schlumberger as a field engineer. I was initially assigned to Argentina and spent four months for my training in Commodoro Rivadavia in Patagonia. After that, I performed oil and gas exploration surveys in Malargue, a village a few hours away from Mendoza, a pleasant city at the foothills of the Andes and the Aconcagua summit. In early 1981, I had to travel to Brazil for additional training. After the flight to Buenos Aires, I ambled in the beautiful Argentinean capital towards the Brazilian consulate, where, I had been told, getting a visa for a few days in Brazil would be a short formality. When I arrived, I was about to enter the building when a platoon of soldiers arrived and put a "closed" sign on the door. I spotted the leader of the group – a sergeant, perhaps? – and went to talk to him. "Excuse me, but I need to get a visa from the Brazilian consulate, since the plane I need to take to go to Brazil leaves in a few hours this afternoon. When do you think this place will be open again?" Next thing I knew, he shoved the butt of his rifle against my back and pushed me violently against the building wall. Then I heard his voice, coarse and threatening: "you know, I could shoot you right now, right here, and nobody would know anything!" I briefly saw my life flash between my eyes, and managed to utter: "no, please do not shoot . . . I will go away 'quietito,' very silently." I was waved away and left the scene, very shaken. Later, calmed down, on my way back to Mendoza – no more trip to Brazil for me, obviously – I came to understand better what some of my workers meant when they whispered to me about "los desaparecidos," the ones who have "disappeared."

A couple of months later, in May 1981, Sanchez, my very competent foreman, took me aside during one of our field works for the local national oil company, Yacimientos Petroliferos Fiscales (YPF). "Ingeniero, let's get away from the derrick and the well site, I have a surprise for you." After a little walk, he produces a nice bottle of Mendoza Malbec wine: "Ingeniero, I just learned that the great socialist Francois Mitterrand has just been elected President of France. Let's have a toast to this wonderful event." Most of the news being heavily censored, I had no idea this had happened. I smiled and marveled at Sanchez's courage in telling me this. The risks he took in sharing this news in such an enthusiastic tone and with a foreigner at that – foreigners were often denounced by the military junta as "part of the international communist conspiracy" – could have cost him his life. But Argentineans are proud, rebel easily, and like to celebrate. Alejandro, our local maintenance engineer, told me about dancing in the streets of Buenos Aires after their national "Albiceleste" football team had won the 1978 World Cup: "we were not necessarily football fans, but could not pass on the first opportunity in years to celebrate in the streets."

How did all this nastiness end? Many people have forgotten that the British helped build a very modern and rich Argentina in the first half of the twentieth century. Railroads; subways; majestic buildings and cities; meat and wool trade; an abundance of posh clubs; even sports like football, but also polo and rugby; all were introduced to Argentina before any other country in South America. Ironically, the British also caused the criminal military dictatorship of Generals and Admirals Videla, Massera, Viola, and Galtieri to collapse in 1983. Their abject defeat in the Falklands War at the hands of an expeditionary force that had sailed for over 8,000 miles to get there precipitated their end and a welcome return to democratically elected governments. I am a private pilot and had flown a little bit while in Patagonia. I was told later that the Argentinean fighter pilots taking off from Rio Gallegos, at the southern tip of Patagonia, had barely enough fuel to get to the Falklands, engage the British aircraft carriers' Harriers defending the Home Fleet, and fly back home. The immensely skillful Royal Air Force pilots knew that if they just kept their Argentineans adversaries a few minutes in air combat, they would have to ditch in the cold ocean before making it back to their base. Even if they survived dogfights with the nimble Harriers, they still would not make it. Which in fact is what happened to most of these pilots, bravely flying missions poorly planned by their incompetent superiors.

The many South American military dictatorships and CIA involvement, open or covert, did not do much to endear the U.S. to the local habitants. For a long time, most of my Argentinean friends referred to Americans as "los Yankis," and it was not an affectionate term. The failed economics pursued under the gun by Pinochet created widespread poverty in Chile, which had been a beacon of democracy and middle-class successes in the region for over thirty years until 1973. Brazil today trades more with China than with the U.S. Fortunately, time heals, countries prosper under democracies, and the turn of the new century has offered many new economic opportunities in the region for Americans.[73]

Outside Latin America, there were brutal dictatorships too, and wars of proxies often determined who between the USSR and the U.S. would gain the upper hand: we had to endure a defeat in minerals-rich Angola, where Soviet-armed and -financed Cuban military "advisors" helped local MPLA war lords win a seven-year civil war during the seventies against U.S.-backed UNITA fighters. This established a communist regime in the country, which morphed into the Dos Santos family regime until August of 2017, when President José Eduardo dos Santos stepped down and was replaced by João Lourenço. Above all, the decade ended with the fall of the Shah in Iran in 1979. This led to the Islamic regime of the Ayatollah Khomeini and a significant loss of influence for the U.S. in the Persian Gulf region. The American hostage crisis in Iran with its failed rescue attempt is one of the factors that contributed to Ronald Reagan's victory against incumbent Jimmy Carter in the presidential elections of 1980.[74]

"To the victor the spoils of war." Ronald Reagan and his government are credited with winning the Cold War without firing a single shot. Just as during the Marshall Plan era, the ultimate U.S. victory owed much more to economics than to battle supremacy. Reagan and his team promoted a confident, sunny, if not always socially equitable version of market economics, to great success. After Watergate, two oil shocks, and inflation well above double digits, America rediscovered economic growth, low inflation, and the almighty dollar: the greenback, worth only 1.7 Deutsche Marks in 1980, soared to 3.2 DM in 1985. In the meantime, the USSR economy was succumbing to the weight of ever more complex and ineffective central economic plans. During the "détente" periods experienced under Soviet premier Brezhnev, the U.S. had to organize several massive grain sale efforts to help avert hunger in the Soviet Union after a succession of failed harvests. Reagan espoused simple economic concepts and was the master communicator in promoting their virtues, but he also possessed a keen sense of global strategic issues, and under him the U.S. moved on to the next gear in terms of armament efforts. And the Soviet Union exhausted its resources trying to follow up aircraft carrier for aircraft carrier, trying to match us in expensive military hardware such as nuclear ballistic submarines and sophisticated fighter airplanes. In particular, Soviet leaders found Reagan's "Star Wars" Strategic Defense Initiative highly threatening to their nuclear deterrence.

Then in 1985 arrived on the scene a young, charismatic Soviet premier, Mikhail Gorbachev. Shortly after Reagan was elected to his second term, and after brief stints by ageing premiers Andropov and Chernenko, Gorbachev became the eighth – and final – leader of the USSR. President Reagan shared with his Secretary of State George Shultz a belief that arms control agreements – from a definite U.S. position of strength – would enhance America's security. They also believed that a strong dialogue had to be maintained with strategic adversaries. In Gorbachev they found a viable negotiating partner. At Reykjavik, Iceland, in October 1986, Reagan, Shultz, Gorbachev, and his minister of foreign affairs Eduard Shevardnadze, discussed the then unthinkable: abolishing all nuclear weapons. On December 8, 1987, in Washington DC, Reagan and Gorbachev signed the Intermediate-Range Nuclear Forces Treaty, which put an end to the SS–20–Pershing missile crisis that had started in 1976 and eliminated an entire class of nuclear missiles. The Reagan and Shultz efforts continued with the 1988 election of President George H.W. Bush, culminating in an encounter in Malta in December 1989, one month after the fall of the Berlin Wall. Bush and Gorbachev then worked together to allow the reunification of Germany; sign a couple of military treaties (CFE on Conventional Forces in Europe and START, the Strategic Arms Reduction Treaty); and help democratic elections take place in former communist countries in Europe.

Gorbachev had determined that the Soviet Union could not go on as it had since the mid-1950s after the Stalinist massacres had ended, even with peace in its land. He knew that keeping up with America in terms of military strength would bankrupt his country and launched massive internal change programs around "Glasnost" (transparency) and "Perestroika" (economic restructuring). Those had some initial success, but also caused the erosion of the tight central control the communist party had all over the Soviet Union. Local dissent, growing regional nationalism outside of Russia, and emerging anti-communism all contributed to the end of the USSR. There were too many vested interests in the centrally planned economy for any type of economic liberalization effort to succeed once the iron hand of the communist party started to relent. Eventually, led by Boris Yeltsin, the president of the Russian Republic, the leaders of several former Soviet republics agreed in December 1991 that the Soviet Union had come to an end. Gorbachev resigned, and independent Russia; Kazakhstan; Ukraine; Azerbaijan; Uzbekistan; Belarus; plus a number of smaller former Soviet republics, replaced the USSR. Unlike so many other partitions in history – think for example of the millions of casualties during the 1947 partition of India and Pakistan – the end of the Soviet Union did not lead to bloodshed, and Gorbachev won the 1990 Nobel Peace Prize. The U.S. had won the Cold War.

The definitive account of the dialogue and negotiations between Reagan and Gorbachev was written by George Shultz in his masterful book *Turmoil and Triumph: My Years as Secretary of State*. Here is how Shultz describes Ronald Reagan in Chapter 51 of the book, "Turning Point":[75]

> The American people liked Ronald Reagan and reelected him in one of the biggest landslides in history because he trusted them and he conveyed to them that they need not to be bound, tied down by class, or race, or childhood misfortune, or poverty, or bureaucracy – they, the people – could make something of themselves; indeed, they could remake themselves, endlessly.
>
> But beneath this pragmatic attitude lay a bedrock of principle and purpose with which I was proud to be associated. He believed in being strong enough to defend one's interests, but he viewed that strength as a means, not an end in itself. He was ready to negotiate with his adversaries. In that readiness, he was sharply different from most of his conservative supporters, who advocated strength for America but who did not want to use

that strength as a basis for the inevitable give-and-take of the negotiating process. All too often, they lacked confidence in the ability of democratic leaders, including Reagan, to negotiate effectively with our adversaries. Ronald Reagan had confidence in himself and his ideas and was ready to negotiate from the strength so evident in the mid-1980s.

He was a fervent anti-Communist who could comprehend and believe that people everywhere would choose to throw off the Communist system if they ever had the chance. And he worked hard to give them that chance. He favored open trade because he had confidence in the ability of Americans to compete, and he had confidence that an integrated world economy would benefit America. He stuck to his agenda.

The points he made, however consummate the delivery, were unmistakably real in his mind and heart, an American creed: defend your country, value your family, make something of yourself, tell the government to get off your back, tell the tyrants to watch their step. Ronald Reagan conveyed simple truths that were especially welcome because "nowadays everything seems so complicated." What he said ran deep and wide among the people.

8 Technology defeats complexity . . . sometimes

Our friendly and can-do attitude to daily service; innovation that helps people

Compared to other countries, we may like to make things more complex than they need to be, but we are very practical people. A lot of what we do in our daily lives aims to allow us to handle mundane tasks quickly and without fuss. Good service is a given, at least when dealing with companies of a reasonable size. When handled by very large corporations, such as airlines, banks and health insurers, where there is a powerful cost-cutting motive to increase profits, service is not what it used to be. For them, the modern notion of service appears to be a customer phone line recording that keeps on saying: "if you do not want to wait an hour for an operator please go to our website at badservicecompany. com." Apart from the frustrations of making airline reservations or getting an erroneous overcharge by your health insurer credited back to your account, getting service is a dream experience in our country.

In Europe, having any type of service done at your home – electricity, plumbing or basic repairs – is a dreaded experience, best postponed until you have no light at all or your floors are getting flooded. I remember that simply having access to a phone line was a multi-month proposition there until the advent of cell phones. In contrast, even before the digital age, getting phone, plumbing or electricity services in the U.S. was amazingly easy. I remember settling in with my roommates in a low-cost apartment in Berkeley almost forty years ago and writing to my parents about it.

> Steve called the phone company from a pay phone at the corner of the street; a few hours later the company representative came in; and for almost no money we had four telephones in the apartment, one for each room plus living room! . . . We also had the kitchen sink plumbing fixed in a day, all with smiles.

In their letter back to me my parents were totally incredulous. Within the next few weeks, I experienced amazing convenience and friendly service in renting a car, allowing me to drive a full-sized V8 automobile for a pittance. I would have never dreamed of even attempting to rent a car in France as a student. In the winter, the small building we were living in needed a new boiler. The landlord reacted to our call with great speed. I stood in front of the boiler room, fascinated, watching the repairmen installing the new unit – gas-fired, unlike the coal or heavy fuel then used in much of Europe.

Even today, we remain the country of fast, convenient and friendly service. Our homes have an array of overly complex fixtures and contraptions (think of programmable lighting switches!), but getting Mike the electrician, Bob the plumber or Joe the locksmith is more a pleasure than a hindrance. Nice folks, impeccable service, all done at a very reasonable price while having friendly chats about the issues of the day. I never cease to be smitten by it. We take all this convenience for granted and do not realize that not all countries share our practical sense. Whenever I go back to France and hear my parents talking about repairs or upgrades to their home, I realize that this transatlantic gap still yawns. This is not just my experience: *A Year in Provence*, the popular book by Peter Mayle, describes the travails of setting up a vacation home near the nice Provence city of Apt in Southern France, and relates it all convincingly and with good humor.[1]

From our history as self-reliant immigrants, we are naturally practical people. Most of the time, this translates into us putting our ingenuity at the service of our customers. What the electricians, plumbers and repairmen serving us have in common is that their business depends upon their courteous, professional and speedy response to our needs. The same is true for the dealerships and garages that service our cars. There again there is a big difference with Europe. The first car I owned in San Francisco after I started working was a beautiful Peugeot 505. From a comfort, balance and road holding point of view, my "Pug" was a much better car than its nearest U.S.-made cousin, the popular Ford Taurus. Peugeot also had an excellent smaller car available for sale here, the 405. But French decision makers never understood that, when it comes to service, Americans are accustomed to much, much higher standards than the folks back in France – and in Europe for that matter. So Peugeot skimped on the number of dealerships: whenever the 505 needed servicing I had to drive 50 miles, all the way to San Jose! Had I owned a Ford Taurus, there would have been a dealer down the street, or close. Among European mass volume car manufacturers, only Volkswagen understood this, which explains their success in this country. The Fiat Group is now back in the U.S., but only after having purchased Chrysler, which gives it access to a large network of dealerships. It started with just one model, the "niche" Fiat 500 type, but now cool-looking Alfa Romeos are also reaching our shores.

Practicality should lead to straightforward, easy to understand products and services, right? Right . . . as long as there remains a healthy balance between the information and power of customers relative to their service providers. Otherwise, companies will feel incentivized to cut all corners in matters of customer service to maximize their profits, without fear of losing business. This is what is happening with airlines, health insurance companies and telecommunication providers. In all three cases, the choices we have are usually limited. If I want to fly from San Francisco to Dallas, it must be on American; there are three large health insurers in California – many states are down to one or two – but only one covers my large hospital of choice; and when it comes to my television and internet needs, it is essentially AT&T or Comcast. No wonder, then, that what passes for service with these large corporations is either waiting hours for a representative to deign to attend you or navigating extremely complex websites. Recently, after waiting in vain to get an airline representative on the line, I decided to spend another hour navigating their website. And then, victory! I had the perfect travel arrangements to get one of my children to his high school summer abroad program and back. Well, close, but no cigar. As I was pressing the "confirm and pay" button, a notice flashed on my screen: "For minors below 18 years of age, you need to talk to a representative." Back to square one.

Of course, this irritating inconvenience is dwarfed by what can happen to airline passengers at the airport, in the boarding area, or within the confines of the planes. "Customer service" there can turn into true nightmares. But that is not a technology or a complexity story. Just old-fashioned power abuses that may arise when there is absolute corporate power over hapless customers.

For over six months in 2017, my health insurer kept charging me for dental fees covering my three children still in the family plan, even though I had requested them to be taken off it. They have good teeth and this dental program is pretty much all high deductible anyway, essentially useless unless you have a ton of work done. Every month, like a ritual, after having received a bill that still showed the children's dental charges, I had to call their customer line. It is in India, everyone was infallibly polite, agents and supervisors alike, and they all always reassured me this would be taken care of. To no avail. In the meantime, my insurer kept charging me, like clockwork. Once I tried not to pay the bill in full, removing these dental fees. It did not take long for a letter to come to my home stating that, unless invoices were paid in full, medical coverage would be suspended within thirty days. After months of this game, they owed me over $1,000. It all eventually stopped when, upon the sage advice from a friend who used to run a hospital system, I threatened to lodge a formal complaint with the California Insurance Commissioner. Two weeks later all was in order: dental fees removed from the monthly invoices, and a check for the monies owed to me duly sent. Service indeed ... I cannot wait for Medicare! When I hear pundits saying on television "we need the private sector to work its magic to solve our health care problems," I cringe.

In all these cases, large corporations enjoying oligopolistic or quasi-monopolistic power over their consumers have paid vast amounts to IT staff and consultants to develop very complex websites that are supposed to represent advanced customer service. Costs of voice-to-voice interactions with customers have been reduced to almost nothing, with minimally staffed call centers in low labor cost countries handling those who still want to talk to human beings about their service needs. Everyone complains about these deteriorated levels of service, but nothing changes. To the contrary, there is always another mega-merger being proposed around the corner that promises more misery for the hapless customers of the companies involved. Technology is the friend of the bottom line of these companies, of their bankers and consultants, but certainly not the friend of their customers or service.

Is this always the case? No, fortunately, because we have, in addition to the friendly local businesses we treasure, an enviable number of entrepreneurs who seek to make a positive difference in our lives through real progress, not cost cutting in a technologist's clothing. These entrepreneurs know their field and apply their genius to find the simplicity on the other side of complexity. And thus, innovations in fields as diverse as communications; energy; and personal mobility, just to mention a few, have made our lives simpler, healthier and more enjoyable.

★   ★   ★   ★   ★

iMac and operating simplicity

In the pantheon of our great inventors, Steve Jobs assuredly has his place alongside the likes of Thomas Edison. He started early with personal computers, having founded Apple at age 21 in 1976 with Steve Wosniack and Ronald Wayne. In 1982, when I was working for Schlumberger in El Tigre, at the heart of Venezuela's heavy oil producing savannah, we used an Apple 2 for all our financial and operational accounts. Simple, convenient, with nice color graphics – revolutionary at the time. By the time I started working as a management consultant in 1985, alas, it was Lotus 123 spreadsheets, running on very heavy and suitcase-like Compaq computers. Steve Jobs, with his crazy ideas of integrated hardware and software, had been booted out of Apple. The road was wide open for Bill Gates and Microsoft to dominate the world of personal computers, or PCs. But Jobs would be begged to back to Apple, and he returned in 1997. Less than two years later, he unveiled the iMac and had Jeff Goldblum of *Jurassic Park* fame do a series of videos still admired today. Let's remember that when Apple launched its iTools web hosting and email services to complement its freshly launched iMac, this was a rare thing, not exactly mainstream. Most businesses, including the giant IT company where I was a global managing partner, would not touch this with a barge pole. We could have any computer we wanted – mine was a sturdy, black and serious-looking ThinkPad from IBM – as long as they operated on Microsoft DOS.[2,3]

Here is one of these first "simplicity shootout" videos with Jeff Goldblum about the Apple iMac G3 and the internet. The pictures show a traditional PC with many tentacles like cables, yielding to a nice color iMac with two hardly visible connections, to the sound of a soothing harmonica. But it is the words that matter:

A PC. Perpetually complicated. Profusely corded. Physically conspicuous. Particularly costly.

Oh, then there is the new iMac. Which is about as unPC as you can get.

Hmm. Two roads diverge on the way to the internet. And I, I took the faster, simpler, less expensive, and far more colorful one. And that made all the difference.

Even more to the point, here is the "There is no step 3!" video showcasing the simplicity of use of the iMac:

Presenting three easy steps to the internet.
Step 1. Plug in.
Step 2. Get connected.
Step 3. [Pause] There is no step 3. There is no step 3! [Laughing]

In another series of videos on the iMac called "Drunk Jeff Goldblum," the actor compared the cost of an iMac to getting $30 worth of pizza every month, to the sound of a slowly playing clarinet:

You know how much a pizza costs. About ten bucks. In a month, if you get three it is thirty bucks. For the same cost, roughly less, you can own a computer! The iMac is less than thirty dollars a month. Can you imagine, for the same cost as three pizzas, you own a computer!

Now you are on the internet, now you are emailing everybody in the world, you are playing the greatest games, you are empowered, your vision is expanded, you are collaborating with people, it changes your life in a million ways.

So budget yourself, skip the pizzas and get the computer! Hot, fresh out of the box. You, hmm, you know, you can put anchovies on it if you want.

Steve Jobs and Apple would continue launching great computers, the iMac G4, today's MacBookPro and MacBookAir, and several others. These have all gained acceptance from the largest corporations, where Apple computers today happily mix with Dell, HP (ex-Compaq), and Lenovo (ex-IBM) PCs. But after the iPod, its first hand-held device, it is the iPhone, launched in January of 2007 that made Apple the global juggernaut it is today. One of the revolutionary features of the iPhone was the now ubiquitous touch screen technology. Most professionals had learned the use of hand-held devices with the PalmPilot, with its small stylus, and later with the quite successful Black-Berry, with its tiny keyboard. Years after the iPhone became the smart phone to have around the world, professionals still hung on to their BlackBerries, most famously President Obama. Now, though, over ten years after the launch of the iPhone, touch screen technology is omnipresent in a number of applications. Touch screen technology is digital, enabled by capacitors, whereas keyboards are analog devices using resistors. So, touch screen feels like home today, in our appliances and cars, not to mention in more sophisticated applications such as airplane flight deck instrumentation. Personal computers are still using keyboards, but for how long? After all, lots of people now prefer an iPad, with its touch screen and stylus for handwriting, to even a light computer with its keyboard and no ability to hand write. Touching a screen is clearly a more natural gesture than typing on a keyboard, and despite the IBM typewriter still in the warm memories of our youth, keyboards are probably on the way out. Steve Jobs did not invent touch screen technology, but, just like Henry Ford hundred years before with his vision of a Ford T for everyone, Jobs assumed correctly that this superior technology would eventually become the norm. Visionaries do not rely on market surveys; they show us the way of the future and we follow their lead.[4,5]

What happens when visionaries like Ford and Jobs pass away? The empires they built survive, even thrive. However, in most cases incrementalism – so much disliked by Jobs – replaces transforming innovation. And incremental features add complexity. Things can improve, yes, like the growing quality of every new iPhone's camera. But how long can Apple stay at the top of the business world by churning out new iPhone versions, now 8 and X, and so forth? One day, the many new features, add-ons, and increased prices will make us look back and barely recognize the original, brilliant product. One of Steve Jobs' many nemeses gave an interesting demonstration of this on May 30, 2017. Andy Rubin, the creator of Android, Google's mobile operating system, against whom Jobs wanted to wage "thermonuclear war," unveiled a new rival for the latest versions of the iPhone, the Essential Phone. The Essential is a high-end Android device that could start denting Apple's domination of the smart phone world, domination that has never looked so strong after all the problems Samsung had with the batteries of its Galaxy 7. The Essential can build upon the two billion devices worldwide running on Android today. In launching the Essential with great fanfare, Andy Rubin said he wanted to simplify a complicated world, one overwhelmed with too many features and products that don't work together. Rather than to go into the details of the Essential's features, let us look at the one-page advert that appeared on the *Wall Street Journal* on May 30.

Hi,
I'm Andy Rubin.
Co-founder of Android.
Today I'm launching a
new kind of company.

I know many people in the media are going to speculate on why I started Essential, so I wanted to take a moment to share the real reason with you. It all started during a night out with an old friend of mine. As the night went on we inevitably began talking about what we didn't like about the current state of technology. Less and less choice. More and more unnecessary features cluttering our lives. An increasing sea of products that didn't work with one another . . .

And just when I was about to drop another criticism, it hit me. **I am partly responsible for all of this.**

For all the good that Android has done, it has also helped create this weird new world where people are forced to fight with the very technology that was supposed to simplify their lives. Was this what we had intended? Was this the best we could do? After a long talk with my friend, we decided that I needed to start a new kind of company to build solutions for the way people want to live in the twenty-first century.

The result is Essential and this is what we believe:

- Devices are your personal property. We won't force you to have anything on them you don't want to have.
- We will always play well with others. Closed ecosystems are divisive and outdated.
- Premium materials and true craftsmanship shouldn't be just for the few.
- Devices shouldn't become outdated every year. They should evolve with you.
- Technology should assist you so that you can get on with enjoying life.
- Simple is always better.

I have used the above principles to inform everything Essential is doing and they have helped me attract some of the best and brightest people from all over the world to join me in bringing this vision to life.

We won't achieve everything we hope on day one, but if you're one of those people who also think it is time for something new, please have a look at www.essential.com to learn more.

Andy Rubin, Founder and CEO, Essential Products TM

Brilliant marketing. Nice credo, too! This is what is wonderful about Silicon Valley. A brilliantly simple product emerges, changes our lives for the better, but then leads to an increasingly complex ecosystem where we feel as trapped as we felt liberated by the original product. New product comes in, with the objective to bring us back simplicity. And the merry go-round goes one more cycle. Wow![6]

If we step back a little further, how much has the Valley and its ultra-deep trove of innovations actually changed our lives?

There is no doubt that the age of Facebook; Instagram; Twitter; WhatsApp; Snapchat; and many others has revolutionized communications. Our ability to reach each other on a local as well as planetary scale has been completely transformed, and with options as simple as they are effective. Just look at how President Trump communicates with all of us. No "fire-side chats," few press conferences, hardly any question and answer sessions. No, just Twitter! Much criticized, but so very effective. In this new age of numerous social media platforms, many complain that they are overwhelmed, feel they have become slaves to their electronic devices, and no longer have enough old-fashioned, in the flesh human interactions. Attention Deficit Disorder is on the rise, and so are road traffic casualties, the main reason being people distracted by texting while driving. Our young people suffer from FOMO, or "fear of missing out"; they need to track their friends and "electronic buddies," wherever they are, in real time, all the time. In more socially advanced Europe, companies are being mandated to allow all their employees "e-mail free" hours, so that they can stay disconnected for a while and recharge their batteries. Well, this may be a little bit overhyped, but we will evolve and learn how to take advantage of instant communications everywhere and not destroy our lives in the process. As a father of five, I have full confidence that the Millennial generation will rise to this challenge. It might just take a few years, and of course more innovation and simpler solutions coming from the future Steve Jobs.

For me, one of the best illustrations of the power of the new information age and also its limitations at the time was what happened in the 2010 to 2012 "Arab Spring." Throughout a region long repressed by autocrats, people using Facebook and Twitter got together in millions, took the streets, and toppled these old autocrats one after another. Nowhere was this truer than in Egypt, the most populated nation in the Middle East. The Arab Spring had started in neighboring Tunisia, following a protester's self-immolation, and where President Ben Ali was ousted in 2011. A wave of unrest and protests then swept Egypt, the largest demonstrations occurring during the Friday afternoon prayers. Protesters outfoxed security forces by relying on texts to keep their place of assembly secret until the last minute and using social medial to mobilize millions effectively. They wanted an end to corruption, brutality from security forces, access to economic opportunities, and freedom of assembly and speech. On February 2011, the Egyptian government was overthrown, with the resignation of long-time ruler president Hosni Mubarak and his Prime Ministers Nazif and Shafik. Mubarak was later convicted of corruption and for ordering the killing of protesters, and was imprisoned. After a brief assumption of power by the country's Armed Forces, the 31-year-long state of emergency was lifted and democratic elections held. Score a major victory here for the new information age and social media.[7]

However, the ensuing election campaign in Egypt showed the limits of the power of the demonstrators, civil society, and their social media weapons. A successful election campaign in a country that had not had one in decades requires true on-the-ground organization. Grassroots. The ability to implement actual changes in how people work, eat, and vote. And there it became clear that the revolution enabled by social media did not possess these capabilities. The long-time opposition to the Mubarak regime, the Muslim Brotherhood, did. And one of their leaders, Mohamed Morsi, was elected and inaugurated as Egypt's president in 2011. His brief rule proved to be a disaster, borne out of overreach in trying to impose a strict Muslim philosophy on a country modern enough not to want it. A new Constitution was voted – not Sharia Law, but fairly close. The governing Muslim Brotherhood refused to compromise on anything and attempted to steer the country to a level of religious fundamentalism that clearly was very unpopular. The Armed Forces then intervened in 2012, ended the rule of the Muslim Brotherhood, put Morsi in jail, got a new Constitution and organized new elections, severely restricted. The former Armed Forces commander Abdel Fattah el-Sisi was elected and is president to this day. As an aside, an interesting philosophical question: is it "democratic" to overthrow by military force a democratically elected regime that has decided to govern undemocratically? Answering this is not the point here, though. The point is that the powers unleashed by the twenty-first-century information age and Silicon Valley are formidable, yet full of unintended consequences.

The new technology giants of our age, the "Fangs" (Facebook, Amazon, Netflix and Google) use our personal data and individual consuming habits, which are extremely valuable to advertisers, giving them the ability to get deeply into our preferences and tastes. But these business models and information, the source of the high valuations of these technology companies, carry with them serious potential vulnerabilities if they fall into the hands of unscrupulous operators, through hacking or other means. Social media may thus bring new dangers to liberty, such as when authoritarian regimes use their citizens' personal data to control information, spread false news and stifle democratic debates, all to hold on to power. This could create real dilemmas for these dominant tech companies: can they beef up their cyber security enough to prevent the hijacking of our personal data for nefarious purposes? Or do they have to re-think their very profitable business models to prevent this at the source? And can they solve this by themselves, or do governments need to start regulating them to protect our privacy? Many important voices in Europe are calling for new regulations to govern social media and privacy issues: the E.U. may enact legislation mandating that social media companies offer their users the tools needed to protect their personal privacy, based on the principle that users own and therefore should have control of their personal data. In the U.S., Congress is not looking at this with a lot of urgency, but this could change if the security and privacy of personal information in social media becomes a widespread concern for voters.

To step back, the changes created in Silicon Valley today are ultra-deep, with a huge impact in some areas, but still take place within a narrow band of activities – the opposite of "a mile wide, an inch deep." This is why it remains to be seen whether the innovations of our new century will change the lives of multitudes as profoundly as did the late nineteenth century innovations we talked about earlier in this book. To quote famous technology entrepreneur and early Facebook investor Peter Thiel: "we wanted flying cars, instead we got 140 characters." More on this with Elon Musk.

★   ★   ★   ★   ★

Magical electric cars: as simple as a flying carpet

Is there a simpler motorized vehicle than an electric car? Think of it: no cylinders; valves; camshafts; fuel injecting system; circulation of high-pressure oil;

water or air-cooling system; gear box; drive shaft. Just a large battery and electric engines driving the wheels directly. And, of course, no noise and no direct
emission of noxious gases. As simple as a flying carpet.

I drive an electric plug-in hybrid called Fisker Karma. It is a strikingly designed
and beautiful car . . . people wave at me when I drive it around town; they give me
thumbs up, atta boys, or cool car, dude! I have driven the Fisker around our local
Bay Area racetrack, which is at the entrance of Sonoma Valley, and hosts Nascar and
Indy Car races every year. Nascar in the wine country! A unique experience. On
this technical track, the Fisker handles beautifully; it will take the 180-degree turn 6
faster than many Porsches and is a delight to drive fast. The Karma also has the most
comfortable seats of any car I know, one of the best automobile stereos, and regen-
erative breaking to add to the brakes – great car for daily city driving, too. But when
it comes to the batteries, it is the Stone Age! There is literally a ton of them, forming
a double "T" chassis for the car, and all that gives me only 50 miles of driving range.
Where were Elon Musk and his Tesla batteries when we needed them? Fortunately,
the Fisker also comes equipped with a GM 2-liter turbocharged engine, so I do not
have to suffer from electric range anxiety. When used, this gasoline engine works at
peak torque, with good 30-mpg fuel economy, and does not drive the wheels but a
generator that in turn sends current to the electric engines on the rear wheels. Of
course, the name of the game is to go electric and use the gasoline engine as rarely
as possible. The gasoline tank is small, at eight gallons, and I typically drive over
2,500 miles before I have to refill it. Concerned about the lack of noise emanating
from electric cars, Henrik Fisker – formerly Chief Designer at Aston Martin – even
added to his car a space ship type of constant frequency sound so that pedestrians
and cyclists know something is coming down the road . . . a magic carpet, if you
ask me. But still a complex contraption, with two electric engines, a generator, a
gasoline engine, and those 2,200-pound batteries. One day, the Karma will go into
a museum, as a showcase of sophisticated efforts straddling the ages of the internal
combustion engine and that of the all-electric vehicle.

I have enjoyed my Fisker Karma for over five years now. A couple of years
ago, it was my wife's turn to have a new car, and she wanted it all-electric!
Great. My wife is an artist. She paints. Forms are important to her. Her car has
to be small, too; she wants to be able to drive in narrow city streets and park in
small spaces. I know it is going to be a challenge: she describes most modern
cars we see on our streets, like the Toyota Prius, as "carros ovos," or "egg shaped
cars" in her native Portuguese. The new Tesla SUV? An enormously bloated
"carro ovo." A friend of mine swears by his Nissan Leaf – they just increased the
battery range to 120 miles. Will not do: "look at the front! It looks like a frog."
The BMW E3 is even uglier, and tiny at that: "where would I put my canvases?"
We still go drive it at the local Beemer dealership, and the salesman does not
help his cause. When asked, diplomatically, about the "unusual looks," he snaps
at us: "you will get used to it." Hmm, the Bavarian brand must be strong enough
since these E3s appear to be selling. The Fiat 500, which has a full electric version, is also too small. The new Chevy Bolt, fully electric with an impressive
range of over 200 miles, is another "egg car." Toyota, Honda, and Hyundai
are not (yet?) offering all-electric cars with batteries, betting instead on new

hydrogen-fueled models, with sophisticated fuel cells. Amazing. I remember testing hydrogen-fueled prototypes in the early 2000s in Sacramento as part of a zero-emission program pushed by then-California Governor Schwarzenegger, and we were told they cost over a million dollars each to build. But Toyota and Hyundai will only release their hydrogen cars for sale to the public late in 2018, and in any case, where are the hydrogen fueling stations?

During our last European vacation, we rented a small A-class Mercedes. Practical, comfortable, roomy, and with acceptable looks. Of course, like most rentals in Europe, ours came with a diesel engine. But wait! We learn that Mercedes is now selling a B-class all-electric car in the U.S. In photos, it looks very much like the A-class we rented in Austria, just a little bigger. Let's go for a test drive. Alas, when we see the car for the first time, it is quite large . . . not at all like the A but very close to the full-sized R-class minivan. It also feels heavy and ponderous while driving, not what one expects from an electric car and its instant torque response. My wife is unhappy:

> I don't want this Mercedes van, it is much too big. The Tesla Model S is too big also. I hate SUVs! And why do small electric cars have to be ugly? Why can't BMW make an electric Mini instead of that tiny and horrendous looking E3?

I have one more card to play, but it is not an ace by any means. All of this takes place a couple of months after the Volkswagen diesel engine emissions control cheating scandal. As mentioned in an earlier chapter in this book, VW literally manufactured millions of engines with software designed to only activate the anti-emission process when their cars were being tested for emissions, and they got caught. A testing lab in West Virginia discovered the "cheating" program, with emissions during actual driving up to forty times those during testing, and by September of 2015 the EPA issued a notice of violation of the Clean Air Act to Volkswagen. VW pledged $16 billion to pay for the avalanche of lawsuits in the U.S. alone, where around 500,000 cars were sold with the culprit engines. Newspapers around the world raged in protest, with the Italian press describing the cheating in the most succinct words. "Hanno truccato il motore!" was the title of an article about the scandal in one Italian daily. My wife has duly followed the VW disaster, noting quite accurately that most drivers of VW models like the Golf buy them because of their small size, convenience, and fuel economy. We are not talking about "flat earthers," climate change deniers here, and it is these environmentally conscious people that have been deceived. So her initial position was that "we are not even going to look at a car from these people."

But . . . VW also makes a fully electric Golf, and somehow I persuade my wife to have a look and test the car. Nirvana! The car drives like a go-kart; it is agile, quick, and silent like another magic carpet. It is small, but roomy; with the rear seats folded it actually has ample cargo room. It has understated but elegant looks as well; the car brochure actually says: "enjoy an electric car without obnoxious looks." And when I look under the hood, wow! There is nothing in there, just a very small electric engine, a few high-voltage cables marked in yellow – that's it; so simple, so clean, sold! The future is here. Eager to make a sale during these tough PR times for the company, the VW salesman offers us a very nice rebate if we take the car home the same day, and my wife has been happy with the car ever since.

Of course, my wife's eGolf does not quite have the 200+ miles range of the Chevy Bolt and the Teslas. A little tribute to Elon Musk, inventor, visionary, and also exceptional businessman is in order here. Mr. Musk wants to change and improve our lives even more than Steve Jobs did. After having made his fortune pioneering e-payments with PayPal, Musk decided that electric cars were the way of the future, hence Tesla, today the most valuable auto company in the U.S. by market capitalization. Yes, ahead of both Ford and GM. But transportation represents only half of the carbon and nitrogen associated emissions in most countries, the other half being the burning of fossil fuels to produce electricity, coal being the most noxious for air quality. We already have a large installed base of solar and wind electric power in California, but if we want to get renewables to account for well over 50% of our electricity production, we need to address the storage issue. The wind blows most strongly at night, and the electricity production from solar panels decreases markedly after 5–6pm in the afternoon when the sun goes down, whereas our peak electricity consumption is typically around 8pm. So Elon Musk has also created large home batteries to store electricity for a few hours, potentially bridging the time gap renewables suffer from and allowing us to use solar panels on our rooftops to meet all our domestic electricity needs. There is also SpaceX: of course we are going to Mars! It is just a question of when. Mindful that the 6–8 months journey – each way – requires a lot of good planning, Musk is thinking ahead. He wants to cut the tremendous waste represented by the loss of the launching rockets inherent to all space missions thus far: think about all these enormous Saturn V rockets lost after just one mission. And Space X has achieved the amazing technology exploit of being able to recuperate the launching rocket by having it land precisely on an offshore platform after its ascent into space, so it can be used again. We all watched over and over again when Space X achieved its first successful launcher retrieval in 2016; this is simply sensational.[8]

Back to the 200+-mile Tesla car batteries. Elon Musk also achieved this performance by challenging conventional wisdom. When it came to batteries, most auto manufacturers were concerned about electric connections and soldering. So, the prevailing idea was to put together as few as possible very large elements of battery. In my Fisker, for example, there are six large battery elements. When thinking about his own future batteries, Musk is rumored to have said: "this makes no sense at all. If we were afraid of soldering, we would never have had semi-conductors or computers!" Following this logic, a Tesla battery is composed of up to 15,000 lithium-ion battery cells, about 3,000 as many as found in a normal laptop computer battery. The Tesla batteries are assembled together in a semi-conductor style "clean room," and manufacturing them involves a gazillion soldering points. But this allows class-leading energy density for batteries (250 watt-hours for the Modal S, versus only 100 watt-hours in my Fisker's large A123 batteries) and the enviable range Tesla cars enjoy. With its Panasonic mass-produced lithium-ion cells, Tesla batteries are the cheapest at about $300 per kilowatt-hour. Tesla's batteries can also get charged more quickly than others: Musk and his automotive team have pioneered an emerging network of charging stations, where DC power is pumped directly into the batteries, allowing 150 new miles of range in a remarkably short twenty minutes. Plus, charging at these stations is absolutely free for Tesla car owners. At home, I have rigged a 220 (AC) volt charging station by putting two 110-volt outlets together, but the best I can do on either the Fisker or the eGolf in twenty minutes of charging is about 10 miles! In addition, the Tesla Model S has won many awards, from car magazines like *Motor Trend* to consumer publications like *Consumer Reports*. Tesla is expected to deliver over 100,000 Model S and X cars in 2017, a 30+% increase over 2016, with the first Model 3 cars also sold in Q3 and Q4.[9] Teslas are built in the New United Motor Manufacturing Inc. plant in Fremont, close to San Francisco and Silicon Valley, which Musk got for a song after GM and Toyota ended their manufacturing joint venture there. Space X rockets are made in the Los Angeles area. The lithium-ion batteries used in Teslas and in the storage units sold by Solar City (now merged with Tesla) are built in Musk's first "Gigafactory" in Nevada, the largest battery plant in the world. How can anyone say that we no longer make great products in America?

Perhaps when the new, smaller Tesla Model 3 comes off rolling the assembly chain in large numbers, my wife will trade her eGolf for one. Or perhaps by then VW will also have a 200-mile range battery. In any case, we are very happy campers driving every day on electric power, and we smile ear to ear as well when the annual service is due. No oil change; no change of filters; no coolant check; no valve train, camshaft, transmission and gearbox maintenance; no worries about a potential malfunction of the fuel injection system or the gas pump; no leaky engine block seals when the car gets old, nada! Just a quick check on the brakes and the battery, and we are good to go. The services are free, and we did not even have to pay extra for that when we bought the car. There is nothing as simple as an electric car in the realm of automobiles.

Tesla's marketing strategy was also quite astute. We are in Northern California, a very rich enclave, and many professionals here drive mid-sized imported sedans that, by the way, would be classified as large cars in Europe. One of Musk's goals for the first years of production of the Tesla Model S was to sell more of them in the Bay Area that any of the Audi A6s, BMW 5 series, or Mercedes E-class sedans. This goal achieved, Tesla had to offer a "SUV cum Minivan," even before a small car. One of the objectives of the expensive (about $100,000) Tesla Model X and its striking rear "gull wing" doors was to allow parents to easily install their babies or toddlers in the third row seat, without hurting their backs or struggling to get through a normal door. Interesting for a car that also claims to beat most Porsches in 0–60mph acceleration performance! Again, this is Northern California, where Sports Utility Vehicles are quite the rage. I have heard many times from friends and local Bay Area habitants that "SUVs are very safe, and this is why I drive one." My translation of this is: "so when you are driving while texting, or generally being sloppy at the wheel and you have an accident, only the other parties will get hurt when you hit them with your tank." These enormous things are also ugly. So large and high on wheels, why, even Michelangelo could not make one of them look good. What about their four-wheel drive ability? We live in San Francisco, where snow is non-existent: when there is a sprinkling of it on the very top of our nearby mountains, Mt Diablo and Mt Tamalpais, everyone gets up early and rushes to take pictures before it melts. Yet it seems like half the city drives gas-guzzling SUVs … sad, and not very good for energy conservation and the environment, either!

SUVs, because of their weight and lack of aerodynamic qualities, are also the last vehicles, Tesla aside, to be considered for an electric version. It is sobering for me as a car buff to see glamorous marques like Jaguar; Maserati; Bentley; and even Lamborghini launch or plan to launch SUVs. What is utilitarian in a Lamborghini? Or is it a return to their roots as the tractor company launched with WWII surplus parts by Ferruccio Lamborghini? I would much rather see their efforts focused on making attractive sports cars riding on electric platforms, to increase choices for environmentally conscious car aficionados. Ironically, this is why my Fisker only sold in small numbers, about 1,000 in total. It is an electric "Muscle Car," which looks just as good as Steve McQueen's Ford Mustang Mach 1 in the movie *Bullitt*. But there lies the rub. Most car enthusiasts, often called "petrol heads" in America, favor deep-throated V8s or screaming V12 Ferraris, not silent electrics. Fortunately, Elon Musk understood this and did his market segmentation well, targeting modern urban professionals interested in the latest clean tech vehicle as opposed to old-fashioned car enthusiasts. After his third and lower priced car, the Model 3, is in full-scale production he will be able to flood the country and the world with the electric cars we should all drive in the age of climate change. This is exactly why the market capitalization of Tesla is skyrocketing, no pun intended.

$$\star \quad \star \quad \star \quad \star \quad \star$$

From iPhones to personal energy: distributed networks and renewables

Ten years ago, well into the twenty-first century, most "serious" energy economists would still decry renewables as unable to make a dent in most countries' total energy matrix. What a difference the last decade has made. In October of 2016, the International Energy Agency (IEA) reported that total renewable energy capacity around the globe had overtaken coal power for the first time. Imagine this. Hydropower, wind, solar, and biomass together contribute more to electricity production than "King Coal." Just as London eventually escaped from its nineteenth-century nightmare of coal pollution and associated thick fog, countries such as China can aspire to cleaner air and clearer skies for their future. The recent progress of renewables in the global energy matrix is illustrated first by the sizable growth of solar and wind capacity in the two largest energy consumers of the world, China and the U.S. According to the IEA, China is the largest producer of wind power today, with the U.S. second; Germany, Spain, and India come next. China has the largest installed base of solar capacity as well, having overtaken Germany in 2015. Japan is third, followed by the U.S. and Italy. China is also the largest producer of hydropower in the world, well ahead of the U.S., with Brazil and Canada coming next.[10,11]

Second, progress in renewables is showcased by a number of European countries where the percentage of the energy matrix represented by renewables has reached very high levels. Germany leads the industrialized world in solar photovoltaic (PV) capacity per capita, has a fair amount of wind power as well, uses biomass extensively, and as such derives 34% of its electric power from renewables, a record among the world's twenty largest economies (G20). Denmark is at 50% of renewable energy, thanks to 42% of its electricity being produced from wind – Danish company Vestas is the largest producer of wind turbines in the world. Denmark aims to be 100% fossil fuel free by 2050, a goal shared by its larger Scandinavian neighbor Sweden. Sweden is also a leader in solar, wind, biomass, energy storage, smart electric grids and clean transport. Finland is also a large user of renewables, with a share of 38% of total energy. (Norway, with its abundant hydropower, is at 98%). Overall, the European Community has set itself a goal to reach 34% use of renewable energies for its total energy consumption by 2020 and is well on its way to reaching it.[12,13]

Traditional utility-based networks involve extremely complex production units, whether nuclear, coal-fired, or combined-cycle gas turbines. The high-voltage transmission grid has to be very sophisticated as well to accommodate the fact that some power units are base load, i.e. running all the time, while others are only used to meet "peak" demand, and voltages have to be kept constant amidst wide variations in demand. Contrast this with electricity self-sufficient homes thanks to solar panels; electric cars getting their batteries charged from surplus electricity at home; wind farms supplying entire towns. Renewables can foster "distributed" electricity networks that free themselves from high-voltage grids and bring to us a much simpler electricity future compared to the complexity of our traditional integrated utility system. America and its strength in technology innovation played a key role in making solar and wind power available on a large scale to the world. Even though we are lagging behind China in absolute renewables capacity and are far from the clean energy percentages seen in Europe, a lot of the needed ongoing technical developments are still taking place here. When it comes to renewables, China is the king of scale, and select European countries the closest to fossil fuel–free environments. But it is the U.S. that keeps pushing the innovation frontiers to help our planet achieve a cleaner and simpler electricity future.

The U.S. launched the solar energy business. It was NASA that first made photovoltaic (PV) solar panels usable, for its early satellite and Apollo missions. Since then we have been manufacturing solar panels in this country for close to fifty years. But we also have experienced ups and downs in the business, driven by changing political and regulatory regimes. The Chinese, on the other hand, took the proverbial ball and ran with it, bringing the scale of the business of PV solar panel manufacturing to a level few would have predicted. The cost of polycrystalline silicon used in solar panels decreased by 80% in less than a decade, allowing much lower costs than anticipated by U.S. solar industry players. This aggressive low-cost competition from China, where over 60% of the world's solar panels are now built, is why California-based Solyndra went bankrupt in 2011. Far from signaling any demise in the solar industry, though, it showed that the prices of solar panels had become so low that the industry could compete on price against other sources of electricity with little or no help from subsidies. But to drive the solar industry forward even faster, scale and low cost will not be enough. New breakthrough technologies will be needed, and those will likely come from Silicon Valley and other American centers of innovations.[14,15]

Hundreds of U.S. start-ups are working on new technologies that can transform the industry. It is riskier than just driving costs down through scale on existing technologies, but the potential payoff is higher. Cheaper and lighter DC to AC invertors needed to convert solar electricity to "home" current can help decrease installed costs; small wireless circuit boards that monitor and control the flow of electric current on solar panels can increase output by 25%; "plug and play," easy to install solar panels can allow large solar farms to be set up quickly even by unskilled workers; panels made of new materials can achieve performance breakthroughs, with giant companies like DuPont and Applied Materials involved in this as well as early stage companies. Stanford University is doing research in nanocrystalline silicon shells, or nanoshells, where more light gets trapped than in conventional photovoltaic panels; thin-film PV panels can displace today's ubiquitous polycrystalline silicon panels; and a number of U.S.-based chemicals and materials companies are seeking to manufacture at scale panels that do not rely on silicon: one of the leaders in the field, Arizona-based First Solar, is manufacturing a large number of solar panels using cadmium tellurium instead of silicon. Other thin-film materials used instead of silicon include amorphous silicon and copper indium gallium selenium (CIGS). Thin-film organic polymer flexible cells, printable inorganic thin-film flexible cells, dye-sensitized cells, and even quantum dots are other innovations for solar panels in the ongoing quest for new materials that trap light better than conventional cells. While all this research is undertaken, large U.S. solar players keep their cost of traditional panels low by manufacturing them abroad, such as First Solar in Malaysia and SunPower in the Philippines. However, there is still a fair number of solar panels manufacturing in America, with large players from abroad building new plants for the U.S. market. SolarWorld from Germany is building a huge plant in Oregon, as is Sanyo Electric from Japan. SolarCity, one of the largest solar installers in the country, produces its own panels in Buffalo, New York. Solar innovation is thriving in America, with funding still abundant despite early setbacks for both the federal government (Solyndra) and venture capitalists. Local state incentives are also plentiful, from states as diverse as Arizona; California; Florida; Nevada; New York; and Oregon. And little by little, this helps large states get an increasing amount of electricity from renewables. California leads the pack at 28%, a European level of renewables as a percentage of total electricity produced.[16,17]

We have many states in the West with ample sunshine. Others can benefit from a lot of wind, in the middle of the country and on the Eastern seaboard. As a result the U.S. is very active in wind turbine innovation. Airborne wind turbines that can access stronger and more consistent winds at altitudes close to 1,000 feet could be a great solution for offshore and sparsely populated onshore wind farms; similarly, helium-filled inflatable shells could allow wind turbines to operate at high altitudes; new models such as vertical axis turbines can help reduce the noise generated by traditional designs, allowing silent wind turbines designed specifically for rooftop use to supplement solar panels in urban areas. Innovations in energy storage, using for example wind powered hydro systems to pump water between lower and upper reservoirs, can help harness wind electricity when it is needed the most, during peak consumption hours. Further ahead, tunnel-based wind energy generators can accelerate the speed of the air, creating higher electricity outputs without large external blades rotating noisily at speed. Other wind innovating centers exist in Denmark; the Netherlands; New Zealand; and the United Kingdom, but the U.S. still leads when it comes to the number and scope of innovations being tested, and potentially brought to market.[18,19,20]

U.S. innovators are also extremely busy in the challenging area of electricity storage. To reach full potential for renewables, this challenge has to be solved. Unlike most other forms of energy, electricity has to be consumed the instant it is generated, since our capability to store it is limited and expensive. Storage can be achieved upstream of electricity production: water stored in reservoirs above dams and gas turbines that can start repeated times, quickly and inexpensively, both represent ways to produce incremental quantities of electricity for peak demand times. But once the electrons start flowing, they better be used. Today, electricity storage is mostly achieved through heavy and expensive batteries that are inadequate for large amounts of power. This is why most traditional utilities use a combination of hydro electricity and gas-fired power turbines to meet peak demand. When it comes to renewables, the wind blows stronger during the night, and solar obviously cannot work after nightfall. Electricity storage on a large scale would allow wind and solar electricity power generated hours before to be used during the hours of peak electricity consumption, around diner time typically in most countries.

I have been an "angel" investor in a company that aimed to use molten salt, then molten glass, to store electricity. The underlying concept was simple, but fiendishly difficult to realize operationally, even more so at scale. Surplus electricity in early afternoons would have been used to melt salt in a first stage, then glass. Molten salt and glass keep very high temperatures for a few hours, so the heat produced from them in the afternoon could be used to drive a steam turbine a little later, just in time for the evening peak demand hours. The company had raised successfully $10 million from the Department of Energy's Advanced Research Projects Agency-Energy (ARPA-E), and another $4 million from a large refiner and an aluminum producer, so the prognosis looked good in early testing. But after a few years of prototype work we all realized that at least a hundred million dollars would be needed to build a first plant at scale, and the project had to be abandoned. This is one example among many. Eventually the electricity storage equation will be solved; the golden question is, how?

Compressed air energy storage may be a potential solution. The technology is not new. Paris used it in the late nineteenth century to drive an assortment of small urban machines, the Eiffel Tower lifts, and engines to help suburban trains climb the hill to the western town of Saint-Germain-en-Laye. Traditionally this storage process has used large underground salt caverns to receive the compressed air when the energy is not needed, to then release it for consumption during periods of high demand. But these set-ups are somewhat inflexible, and therefore not much in use today. Developing smaller compressed air systems might allow them to be placed on the grid where they might be the most useful.

Fuel cells using hydrogen represent another technology that could be close to prime time. Again, fuel cells are not new: the Germans used them in the first half of the twentieth century; and there was a boom in fuel cell investments in the first years of the twenty-first century. A Canadian company based in Vancouver, BC, Ballard Systems, received around that time hundreds of millions of dollars in funding from blue-chip companies such as Daimler Benz and General Motors. The Ballard fuel cells did not take off – too expensive to make. But as we saw earlier, auto giants Toyota, Honda, and Hyundai are now betting on them and are poised to introduce hydrogen-powered cars in 2018. There are quite a few hydrogen fuel cell–powered buses in a number of cities worldwide. And in electricity storage, fuel cells may soon play a bigger role. On the research front, liquid methanol fuel cells are being developed at the University of Southern California and Caltech's Jet Propulsion Laboratory, the funding originally coming from the U.S. Defense Advanced Research Projects Agency (DARPA) in the late 1980s. DARPA is very interested in such applications, which would allow U.S. soldiers to carry less weight with much lighter power supplies. A significant amount of power supply is needed for all the sophisticated equipment a modern soldier brings along, and weight is becoming a significant issue. The idea of new fuel cells is again to create new forms of electricity storage that are smaller and lighter, so they can be moved close to where electricity is used – homes and people – as opposed to where it is produced. Just like with solar panels, materials play a huge role in fuel cells. In particular, the high price of the platinum catalysts used in today's fuel cells has limited their application. There is a lot of academic and industrial effort aiming to find a substitute for platinum, and a potential alternative being researched at Stanford is carbon nanotube, also called graphene.[21]

Longer-term, supercapacitors packed with a compound having good energy storage properties, vanadium nitride, could also play a role in smart grid electricity storage. Capacitors can store and release electricity much more quickly than batteries, so most of their applications today are restricted to operations with a high frequency of energy storage and release. For example, Formula One racing cars use them in ultra-sophisticated electricity modules that allow braking energy to be stored and released several times per lap. With carbon fiber brakes allowing deceleration of up to 5 Gs and therefore producing a lot of energy, these regenerating units harness braking energy and can increase the power of their engine from 600 horsepower or so to over 1,000 for several seconds, until the next strong application of the brakes. The new supercapacitors using vanadium nitride being developed at the University of Michigan could dramatically expand their potential range of applications and thus become part of the solution for electricity storage.

And then, there is a very simple (yes!) application showing much progress and potential for electricity storage. This application stands at the end-user level, downstream of the electricity supply chain. "Demand Response," or DR, is increasingly viewed as a very useful component of the panoply of distributed energy resources available to us. Charging stations for electric vehicles, rooftop solar panels, home batteries for electricity storage, and microgrids at the urban level are all part of this distributed energy equation. In many parts of the country, local electric utilities, mainly electric cooperatives, are using DR to complement wholesale markets and this panoply of distributed energy resources through the use of residential electric water heaters. Yes, the simple heating tank in your basement that guarantees you don't have to take a cold shower in the morning can also help create electricity storage on a good scale. Utilities have already used for a long time direct load control programs to optimize the timing of resistance heating in domestic water heaters, to achieve a cost-effective way to manage peak capacity. Today, with the evolution of the "Internet of Things," there is a cost-effective way to achieve two-way communications between the utilities and a whole range of home devices such as thermostats for floor heating, electric water heaters, water pumps, and other connected appliances. This allows two-way communication with water heaters to provide real time electricity usage measurement. Utilities can also monitor water heaters during charging cycles to ensure that load management is truly dynamic, without risk of such a program causing customers not to have hot water available due to load constraints. Residential water heating can thus become part of distributed energy for our electric grids.

This is particularly helpful in the increasing number of states that have a high share of solar and wind power in their energy production matrix. When this share of renewables – hydro excluded – starts approaching 50% during periods of the day, a large component of distributed energy resources at the end-user level becomes indispensable to avoid overproduction during periods of weak demand, and generation of non-dispatchable electricity. Such instances of overproduction, which have already occurred frequently in the Midwest and

Texas, lead to negative energy prices and the curtailing of renewable energy generation, two bad outcomes. In these regions and states where there is a large Federal Production Tax Credit available to wind generators ($20–24 per megawatt-hour), wind electricity producers will continue producing electricity even when wholesale prices are negative. California is getting there, too. In the state, a large excess of solar generation capacity – up to five gigawatts – may start causing negative electricity prices in the afternoon. Innovations in distributed energy, some as simple as water heater usage optimization and others more distant in the future, are needed in relative short order to help states and utilities manage the positive trend of growth in production of electricity from renewable sources.

Returning to sophisticated technologies for the future, one has to mention the harnessing of magnetic fields, with a very long-term but virtually limitless field of applications. High-efficiency charging systems using magnetic fields could be used to transmit wirelessly large electric currents between metal coils placed several feet apart along a roadway. This would create an "electric highway" that would allow electric vehicles to have their batteries charged as they cruise down the highway. Today's best demonstration of the power from magnetic fields is the 275 mph (440 kmh) Chinese Maglev train linking Shanghai airport to the city. Japan is preparing its own Maglev train, on the much longer Tokyo to Nagoya route (220 miles or 350 km), so that it is ready for the upcoming 2020 Tokyo Olympics – just like when the country inaugurated the world's first high speed railway, the Shinkansen, for the 1964 Tokyo Olympics. Efforts are underway to bring this Japanese Maglev technology to the U.S. with a potential New York to Washington DC line, which will be amazing when realized. Planning for the DC to Baltimore section has already been approved. Further out in time and performance, there is Elon Musk (always him!) at the vanguard of magnetic field technology with his Hyperloop concept that would leapfrog existing Maglevs in terms of speed. The Hyperloop proposes to propel passenger-carrying capsules inside a sealed tube at speeds up to 700 mph (1,100 kmh). The capsules would ride on an air cushion and be propelled by linear induction motors, a kind of closed and sealed Maglev.

★　★　★　★　★

Promise and pitfalls of artificial intelligence and automation

In his 1930 "Economic Possibilities" essay, the great English twentieth-century economist John Maynard Keynes wrote that by 2030, developed economies would be wealthy enough so that leisure time, rather than work, would characterize the lifestyles of their citizens. With perfect timing, artificial intelligence (AI), and systematic, robotized automation should bring to us the era of prosperity and leisure Keynes promised us for 2030, right? Think again.[22,23]

When it comes to AI and automation, like many innovations from the "sharing economy," the initial steps are always full of promise. Who can argue against a domestic robot facilitating house-cleaning chores for today's busy couples? Or against AI programs in automobiles that may allow us to be on "auto-pilot" mode while cruising down highways so that we can eat, read, or fiddle with our iPhones while "driving?" It is when these AI technological innovations become widespread that societal problems start occurring. Then the world suddenly awakens to realize that, essentially, the "revolution" that actually took place is replacing whole professions enjoying a complete array of social benefits – health care, retirement, etc. – with automation and robots. Today we are still decades away from a world of ubiquitous robots. Instead, we have the new sharing economy, in which millions are part-time contrac- tors. Contractors who have no benefits, no employment rights, and are at the total mercy of their employer even for the total amount of hours they work. The sharing economy is a complete misnomer. It is innovative in the sophis- ticated software programs it uses to function, and it helps provide flexible and responsive services to millions. But when it comes to those trying to make a living through it, it is more like a return to the Oliver Twist Industrial Age. The key new word here is "precariat." Taxi drivers; chambermaids; hotel staff and waiters; professions that typically have been pillars of local communities, are all being replaced by "on-demand" contractors, with little or no guarantees in their work. The losses of health and retirement benefits for millions earning meager wages in casual labor have morphed into gains for the Airbnb, Lyft, and Uber management teams and shareholders. That is the hidden "sharing" that is taking place: large investment gains for a few in exchange for foregone social benefits and increasingly precarious work for many. "Uberworked and Underpaid" has become a famous line.

Countries and cities around the world are, slowly, recognizing there is a fun- damental problem with the sharing economy and its legions of contractors with only hourly pay replacing real jobs with real benefits. Some have banned Uber outright, or at least some of its services, like many cities in India, as well as Aus- tin, Texas. Others, such as San Francisco, have started to regulate Airbnb short- term type rentals so that developers cannot buy apartments just to transform them into cheap alternative to hotels, staffed with contractors suffering from precarious working conditions. Taxis around the world have organized against the "Uberization" of their working world, with mixed success: virtually none in the U.S.; some in Germany, France, and Italy, countries that have banned some of the group's lowest cost services. For example, France's Constitutional Court upheld in September 2015 a ban on Uber using non-professional drivers in the country. Recently, the advocate-general for the European Court of Justice has declared Uber to be a transport group, which if upheld by the Court will force the company to comply with local taxi rules everywhere within the E.U. But it is London, the company's largest market in Europe, where the famous black cabs and their cabbies are an institution to reckon with, that is giving Uber its biggest challenge. On September 22, 2017, London stripped Uber of its license to operate due to "lack of corporate responsibility." The company has both apologized and appealed the ruling, a process that may take years before a final decision is reached. A tribunal in London also ruled that Uber's drivers are entitled to the minimum wage, sickness payments, and holidays. The company replied and appealed again, saying this ruling would prevent it from offering its drivers the flexibility of work they desire. Tough going, but while appeals proceed, Uber continues to operate ... China, on the other hand, has elected to help launch rival platforms to Uber, the company opting to sell out to one of them and exit this giant market. Taxi cooperatives, like Yellow Cab in California, now have their own taxi apps. Unlike with Uber, Yellow Cab drivers share in the new benefits brought by these apps through the cooperative.

The damage done by the sharing economy to the quality of low–middle-class jobs around the world pales against what can happen with widespread automation, however. Longer term, for Uber executives and shareholders, driver contractors – even low-paid and with no benefits – can advantageously be replaced by driverless cars. No more embarrassing PR moments for Uber founder Travis Kalanick when discussing with his drivers! There are many well-financed early stage companies in Silicon Valley working feverishly on driving automation under the umbrella of huge companies like Apple, Ford, GM, Google and Uber, or independently. There are also many start-ups building the domestic robots of the future, to clean rooms, deliver room service or do the laundry. Some business managers cannot wait: as Donald Trump's first nominee for Labor Secretary, CKE Restaurants (Carl's Jr. and Hardee's) CEO Andrew Puzder, was reported to have said about robots replacing workers, "they are always polite, they always upsell, they never take a vacation, they never show up late, there is never a slip-and-fall, or an age, sex or race discrimination case." In the U.S. in particular, where the relative power of corporations against their employees has increased massively over the last thirty-five years, one can easily imagine how automation is viewed as a future Eldorado for company executives and investors alike.[24]

Let's leave cars and hotel rooms and look at trucking in America. The industry moves over 70% of the freight tonnage in the U.S. (10.5 billion tons in 2016) and employs no less than 3.5 million professional truck drivers, with about nine million employed in this giant industry. Truck drivers represent the largest remaining bastion of relatively well-paid blue-collar jobs in the country, with many drivers earning between $50,000 and $75,000 per year. Beyond those employed by numerous small and large trucking operators, there are also 350,000 truck owner–operators. What happens when automation replaces these drivers? This is not for tomorrow, since handling a large semi requires a fair amount of skill not easily transferrable to a robot, but the number of livelihoods potentially involved dwarfs any other profession subject to displacement by AI and automation.

There are three ways AI and automation can impact our future. One, they can be used to replace wholesale activities performed by workers today, blue- and white-collar. Two, in a more positive trend for employment prospects in America, they can improve the competitiveness of selected industries to a degree that we start seeing "re-shoring" of underlying activities, i.e. bringing back to the U.S. activities that were previously outsourced to low income countries. Three, they can open new paths to activities or whole industries that do not even exist today, solving seemingly intractable problems such as climate change and water availability, as well as universal access to food, health care and sanitized conditions for all. Let's have a quick look at each one of these three scenarios.

The replacement of wholesale activities performed by workers today through the massive use of robots poses fundamental, even existential, societal issues as we saw earlier. If pushed to the limits we can see today, this replacement of workers by automatons could lead to unemployment levels of 20–40% in developed countries. How would our traditional democratic political process cope with such disruption? Hard to predict. However, as long as we live in democracies, we can be sure of one thing: working people vote, robots do not. And voting patterns may be exacerbated – towards xenophobism, protectionism, and more generally speaking towards a retrenchment within one's borders – by what we have seen in terms of employment shifts in little more than one generation. A very significant number of manufacturing positions left the U.S. to go to Mexico after NAFTA was signed, then to China, and beyond China to yet lower income countries such as Vietnam and the Philippines. Despite the recent election of Donald Trump and the openly protectionist voices among his cabinet members and advisors (e.g. Robert Lighthizer; Peter Navarro; and Wilbur Ross), it is by no means certain that this offshoring manufacturing trend has abated or will do so within the next few years. Beyond manufacturing, offshoring has also affected millions of white-collar jobs, from call centers to software programming, when millions of jobs left America to go to India, Southeast Asia, and even Central Europe and South America over the last twenty years. This trend, which interestingly has not received much attention from the Trump administration except for a mild change in how working visas (H1s) are handled in the U.S., is very much alive. Ask any start-up in Silicon Valley where its team of programmers is located, and the response will almost look like a world map: India, of course, but also countries as diverse as Argentina and Estonia; Brazil and Latvia; the Czech Republic and Slovakia; Russia and Ukraine; Spain and South Korea; and so forth. This is obviously not limited to start-ups and is one of the reasons – along with offshore manufacturing – why the giants of Silicon Valley have not added nearly as many U.S. jobs as their size would suggest. This is evolving, with the fast growing need for data centers providing tens of thousands of new jobs across the country. New economy Amazon is now the second largest U.S. company by headcount, but with less than a quarter of the jobs of Wal-Mart and its 2.3 million employees.[25] Create a "local employment intensity" index tracking American jobs, divided by market capitalization: the likes of Apple; Facebook; Google, Netflix, and Twitter will be at the bottom of it. What about scenarios where technology works for us instead?[26]

★   ★   ★   ★   ★

Making technology work for us

In an age where Corporate Social Responsibility appears to have died without ever being much alive, there is a growing chasm between corporations and societies in the western democratic world, because the fundamental issue of employment is seen as completely disconnected from new business models. Trust between the public and the business world is at an all-time low. Beyond the well-maligned banking and financial sector, it is now affecting even the perception of Silicon Valley. In a short decade, the Valley has started to lose its shine as a hotbed of innovation for the advancement of mankind. It is increasingly perceived as a rich club of faceless behemoths that play against the public interest in areas as diverse as privacy (AI being used to read our minds for advertising, commercial and even political purposes); rampant sexism; unpaid taxes; and, of course, robots taking jobs. This is very much an emerging development, since by and large Silicon Valley and its band of plucky entrepreneurs still enjoy more trust in the public's eyes than many other businesses and industries. To keep that trust from eroding further, though, Northern California entrepreneurs will all have to focus much more on improving the competitiveness of existing industries across America, local employment, social conditions, and blaze new paths to solve the planet's most pressing issues.[27]

AI and global data–based analytics can make simple businesses like call centers as well as very complex activities like medical diagnostics much more effective, with less reliance on low-cost labor. Robots can help factories in the Midwest and the Southeast manufacture cars much more efficiently. It is not a stretch of imagination to anticipate that in the medium-term whole industries like call centers; software writing; and traditional manufacturing could be "de-offshored," with large numbers of U.S. companies electing to bring these activities back to America. These activities would not be as employment intensive as they used to be. Still, their repatriation would likely enhance our own economy and employment patterns. CEOs rediscovering their companies' local community roots, as well as the technology world making this possible, would see their reputations enhanced as a result. Short-term transitions may be challenging, with current industrial winners like China experiencing some of the difficulties our Appalachia and Midwest regions experienced during the last few decades. But this new equilibrium, with a better convergence of corporate and public interests in America, might be more sustainable than the current one.

The big prize for AI and automation, though, is being the new key to solve the world's most pressing and intractable issues. Climate change. Water availability. Distribution of crops to eradicate hunger for the billion-plus people who still suffer from hunger or malnutrition today. Health care, sanitized conditions and vaccines for all. Of course, these are all interrelated. The stakes are very high. Absence of real solutions within the next 50–100 years means that we may really have to colonize Mars after all, or to retreat to New Zealand – for those who can afford it – to avoid new global wars triggered by desertification, flooding, and resulting famines. There is little doubt that the talent exists to tackle these enormous issues successfully. At a number of California universities and start-up incubators entrepreneurs are given a set of problems to solve, e.g. how to bring sanitized toilets and clean water to the two billion people who do not have access to them. This helps channel entrepreneurial energy towards addressing urgent global issues as opposed to attempting to create yet another unicorn in social media.[28]

Even though the required capabilities are here, success is by no means a foregone conclusion. Political will is uneven, to say the least. The "Big Tech" pioneers, in their ambition to create a more open and transparent world, one in which technology could potentially help alleviate diseases, hunger and poverty, may have had a more idealistic view of their mission than traditional corporate CEOs. But today's technology leaders struggle to articulate their ambitions in terms of contributions to society, and serial problems are emerging. They built ultra-sophisticated AI engines to extract – at no cost – their users' personal information. This (private?) data is then sold to advertisers in high-speed types of auctions that are as unregulated and opaque as they are profitable – remember the dark pools of finance? And technology companies have proved incapable of preventing the manipulation of information shared with millions. In one glaring case, Russian interference in the 2016 U.S. presidential election relied heavily on the manipulation of social media channels. This was so well hidden within the zillions of social media interactions that the companies involved did not see it happening, first denying any issue, and then reluctantly admitting this was a serious problem.[29,30]

The necessary dialogue between these technology leaders, the political world, and NGOs is strikingly absent from most debates today. This lack of dialogue has created many avoidable barriers. Thus, when it comes to genetically modified (GM) foods, the world is divided. Large agricultural producers like Argentina, Brazil, Canada, and the U.S. essentially allow everything, while preventing even the most basic public education such as the labeling of GM food in supermarkets. All the power to agribusinesses, none to consumers. At the other extreme, GM foods are not allowed in Continental Europe. This issue is one of the biggest stumbling blocks preventing a trade agreement between the E.U. and the U.S. When it comes to food, I personally tend to trust the French (or the Japanese) more than American industrial food producers. I also like the European Union's very public stand that "the health of our citizens is more important than the profits of American processed food companies." But I also deplore the absence of dialogue, the consequence of profound mistrust between the political world, business, and NGOs. Surely science has a role to play in ensuring there is food for everyone in our planet, even amidst changing climate conditions? Similarly, the political world and Northern California's biotech companies have to improve their interactions to ensure that advances in understanding the human genome lead to advances for all, not just expensive cures for a few. Technology will be an indispensable partner to society in tackling climate change, provided that politicians and fossil fuel industry lobbyists do not get in the way by denying this is an urgent issue. One day, entrepreneurs and industrialists like those who helped over a billion Indians get smart phones will also help the hundreds of million Indians who do not have access to sanitized toilets get them, too. And clean water; and vaccines; and basic primary care health services, not yet widely available to 2.5 billion people in poor areas of the world. Meeting these challenges through modern science is how the tech industry can help create a world that works for all of us. Technology may be at a critical crossroads, one that the industry and its leaders may or may not see. One fork leads to the continuation of current trends of so-called disruptive innovation pitching wealthy entrepreneurs and investors against the interests of millions of working people. From a social point of view, the disruption here is reactionary, and if left unchecked may lead to much misery for "on-demand" working people. The other fork of the road leads to a much better world where automation and AI serve mankind. Tech luminaries such as Eric Schmidt (Alphabet, Google) believe AI can be harnessed to help solve climate change and food security. Google's "Intelligence Designer" aims to use machine learning advances to create an "artificial general intelligence" that would be broad enough to help solve problems at the planetary scale. Many executives from the dominant five technology giants – Alphabet, Amazon, Apple, Facebook, and Microsoft – have made talks on this theme, without offering much in terms of specifics. We are still many years away from driverless flying cars, but perhaps can solve world hunger?[31,32]

Technology can and should take a leading role in tackling global issues. Solar panels on every roof, water filters in every house, millions of electric cars, conservation, and broad availability of water for all can help put the brakes on climate change. Global health challenges can also be addressed at the same time, since water issues cause many deaths in low-income countries. A more decentralized, diverse and sustainable agriculture, and better conceived food supply chains, can also lead to improved availability of food for the world's poorest people while improving the environment. New devices can extract water from human waste, achieving the trifecta of bringing clean water and sanitation to those who do not have access to them while producing energy. Two billion people could see their lives changed as a result, with lower infant mortality, longer life expectancy as well as access to electricity. The Bill and Melinda Gates Foundation is supporting such an initiative, to build and install "Omniprocessors" around the world's poorest countries.[33,34] Mobile telecommunications are, slowly but surely, opening education and telemedicine even to the most destitute. Once telemedicine is widespread, advances in AI may allow medical diagnostics to be instant and effective, reaching remote villages everywhere. The combination of e-reading and AI can eventually help patients manage directly nutrition issues, chronic diseases, and pediatric and maternal health, enabling prevention to have a much bigger impact on health care than today.

We do need to be careful, though: as seen above, technology can be a double-edged-sword, and if poorly harnessed will exacerbate our problems. Back to Uber and Lyft – the real convenience achieved for their customers requires many more cars on the streets than actual passengers, so that waiting times are minimized. As a result, many cities in the U.S. are experiencing unprecedented traffic congestion. In a September 8, 2017 report titled "Uber and Lyft Bloating SF Traffic by 15–20 Percent," the SFCTA deputy director Joe Castiglione is quoted as having told the *San Francisco Chronicle*:

> The perception that there are a tremendous number of (Uber and Lyft) vehicles out on the streets today is, in fact, true. We see huge numbers of trips across all days of the week, primarily concentrated in the most congested parts of the city and at the most congested times of day.[35]

The late and much regretted San Francisco Mayor Ed Lee is also quoted in the article: "there's too many reports about double parking, picking up people in the wrong places, compromising bike paths and bike lanes." San Francisco District 6 Supervisor Jane Kim, who is studying the imposition of a small per-ride tax on Lyft and Uber, issued a press release on the same problem:

> Ride-sharing companies are logging more than a half million vehicle miles on our streets every day. This is having an effect on our quality of life as well as creating serious public safety concerns – no one wants the ambulance that might save their life to be stuck in a traffic jam.[36]

This excess of individual vehicles leads to a very negative environmental impact – air pollution, noise and safety issues. Far from solving the urban transportation issues of tomorrow, the new ride companies may instead exacerbate the traditional problem – well over fifty years old – created by too many automobiles in our cities.

To achieve world-improving outcomes, the technology world needs to serve as a catalyst to fundamental changes in awareness, attitudes, and behavior across whole populations and their political leaders. A step change in societal engagement by the "disrupters" is a necessary condition to jump-start this positive evolution. The resources, creativity and practical sense of the technological giants of our era should be directed towards our biggest issues. Hackathons to solve social and environmental issues, anyone? Artificial intelligence and robots – by themselves very complicated – can make our lives simpler and healthier if we discover how to adjust to the social disruptions they may cause. This is a huge challenge, but there is no other country on earth that is dedicating so much thought to a future where robots perform a lot of our work. President Obama invested a lot of time on this while in office, meeting frequently with technology CEOs to think ahead about societal transformations in an increasingly automated future. Clearly, this is a topic he felt compelled to study, to anticipate potential fundamental changes in our country and the world. He talked about that to reporters during his last G7 summit, and most European journalists were stunned: "wow, none of our politicians here at home has even started to think about these issues. To hear President Obama talk about them is to realize that we are (in France; in Germany; in the U.K.; etc.) at ground zero in terms of the much required thinking we need to do in this area." President Obama is no longer in office, but the dialogue he started will continue, with many American companies, states and constituencies leading the way. We are both very close to and very far from Keynes' projected 2030 leisure world. Some technology innovations and the companies that promote them pull us relentlessly towards it, whereas others are pushing us back to the old social servitudes Keynes thought would be eradicated in the developed world. But Keynes himself had not anticipated the great progress achieved during the last thirty years in the developing world. He never foresaw that over 80% of humanity today would have food, a solid roof and basic education. Can new advances in automation and AI help us achieve this for 100% of mankind, without destroying living standards for millions in the developed world and, most importantly, our planet itself? This is the challenge confronting the technology titans of the twenty-first century, and also all of us.

Image 6.1 Secretary George Shultz and Author in San Francisco on November 15, 2017

Image 6.2 U.S. Senators Paul Wellstone, Ted Kennedy, and Tom Harkin with Senate Minority Leader Tom Daschle at the podium, April 25, 2001

Image 7.1 The Founding Fathers signing the Constitution in Philadelphia on September 17, 1787, oil on canvas painting by Howard Chandler Christy, located on the House Wing, East Stairway, US Capitol

Credit: Architect of the Capitol.

Image 7.2 First transcontinental railroad: golden spike ceremony, Promontory Summit, Utah Territory, May 10, 1869

Image 7.3 From train to ocean: double stacked containers cross the U.S. by rail, from East Coast and Midwest to Pacific Ocean ports, where ships take them to Asia. A container ship is shown here leaving San Francisco and the Golden Gate

Image 8.1 Original wind power and Fisker Karma

Image 10.1 Industrial solar farm

Image 10.2 Offshore wind farm

Image 10.3 Senator Tom Daschle and Author in New York City, December 5, 2017

9 How did we get here?

Five major causes

Complexity is not in our historical, political, or economic DNA. Our founding fathers devised the simplest yet most effective constitution of any republic; for a couple of centuries our political system helped us overcome two World Wars, the Great Depression, and the Cold War; most of our successful businesses were built upon simple and winning premises; our greatest business and scientific pioneers, from Alexander Bell and Thomas Edison to Steve Jobs and Elon Musk, promoted non-incremental inventions that rendered more complex incumbent systems obsolete. The telegraph eliminated pony expresses; electricity displaced gas-fired lamps; everyone wants an iPhone; we will go to Mars with re-usable rockets; and electric vehicles will eventually relegate internal combustion engines to the museums of industry. So how did we get to the current state of affairs, where we are literally surrounded by complexity in pretty much all aspects of our lives? It was a complex path as well ... full of incremental changes, one on top of each other. I see five major causes for the intrusion of complexity in our society, spanning over seventy years.

One: our recent history and politics

After our success in World War II, legislative battles paved the way for many of the complex challenges that afflict us today. For example, our government and opposing parties could never agree to establish a simple form of universal health care coverage. This could have been achieved through a state-driven system like in the U.K., Australia, and Canada, or a system with clearly delineated roles for the public and private sectors like those found throughout Continental Europe and in Japan. Back in 1945, President Harry Truman proposed a universal national health insurance program. In his remarks to Congress, he declared,

> Millions of our citizens do not have a full measure of opportunity to achieve and enjoy good health. Millions do not now have protection or security against the economic effects of sickness. The time has arrived for action to help them attain that opportunity and that protection.

We know what happened to Truman's proposal. Fierce opposition arose to the idea of a national health insurance plan and its funding by a monthly fee to be paid by all working Americans. The plan would have also covered those unemployed, as well as retirees. Even after winning the 1948 election, Truman could not muster the political votes to get his national health insurance plan passed through Congress, where the opposition from both Republicans and conservative Democrats was just too strong.[1,2]

Therefore, health insurance became tied to work, as Truman was able to cobble together a majority in Congress to achieve this. White-collar professionals got good health packages from their employers, and blue-collar workers got theirs through labor unions bargaining for their members' collective health benefits. Inevitably, this led to the plight of retired Americans: no longer employed, they lost access to health care coverage when they needed it the most. Lyndon Johnson and his Great Society remedied that in 1965, with the creation of the federal and universal Medicare for those above 65, and the state administrated Medicaid programs for the needy. Work-related insurance; Medicare; and fifty Medicaid programs: layer upon layer, our health care system piled complexity on top of complexity. It did not stop there, not in health care and not in most government activities. The Ronald Reagan presidency marked a triumphant return for conservative political ideals, the main one being that the private sector has to be involved in everything. This was emphasized in powerful terms by Reagan's assertion that "the government is not the solution, it is the problem." Incremental complexity was a direct corollary. Having the private sector involved in government social programs adds to complexity and costs, since it is complicated for companies to square the need to maximize profits with the mission to help those at the bottom of our economic ladder. And this mission is often unfulfilled: throughout the Reagan era, millions of Americans still suffered from lack of medical insurance, their number growing year after year.

Hence, thirty years later, Obamacare and its complex network of health marketplaces or exchanges, an idea directly borrowed from the conservative Heritage Foundation think tank and first applied in Massachusetts under a Republican governor, Mitt Romney. With Obamacare's long-term existence in doubt after the 2016 election of Donald Trump, the potential post-mortems all agree on one point. It is the simple components of the ACA that have worked, not the exchanges: the Medicaid expansion; the ability for young adults under 26 to stay on their parents' health insurance; and the obligation for insurance companies to cover pre-existing conditions, all of which remain very popular across the land and the political spectrum. There is no doubt that President Obama would have gone for a type of universal single payer system, or "Medicare for all," infinitely simpler than the fifty state health exchanges (plus the federal one), if he was even close to having the votes in Congress for this solution. The ACA may become history one day, but one thing is certain: its proposed replacement, or AHCA, narrowly passed by House Republicans on May 4, 2017, would have added further complexity to our health care system.

In particular, the proposed way to deal with pre-existing conditions was such a complex game of "Russian dolls" that few commentators attempted to describe it in detail. It kind of went like an old computer program, based upon "if" conditions: (a) if you suffer from a pre-existing condition; (b) if you live in a state that voted to opt-out of the pre-existing conditions federal mandate; (c) if this state got its pre-existing waiver approved by the U.S. Health and Human Services Department; and (d) if you have interrupted your health insurance payments for more than three months; then you will be placed in your state's high-risk pool, with its share of available federal funding subject to some uncertainty at this stage; (e) if there are enough such high-risk pool dollars available to help you purchase insurance, then you will be covered. Simple!

The ever-increasing polarization of American politics, fueled by economic resentment felt by millions, quasi-tribal anger at complex changes many cannot grasp, and enthusiastic embrace of diversity on the opposite side, also makes simple political compromises virtually impossible to achieve. President Reagan passed his landmark tax reform by working closely with Democratic Speaker of the House Tip O'Neill. A decade later, no such working relationship existed between President Clinton and Republican Speaker Newt Gingrich. Partisanship increased further when the Supreme Court decided the election of George W. Bush in 2000, and then went up a notch again during the two Obama terms, with the Republican-led Senate leaving a Supreme Court seat vacant for almost a year instead of voting on an Obama nominee, Judge Merrick Garland. This is also why Obama's ACA, even with its foundation coming from a conservative think tank, passed Congress without a single Republican vote. Aren't compromises usually messy? Perhaps, but less so when occurring across the aisle, usually towards the center of political ideas. When center of right Republicans work with center of left Democrats, pragmatism tend to carry the day. Simpler solutions emerge then, since pragmatism, as opposed to ideology, is built upon practicality.

The opposite becomes true when partisanship becomes so strong that laws can only be passed with the votes from a single party. Assuming, as is the case today, that single party majorities are narrow, legislation then becomes hostage to the most extreme members of that party, and compromises have to factor in ideological demands instead of practical ones. Looking again at the AHCA for illustration, the original package that Speaker Ryan could not pass through the House in March 2017 was certainly not simple. When the ideologues of the "Freedom Caucus" became involved in amending the AHCA, to get the few additional votes needed, complexity went up a notch. Evidence of this was the "Russian dolls" attempt to eliminate the universality of insurance for patients with pre-existing conditions. The need to pass laws "on a wire," with razor-thin majorities, leads to a patchwork of last minute "add-ons" to legislation. At the margin, when the approval of two or three congress people is needed, these representatives or senators can dictate a lot of incremental changes, always adding to complexity.

On taxes, one of the few mantras both Democrats and Republicans adhere to is the imperative to simplify our tax code. Would it be so simple . . . the "how to" solutions are totally divergent across the aisle. The late 2017 GOP tax law is strictly a partisan exercise, even though its attempt to trigger the repatriation of the trillions of corporate dollars parked offshore had some bi-partisanship potential. When it comes to reforming taxes, we are back to the conundrum of our partisan age: how to get the majority party's members to vote together, as opposed to fashioning a practical bi-partisan compromise in the center. The incentive for Congress Republicans to vote together on taxes is certainly there: most of them, principally in the House, egged on by their interested donors, support deep tax cuts for corporations and wealthy individuals passionately. The House Republicans' play book calls for such tax cuts to be financed by the shredding of the nation's safety net if politically possible, through budget deficits if not – "Reagan showed that deficits do not matter," said former Vice President Dick Cheney.[3,4] And indeed most economists agree the 2017 GOP tax package will increase our debt over the next ten years, by some $1.5 trillion. Pragmatic proposals calling for fiscal responsibility both in taxation and through "entitlement reform" are not part of the current debate in Congress.

But what happens beyond taxes? Little new legislation is likely to pass in 2018. Democrats will be hardened in their opposition after the partisan tax law, and legislation outside the budget reconciliation process requires 60 votes, which the Republicans do not have. The November 2018 mid-term elections will start to loom large, slowing down congressional activities even more. Hopefully government budgets will still be passed, most likely at the cost of yet bigger deficits, the least difficult path to approval being agreement on increased spending – in defense (for Republican votes) as well as on social programs (for Democratic votes).

Two: the increased role of finance in our economy

Let's leave our politicians alone for a minute, and in the era of "Citizens United" focus on those who bankroll their election campaigns. Since the early 1990s, we have lived in an era that increasingly resembles the "Gilded Age" and the "Roaring Twenties," which of course ended with the 1929 Wall Street Crash and the Great Depression that followed. During the last twenty years the role of finance has steadily increased in our economy, fueled by a proliferation of very complex financial instruments. These instruments have two main objectives: extract rent for those who design them and insulate the finance "rentiers" from risk, usually by leveraging some type of federal protection such as the one guaranteeing retail banking deposits. True, a number of large finance institutions such as private equity firms and hedge funds do not benefit from federal insurance. However, less directly but just as effectively, they benefit from our very complex tax code, foremost the tax deductibility of interest rates and the favorable tax treatment of their "carried interest" profits. The tax deductibility of interest rates leads to the "flipping" of companies several times across various private equity groups, just like the hamburgers of one such company, Burger

King. Little or no value is created except for the private equity investors, and if this debt leverage leads to bankruptcies, early dividends payouts usually leave these investors relatively unscathed, as opposed to the company employees who are left holding the can. To listen to the finance lobbyists advocating fiercely for the status quo, our economy could never have worked without hedge funds and other shadow finance firms with complex instruments providing "liquidity." One wonders how we went through the 1950s, 1960s, and 1980s without them, decades during which productivity and the economy grew at a faster clip than during the last twenty years. However, big donors and their lobbyists carry a lot of weight today, and the role of finance in our economy continues to grow, Paul Volcker's skepticism notwithstanding. With regulations being relaxed, financial engineering will get a much-unneeded boost, and new complicated derivatives will mushroom, hopefully without leading us to a crash.

We saw it earlier: Dodd–Frank regulations are being watered down by the new Trump administration. For example, a provision allowing class action suits against large financial institutions was recently eliminated. In the middle of the Wells Fargo scandal! This leads us to the Consumers Financial Protection Bureau (CFPB): its head, Richard Cordray, announced he was stepping down at the end of November. No time was wasted, and on November 24 Mick Mulvaney, former member of the House's right-wing "Freedom Caucus" and currently the Director of the Office of Management and Budget (OMB), was named acting head of the CFPB. When in the House, Mulvaney was one of the fiercest opponents of the CFPB ...

He also experienced controversy with budgeting this year: in the first budget from OMB in May 2017, the two trillion in potential economic stimulus from the proposed tax cuts appeared to have been counted twice, which would represent a stunning arithmetic error.[5,6] Relying on a steady 3% annual GDP growth, an assumption derided as too optimistic by pretty much all economists of the land, the budget estimated about $2 trillion in extra federal revenue growth, to "pay for the Trump tax cuts"; then the same $2 trillion were used to balance the budget.[7,8]

All of this does not augur well for the other tough discussions needed on how to keep large banks safe and shadow finance debt at a reasonable level, and how to pay (closing loopholes!) for the proposed large tax cuts for corporations and high earners. Amidst all this, it is useful to remember that our economy is 70% retail consumer based: as a result, the tax cuts that are most effective in fueling growth are those that favor overwhelmingly the middle class, instead of high income people who tend not to spend a large proportion of their earnings. A tax dollar saved for a middle-class family usually goes straight back into the economy, with a high multiplier effect. But sound economic policy does not appear to play a major role in these budget and tax discussions: it is all about political power. And it looks like complex finance institutions and their instruments will emerge out of this doing quite well, with encouragements, fewer regulations and lower taxes from the government. In particular, it is ominous that we are no longer hearing from either Donald Trump or his White

House staff about "reinstating a version of Glass–Steagall," not that the rumors to that effect were very loud to start with. Instead, it is "payback time" for those wealthy donors who bankrolled Republican campaigns …

Complexity may also triumph if we ever get to one of the great promises of the Trump presidential campaign: infrastructure. In an era of low interest rates by historical standards, how about financing a much-needed infrastructure renewal with ten, thirty, even fifty-year treasury bonds? Nay, that appears to be too simple. Rather, we may do this through a complex web of targeted tax incentives and public–private partnerships. The finance sector will obviously love that. Giant banks are looking with much anticipation at complex debt instruments – and great returns – to help construction companies. Blackstone, one of the largest private equity groups, has already announced a large infrastructure fund. Of course, this may work for assets coveted by the private sector, such as airports, freeways, perhaps a few bridges here and there. Congested Pennsylvania station in New York serving 300 million people a year? The tunnels under the Hudson River that connect it to New Jersey? Solving health-threatening water infrastructure problems such as the ones plaguing Flint in Michigan? Or water dams crumbling under lack of repairs? Perhaps later, if ever. In the meantime, the financial sector will continue to grow and thrive through its myriad of complex global tools, providing outsized economic rewards for financiers, with little value and much needless complexity added to our economy.

Three: the combination of globalization forces and outsized CEO pay packages

The mid to late-1990s saw the acceleration of globalization trends, fueled by China's rapid industrialization and transformation. More or less at the same time, Wall Street incomes started soaring, due in no small part to the repeal of Glass–Steagall. Large corporate CEOs, not wanting to be left behind and eager to emulate their bankers, started making tens or even hundreds of millions. Many of them had been content making only millions up to then, and it is interesting to note that this step change in compensation did not go in lock step with a dramatic increase in companies' profits over the medium and long-term. This combination of accelerating globalization and vastly increased compensation led to many CEO decisions favoring complex supply-chain arrangements and outsourcing. Wait, one may say, what do globalization and CEO pay packages have to do with each other? Actually, a lot, when one looks at the decisions made by American CEOs during the last twenty years and compare them with those made by their German or Japanese counterparts. If we take globalization for granted, the impact should be roughly the same for every large developed country, right?

Globalization has led to the emergence of very competent and skilled labor in China, Southeast Asia, India, Mexico, Brazil, Argentina, and Central Europe, earning a fraction of what equivalent labor is paid in Japan, the U.S., and Western Europe. One could think that this would lead not just to the hollowing out of our Midwest and Great Lakes regions' manufacturing base, but to similar consequences in other traditional industrial regions such as Germany's Ruhr, or Japan's Kawasaki and Yokohama urban areas. Happily for Germany and Japan, and sadly for us, this is not the case. The Ruhr is thriving, as are neighbors Bad Wurttemberg and Bavaria. All are industrial strongholds. The mega urban conglomeration of Tokyo, Kawasaki, and Yokohama remains the most populated metro area in the world and enjoys enviable prosperity, due in no small part to a thriving manufacturing industry. Germany has successfully integrated the former East Germany and rebuilt it anew in a spectacular fashion through massive infrastructure spending financed by income tax increases. It is the world's third exporter after China and the U.S., just ahead of Japan. Germans trade more goods as a percentage of their economy than any other developed country. According to the World Bank, exports plus imports accounted for 47% of Germany's GDP in 2015, versus only 12% for the U.S.[9,10]

Not only do Germans and Japanese make a lot of things other people around the world want to buy, they also have a lock on the market of machine tools and robots used by manufacturers in other countries. They not only make things but also the things that make things – awesome! Their blue-collar workforces have also thrived in this era of globalization, unlike ours. In Germany, industrial apprenticeships provide clearly developed paths to well-paid middle-class jobs, so that not everyone feels the only route to a prosperous future goes through a university degree. In Japan, demand for industrial and construction jobs has been such recently that it has helped crack the long-held barrier of female participation in the workforce: today it is common to see Japanese women in a variety of manufacturing jobs and wearing hard hats in construction sites. As a result, the percentage of women working is increasing steadily and getting close to the U.S. rate.

But when it comes to German and Japanese CEOs, what are the main differences with their American counterparts? First, their relationship with employees. Unlike their American counterparts, German CEOs are used to having workers and their unions represented on their board of directors. Key decisions such as layoffs are taken in a consensual manner and with a long-term horizon in mind. If a company can avoid layoffs by having its workforce working shorter hours or for lower pay during a certain period of low demand, that is the preferred solution. Over the long-term, such pragmatic solutions will make the company stronger. In Japan, too, consensus is sought between management and employees. In both countries outsourcing options are studied exhaustively, with local alternative plans sought before any implementation. Second, their constituents. CEOs in Germany and Japan have to deal with a vast array of constituents, not just their board of directors. They are viewed as pillars of their communities, with corresponding obligations to these communities. Third, the stock markets. The role of the Deutsche Börse and the Tokyo Tosho is important, but not dominant – these are much smaller exchanges than the NYSE. As such, local companies do not suffer as much as their American counterparts from the short-term "dictatorship" of quarterly results imposed by financial markets. Fourth, most importantly, their compensation. German and Japanese CEOs are paid in millions of dollars equivalents, but not tens or even hundreds of millions like their U.S. peers. CEOs of large U.S. companies enjoy compensation packages that are hugely complex contraptions devised by consultants and approved by compensation committees populated by other fellow CEOs. The complexity is usually designed to ensure that if the company manages to have two or three years of decent growth in profits and that the company's stock price takes off accordingly, the CEO will make tens of millions of dollars or even an order of magnitude more.

A shocking aspect of this took place in the auto industry in Detroit over the last three decades. Our national automakers have been bailed out umpteenth times, the most recent cycle occurring after the 2008 financial crisis. GM and Chrysler got bailed out by the federal government, which to be fair recouped all its loan money, even making a small profit on its equity shares. GM remains a U.S. company, but not Chrysler, which became the American division of an Italian company when Fiat purchased the U.S. Treasury shares in the company in 2011. Over these thirty years, throughout this repeated cycle of bailouts and times of respite, Detroit and adjoining cities like Flint got decimated. But most of our automakers' various CEOs did quite well, thank you. All it took was two to three years of good profits selling SUVs in between crises for the CEOs of Chrysler, Ford, and GM to make tens of millions in between bailouts. Of course, compensation plans allowing that are not simple, which is why you need the highly paid consultants to engineer them.

These complex compensation plans motivate U.S. companies' CEOs in many instances to engage in ever more complex cross-border supply-chain and outsourcing transactions, involving whole divisions or specific components in the companies they manage. Never mind that many studies show that over the medium and long term those outsourcing arrangements do not create much financial value. Transaction costs are always underestimated in the complex plans underlying these arrangements; over longer periods of time, the training costs of the new workforces are also underestimated; and when the critical mass of such transactions increases, labor costs in places like China increase as well, reducing the original advantage. There are also logistics risks, not to mention political ones. But Wall Street and "activist" hedge fund type investors love a "decisive" outsourcing plan and a focus on short-term results. Financiers have a tendency to bid up the involved company's stock, even if it will eventually deflate within a few years, like a bad soufflé. And all it takes for a CEO to make outsized compensation is a few years of high stock price, so let's go! If in the process whole communities in the U.S. are devastated, well, that is just the price to pay in the name of shareholder value, right? The CEOs are making the "tough" decisions and should be rewarded handsomely, even when thousands lose their jobs as result of their decisions.[11]

Complexity abounds here: in the CEO compensation plans that allow these short-term spikes in rewards while being just opaque enough to avoid lawsuits when profits and stock gains prove to be short-lived; in the complex outsourcing transactions that prevent independent analysts from going beyond headline level differences in hourly wages to assess the true total costs of these transactions; and in the involvement of large short-term investors like hedge funds or "arbitrageurs" that will use complex proxy-fights to place their board members and help dictate short-term agendas at the companies they target. With such opportunities to strike it rich quickly for executives and investors alike, the welfare of local communities in the U.S. does not weigh much in these decisions. This complexity is also long-lasting. For example, once set-up, complex global supply chain arrangements are equally complex to unwind and therefore often outlast their economic usefulness. Sad!

Four: our education system and its "college for all" mentality

Providing an opportunity for all our people to have access to a university education is an admirable concept in itself, but one that often leads to disillusions when it comes to employment prospects. Our universities are clearly the best in the world, as measured by a number of metrics, whether by the number of Nobel Prizes won, the degree by which their education is sought after by the best minds around the world, or their impact on global research. They dominate international rankings such as the Shanghai Academic Ranking of World Universities – usually led by the likes of Harvard, Berkeley, Stanford, Princeton, MIT and Caltech, with England's Cambridge and Oxford as the only interlopers in the top ten. But rightfully so, given their relentless focus on improving their students' minds, U.S. universities balk at serving as pre-employment triage centers for industry, principally at the undergraduate level. This is why students have a vast array of choices between potential diplomas, ranging from computer science degrees leading to highly paid jobs in the tech industry to anthropology majors that will lead to few opportunities outside academia. Beyond undergraduate degrees, universities offer a variety of professional degrees, from JDs to MBAs and MDs that lead to specialized careers, but those cater to an already much smaller proportion of students. There is widespread support in our country for the idea that a college education is the required passport to a prosperous economic future, an idea that is strongly supported by statistics on average employment incomes.

However, over the last ten or fifteen years, even college graduates have suffered from headwinds on the compensation front. The information technology outsourcing wave of the early twenty-first century has decimated the earning power of many computer science graduates, those who could only code at a basic level, for example. Others on the global scene, foremost in the huge Indian centers of Bangalore, Hyderabad and Gurgaon, can do the work just as well for a tenth of the cost. And compared to manufacturing, the transitions are simpler, thanks to the ease with which information is shared over the global internet. Plus, education costs have outpaced inflation by a huge amount, and most American college graduates are saddled with debt. The outstanding student loan debt amounted to 10% of total U.S. household debt in 2016, or

$1.4 trillion for over forty-four million students! The average graduate had over $37,000 in student loans, up 6% from the year before, and more than double of a decade ago. If you add to this a graduate degree, student debt can go through the roof.[12]

This may be OK if you pursue a 1–2-year master's degree leading to highly paid jobs such as an MBA or a JD. But if you have a medical vocation, the seven to twelve years of required graduate studies may mean that you can never afford to be a generalist or primary care physician. The earning power of specialty physicians is for many students the only viable path to reimbursement of medical school fees. A negative consequence of this is that the excessive number of specialists and the shortage of generalists are a leading cause of excess health care costs in the country.

Still, increasing numbers of high school graduates view a college education as the only way to avoid low paid and precarious jobs as fast food workers or Uber drivers. This is not irrational: despite the increasing costs of university education, this is the choice many of our youngsters face. They also read opinions by the vast majority of our pundits, left and right, who say the only way to be "relevant" in our modern, disrupted and globalized world is to achieve higher education. These pundits also tend to debase blue-collar jobs, forgetting that many white-collar jobs may be even less secure over the short-medium term – again, nothing is easier to outsource than a computer programmer's work. With a coveted university degree in hand and the need to pay for tuition loans, a young graduate may also gravitate into professions and occupations that fuel our existing complexity, such as finance and the law.

What is missing in all of this are apprenticeships. These are at the heart of the success of Germany in maintaining millions of well-paid middle-class blue-collar jobs. Apprenticeship, at heart, is a straightforward concept that dates from the Middle Ages. Crafts are taught from generation to generation; no wonder it thrives on the German "Mittlestand," with its many small to large family-owned companies. In Japan, too, the skill of mastering a craft is hugely respected; witness the acclaimed film about sushi Chef Jiro Ono and his three Michelin stars restaurant, *Jiro Dreams of Sushi*. Apprenticeships exist in America, but they are not as widespread as should be. As a result, many students engage in academic studies that are both too long and complex for their abilities, with disappointing employment outcomes. Everyone among us knows a college graduate who has to earn a meager living performing menial tasks while waiting for an opportunity commensurate with her or his education – for how many years? In Japan, the same young adult, without a college degree but with several years of apprenticeship, would have for example started at the bottom of the ladder at Fanuc, the Japanese manufacturing robot maker, with an already interesting job and a wealth of advancement prospects. Why the Fanucs and Boschs have succeeded with apprenticeships when most U.S. industrial companies fail to take advantage of them is a bit of a mystery, although the short-term financial horizons of U.S. CEOs mentioned earlier may be a potential explanation. Setting up apprenticeship is an investment in the future, the costs of which are directly borne by the companies concerned, as opposed to donor, government and student funded institutions of higher learning.

I applaud the many people who drive efforts and political movements to make a university education much cheaper, even free, for young Americans. In the developed world outside America, college education is either free or cheap enough that students are not burdened with tuition debt that will take years to pay back. However, in large areas of our country, less than a third of residents have a university degree, and these efforts to make higher education affordable to all may sound meaningless, perhaps even "elitist" to them. Also, many students enroll into a four-year college program and do not complete it, leading to much frustration and stigma. This is why I think a strong push towards apprenticeships should be one of the country's top priorities. This would make the path between post–high school education and productive employment much simpler and more productive than experienced today by many of our young.

Five: America's insulation relative to the rest of the world

Quick, how many American citizens actually have a valid passport? According to the State Department, 138 million, or 46% of U.S. citizens. This percentage assumes the eligible population is not the 325 million from the 2016 census, but only about 300 million, once the fourteen million legal permanent residents (green card holders) and the estimated eleven million undocumented residents are removed from the total. This is quite a lot, even if less than half our population. The question one should ask, though, is how many actually use their passports to travel abroad? This is much harder to assess. It is easy to tally the number of individual trips overseas, which stands at about thirty million per year. But how many of these trips are multiple ones taken by the same traveler in a year? When I was a global consultant, I used to travel internationally twenty-plus times per year. And it is not only high-frequency business travelers. Many individuals, principally retired ones, will take several leisure trips abroad every year. So the number of Americans actually traveling abroad in a given year is much lower than the number of actual international trips involving U.S. passport holders. Estimates vary, but center around fifteen million American travelers, or a mere 5% of U.S. citizens! That is a very low number. This statistic is important because it shows that only a small fraction of American citizens experience how people live in other countries.[13,14]

From our parents, and increasingly grandparents, we know that in the aftermath of World War II no one had it as good as we did. If we do not travel abroad, why assume this has changed, principally when our politicians keep repeating that we are the greatest nation on earth? We most certainly are, in terms of military and economic power, but what about the day-to-day comforts for all of us? Are we getting a better or worse deal than the Europeans or the Japanese? Yes, Donald Trump did campaign on how bad our airports and infrastructure are compared to China, and explained that our main trading partners take us to the cleaners. He continues to stress this as president. On

May 26, 2017, it was: "the Germans are bad, very bad," because we import so many BMWs, Mercedes and VWs. "Terrible. We will stop this." There is the occasional quip such as "you have a better health care system than we do," when talking to the Australian Prime Minister Malcolm Turnbull – our current president is clearly an admirer of socialized medicine, having already heaped praise on the Canadian health system during his campaign. But even Trump did not expand on the details of our daily lives relative to those of our economic peers in Europe and Asia–Pacific.

And yet. Without traveling to Europe, how can Americans realize that most European university students pay little or no tuition fees? That countries like France and Germany have paperless physicians' offices, universal care, and an extremely simple way to access medical services through the "Carte Vitale" and the "Gesundheitskarte or eGK?" In these countries, information technology has actually led to much administrative simplification, whereas in the U.S. IT has more often than not added layer upon layer of complexity to health care, increasing our $100–150 billion per year of excess administrative costs. Can most Americans understand how complex, user-unfriendly and financially challenging access to medical care is for us relative to all other developed nations? We are so used to complexity in our health care system, and the time and expense it causes us to navigate it, that we take it for granted that a better and simpler system cannot exist elsewhere. This helps to understand why there is not more of a massive popular outcry about this and people in the streets chanting "health care for all!"

Similarly, we are used to seeing complex regulations governing most of the companies that provide us with electricity, natural gas, telecommunications, and transportation. Again, this is the world we live in, so we do not pause to ask ourselves why services levels keep deteriorating and prices going up. Many other developed countries have a lighter regulatory blanket that targets a few major outcomes as opposed to constraining industry through many inputs and rules. Cheap electricity, produced increasingly by non-polluting solar and wind installations, is the result of a few broad government incentives, giving industry stable incentives to invest over the long-term.

Here, we are used to taking the car and trying to avoid potholes in our very tired roadways. Or we can fly and spend a horrendous time queuing up at the airport, when not being manhandled by either TSA or the airlines. If 50% of our population, as opposed to 5%, visited Europe, Japan, and China, they would marvel at sparkling new infrastructure everywhere. They would discover airports looking like glass cathedrals, smooth autobahns, and 200 mph TGV trains as easy to board as the subway – great public infrastructure that is reliable, cheap and easy to use, for everyone. The reaction coming home would naturally be, "how come we do not have any of this?" and then, "what is wrong with those who govern us?" Five percent of our people saying that will not lead to change, but 50% would. They would refuse the current status quo that makes building new infrastructure so difficult. The unbelievably complex imbroglio of getting funding approved at the federal and state level; the endless permit battles; the slow awarding of construction contracts following convoluted bidding processes – these all mean that we cannot build any significant infrastructure in less than a decade. Most of the time, we don't even try. And so our roads and bridges crumble, our airports feel like subways at rush hour, and we . . . just cope. Given that 95% of us do not know any better, we do not demand the changes those who govern us should make to this sad state of affairs. Building infrastructure as investment for the future is a simple concept, isn't it? But only a strong push by voters would motivate our presidents and Congress to do something about it, and cut through the complex maze of red tape to achieve results and actually rebuild our country. Without this push, there is unfortunately no reason to expect any change.

★　★　★　★　★

Re-defining the boundaries between government and the private sector

One common factor in the many complex processes we have to deal with in our daily lives is that our governments, federal and local, are more often than not intertwined with the private sector in many ways. This leads to complex collages of overlapping activities and a very large number of costly interfaces, with much expense, energy and time wasted as a result. We have seen how our polarized politics add complexity through increasingly elusive, and complex, legislation. These complex laws, and the weight of recent history, blur further the already diffuse delineation between the roles and activities of our government and the private sector. What do I mean by that? Well, the private sector has to be involved everywhere (say conservatives). Then it better be regulated in most places (say liberals). With neither side giving an inch to the other, vast inefficiencies emerge and grow. Areas where the government likely has no business being involved are added when Democrats rule the show; regulations needed to control emerging private monopolies are removed when it is the Republicans' turn. This back and forth movement between government and the private sector, including regulations that govern their interactions, always brings incremental complexities. The result? A gigantic number of intersections between federal government agencies and departments, their statewide equivalents, and the private sector. This huge complexity of interface points leads to lots of red tape, large bureaucracies, and poor results in terms of what the government and private enterprise both have to achieve.

The government is not looking after our poor, aging, and sick citizens very well; it is not regulating properly the excesses of companies enjoying quasi-monopolistic powers in their industries; many groups of employees and customers suffer from raw deals in those "consolidated" businesses – think airlines, for example. Major societal issues are not addressed, such as the outsized impact of Wall Street on our economy; CEOs earning thousands of times more than their average employee; "starvation" wages; galloping inequality, not only of wealth, but also of health, education and opportunities for the future; communities devastated by abandoned industries and rampant opioid epidemics. The private sector is hurt, too. Businesses suffer from an avalanche of both federal and local regulations, some of them focusing on such tiny aspects of their operations as to be laughable; regulators are constantly telling businesses what they need to do and produce, or not, as opposed to helping steer outcomes in the right direction; and fundamental issues such as a level playing field in global trade for our companies; international taxation; access to the talent needed to compete effectively; and lack of a world class infrastructure, are left in limbo. Unhappiness rises for virtually everyone, and once this is prevalent enough, watch out! When a group of aggrieved citizens and parties get their turn in power, they are much more interested in "sticking it to the other side" than in devising solutions to all the problems we face, including theirs. Tribal attitudes supersede a productive dialogue of ideas. Overall, we are trapped in a doom loop of politically created regulatory complexity that leads to more complexity from the private sector to address it or go around it, and then to increased demands for yet more complex regulations to moderate the private sector, and so forth.

Allow me a simple illustration through a few questions. Does the federal government, and its U.S. Treasury and the Federal Housing Finance Agency, need to be involved in home mortgages through its control of Fannie Mae and Freddie Mac? These are giant institutions, key players in one of the largest sectors of the economy, one that drives success as well as triggers catastrophes. But does the government really need to be involved in such business operations? Could the same sound objective, which is to ensure that our less well-off countrymen have access to low cost mortgages, not be achieved through a focused set of rules as opposed to actual government participation in originating home loans? Staying in finance, most developed countries only tax those who reside on their soil. Do we really have to tax U.S. citizens living abroad, submitting them to double taxation since they also have to pay the taxes of the country they live in? Couldn't we also find a simpler way to deal with international taxation for our companies operating abroad, one that would be both straightforward and not so easily gamed? We should not pass judgment on the giant government utility TVA because of its successful history – it was created by a liberal icon, FDR, but is still revered by the citizens of red states like Tennessee. The TVA is successful because it is operated very competently and provides its customers with reliable electricity at affordable prices. But when citizens are so fed up with the poor services and high costs they get from their private sector utility, that they take matters in their own hands and form a utility cooperative owned by their county, is it really such a good thing? Yes, the citizens get to own more or less directly the delivery of electricity, natural gas or water in their county, but they also forego a fair amount of technical and operating knowhow, as well as benefits brought by scale and experience. No matter what the shortfalls of our public utilities are, imagine if we citizens had to take all these operations into our own hands, everywhere. Anybody out there want to be responsible for the operation of an aging nuclear plant? Negotiate a complex multi-year natural supply contract? Anyone?

Ah, let's not forget health care. Does the federal government really need to operate a gigantic network of hospitals on a national scale? Wouldn't our veterans be better served with a prioritized access to our best hospitals than by VA hospitals? These always seem to be under negative news coverage, with queues sometimes worse than those experienced by indigents in emergency rooms. I know, this question is a political minefield, but it should be asked, since no one likes the current state of health care affairs for our veterans, who need and deserve better care than they currently get. Talking about veterans, under certain conditions of age and income, some of them could have access to Medicare, Medicaid, and VA coverage. All covering different treatments, hospitals and doctors, of course. Wow! But wait a second; is this really a good thing? Just determining what health plan to use, and when, could tax the readiest and most relaxed of minds. Weeks could be spent studying alternative paths. Not ideal for someone just coming back from a multi-year tour of duty in Afghanistan.[15,16]

The above questions all point to examples of government-controlled operations that should be questioned and potentially replaced by private sector activities, even if tightly – and simply, please – regulated. But the "private sector involved everywhere" mentality has also led to many suboptimal solutions. Take the financing of much needed new infrastructure. It is hard, even in bi-partisan settings, not to hear "infrastructure" and "public–private partnership" in the same sentence. Well, sure, these partnerships or PPPs have had good success in many instances. But finance 101 will tell you that, all other things being equal, the first consequence of a public–private partnership is more expensive financing costs because of the need to accommodate private enterprise financial returns. The financing of infrastructure projects with long-term government debt or tax-exempt municipal bonds costs by definition less than financing through PPPs. This is especially true today, when a thirty-year T-bill yields (costs) about 3%, and when there is a huge market of tax-exempt state bonds and local munis in the country. Does the private sector really need to operate our new highways of the future, or our new airports? For those who travel abroad, does one see a big difference of quality between the German autobahns and the French autoroutes? Well, beyond the fact that, traffic permitting, one can floor it in Germany while in France the gendarmes will fine you if you exceed 81 mph. The autobahns are public (and free), while most autoroutes are public–private partnerships. Not that much difference between them, right? Apart, of course, from the hefty tolls paid in France for the right to cruise at 81 mph. If the private sector is involved in the financing of infrastructure, typically it costs more for those who use it – the construction companies doing the work are often the same, but private finance must make its profits. Hence the users' fees.

In health care, we have allowed a huge variety of private sector information technology companies, from multi-billion-dollar multinationals to a myriad of start-ups, to attempt to solve the nightmarish complexity of our patient accounting systems and electronic medical records (EMRs). Well over a hundred billion dollars later, where are we? We have hospital systems that cannot "talk" to each other. EMRs are a hodgepodge of electronic systems hard to access by those at the center of them, the patients. New systems! New passwords! New privacy concerns! Most patients are lost in a sea of different databases and still rely on paper for what they want to know about their health. Physicians complain, my very skillful cancer surgeon telling me recently, "I spend far too much time every day as a data entry clerk." Start-ups, well financed by eager venture capitalists, try to find a niche and address it, and in aggregate add to the complexity of the whole health information technology edifice. And there are still a lot of paper, PDFs and faxes, everywhere, at the doctor's office, in hospitals and in the mail, from your hospital co-pays to the many invoices and statements from your health insurance company. A success it definitely is not. This failure to bring health data together in a simple and efficient manner to those who need it also impedes progress through artificial intelligence. When they hear an entrepreneur say the words "Big Data, AI and EMRs," VCs rush to their check-books. I have a less enthused reaction, more along the lines of, "here we go again, more complexity and costs in our health system; and where are the tangible benefits at the all-important point of care?" All of this has unfortunately meant that, to date, IT has been a cause of negative productivity improvement in U.S. health care. This is unlike any other industry I can think of. Information technology is attempting but failing to move us towards a new health care system based upon prevention, ease of access, and personalization of care. And beyond that, it created such complexity that most people in the country no longer understand health care. During the launch of the Obamacare exchanges, the new users were first challenged by accessing the new IT systems, principally the federal government one. Then there was a sticker shock: huge monthly premiums! But wait, there are subsidies available, ones that could be discovered after a few lengthy phone calls or a challenging website navigation exercise. The rates, and subsidies, would change every year. People became angry. President Obama, why did you trust the Heritage Foundation ideas? Couldn't you have just extended Medicaid even more, and lowered the entry age to Medicare ten years or so? Just kidding . . . I know this was hardly feasible politically. However, the ACA exchanges provide us with another powerful example of legislation creating additional government–private sector interfaces that increase complexity without solving the problem at hand. One of the reasons for Trump's election is that many people became fed up with the ever increasing challenges in important aspects of their lives, challenges they struggled to address. In particular, applicants using the exchanges to find coverage felt trapped in a system they did not understand, and one that always seemed to offer negative surprises, either rising premiums or health insurance companies exiting their state.

Complex government private sector interfaces may also allow sophisticated players to game the system – remember Enron? Many such suspicions turn out to be unfounded, but at a minimum they lead to lengthy legal proceedings – time and energy not spent on productive activities such as improving outcomes for customers.

The *New York Times* reported on May 15, 2017 a whistle-blower story describing a sophisticated scheme by big health insurers, allegedly to defraud

Medicare through its privately run Medicare Advantage program, created during the George W. Bush presidency. The concept behind the alleged scheme is simple, even if complex to execute. As written in the *New York Times*, in Medicare Advantage the government contracts with for-profit health insurers to manage health care for patients above 65 years of age and pays insurers a yearly fee for each member they enroll. The fee is higher for patients recently treated for certain conditions, creating a perverse incentive for Medicare Advantage insurers to search for diagnoses of illness in their patients, even where none may exist. Auditors and analysts have warned for a decade that Medicare Advantage has been vulnerable to cheating since this illness diagnosis–based risk scoring was phased in from 2004 to 2008. This whistle-blower story also alleged that the Centers for Medicare and Medicaid Services tried to recoup large amounts from such schemes in 2007, only to settle for a very small sum in 2012.

According to a second article on this issue in the same week, the *New York Times* mentioned on May 19 that the Justice Department (DOJ) had sued the whistle-blower's employer, a large health insurer, saying that "senior executives knew the company was overbilling Medicare by hundreds of millions of dollars a year." The complaint was filed in the U.S. District Court of Los Angeles, with the DOJ claiming the insurer "routinely combed through millions of patients' medical charts, searching for data it could use to make patients look sicker than they really were."

Congress had also spoken out about this issue of Medicare overpayment: Senator Charles Grassley, the chairman of the Senate Judiciary Committee, demanded explanations from the new CMS administrator, Seema Verma, questioning CMS plans to "implement safeguards to reduce score fraud, waste and abuse" in an April 2017 letter. In July, the large health insurer filed a motion in federal court asking the court to dismiss that whistle-blower lawsuit. In the meantime, a federal judge had unsealed another whistle-blower lawsuit joined by the DOJ on Medicare Advantage overpayments, filed in October 2016 by a sales agent working for the same insurer. That False Claims Act lawsuit was dismissed on October 5, 2017 by a federal judge of California's Central District. The judge decided for the health insurer, saying that the DOJ had not shown the insurer knew the claims submitted were false, and had failed to prove that CMS would not have made the Medicare Advantage payments to the insurer had the government agency been aware of the practices alleged in the suit.[17,18,19,20] This was a major legal victory for the health insurer, which could gain confidence that the other whistle-blower lawsuit filed by DOJ in May 2017 might be dismissed as well. But DOJ is also pursuing similar cases against other, smaller health insurers, and has obtained a couple of minor settlements. The legal battles continue . . .[21]

All of this is terrible for costs, in health care and elsewhere in our economy. Not only does complexity inexorably build costs, it also makes solutions quasi-impossible to find, let alone implement. Even if a desired, simpler end-objective is determined and agreed upon by warring political parties, the transitions to the objective could be fraught with millions of people losing employment and assorted other disasters. This is why we never seem to be able to get out of our infrastructure and health care conundrums. We cannot see any path to reduce complexity and costs. Adding incremental complexity is politically expedient, but also much simpler in the short-term, with less risk of unforeseen and unintended consequences. Therefore, the trade-off is always the same. Democrats want to rebuild infrastructure and provide health insurance to everyone (among other things), which carries such costs that only additional taxes can provide the required funding at the national level. Republicans want above all to eliminate these taxes, and then in doing so vote for laws that subject millions to losing their health coverage, while our infrastructure stays in its decrepit state of abandon. But yes, there is a way out of this conundrum. It involves nothing less than the complete re-thinking of how our government works and interacts with the private sector.

It is imperative that we think collectively – all good hands on deck – on how we can re-invent our system of government to delineate very clearly what our federal institutions, their state counterparts, and the private sector do. And, most importantly, what they should no longer do. Only then will we be able to have a country where the government is no longer doing things that are better done by the private sector, and vice versa. In the next and final chapter of this book, I offer solutions to achieve this. Industry sector by sector, one can view this as a heuristic that identifies what the government can do best, and should do; and what the private sector excels at, and should run unencumbered with.

10 Proposed solutions to improve our lives

An effective, focused, and strong government

Chapter 9 concluded with the need to re-invent our government, to streamline its too numerous and too complex interactions with the private sector. What does a re-invented system of government for our country look like? One initial thought is that our federal government should emulate the spirit of our Constitution. We saw earlier that de Tocqueville stressed that our Founding Fathers wanted federal and state power to be shared in a way that would allow the states to address all their local government needs without undue interference from the Union. Everything that was not defined explicitly as a federal government attribute belonged to the state governments. This did not mean the federal government was not strong or without powers. Its very focus on the major issues facing our young republic, such as commerce, the money, foreign affairs, and war, ensured clarity of rule and thus a strong authority.

Our federal government has expanded steadily over the last century or so, at least in terms of manpower. Wrong, one may say, since the rolls of federal civil servants have remained relatively flat over the last four decades at around two and a half million. But the federal civil servants have been supplemented by hundreds of thousands of contractors who perform many inherent government functions. These contractors are typically costlier – their employers make a nice "mark-up" or profit on every hour they work. They are also less accountable and less subject to scrutiny than federal employees. However, they do not exist just to appease those concerned about the expansion of the federal work force. They are needed because complicated missions are constantly added to the federal agenda, whatever the administration. These new complex missions vary when we have a Democratic government, or a Republican one, but they increase in number steadily. A Democratic president means new missions in social programs, education, protection of the environment, regulatory initiatives, and perhaps global initiatives. A Republican president will add new missions to the forces of enforcement, security, immigration control, defense, and perhaps war. And so the actual size of our government grows well beyond the headcount of federal employees, almost inexorably.

This expansion of total headcount serving the federal government has not made it more effective or more powerful. Rather, it has led to a conundrum where:

1) When the Democrats are in power, social programs (and a few others) increase in number and scope, but at the cost of inflated bureaucracies and inefficiencies.
2) When Republicans are in office, they attempt to cut into the bureaucracy of government – except in the Defense Department and the Pentagon – with catastrophic consequences for the poor, old, and sick.

The choice we face collectively is social justice, at the cost of expensive government programs; or lower federal taxes, at the cost of grotesque inequality and leaving millions uncared for. Alas, this choice does not involve shrinking the government or increasing its effectiveness. Since the 1980s, Republican governments have cut taxes (except during the George H. W. Bush presidency), but not the weight of the federal government on the economy. The best illustration of this is the George W. Bush presidency. Large increases in defense and war spending went theoretically hand in hand with some attempts to reduce federal staffing in other areas of the government. But these attempted cuts were never backed up by an actual decrease of scope and work at the agencies concerned, and the overall size of government grew significantly under Bush the 43rd. This is one of the factors that have led to the creation and rise of the Republican Tea Party, which defines itself as "anti-government." Under President Trump, a number of Tea Party leaders find themselves heading agencies and departments of the federal government. A freeze in new federal government hiring is in effect. Apart from defense, of course. The first proposed White House budget included severe cuts in just about every area except defense, Medicare, and Social Security. This proposed budget was also declared "dead on arrival" by many influential Republican Senators, who essentially said: "when it comes to the budget, the government proposes, Congress disposes." How will this end? More likely than not, by increased budget deficits as opposed to a shrinking of the overall number of career civil servants and contractors serving the federal government. No wonder Washington DC is one of the fastest growing large metropolitan areas in the country!

Let's step back a moment, forget our domestic political travails, and fill our lungs with the air of optimism. Imagine that our Congress has just passed a carbon tax law, tripled capital requirements for our banking sector, and is looking seriously at universal health care coverage. The President has promised to sign all this new legislation. Now think how many regulations we could eliminate with a carbon tax levied on all fossil fuels at the point of consumption! We could streamline the many federal and state agencies dealing with CAFE standards for vehicles and clean air mandates for fossil fuel electricity power plants; Americans hooked on gas guzzling SUVs could rediscover the joy of driving small and nimble vehicles. Imagine how much of Dodd–Frank and the armies of lawyers working to interpret it could be made redundant by tripling the current leverage ratios, or equity relative to total assets, required of our many banks that are deemed "too big to fail." There would no longer be a need for complex "stress tests" for financial institutions; for endless dialogue on whether JP Morgan, Citigroup, and Bank of America ought to be broken up into smaller components, easier to understand and manage; and for concerns on how the vast array of financial regulations targeting very big institutions is choking the important layer of mid-sized regional banks. With universal health coverage in place, would there be a need for the fifty state-level Medicaid programs? Would the VA still be needed? Tens of billions of dollars in administrative costs could be eliminated. Countless regulations set up by CMS, as well as individual Medicaid programs within each state, would no longer be necessary. Our health care dollars would focus a lot more on prevention and cure as opposed to administration and regulating.

More generally, think of all the federal regulations that could be eliminated or simplified if Congress mandated that regulations focus on clear price signals and outcomes, as opposed to inputs to businesses. This would not only simplify our legislative and regulatory frameworks, but would also provide incentives for business to focus on simpler products and services instead of devising complex solutions to fend off regulations viewed as too cumbersome. To take the example of mandated increased equity levels for the balance sheets of our large banks: this type of straightforward mandate not only achieves simplicity at the legislative level, but also discourages the elaboration of complex schemes by the financial sector to go around complex regulations and attempt to "game" the system for its own profit. How do you go around equity requirements? They focus on such a basic aspect of accounting and finance that any shortcut or attempt at manipulation is by definition futile. Simple regulations impacting the fundamentals of major businesses, to steer them towards favorable outcomes such as reducing the risk of another major financial crisis, should be the way forward for a focused and effective government. In energy, a carbon tax is much simpler than "cap-and-trade" frameworks, and also much more effective. It provides a strong answer to the triple challenge of national security, dependency on foreign oil, and protecting the environment. Mandated equity levels for banks and a carbon tax on fossil fuels do not attempt to tell business what to do and how to do it. They just represent new, simple, and powerful rules of the game to ensure that climate change does not destroy our planet and financial crises do not demolish our economy. The rest is left to the creativity and innovation of the private sector, which is the one that should determine winners and losers through increased competition within these new simple rules.

Following such a philosophy, and creating simple, overarching policies governing those industries that need high level regulatory and price signals can transform our federal government into an entirely new animal. Focused. Streamlined. Effective. And also stronger, even with smaller armies of civil servants and contractors at its disposal. Politicians across the aisle think the strength of government is proportional to its size. Grow it, say Democrats. Shrink it, respond Republicans. How about making our government both stronger and smaller? Isn't this worthy of bi-partisan appeal? Such a government would also transform, directly and by osmosis, how the private sector operates. Major drivers of complexity flagged in the prior chapter, such as the combination of globalization forces and outsized executive pay packages; the role of finance in our economy; and even higher education, which might be incentivized to produce fewer lawyers and more engineers, could be addressed in a simpler but more effective manner than today.

The devil here would not be in the "details," but in the transition to this smaller yet stronger federal government. Let's now explore how we could get there in the areas of government social programs targeted at low income and poor people; health care; electricity and energy; finance; taxes; and new regulatory frameworks.

★   ★   ★   ★   ★

A universal basic income

The future belongs to artificial intelligence enabled robots. They clean our homes and hotel rooms. They serve our meals in restaurants and deliver them at home. They stretch their artificial limbs to bring us our medicines when we need to take them. They select in giant warehouses the goods we have purchased online that drones will deliver to our doorsteps. Driverless cars and trucks dominate our streets and highways. Engineers are no longer needed to operate our trains. Fewer and fewer pilots sit in cockpits of airplanes; they are just watching a sequence of indicators showing the autopilot is performing flawlessly. Needless to say, there is hardly anyone in manufacturing plants, where robots, supervised by other robots, assemble automobiles and millions of other products from A to Z.

This future is not yet with us and may not be for several decades. But it is coming, surely. Already in manufacturing giant South Korea there are about five robots for each hundred workers. Countries with the highest intensity of manufacturing in their economies, and those where low-skilled workers perform tasks that are easy to automate, may be the first ones to bear the brunt of the automation tsunami being announced. The U.S. will not be immune from it. We still have a fair amount of manufacturing left; driverless cars and trucks will replace professional drivers; artificial intelligence may displace an increasingly large number of entry level software programmers; and many new jobs created in hospitality and restaurants are simple enough that they too could get displaced by domestic robots. Even before this future becomes reality, online shopping, supported by giant automated warehouses, is already killing countless retail jobs. The emerging consensus is that tens of millions are likely to lose their current way to earn a living in a world dominated by automation, with little or no prospect of alternative employment, even if we get our act together with apprenticeships and retraining programs.

This is why a number of prominent voices are promoting the idea of a Universal Basic Income. Elon Musk has endorsed it. So have many of his fellow high technology luminaries, such as leading venture capitalists Mark Andreessen and Tim Draper. Sam Altman, president of the start-up accelerator Y Combinator, is leading a Basic Income experiment with 1,000 families in Oakland, across the bay from Silicon Valley, and is funding a Basic Income Lab with $10 million. Facebook founder and CEO Mark Zuckerberg said at his May 25, 2017 Harvard Commencement address:"We should explore ideas like universal basic income to make sure that everyone has a cushion to try new ideas."[1]

Even though it is embraced widely within the high-technology community in Silicon Valley, Universal Basic Income is not a new idea – far from it. The English–American revolutionary Thomas Paine endorsed it in 1795, talking about "asset-based egalitarianism" in his "Agrarian Justice" pamphlet. Thinkers as different as Austrian economist Friedrich Hayek, defender of market liberalism; British philosopher Bertrand Russell; Economy Nobel Prize winner and free markets apostle Milton Friedman; Civil Rights icon Martin Luther King, Jr., all supported the idea. More recently, it is not just the tech community that is touting the concept. The unlikely duo of the former president of the Service Employees International Union, Andy Stern, and vocal critic of the welfare state Charles Murray appeared together in the fall of 2016 at the Cato Institute in Washington DC to discuss the idea of keeping people out of poverty by giving them regular unconditional cash payments. What Stern, Murray, and Silicon Valley celebrities have in common is the belief that automation will bring great turmoil to our economy. In a 2016 book written with Lee Kravitz, *Raising the Floor*, Stern predicts that tens of millions of jobs will disappear, with much of the country left with work that "is contingent, part-time, and driven largely by people's own motivation, creativity, and the ability to make a job out of 'nothing.'" Kravitz, Stern, Altman, Musk et al. want to give people enough money so they can eat, have a roof on their heads, and a reasonable quality of life.[2,3]

These leaders all realize that the current trends of employment in America, whether due to today's globalization forces or tomorrow's automation, are not sustainable. Unemployment is low, yes, but millions subsist on extremely low wages, and the percentage of the working age population that has stopped looking for work has not been so high since the Great Depression. The OECD launched this year new metrics to measure labor market performance beyond unemployment and employment rates. There are nine metrics, three for the quantity of jobs; three for their quality – wage levels being a key factor; and three for their inclusiveness. The U.S. ranks at the very top of OECD countries in quantity of jobs, but when it comes to quality, we suffer from Portuguese or Greek levels of low income. Our economy produces lots of jobs, but it is failing to lift a large number of people – the "working poor" – out of poverty.[4,5]

In a democratic society, people choose. If they are fed up enough, they can choose to ditch open trade and transforming innovations promoted by global competition, and vote for a sour retrenchment to protectionism, everything made in U.S.A. and the end of the global economy. Make no mistake, this is a real choice. Globalization and free trade apologists always err in assuming there is no alternative. There is. Protectionism and the closing of borders represent a feasible option for an economy as large as ours, very diverse, self-reliant, and where external trade only accounts for 12% of GDP. Yes, in aggregate our economy would suffer. But less so than China's, Germany's, or Japan's. And the new winners of protectionism would be many of globalization's losers. Conversely, the business executives, consultants, and bankers who laughed all the way to the bank during the last thirty years would see their opportunities and financial rewards diminish. Who would cry for them? Politically, there is a potential majority for a more closed economy in the U.S. – think of Bernie Sanders' voters added to Donald Trump's. Most people in the U.S. are already angry, and this is not the time for incremental changes. If we want to preserve an open economy and society, bold solutions like the Basic Universal Income (UBI) have to be on the table.

With so many proponents coming from such different quarters, it is hardly surprising that several versions of the UBI are being floated. In terms of semantics, I have taken the liberty of using the single word "universal" instead of the more accurate "universal for all Americans." That is how most in Silicon Valley see the idea. In their words, UBI would accrue to everyone in the land, whether they are unemployed, work at a McDonald's, or belong to the select club of billionaire entrepreneurs. Following this logic, to avoid making the UBI a regressive policy, the tax code and progressive rates for the upper brackets would be used to ensure that wealthy people's taxes go up at least enough to cancel their basic income payments. An acceptable and simpler alternative can be to means test the UBI so that only Americans below a certain income – $100,000 per year, for example – would receive it. If we view the future, as some Silicon Valley and union leaders do, as an economy than cannot modernize and provide jobs for everyone at the same time, then the appeal of a basic income is easy to understand. It becomes Social Security for everyone. UBI would not be just a tool to fight poverty, though. What Zuckerberg meant in his Harvard speech is that an income "cushion" can also help people take risks with their career choices, invest in their own education, or, even better, follow the Harvard dropout and founder of Facebook's example and become an entrepreneur. The UBI is thus viewed both as a means to ending poverty and freeing workers from lousy dead-end jobs, and as a very simple, direct alternative to bureaucratic social welfare programs. This is why conservative, libertarian, technology, and liberal thinkers all like the UBI concept. This is also the best answer to those who would raise the issues of incentive ("why would anyone work?") and fairness ("why should I work to support someone who doesn't?").

A number of UBI experiments and pilot programs have taken place in the U.S. and worldwide, ranging from low income Kenya to wealthy Switzerland. Just to mention a few, Finland is experimenting with an UBI of about $660 per month;[6] Netherlands with one of $1,000 per month; closer to home, Ontario in Canada launched in April of 2017 an UBI pilot program amounting to $12,600 per year, targeting 4,000 individuals between 18 and 64 years of age who were living on very limited income. Alaska has used its large oil and gas production to have its own UBI of sorts, financed by the Alaska Permanent Fund, set up in 1982 with hydrocarbon royalties accruing to the state. Since then, Alaskans receive annual checks amounting up to several thousand dollars each year. As long as local oil and gas discoveries and production continue, and the price of a barrel of oil does not fall too low, the checks keep coming.[7]

A clear sign that an idea is coming to maturity and could become widespread in the future is when it is put for approval to voters through the ballot box. You may remember this is how in gay marriage evolved in America. First it was the subject of ballot box propositions in some states, notably California; then it got approved in a growing number of states; and finally it became legal throughout the nation after a landmark Supreme Court decision. And the rapidity of the timing between the first statewide gay marriage propositions and the ultimate Supreme Court approval surprised many experienced social and political pundits. Similarly, one can take the fact that Switzerland put the UBI on a national referendum in June of 2016, at a generous $2,600 income per month, as a harbinger of UBI things to come. Even though that referendum clearly failed, with only 23% for the proposed initiative versus 77% opposing it, it is likely that further such initiatives will make it to other ballots, in Switzerland or elsewhere, quite possibly with much more positive results. It is the first step that counts. After all, California's Proposition 8, eliminating the right of same-sex couples to marry in California, was approved by 52% of voters in November 2008. Less than two years later, a U.S. District Court declared Proposition 8 unconstitutional, a decision upheld by the Ninth Circuit Court of Appeals in February 2012. The Supreme Court issued its decision to make gay marriage legal (*Hollingsworth v. Perry*) on June 26, 2013, less than five years after the negative California vote. UBI is coming, people.

The next question is how to pay for a Universal Basic Income. If taken in isolation, it is frightfully expensive. In the U.S. it would cost $3.24 trillion to distribute $10,000 per year of UBI to anyone – very simple math, considering a population of about 324 million habitants in the country at the end of 2016. However, many people agree a very simple and fair adjustment to UBI eligibility could be implemented within the program. If children and households earning more than $100,000 per year were excluded, as well as undocumented immigrants and permanent visa holders, plus recipients of Social Security, the original amount would decrease by about 60%, to $1.3 trillion.[8] A less generous UBI at the level of the Finnish experiment mentioned above would lead to a cost of $1 trillion. And for the purpose of this book, one of the most intriguing potential features of the UBI is that, when paying for that $1 trillion plus, we would simplify all our social programs on an epic scale. Let's look at this in more detail.

With a nationwide UBI in place, a number of federal and state welfare programs could be streamlined, if not eliminated outright. The number and complexity of these programs at the federal level is very high. Of course, complexity and costs increase further if state welfare programs are included. Staying at the national level, our federal safety net may not be as effective as those found in Europe, but it is much more complex and as a result carries hefty administrative costs. From the U.S. government's own website, we can list the following programs, with their annual spending for the 2016 fiscal year.[9,10]

- Negative Income Tax or Earned Income Tax Credit (EITC, cash paid to working families who pay no income tax) – $83 billion
- Supplemental Nutritional Assistance Program (SNAP, debit cards distributed to the poor, colloquially known as food stamps) – $78 billion
- Supplemental Security Income (SSI, cash paid to aged, blind, or disabled people with little or no income) – $62 billion
- Housing Assistance (HUD housing programs) – $49 billion
- Pell Grants (to help students pay for college tuition) – $29 billion
- Child Nutrition (school breakfast, lunch, and after school food) – $22 billion
- Temporary Assistance for Needy Families (TANF, to move families from welfare to work) – $16 billion
- Head Start (preschool program) – $11 billion
- Job Training (for youth, adults, and seniors) – $6 billion
- Women, Infants, and Children (WIC, high protein food for pregnant women and children up to 5 years old) – $6 billion
- Child Care (child care and after school programs) – $6 billion
- Low Income Home Energy Assistance Program (LIHEAP) – $3 billion
- Lifeline (phone subsidy including cell phones) – $2 billion
- Medicaid (federal share of health care for low income people) – $367 billion

The total amount? A whopping $740 billion.[11] When state and local governments' anti-poverty programs ($162 billion) and local welfare expenditures are added ($50–70 billion), we spent almost $1 trillion in 2016 to fight poverty – that is of course without including private charity amounts, which are substantial in our country. No less than eight federal agencies are involved in welfare: the Department of Agriculture (SNAP; child nutrition; WIC); the Social Security Administration (SSI); the Internal Revenue Service or IRS; the Department of Housing and Urban Development (housing assistance); the Department of Health and Human Services (TANF; Head Start; child care; and LIHEAP); the Department of Education (Pell Grants); the Department of Labor (job training); and the Federal Communications Commission (Lifeline). The above does not include a number of programs under the VA to help our veterans with a variety of forms of economic aid.

Eligibility for these programs is all over the place, ranging from 50% of poverty threshold (TANF) to 130% (SNAP; child nutrition; Lifeline), all the way to 185% (WIC). In terms of individual income limit, it varies from $13,460 (EITC) to $24,888 (Housing Assistance). States have their own eligibility rules in terms of percentages of local poverty thresholds or median incomes. And that is just for income qualifications. There are also resource qualification rules: for example, in the cases of SNAP and SSI, a person cannot have more than $2,000 in cash or equivalent savings to be eligible. Since the Bill Clinton presidency, work requirement conditions have been added as well. With these eligibility rules, the government estimates that $14,194 per person was spent in 2016 on low-income individuals receiving funds from components of the federal safety net. The trillion-dollar question is, given this complex mosaic of programs, eligibility rules and resulting high administrative costs, how much of this spending used to fight poverty reaches its intended recipients? It is likely only a fraction of the total amount, which might explain why the poverty level in the U.S. has stubbornly stayed at 12%–15% of the population over the last fifty years.

Given these numbers, the proposed UBI described above does not actually cost much more than our federal safety net plus its add-ons from the states and local governments. The gap is about $300 billion for the UBI of $10,000 per year mentioned earlier. Even when not including Medicaid in these figures, the gap between a Finnish style UBI and our current welfare spending is around $400 billion per year. If one takes into account that a significant proportion of UBI recipients would pay income tax on it – given our generous $100,000 household income per year ceiling for eligibility – then this $300–400 billion gap is actually much smaller, probably in the range of $100–200 billion. A slightly more progressive income tax framework can easily finance this.

A national UBI would also generate true added benefits to our economy. In our country, as seen earlier, 70% of the GDP is household retail spending. With the UBI dollars reaching low and middle-income households who tend to spend a very large proportion of their income, a large chunk of that trillion dollars plus of UBI would quickly and directly find its way into our local economy, unlike tax cuts for multi-millionaires. The UBI would also benefit our economy through its simplicity. One federal agency could administrate it, with likely fewer staff than its nearest existing equivalent, the Social Security Administration or SSA. This is because the SSA has to track our incomes and contributions throughout our professional lives, work with the IRS, and follow changes from full-time to part-time employment, actual retirement age, etc., whereas the "UBI Administration" would just have to control eligibility with the IRS and SSA.

Last but not least, the UBI shines in its simplicity of concept and potential implementation, principally when compared to the extraordinary complexity of our federal, state and local safety net described above. In practical terms, this means that the UBI would have much, much lower administrative costs than our current safety net. Virtually 100% of UBI dollars would reach their targeted recipients, relative to a much lower percentage of the trillion dollars we spend fighting poverty. Think about most modern charities and non-governmental organizations (NGOs). One of the first statistics they advertise is the percentage (hopefully high) of your donations reaching the intended targets. Scandals occur periodically when charity officers are viewed as spending too much money on themselves, or on "administration." Well, a national UBI program would be unlikely to suffer from this, again on account of its simplicity.

Can we transition smoothly from today's safety net to the UBI? As with any transition from a complex state of affairs to a simpler end-state, there would be challenges, including the potential conversion of well over one hundred thousand federal employees from their positions at welfare agencies to other occupations. However, a smooth transition could start taking place through the combination of existing welfare programs into fewer ones, and a gradual shift of program specific benefits to aggregate welfare dollars. In other words, this transition would first make our existing welfare state more like a basic income. For example, in a first stage SNAP (food stamps); child nutrition; Head Start; WIC; and child care programs could be aggregated, sending a single monthly check to the eligible individuals and families. Housing assistance; TANF; LIHEAP; and Lifeline programs could be merged as well. Over time, all federal and state assistance benefits could be transformed into cash grants with limited and simple eligibility criteria. Instead of helping the poor with specific credit, education, food, health, and housing assistance, the government would just hand them one form of assistance, cash. This would turn the needy into more active participants in the economy, with a much simpler, less intrusive and administratively cheaper form of welfare. Over time, this simplified set of anti-poverty grants could easily morph into the national UBI program described above.

The strength of the UBI idea comes from having well-known supporters from the business, union and academic communities, as well as from libertarian, conservative and liberal politicians. What would be needed to spur Congress and government into action? In the current political environment, I would place my bet on specific state ballot initiatives. Given the widespread support within Silicon Valley for the idea, and the very deep pockets of UBI proponents there, the most likely next step appears to be a California ballot initiative or proposition. UBI "Prop X" is coming! Who will be its sponsors? Mark Zuckerberg and Elon Musk? Who will lead the opposition to it? Interests from outside the state, like in past anti-pollution and gay marriage initiatives? Will the California governor endorse it? Possibly: a leading candidate to replace Jerry Brown when he ends his current second term – and fourth overall! – is Lieutenant Governor Gavin Newsom, who has already spoken eloquently about the need to plan for the automation wave and mitigate its social impact. If California takes the lead, other states are likely to follow suit. There will be challenges to the constitutionality of the UBI. It may end up being decided for the country by the Supreme Court. In that case, the number of states having adopted it would weigh heavily in the balance. Could the U.S. move from being the laggard in safety net relative to all developed nations to UBI leader? This will be fascinating to follow, but one thing is certain. The UBI is quickly moving from chimera to viable idea, and it could become reality sooner than expected.[12]

★　★　★　★　★

Transforming health care: basic Medicare for all and a thriving private sector

When it comes to health care, and our convoluted and partisan politics of this day, where are we at the end of 2017? Well, as already related in the health care chapter of this book, the House passed its AHCA bill on May 4 of 2017. Trump celebrated the very narrow – three-vote margin – passage of the bill in the House as a "great victory." It was then the U.S. Senate's turn. Between extremely conservative senators like Ted Cruz and Mike Lee, a "libertarian" like Ron Paul, and a few moderates like Susan Collins, Dean Heller, and Lisa Murkowski, Senate Majority Leader Mitch McConnell faced a complex challenge. He had to walk a tightrope to achieve some type of compromise apt to garner at least fifty Republican votes, with Vice President Mike Pence providing the tie-breaker. In late May, McConnell professed in media interviews that he was "unsure how to get a majority to pass the GOP health bill." No help was forthcoming from Democrats. Democratic senators were unanimous in their opposition to the AHCA, in a stand best defined by what Iraq war veteran and Massachusetts Congressman Seth Moulton wrote after the May 4 House Republican vote, channeling his inner Churchill:

> Never has the GOP acted with such little information to take so much away from so many to benefit so few. This is a tax cut for the wealthy paid for by the lives and welfare of working Americans. This is a vote that should forever stain their political careers.[13]

After weeks of debate behind closed doors, to the frustration of Democratic and Republican senators alike, McConnell unveiled his health bill, called the "Better Care Reconciliation Act," on June 22, 2017. The bill was very similar to the AHCA, with a couple of noteworthy changes. On Medicaid, the Senate bill would slow down the timing of the significant cuts in the popular program covering seventy-four million Americans. These cuts would not start to take effect until 2021, with most Medicaid expansion funding ending in 2024. This would allow the Republican senators scheduled for re-election in 2018 and also 2020 to face their electors before the cuts in Medicaid took place, an astute if cynical political move. After 2021, though, the Senate bill would slash more deeply into Medicaid funding than the House bill, using a less generous "cost of living" adjustment formula. Over ten years, there would be $772 billion in Medicaid cuts relative to Obamacare, to pay for $700 billion in Medicare and investment tax cuts for those making over $250,000 per year. On the health exchanges, the Senate bill would eliminate the individual mandate like in the AHCA. But whereas the AHCA proposed tax credits replacing the Obamacare subsidies only increased with age, ignoring income differences, the "Better Care" bill would be more progressive, allowing tax credits to be higher for lower incomes.

A mere couple of days after the bill release, five Republican senators stated they would not vote for it in its present shape, underscoring McConnell's challenge. Four (Cruz – TX; Lee – UT; Paul – KY; and Johnson – WI) said the bill was too much like Obamacare to their liking. I cannot vote for "Obamacare-lite," commented Paul. From an opposite point of view, Dean Heller (NV), standing beside his fellow Republican and governor of Nevada Brian Sandoval, said: "I cannot support a piece of legislation that takes away insurance from tens of millions of Americans and hundreds of thousands of Nevadans."

On June 26, the much-awaited Congressional Budget Office (CBO) report came out. The "Better Care" Senate bill did score better than the House's AHCA, but not by much: twenty-two million Americans would lose insurance by 2026 (instead of twenty-three million in the AHCA), and the ten-year budget savings would amount to $321 billion. Upon the release of the CBO report, a sixth Republican senator, Susan Collins of Maine, declared her opposition to the bill, saying she would vote against "motion to proceed" (to the Senate floor for debate and a vote). With such opposition, McConnell abandoned his plan to vote on the bill before the July 4 recess, giving his leadership more time to negotiate with the holdouts. As soon as this was announced, three more Republican senators announced their opposition to the bill: Shelley Moore Capito (WV), Jerry Moran (KS), and Rob Portman (OH). Would Senate Republicans manage to "repeal and replace" Obamacare?

Mitch McConnell had one more go. But what happened in the Senate during the last week of July was all about larger than life John McCain, with quite a bit of theater. Vietnam War hero, "maverick" Navy pilot, U.S. senator, 2008 Republican presidential nominee, and now fighting recently diagnosed brain cancer, McCain rushed back to Washington DC after his first medical treatment. His vote on July 25 was the 50th Republican Senate vote, needed to allow Vice President Mike Pence to break a tie and let the health care debate proceed on the Senate floor. Bravo, said all Republicans committed to the repeal of the ACA. McCain followed his vote with a heartfelt speech admonishing his fellow Senators that "we are getting nothing done here," and that it was time to go back to a long tradition of bi-partisan legislative efforts in the U.S. Senate. On July 26, seven Republican senators heeded McCain's call for bi-partisanship, but not in the direction McConnell hoped for. These Republicans joined the unanimous Democrats in voting 55–45 against a proposal that would have ended major parts of the Affordable Care Act, with a two-year delay to allow time for lawmakers to design new health care legislation.

The outright repeal of Obamacare having failed to pass the Senate (unlike in 2016, when Obama was still president), McConnell and his leadership decided to go for a "skinny repeal." This new, eight-page short bill would have ended the ACA's individual mandate and its requirement that large employers provide coverage to their employees, and delayed the tax on medical devices. It would have made it easier for states to waive federal requirements for insurance plans to offer a minimum package of benefits, a key demand from conservative Republican senators like Ted Cruz. Planned Parenthood federal funds would have been cut for a year, compensated by increased federal monies to community health centers, and contributions to health savings accounts would have been encouraged through increased limits for tax-free contributions. The CBO calculated that even the "skinny repeal" would put fifteen million Americans out of health insurance, and several Republican senators revolted. In particular, John McCain, Lindsey Graham, and Ron Johnson demanded assurances that this Senate legislation would only be used to re-open the dialogue with the House, and never become law. Think about it: voting for a bill under the guarantee that it would never be enacted . . . amazing. Calling the stripped-down bill a "disaster," Graham said at a news conference, "I'm not going to vote for a bill that is terrible policy and horrible politics just because we have to get something done."[14] House Speaker Paul Ryan provided enough assurance to mollify Graham and Johnson. Alaska's Lisa Murkowski and Maine's Susan Collins remained undeterred in opposition.

And McCain? On July 27, around 11pm, he told reporters asking him about his vote to "wait for the show" and ostensibly accepted to confer for over half an hour with Mike Pence. And then, with a very visible thumbs-down, like a Roman consul at the Coliseum sealing someone's fate, he voted against the bill, joining Ms. Collins, Ms. Murkowski, and the forty-eight Democrats. The last word belonged to the senator from Arizona:

> I've stated time and time again that one of the major failures of Obamacare was that it was rammed through Congress by Democrats on a strict party-line basis without a single Republican vote. We must now return to the correct way of legislating and send the bill back to committee, hold hearings, receive input from both sides of aisle, heed the recommendations of the nation's governors, and produce a bill that finally delivers affordable care for the American people. We must do the hard work our citizens expect of us and deserve.[15]

The last word? Not so fast. One should never underestimate the determination of the Republican Congress to make good on a campaign promise made to its voters, over and over again, for seven years. No matter what the consequences might be for one-sixth of our economy. And so, first in a very stealthy way, like a snake in the grass, a new effort gathered steam during the last two weeks of September. Why then? Because the ability of Republican senators to pass a "repeal and replace Obamacare" bill under "budget reconciliation rules," i.e. needing only 50 votes (plus Vice-President Pence's tie-breaking vote) would expire on September 30, at least for 2017. And thus came for debate the Graham–Cassidy bill, named after its two main sponsors Lindsey Graham (from South Carolina, already mentioned above) and Bill Cassidy (from Louisiana). Two other sponsors, Ron Johnson (Wisconsin) and Dean Heller (yes! The senator from Nevada quoted earlier in his opposition to Medicaid cuts . . .) cut a much lower profile. Graham–Cassidy was even more radical than earlier Republican health care proposals: not only would guarantees of coverage for pre-existing conditions be left totally at the discretion of the states, without any need for federal government waivers in the last iteration of the bill; not only would Medicaid expansion be stopped; but Medicaid also would stop existing as we know it, replaced by "block grants" to each of the fifty states, with these federal funds being totally abolished after 2026. Graham–Cassidy would remove all the Medicaid expansion dollars and follow a per capita formula for the block grants, handing a windfall to states that had refused Medicaid expansion, such as Texas, Mississippi and Kansas. "Blue" states like California and New York would be hit the hardest.

Graham–Cassidy broke all prior records of unpopularity: only 20% of those polled supported it; all medical associations known in the land came against it from day one, starting with the American Medical Association; the AARP voiced its total opposition on behalf of our retirees; even health care insurance companies like Blue Cross Blue Shield, usually very cautious, came out against the proposal. In terms of complexity, the proposed law was a doozy: imagine, fifty states creating their own systems to replace Medicaid! Over time we could see anything from no coverage at all to statewide single payer systems covering everyone. Most likely, though, chaos would prevail. It took Massachusetts under Republican Governor Mitt Romney four years to establish its own, quasi-universal health care system – the precursor of Obamacare. Would all fifty states get ready within the two years allowed? Doubtful.

This time, Senator McCain led. A few days after the details of Graham–Cassidy became known, he opposed the bill forcefully, exactly on the same principled grounds he had voiced on July 27, with added criticism that the short time frame had not allowed the CBO to perform its review. Rand Paul of Kentucky also voiced his opposition, from the angle that this proposed bill was still too much like Obamacare, "essentially redistributing the funds from blue states to red states." When Susan Collins declared her opposition on September 25, Graham–Cassidy collapsed, Mitch McConnell confirming on September 26 no vote would take place on the bill.

The Republican Congress moved on to tax reform. Will there be further attempts to "repeal and replace" the ACA in 2018? Only time will tell. In the meantime, the ACA's Medicaid expansion is safe – as well as the resulting health care coverage for millions of Americans. On another front in the battle against Obamacare, President Trump signed two executive orders in October 2017 to allow "low frills" health insurance plans across state lines and to eliminate federal funding of ACA subsidies for low income people not qualifying for Medicaid. These subsidies could be reinstated if Democrats and Republicans reached a bi-partisan deal on health care, Trump said, although such an agreement remains elusive. Two brave and patriotic senators, Lamar Alexander (R-TN) and Patty Murray (D-WA), did reach a bi-partisan compromise solution, but the Republican leadership in the Senate did not take it up. Later in the year, against opposition from health insurers, the GOP tax plan repealed the Obamacare individual mandate (i.e. penalty for not having health insurance), likely leading to a big increase in the number of Americans without coverage. Our health care saga goes on. Stay tuned!

There is no doubt our health care system is broken, its ever-increasing complexity causing the high costs and poor outcomes so many Americans suffer from. The current efforts by the Trump administration and Congressional Republicans confirm the trend of the last seventy years, of changes that always add to the complexity of the system. The AHCA law voted by House Republicans and the failed Senate bills all eliminated or curtailed the simplest and most effective components of President Obama's Affordable Care Act: the expansion of Medicaid and the obligation for insurers to cover pre-existing conditions.

In a less polarized world, one could easily imagine a bi-partisan reform of the ACA focusing on tax credits, increased competition across state lines, expansion of group insurance, and lower cost insurance targeted for the young. That bi-partisan reform would keep coverage of pre-existing conditions; children up to 26 years of age insured within their parents' plans; and the popular Medicaid expansion as they are today, investment taxes for the wealthy included. In other words, keep what is simple in the ACA and reform the complex health exchange marketplaces that clearly are not working well. That would be the key to a popular reform, even within our current and suboptimal health care system.

The U.S. health care dilemma today is that no proposed reform within the last fifty years has addressed the fundamental problem of costs. Our health care costs never go down, so the tradeoff is always between increasing coverage (Democrats' objective) or lower taxes (Republicans' objective). Democrats claimed after their vote on the ACA that millions of Americans would get access to health care for the first time – true – and that costs would also go down, thanks to complex innovations like Accountable Health Organizations (ACOs) – this did not materialize. There were winners and losers under the ACA: insurance became much cheaper for low income and sick people, but the healthy and well off ended paying more for insurance, and tax rates for the wealthy went up 4%. In voting for the AHCA, House Republicans aimed to cut taxes for the wealthy and health care device companies – true – and claimed as well that "everyone will have 'access' to health care" – patently untrue, given the increase of the cost of coverage for millions, foremost low-income people of just below Medicare age in rural areas. The CBO report assessing the potential impact of the House passed AHCA defined clearly its winners and losers: older, low-income people and patients with pre-existing conditions would lose; the young and the affluent would win. Short-term, the prognosis for genuine progress is not good. More of the same, or worse, appears to be on the menu for America's health care.

The only way to break this zero-sum game is to bring our health care costs down first. To achieve this the major pockets of excessive costs in our system identified in Chapter 2 on health care need to be squeezed. Administrative complexity; IT costs; galloping drug prices; the prevalent fee for service pricing framework; the shortage of primary care physicians (PCPs)' and overabundance of specialists, all have to be tackled. Incremental initiatives targeting this or that piece of the health care puzzle are doomed to failure, since any gain in one area is offset by losses in another due to the complexity added incrementally to the system. Bringing health care costs down in a comprehensive way requires a fundamental re-thinking of our system, one that leaves political ideologies behind – quite a challenge. The following statistic illustrates its magnitude. The U.S. is the country of free markets, and Europeans drown under the weight of socialism and statism in health care, right? Well, the fact is that when we add together direct government funding for Medicare ($672 billion); Medicaid ($565 billion); public health activities ($82 billion); the VA ($67 billion); the Department of Defense Health spending ($41 billion); medical research ($42 billion); CHIP ($17 billion); the Indian Health Services ($4 billion); a number of other federal and state programs ($54 billion); plus two often overlooked factors, government outlays for public employees' private health insurance coverage ($200 billion) and the tax subsidy for all employer-based health care plans ($300 billion), 62% of all 2016 health care expenditures in the U.S. were paid by Uncle Sam. Over 60%![16] That is significantly more than the Dutch, German, or Swiss governments spend on their own systems, and roughly on par with France.[17] We manage to cover fewer people and suffer from worse outcomes while having a higher relative participation of the state in health care than many other developed countries. Amazing. This is a sobering finding for the advocates of free markets. Surely it can help all of us be bolder in finding new solutions?

How can we transform health care in our country? What could a new, simpler system based upon effectiveness and lower costs look like? Which proposals can garner approval from industry, patients, and both sides of the aisle, at least from elected officials driven by the need to put practical solutions in place, the other side of complexity and ideology? These are the questions I want to answer in this chapter. To start with, though, allow me to list several often-proposed alternatives that will not work, and explain why.

The first such alternative to our current health system can be called "put health care in the hands of the 'consumer' and let markets work." Indeed, why shouldn't free markets work in health care? They do a pretty good job just about everywhere else, where competition always leads to lower prices and higher quality. So, let's hand off health care to the private sector. Lower prices with better outcomes will follow, right? Yes . . . but. There are major issues with this type of solution, which amounts essentially to handing the whole health care mess to the "consumers," trusting that they, or we, with the infinite wisdom we show in buying food, appliances and cars, will sort it all out. The main "but" is that, for free markets to work, there has to be symmetry of information between the sellers of goods and services and those who buy them. With very basic homework, I can get to know enough about cars, for example, so that I can choose the model I want without becoming prey to the slickest car salesman and without making a catastrophic mistake. There is enough available information to let me know that if I care about exhaust pollution I should not buy a second-hand diesel engine VW. I also know to the nearest cent the price I will pay before I buy the fine automobile I selected. Prices are very transparent for pretty much everything we buy. Except in health care, that is. In most countries around the world, you go to the doctor, and . . . there are price lists on the wall, clear and legible! What a novel concept. Not here, though. Here, our health care system has no price transparency at all. Not only does one get a bill at least a month after the visit to the doctor or intervention at the hospital, but also when it eventually arrives it is hardly self-explanatory. Lots of numbers in that bill: what the actual charges were; what the insurance company paid on your behalf after the mysterious discounts they enjoy; what you may have paid, or not, in co-pay at the doctor's office or hospital registration; and then, an amount, preceded by the words "please pay." Crystal clear! Oh, I forgot: before one receives the actual bill, there are mailings related to the same medical intervention explaining a number of things that are quite opaque. But those have a bold statement on top of their first page that says: "EXPLANATION OF BENEFITS. This is NOT a bill." Phew! I do not have to pay yet ... but when the real bill arrives, my reaction will be: ouch! Why so much?[18]

When I buy a car, I feel completely in charge. After I get treated for a health issue, when it comes to payment, I feel completely under the control of my insurance company. With time and experience, I may be able to anticipate what the cost will be for me of a given visit to the doctor, or a given lab test. But for a whole treatment? No way. Of course, if one is lucky enough to be relatively affluent, "it is only money." Before that, when it comes to my precious health, I feel completely under the control of another party, this time my physician and her or his colleagues. Fortunately, I trust them a lot more than any health insurance company. It better be that way: how could I ever hope to match the accumulated knowledge of physicians who have spent a dozen years at top medical schools, then practiced under brilliant surgeons or professors of medicine, while attending top level seminars around the world on the latest science and techniques? These are some of the most learned and skilled professionals on earth. Obviously, the symmetry of information between them and me, the patient – sorry, I meant to say 'consumer' – is inexistent. The economic theory behind free markets says that competition works when buyers can compare, knowledgeably, the prices and qualities of different offerings from different goods or services providers. With competition, and symmetry of information, prices go down and quality up – only oligopolies or monopolies can prevent this positive outcome. To be fair, there are a few simple care procedures that do benefit from competition and genuine customer choices. Cosmetic work, some laser eye surgeries, and corrective lenses have become better and cheaper over the years, even though (or because?) they are not typically covered by insurance. But they represent a relatively small part of our health care sector.

For most health issues, because I simply do not have enough medical knowledge, it is hard for me to make an informed choice on the treatment alternatives offered to me. Again, I will trust my physician(s) there. I will only go seek another opinion, at significant cost of time and money, if they suggest something that appears outlandish, such as complex surgery to treat something that seems benign to me. As we saw in the health care chapter of this book (when talking about overtreatment), most of our fellow citizens rarely even do that, always trusting their physicians and hardly ever second-guessing them. Well, surely this should be easier with competing offerings from insurance companies, right? After all, I did earn a fair amount of my living as a business executive. Yes ... but, again. When one "shops" for an insurance company – assuming there is a choice in one's state, which is not always the case – first one has to master complex and technical language. Second, one has to navigate half a dozen plan offerings, each one with a monthly cost (premium) for you, your wife, children, and also, for a large number of listed procedures, different maximum out of pocket amounts, co-payments, caps, and deductibles. When the latter reach $15,000, or $20,000 for you and your family, it means essentially that you have "catastrophic health coverage," but not much more. Even at today's inflated medical costs, it will take a lot of doctor's visits and minor interventions to reach $20,000 in costs. In this case, of course, the insurer will tout a relatively low monthly cost of insurance. However, if you decide you want real insurance, with deductibles around a few thousand dollars, then the monthly cost goes up a lot. To make an informed decision I would have to go to my crystal ball, and anticipate correctly what health ailments will affect each member of my family and me within the next year. Also, whether we will be able to get treatment at "in network" or "out of network" hospitals - the latter increasing deductibles and out of pocket costs significantly. In the absence of that foresight, it is guess work. Even looking back, with perfect hindsight, it is not all that easy to assess which plan would have been the best. And that is just with one payer. If I have to compare with another one, it becomes even more of a guessing game. To add to the confusion, some insurers which offer lower rates may on the other hand have internal policies that direct their staff to deny procedures their policies appear to cover, every time they can get away with it.

Case in point: on my father's side, my grandmother and first cousin had breast cancer when in their 40s. So did my only sister, a few years younger than me. All survived the disease well. Still, when my daughter was born, I thought it prudent at the time to take a test that could tell me whether I had the mutated gene causing this, or not. This was fifteen years ago, and DNA testing was not what it is today. But the test existed, at a cost of $3,000, and my insurer told me they would cover it – after I filled a whole bunch of information about my grandmother, sister and cousin. I go get tested, good news, I don't have the mutated gene, and my daughter appears to be safe. Then a month later, I receive a piece of mail from the insurer, denying the payment, without explanation. Undeterred, I call the number listed on the letter, and wait an hour for a person to deign to talk to me. "We denied you because you did not list on your application the tests results for your grandmother." Silence from me. Then screaming. My grandmother was born in 1905, and she had cancer at 45; how could I possibly know whatever tests they used in 1950? No go. I ask to talk to a supervisor. No go. Then I try calling two days later. More screaming, and another supervisor. "Well, if you write us a letter explaining to us why your grandmother could not have had access to modern cancer screening techniques in 1950, we may reimburse you." Letter sent. Another letter received, asking for more questions. Duly answered. And, finally, I get my $3,000 another month later, minus of course my patient-pay after insurance. Wow! And this was a case where I had taken the pains to ask specifically whether the procedure would be covered before taking it. Would Medicare ever behave like this? The saving grace out of this whole saga is that my numerous relatives back in France never tire of hearing the story ... "Really? Are you serious? You are exaggerating again!"

Seriously, can anyone really propose a coherent health care plan just based upon empowering the patient customers to transform the system? Speaker Paul Ryan is one such advocate, but even he does not practice what he preaches – no matter of how much one may disagree with his theories. If one looks at the AHCA he and his House Republican colleagues cobbled together, it is a far cry from his repeated assertions that "competition and the private markets will lower health care prices and improve accessibility for all." There was very little in the AHCA detail that would have allowed one to think it could have led to a nirvana of healthy competition and customer choices, as we saw earlier in the book. Let's also not forget that, unlike in consumer goods, when it comes to health care, lives are at stake! To mention other professions involved in saving lives, I have never heard any proponent of "consumer driven" health care also advocate for the privatization of fire departments and police forces. Curiously, we "customers" are not deemed as capable of choosing our fire people or police precinct as to decide which treatment to pursue when facing a life-threatening illness.

An extreme version of transferring most of our health care system to the private sector has already been mentioned in this book: it is the idea of replacing Medicare as we know it by a system of vouchers to buy private insurance. This idea, promoted by conservative ideologues and called "Voucher Care" by its many detractors, has little chance of ever becoming reality because of the strong and enduring popularity of Medicare. Medicare's popularity transcends all political cleavages; even avowed anti-government individuals love Medicare. Remember the famous line from a Tea Party activist, "do not let the government touch my Medicare?" Private insurance companies often overcharge for insurance; they suffer from inefficiencies and high administrative costs; and have not shown much ability in lowering costs when procuring medical devices or dealing with pharmaceutical companies about the high cost of drugs. As a result, "Voucher Care" would likely result in yet higher costs for our health system, or much diminished quality of coverage, or both.

Health care cannot be reduced to customer choice. For those who do not want their Medicare replaced by vouchers that would allow them to buy the "right" to be in the tender and loving care of private insurance plans, there is a completely different alternative. This alternative manages to combine statism and state rights. It is "Medicaid for all." Yes, Medicaid, or rather, the fifty state-administrated systems that were created alongside their big federal brother Medicare during the Johnson presidency in 1965. Most Medicaid programs have a rather low profile compared to Medicare. Yet they work very well in most states, providing access to decent quality care to millions of low-income Americans of all ages. Medicaid programs are lower cost than Medicare or private insurance programs. This is a plus, but also explains why many physicians and hospitals do not take Medicaid patients, being put off by the low reimbursements. As a result, many Medicaid beneficiaries often have trouble finding high quality care. Yet, several states have attempted to correct this by innovating their state health care program. These innovations are as diverse as our states, ranging from efforts to work with groups helping immigrants in New York and California, to an Indiana experiment with cheap, high-deductible plans and health savings accounts. Even to its critics, Medicaid cannot be tainted with the "big and wasteful government program" label, since each state has the latitude to administrate its local Medicaid as it – and local voters – see fit.

A vastly expanded Medicaid would likely have at least some bi-partisan appeal, since conservatives would applaud the increased state role in health care, while liberals would support Medicaid's ability to enroll most individuals and families at low cost. "Medicaid for all" proponents also point out at the potential ease of transition to such a model. In a transition period, we would keep Medicare, Medicaid targeting everyone below 65 who would not have access to employment-related health coverage. Obamacare's subsidies or the proposed AHCA's tax credits could be used to pay Medicaid premiums. Over time, there might be a phase-out of both Medicare and work-related insurance, but that likely would trigger a volley of opposition fire from pretty much all quarters. Complexity in health care would remain undiminished, and adminis-trative costs as states took on a bigger role in health care might increase as well. California could spread the administrative costs of its Medi-Cal program over its thirty-nine million people, and also command good negotiating power with hospitals and drug companies, but what about states with fewer than a million people? Their per capita health costs might rise a lot, lest they offer very subpar coverage. That would be the biggest negative of such a state-by-state decen-tralized health program. We could wake up one day with a two-speed health system, with some of our people well taken care of, and others having little or no coverage. Many more Americans than today could become second-class citizens with very limited access to decent health care, a very negative outcome.

Then there is the well-known "single-payer" alternative, and the end of pri-vate health insurance as we know it. In health care, this is like abolishing the border with Canada. Our health system would essentially be like Canada's, at least from the coverage standpoint, with one very large, single federal insurance system. Finally, universal health care in the U.S.! Physicians and hospitals could remain like they are today in America, since I have never heard anyone advocat-ing for the U.S. a full "National Health Service" à la Britain, where both payers and providers are state-owned and administrated. In the single-payer alterna-tive, the only part of medicine that is "socialized" is insurance. Proponents of a single-payer system point at much lower health costs per capita in Canada than in America. They sometimes point at the even lower per capita costs of the U.K. system, although again the NHS is a different system. Here is what one advocate of a single-payer public system says:

> These savings (from a single-payer public health system) would be more than enough to fund $343 billion in improvements to our health system, including the achievement of truly universal coverage, improved benefits, and the elimination of premiums, co-payments and deductibles, which are major barriers to people seeking care.[19]

The author of these comments is Gerald Friedman, Professor of Economics at the University of Massachusetts, Amherst. He also quantifies in his research the potential savings obtained through a single-payer system. They would come from cutting the excess administrative costs associated with today's private health insurance industry (estimated at $476 billion) and using the new public system's bargaining power to negotiate pharmaceutical drug prices down to European levels ($166 billion). Friedman's research was commissioned by Physicians for a National Health Program, a not-for-profit research and educational organization of more than 18,000 doctors nationwide, to find out how much a single-payer system would cost today in the U.S. and how it could be financed.

Yes, all this could be true, if we suddenly woke up, pronto, with a Canadian type single-payer system. In reality, the transition costs would be horrendous. What are we supposed to do with Aetna, Anthem, and United Health? Nationalize them? How, and at what price per share? Gains or losses for their shareholders? Politically, I do not know how this could be feasible in this country, even with a Washington entirely controlled by Democrats. Then let's not forget that the Canadian health care system is far from perfect. Its main issue is the "rationing" of care, principally when national budgets are tight. Everyone would be covered, yes, but if there are not enough federal dollars to give everyone unlimited access to our best hospitals, how would decisions be made that would direct some patients to lower quality care and ask others to wait years for an operation such as hip replacement?[20,21,22]

I believe that some type of "Medicare for all" has a key role to play in solving the issues of our health care system, but not on an exclusive basis. What we need is to combine the universality of health coverage achieved by Medicare for all with market-based competition. It is important to keep the ability of the private sector to innovate in the area of leading edge medical treatments and provide enough capacity so that no queuing exists, even for medical operations that merely improve our physical comfort. We need to do this with particular attention on the overall costs of the system to prevent our health care costs from crashing the barrier of 20% of our GDP, something that could well happen within a decade if current trends continue. My proposed solution, which would include a thriving private sector, can be named **Basic Medicare for All**, or **Universal Public Option**.

How would such a solution and its universal public option work?

- Medicare would be extended as government-guaranteed health insurance to everyone above 26 years of age, younger individuals keeping the option to stay on their parents' insurance plans, as they have today.
- As a cost containment measure, today's Medicare, which is a very generous and comprehensive plan, would remain available only to those 65 years of age and older. It would be called "Comprehensive" or "Platinum."
- There would be three lower cost but higher co-pay and deductible plans. A "Basic" Medicare, akin to a "Bronze" plan, available to those between 26 and 40, with the lowest fees but highest co-pays and deductibles; a "Silver" plan, available to those between 40 and 55; and a "Gold" plan, available to

those between 55 and 65. The health exchanges set up as part of the ACA would be closed.

- Anyone wishing to get better quality coverage and access than provided in the Basic, Silver, Gold or Comprehensive Medicare plans would have to go to the private sector for supplementary coverage providing lower co-pays and deductibles. All such private sector supplementary plans, as well as employer-based insurance, would be allowed to operate across state lines. Private health insurers would be encouraged to compete nationally, just like any other form of insurance such as for homes or cars.

- The tax-deductibility of employer-provided private insurance would be eliminated, saving the U.S. treasury $250–300 billion per year (according to the Kaiser Family Foundation; the Tax Policy Center; and PNHP), and thus helping finance the proposed solution.[23,24] This would also redirect the efforts of most private insurers to Medicare Advantage types of plans. Employers could still award "Cadillac" private health plans to employees as part of their benefits package, but they would have to pay taxes on them like on payroll. Most employers would offer Medicare supplemental plans as benefits, but more sparingly in terms of costs than today. This would provide an incentive to prevent overuse of health care services.

- The private sector would thus gradually focus on "Medicare Advantage" or "Supplemental" plans, which would be available to all, the fees charged by private insurance companies essentially determined by competition forces. With Basic Medicare for All covering by definition all individuals to some degree, the rules on pre-existing conditions would be very simple. Private insurers would be not be allowed to deny coverage to anyone or to charge more than five times the cost of a Basic plan, four times that of a Silver plan, and three times that of a Gold plan to the individuals eligible for such plans. This way no one with a pre-existing condition would be priced out of supplemental Medicare coverage.

- The federal government and CMS would be responsible for setting the guidelines, standards, co-pays, deductibles, and fees for Medicare plans. The administration of Medicare plans would be modeled on today's Medicare, with a few changes mentioned in the following points.

- The federal government (HHS Department and CMS) would be responsible for negotiating reimbursement schedules with hospitals. There would be a renewed, nationwide focus on an outcome-based pricing system that would gradually eliminate fee for service over a ten-year period, leveraging the success of the few Medicare Advantage plans that have already implemented "capitated" pricing for given populations.

- As part of this renewed focus on relationships with hospitals throughout the country, CMS would launch a national information technology program that would aim at creating a "National Health Card." This health card would allow all Americans to keep their personal health and medical data in a simple IT format that would be compatible with most, if not all, existing hospital patient accounting systems. CMS would dictate the standards required, and this program would be financed by private IT companies currently involved in the health sector, against a small recurring fee paid by health card holders.

- HHS and CMS would be responsible for negotiating the pricing of drugs for Medicare plans with pharmaceutical companies, ending the current Medicare Part D restriction in this area. A key lever to be used by the relevant government entities to lower supply costs would be allowing more imports of lower priced drugs from other countries with high health standards, such as Canada, Japan, and E.U. members.
- HHS, in conjunction with the Department of Education and leading U.S. universities, would launch a medical school initiative aimed at creating graduate programs forming primary care physicians in fewer years than today, and at a much lower tuition cost to students opting to become generalists.
- State-level Medicaid plans would be eliminated. However, individual states would have the option to administrate Medicare for All in their state, as long as they met the universal standards set by HHS and CMS at the federal level. In particular, states would be encouraged to develop their own arrangements with local providers, Medicare, and private insurers to monitor patient outcomes in an integrated way for segments of their population.
- Veterans' hospitals and the VA's involvement in health operations could remain, but in terms of coverage the VA would focus on financing Medicare Advantage plans for veterans of all ages to ensure their current level of health coverage is maintained, beyond the new Medicare levels.
- The National Institutes of Health would continue to be well financed, just like during the Obama administration. A new national effort would be launched to help develop new innovative medical devices and drugs, working with young biotech companies and funding them along the lines of DARPA for scientific ones and ARPA-E in energy and cleantech.
- The federal government, with HHS, the FDA and the National Institutes of Health, would launch a national initiative on prevention, working closely with Academic Medical Centers and biotech companies throughout the U.S.

This "Basic Medicare for All" or "Universal Public Option" system would be a lot simpler than today's health care in our country. The administrative costs of the existing multi private insurance plans within each state (remember, our current private system of private insurance does not cross state lines) would be greatly simplified with one national, Universal Medicare Option plan. Private Medicare supplemental plans would operate across state lines, transforming a multi-state system into a national one and also simplifying administrative processes significantly. The fifty state Medicaid programs, with their enormous differences, would essentially disappear. States that would elect to administrate the Basic Medicare for All in their state would do so under a unified set of national guidelines. The mosaic of interactions between the governments – federal and fifty states – and the private health sector would be replaced by a much smaller number of interactions between Medicare and private plans operating at a national level. The ACA's health exchanges at the federal and state level, a source of much complexity and poor results, would cease to exist. With them a whole lot of very complicated and confusing set of eligibility rules, subsidies, and tax credits would disappear. The roles of the federal government and the private sector in health care would no longer overlap significantly like today. The government would focus on universal health care with basic coverage, the operations of VA hospitals (which could be reversed to the private sector without changing the proposed system fundamentally), some medical research, and the regulatory role played by the FDA. The private sector would do all the rest, including operating most of our hospitals. With this simplification of state–private interactions in health care, information systems could also become much simpler over time.

How would "Basic Medicare for All" be financed?

In Chapter 2 on health care, when reviewing the major reasons behind the much higher costs in America relative to other developing countries, a few major ones stood out that were inherent to our current system, and not due to medical exploits keeping us healthy into advanced ages: administrative costs; growing IT costs; fee for service pricing; the quickly increasing costs of drugs; a shortage of primary care physicians (PCPs), and needless practice variations across state lines. It was estimated that complexity in health care, with its systematic use of expensive drugs and technologies; redundant administrative and IT activities; dysfunctional pricing; and state-by-state practice variation must cost us $500–600 billion per year. Today we still have about thirty million people without health insurance in the country. Assuming our current and very high health care cost per capita of about $10,000 per year, all other things being equal, insuring the thirty million would cost $300 billion. Given that with Obamacare having been implemented today's uninsured are healthier than the average population, that $300 billion is probably lower, perhaps as low as $150–$200 billion. Therefore, the cost of complexity in our current system dwarfs the cost of insuring everyone in America, by a factor of about 3x. The main question then becomes, how would the proposed solution help achieve the identified reductions in our excessive health costs?

In administrative costs, we already have strong evidence that our current Medicare is much more frugal than private plans. According to the Kaiser Family Foundation, administrative costs are only about 2% of Medicare's total operating expenditures, less than one-sixth of the rate estimated for the private insurance industry. Why? Because Medicare does not have to spend anything on advertising and other promotional efforts like private insurers. It operates across state lines, with huge scale. It also does not have to make a double-digit profit margin to keep shareholders happy. Like in all public–private partnerships, entrusting health care coverage to the private sector for the majority of our citizens inflates administrative costs a great deal: in the health care chapter, we estimated the excess administrative costs in our system at $100–150 billion per year. Having a single entity, CMS, define national standards and rate schedules for the majority of the population would also vastly simplify the current administrative burden inflicted upon our hospitals. Think about it. Today, the average U.S. hospital has contracts with around one hundred payers, many of these contracts over a thousand pages long. Having a national public plan as benchmark would also help competition work among private plans nationwide, something that is not happening enough today. Private insurers already operate successfully alongside a national public health program, Medicare. Essentially, the proposed model here replicates something that works well already at the national level, for everyone – not just for those over 65 years of age. It is also worth mentioning that systems involving government-sponsored universal health insurance alongside private insurers and providers, are successful throughout Continental Europe and Asia–Pacific, with costs much lower than ours and better outcomes.

In terms of growing IT and principally drug costs, a significant advantage in having a national public plan such as Basic Medicare for All is its strong ability to keep a lid on prices. Today, Medicare hospital reimbursements vary less and are lower than those from private plans. As a result, Medicare has experienced slower cost growth per insured person than private plans in recent years. A new initiative sponsored by CMS to give all Americans a National Health Card, focusing on straightforward nationwide data standards and the essentials in one's medical record, would also put an end to the absurd levels of spending by hospitals on IT systems that cannot even "talk to each other." The CMS initiative would help our information sector, the most dynamic in the world, focus on a set of inexpensive national standards, as opposed to spending all its creativity on "Band-Aid" applications that only address a small part of the data problem, always increasing overall complexity.

One of the biggest cost advantages of a Universal Public Option solution would be the enhanced ability of CMS to negotiate drug prices with an enormous purchasing power. The Medicare Part D program is much appreciated by Medicare recipients today, and it is not proposed in this book to eliminate it. But the absurd Part D clause governing Medicare's purchasing relationships with pharmaceuticals companies must be eliminated. This clause stipulates that the federal government is not permitted to negotiate prices of drugs with pharma companies, unlike what other federal agencies do in many activities. In the same health care sector, the Department of Veterans Affairs is allowed to negotiate drug prices and has been estimated to pay between 40% and 60% less for drugs on average than Medicare Part D. There is so little purchasing power by patients facing pharma companies today that a group of twenty large employers recently created the "Health Transformation Alliance" to use the purchasing power represented by their four million employees to negotiate better deals with pharmaceutical companies. As part of this proposed new negotiating muscle with drug manufacturers, HHS and the FDA should also allow the sale in the U.S. of imported drugs manufactured at much lower cost in countries such as Canada, where safety standards are just as high as here. It is estimated that even today, 25% of drugs labeled "American-made" are actually manufactured in other developed countries, in FDA-inspected plants. Allowing our hospitals and drugstores to get much lower priced supplies from trusted nations overseas would save us a lot of money, and also put an end to the current trend of abusive price increases by a number of U.S. drug companies.[25]

We also saw in Chapter 2 that a shortage of PCPs contributes to our excessive health costs. The initiative described above would create a special PCP track within the medical curriculum of our universities, with increased emphasis on shorter duration and lower tuition costs, perhaps with special grants from the federal government and states where the shortage of PCPs is most acute. Availability of PCPs is key to improving U.S. patients' ability to get an appointment with a provider at short notice. We do not fare well in this area: in a survey conducted by the Commonwealth Fund in 2013, covering patients in eleven countries, 52% of Americans said they could not get a same-day or next-day appointment with their provider when they were sick. The only country that was worse than the U.S. in this survey was Canada, where 59% of patients answered no to the same question – remember the queuing issues of the single-payer Canadian system? The same survey noted that America in 2013 had half as many primary care physicians per 1,000 people as Sweden (which was ranked just above the U.S. in the survey), and only one-fifth as best performers France and Germany.

Last but not least, there would be a strong national initiative to wean our hospitals and providers from fee for service, perhaps the biggest culprit in our excessive health care costs today. Let's face it, the current array of decentralized and complex initiatives around Accountable Health Care Organizations or ACOs is not working, or at best is working at a glacial speed. Clearly, we need a stronger push, and CMS under the proposed Medicare for All solution would be well placed to sponsor a national solution based upon the success of private sector experiments in this area, which are unfortunately far too few in number and scope. A few Medicare Advantage plans have reduced health care costs through "capitated" contracts with given populations. These contracts place a cap on how much the plan can spend per insured "life," and where successful provide a good blueprint to reduce costs by replacing fee for service with a pre-determined amount per patient. These solutions are very powerful, because they can incentivize payers and providers to work together with patients to eliminate wasteful costs. A telehealth consultation instead of a visit to the hospital; systematic follow-up to ensure patients take their prescribed meds to avoid costly hospital readmissions; use of simple communication techniques with patients, based on texting and smart phones; focus of PCPs on patients who need the most medical attention, as opposed to a standard half-hour for every patient; and increased use of skilled nursing staff for interactions with patients where a physician is not needed. Such are some of the innovative elements put in place by the few Medicare Advantage plans that have pursued "capitated" pricing models. This unfortunately has been very limited, because today's pricing of Medicare Advantage plans gives a fixed percentage above Medicare fees to the private insurers involved, without much incentive for them to beat the Medicare costs. Such an incentive would have to become widespread as part of a push away from fee for service, but the existing best practices to lower costs of insuring patients without compromising their health outcomes already exist. They just have to become the prevailing norm in our system, to consign our expensive fee for service model to history.[26]

Having Medicare set national standards in health care administrative and IT costs; a much cheaper supply of drugs; more PCPs; and capitated pricing of provider services, would all help reduce our excessive system costs. In addition, these initiatives would reduce the high level of medical practice variation observed across the U.S. and help us adopt proven best practices nationwide. Overall, eliminating the $500–600 billion in excess costs of today's U.S. health care would be more than enough to pay for this proposed new system with universal health insurance. Let's review this in a little more detail.[27,28,29]

On the funding side, on an annualized basis, we have around $1.4 trillion available (based upon 2016 figures from the Kaiser Foundation, CMS, and the federal government, with rounded up numbers):

- $550 billion in cost savings (16.7% of total spending)
- $550 billion in Medicaid federal and state funds, including extensions
- $250 billion with the elimination of tax deductions for employers' plans
- $50 billion in subsidies for patients using the ACA's exchanges

In terms of the 324 million people in the U.S. in 2016 and their health coverage, we have:

- 55 million covered by Medicare (public)
- 150 million covered by employment related insurance (private)
- 9 million enrolled in the VA health care system (public)
- 74 million covered by Medicaid (public)
- 12 million covered by ACA plans sold in federal and state exchanges (private)
- About 30 million uninsured and 6 million "double counted" due to overlapping coverage between Medicare, Medicaid, and the VA (e.g. "dual eligible" Medicaid - Medicare enrollees)

With the current Medicare and VA coverage staying as is, the proposed new health system needs to provide coverage to the following people, under the new Basic, Silver, and Gold plans: seventy-four million people covered by Medicaid today; twelve million covered by private plans sold on exchanges; thirty million uninsured; and 105 million people covered today by employment related insurance, assuming that forty-five million of those, or 30% of the total, will remain under private insurance provided through their employer. That is a total of 221 million people; 215 million after removing the six million "double counted." We have $1.4 trillion available on the funding side, which amounts to $6,500 per individual for 215 million people. This can be compared with $7,200 spent per individual on Medicaid today, consistent with the emphasis on "basic" Bronze and Silver plans for those under 55 years of age – the vast majority of these 216 million insured when looking at the relevant age pyramids. Furthermore, with the identified cost savings amounting to 16.7% of our current care health care costs, the equivalent of $7,200 under the new proposed system would only be $6,000 per individual ($7,200 × 0.833), or $1.3 trillion in total. So with the cost savings implemented there could be a $100 billion cushion relative to the $1.4 trillion ($6,500 per individual) mentioned above.

The $6,500 per individual available on the funding side could also be increased with (modest) deductibles and premiums charged to those enrolling in the Bronze, Silver and Gold plans. Most Medicare beneficiaries (with annual incomes up to $107,000) were paying monthly premiums between $120 and $170 in 2016. Even assuming a very low average level of premiums for the new plans, say around $80 per month (taking into account that low-income beneficiaries would pay very low or no premiums, like with Medicaid today), another $200 billion would be added on the funding side. This would represent another $200 billion cushion, which could serve as a funding "buffer" during the transition period, until the full implementation of the anticipated cost savings. Additional federal savings – difficult to quantify – would come from reduced government outlays for the current public employees' private health insurance coverage.[30,31]

The proposed system could therefore be financed without tax increases beyond those that already took place under the ACA. It would achieve universal health care in our country for the first time, and our per capita health costs would go down from over $10,000 today to about $8,500.[32,33,34]

This would still be more than in most western countries but would represent a decisive reversal of our inflationary spiral in health care costs, paving the path for even more significant cost reductions over the long-term. With additional cost reductions in the system, the remaining people covered by private plans through their employers could also go to the new Medicare for All plans, should fewer employers decide to offer health coverage that would no longer be tax-subsidized. These results would be achieved without any compromise in health outcomes – far to the contrary, since a country where everyone has access to health coverage typically also has better health outcomes. The new Medicare and CMS would also have at its disposal an extraordinary trove of patient data across the country, which could be used in conjunction with universities as well as public and private institutions to increase prevention efforts and find new innovative ways to improve health for all in the U.S.

How challenging would be the transition to the new proposed health system?

The private sector would continue playing a key role in the system, which would help ease transition pains to this new, transformed health care regime in the country. The expansion of today's Medicare into the proposed Basic Medicare for All is relatively straightforward to achieve, since the fundamental pillars of Medicare and private sector Medicare Advantage would be maintained. The creation of a few new Medicare plans with lower costs and lesser levels of coverage is a very easy thing to do. At the state level, local Medicaid programs could easily serve as operators of the new Medicare for All program. Pretty much all private insurers participate in Medicare Advantage plans already. Current Health Saving Accounts could be used, and expanded, to allow individuals and families to use tax incentives to purchase Medicare Advantage plans on a larger scale than today. Still, costs may spike during the transition to the new health system, as is often the case when a large chunk of our economy is being transformed. If during the first few years of transition the above identified cost savings, including the additional revenues from eliminating the tax exclusion of employer health insurance premiums, were not enough, the ceiling on the FICA payroll tax could be raised temporarily, until smooth running of the new system is achieved.[35,36]

In terms of transition, some progressive states may not wait for a Basic Medicare for All or Universal Public Option health care system, and could very well lead the way into universal coverage before Washington is ready for it. As seen earlier, this already happened with gay rights. There are single-payer initiatives already in seventeen states: Colorado; Illinois; Maine; Maryland; Massachusetts; Minnesota; New Mexico; Ohio; Oregon; Pennsylvania; Rhode Island; South Carolina; Vermont; Washington; and in California, Nevada, and New York, where significant landmark votes have already taken place.

In New York, the State Assembly passed a Medicare for All bill on May 16, 2017, by a vote of 92 to 52. The "New York Health Act" would afford all state residents "access to comprehensive inpatient and outpatient care, primary and preventative, prescription drugs, behavioral health services, laboratory testing and rehabilitative care, as well as dental, vision, and hearing coverage." There would be no premiums, deductibles, or co-pays; the plan would be funded through progressively raised taxes, including a surcharge that would be shared 80–20 between employers and employees. The legislation's lead sponsor, NY Assemblyman Richard Gottfried, said: "almost all New Yorkers would pay less than they currently do because they would be able to replace their current plans with this more affordable state-based plan." However, the NY Health Act stalled in the state's Republican-leaning Senate, which is more representative of rural and upstate New York, and much more conservative than the State Assembly. The Democrats will have to gain voting control of the Senate in 2018 to move the state further in the direction of single-payer legislation. Should this happen, it would then be Governor Andrew Cuomo's turn to decide.[37,38,39]

Not to be outdone, the California Senate approved on June 1, 2017 by a 23–14 vote a $400 billion per year single-payer program for the Golden State, sponsored by Senators Ricardo Lara and Toni Atkins. This legislation would create a single-payer, government-run, universal care system for everyone in the state. Like in New York, premiums, co-pays, and deductibles would be eliminated. Initial legislative analysis shows that $200 billion could be raised to finance half the annual cost of the new plan from a new 15% payroll tax, which would require a two-thirds vote from both houses. This hurdle is significant, but one has to consider that Democrats hold such a "super majority" in both the California Senate and Assembly. An alternative way to finance the $200 billion would be through a 2.3% sales tax and a 2.3% gross receipts tax on businesses – this too would be a challenge since it would bring the state's sales tax close to 10%. The other $200 billion would come from the existing federal, state and local funding on health care in the state.[40,41,42]

The single-payer legislation would take California into unchartered territory, with many unknowns on how enrollees, employers, health providers, and the state would adapt to this new regime. There would also be the issue of all the private health insurance employees, who either would have to join the new single-payer administration or be retrained into other activities. There would be a need for additional funds to retrain part of this workforce. The Healthy California legislation would need to pass the state Assembly, and then potentially go to Governor Jerry Brown. Assuming Brown's current concerns about funding for a single-payer system in California could be overcome, the proposed law would still need to face two additional obstacles. California voters would have to approve Healthy California, to exempt it from budget and spending limits enshrined in the state's constitution, since the law's $400 billion spending requirements exceed the $180 billion state budget. California would also have to get federal approval to repurpose existing funds for Medicare and Medicaid in the state towards the new single-payer system. Because of all these challenges, Assembly Speaker Anthony Rendon decided to shelve the single-payer measure on June 23, calling it "woefully incomplete." This means the effort is halted, at least for the current legislative session.[43,44,45,46]

It is in neighboring Nevada that a statewide public option came the closest to adoption. After passing the Nevada legislature on June 7, 2017, a landmark Medicaid for All health care bill sat for nine days on Republican Governor Brian Sandoval's desk, waiting for his potential signature. Note a couple of twists here. Medicaid, not Medicare for All. And in a state led by a Republican governor! The Democrat sponsor of the bill, Assemblyman Mike Sprinkle, saw states stepping in to help the uninsured, should the AHCA become law and existing benefits of Obamacare rolled back:

> With the uncertainty and mixed messages coming from our current federal administration in regard to health care and health care accessibility, there is an absolute need for states to become more reliant on providing insurance options to citizens ... It's the responsibility of government to be more involved in providing adequate health care to its citizenry. So we spit-balled some ideas around and came up with this: The one package people are highly pleased with is Medicaid. Let's mirror that.[47]

Governor Sandoval had approved Medicaid expansion in Nevada, one of only half a dozen Republican governors to do so. He also had stated clearly his opposition to the House Republicans' vote on the AHCA to repeal Medicaid expansion, which would have caused 300,000 Nevadans to lose health coverage. Sandoval issued a cautious statement on June 7:

> I will review the final language this week and work with healthcare experts to evaluate how this would impact the current market, potential state costs and risks, make a determination if this is needed, and whether or not this is something that can be effectively implemented.[48]

In the end, Sandoval waited until the last possible moment and vetoed the Medicaid for All measure on Friday, June 16. Had he not done so, at midnight that day the bill would have become law in Nevada. Governor Sandoval did praise Assemblyman Sprinkle for his "creativity," but said in a statement that ultimately there were too many unanswered questions. The road ahead would have been challenging indeed, with issues on eligibility, potential coverage premiums, impact on health providers, and needed approval in Washington DC for the use of federal Medicaid funds to finance the program. In a statement, Sprinkle expressed his disappointment, saying: "healthcare is a right, not a privilege or a product. With this veto, Governor Sandoval has actively decided to veto a right that all Nevadans should have."[49,50]

Lots of political hurdles at the state and federal level. But clearly the idea of a single-payer is advancing steadily in some of our larger states, its progress somewhat overshadowed by the sad health care political show in Washington. A U.S. health care regime with some version of the AHCA at the federal level, and populous states like California and New York implementing single-payer systems in the perfect opposite direction, would be a cacophony of complexity, with huge transition challenges. The most interesting thing coming out of this would be the very visible comparison between single-payer systems touching sixty million or more Americans living on the coasts, versus "Trump–Ryan–McConnell care." At the very least, data on comparative enrollment; coverage; costs; outcomes; and not least popularity of such different health systems would yield a lot of lessons learned. However, if we end up in a country where every state has a different health care system, with private insurers that do not operate across state lines, plus Medicare and the VA, complexity and costs will grow even further.[51,52,53,54]

A far better outcome would be a scenario in which successful single-payer experiments in large states prompt voters nationwide to elect U.S. Representatives and Senators favorable to a national solution involving a public (but not single) option for all citizens. This is how Canada adopted universal health care and a single-payer system. A province level experiment started in 1946 in Saskatchewan proved to be so successful it compelled the other provinces and the government in Ottawa to adopt it nationally, fifteen years later. Statewide initiatives promoting "health care for all" public options may also represent a harbinger of things to come with universal health care in our country.[55,56,57,58]

In an age where millions have part-time, freelance or contractor jobs, our traditional employer-based health insurance no longer works, and risks over time to leave tens of millions without coverage - in addition to the thirty million uninsured we already have today. This would be a disastrous throwback to the early 1920s, basically a century ago, when access to health care was almost a luxury. We therefore need to transform our health care regime radically, but in a way that is implementable, and does not cause transition convulsions in terms of costs and employment losses in the sector. The proposed Basic Medicare for All, or Universal Public Option, would give all Americans health care for the first time in our history. It would dramatically simplify our existing system, save costs by at least 15%, and improve health outcomes for all Americans. The new system would also keep a thriving private sector very involved in our health care, alongside the public option. This would help achieve bipartisan consensus, and support from legislators across the aisle who would put practical and results-oriented solutions ahead of political ideology. We should look forward to having a future for the country where our patchy current safety net is replaced by a Universal Basic Income and Basic Medicare for All. Everyone with some income and health care! This should help Americans free themselves from existential and health worries, and focus on re-inventing our economy with automation, artificial intelligence and other new technologies.

*   *   *   *   *

A carbon tax and a nationwide flexible grid, enabling clean tech progress

The electricity and utilities chapter of this book concluded with the key issues we face in our energy markets today. In our utility sector, complex regulatory strategies are sometimes more important than running operations optimally. With constant changes in federal and state regulations, implementing any type of national energy policy is near impossible. This is a grave handicap since energy is by definition a long-term game, where strategic decisions take decades to be validated or proven wrong. These issues mean that, when it comes to the triple imperative of maintaining reliable energy supplies, addressing climate change and growing our economy, we kind of play the global energy game with our hands tied behind our back. Incentives at the federal and state levels change all the time, with the exception of large ongoing extraction subsidies for our oil & gas explorers and producers. When it comes to renewables, in particular solar and wind, it is "stop and go," or "two steps forward, one step back." There was a first wave of incentives in the late 1970s and early 1980s, after the 1973 and 1978 global oil shocks. Then another push during the mid-1990s. Now it seems like the renewables train has left the station for good and is accelerating fast . . . although clearly the Trump administration is sending every possible signal that it wants to slam the brakes on it. We have seen the appointment of a skeptic of climate science as EPA administrator, an Energy Secretary who initially thought the mission of his federal department was to promote fossil fuels, and the much-criticized U.S. exit of the global Paris climate agreement. Amidst all of this, a select group of Republican statesmen, business executives, academics, and environmentalists raised their voices to promote a "Conservative Case for Climate Action." Let's listen to them and read what Martin S. Feldstein (Chairman of the Council of Economic Advisers under President Ronald Reagan), N. Gregory Mankiw (Chairman of the same council under President George W. Bush), and Ted Halstead (Founder and Chief Executive of the Climate Leadership Council) wrote in their op-ed in the Wednesday, February 8, 2017 edition of the *New York Times*:[59]

> Crazy as it may sound, this is the perfect time to enact a sensible policy to address the dangerous threat of climate change. Before you call us nuts, hear us out.
>
> During his eight years in office, President Obama regularly warned us of the very real dangers of global warming, but he did not sign any meaningful domestic legislation to address the problem, largely because he and Congress did not see eye to eye. Instead, Mr. Obama left us with a grab bag of regulations aimed at reducing carbon emissions, often established by executive order.
>
> In comes in President Trump, who seems much less concerned about the risks of climate change, and more worried about how excessive regulation impedes economic growth and depresses living standards. As Democrats are learning the hard way, it is all too easy for a new administration to reverse the executive orders of its predecessors.
>
> On-again-off-again regulation is a poor way to protect the environment. And by creating needless uncertainty for businesses that are planning long-term capital investments, it is also a poor way to promote robust economic growth.
>
> By contrast, an ideal climate policy would reduce carbon emissions, limit regulatory intrusion, promote economic growth, help working-class Americans and prove durable when the political winds change. We have laid out such a plan in a paper to be released Wednesday by the Climate Leadership Council.
>
> Our co-authors include James A. Baker III, Treasury secretary for President Ronald Reagan and secretary of state for President H. W. Bush; Henry M. Paulson Jr., Treasury secretary for President George W. Bush; George P. Shultz, Treasury secretary for President Richard Nixon and secretary of state for Mr. Reagan; Thomas Stephenson, a partner at Sequoia capital, a venture-capital firm; and Rob Walton, who recently completed 23 years as chairman of Walmart.
>
> Our plan is built on four pillars.
>
> > First, the federal government would impose a gradually increasing tax on carbon dioxide emissions. It might begin at $40 per ton and increase steadily. This tax would send a powerful signal to businesses and consumers to reduce their carbon footprints.

Second, the proceeds would be returned to the American people on an equal basis via quarterly dividend checks. With a carbon tax of $40 per ton, a family of four would receive about $2,000 in the first year. As the tax rate rose over time to further reduce emissions, so would the dividend payments.

Third, American companies exporting to countries without comparable carbon pricing would receive rebates on the carbon taxes they've paid on these products, while imports from such countries would face fees on the carbon content of their products. This would protect American competitiveness and punish free-riding by other nations, encouraging them to adopt their own carbon pricing.

Finally, regulations made unnecessary by the carbon tax would be eliminated, including an outright repeal of the Clean Power Plan.

Our own analysis finds that a carbon dividends program starting at $40 per ton would achieve nearly twice the emissions reductions of all Obama-era climate regulations combined. Provided all four elements are put in force in unison, this plan could meet America's commitment under the Paris climate agreement, all by itself. Democrats and environmentalists may bemoan the accompanying regulatory rollback. But they should pause to consider the environment value proposition.

These four pillars, combined, invite novel coalitions. Environmentalists should like the long-overdue commitment to carbon pricing. Growth advocates should embrace the reduced regulation and increased policy certainty, which would encourage long-term investments, especially in clean technologies. Libertarians should applaud a plan premised on getting the incentives right and government out of the way. Populists should welcome the distributive impact.

According to a recent Treasury Department study, the bottom 70 percent of Americans would come ahead under a carbon dividend plan. Some 223 million Americans stand to benefit.

The idea of using taxes to correct a problem like pollution is an old one with wide support among economists. But it is our unique political moment, combined with the populist appeal of dividends, that may turn the concept into reality.

Republicans are in charge of both Congress and the White House. If they do nothing other than reverse regulations from the Obama administration, they will squander the opportunity to show the full power of the conservative canon, and its core principles of free markets, limited government and stewardship.

A repeal-only climate strategy would prove quite unpopular. Recent polls show that 64 percent of Americans are concerned about climate change, 71 percent want America to remain in the Paris agreement, and an even larger share favor clean energy. If the Republican Party fails to exercise leadership on our climate challenge, they risk a return to heavy-handed regulation when Democrats return to power.

Much better would be a strategy of "repeal and replace." This would be pro-growth, pro-competitiveness and pro-working class, which aligns perfectly with President Trump's stated agenda.

Beautifully written. The authors of this courageous and convincing manifesto put country before party; practical results before ideology; and simplicity at the heart of their argument. In a few sentences, they address everything that matters in energy, economics, and the environment. As stated, their proposal should indeed appeal to a plurality of congress people across the aisle.

The idea of a carbon tax is not a new one. George Shultz himself has written repeatedly about it, as we saw in Chapter 6 on laws and regulations of this book. Harvard Business School professor Michael Porter and Yale University professor Dan Esty offered a similar policy recommendation in another *New York Times* op-ed, written on April 27, 2011: "Pain at the Pump? Try a Charge on Carbon Emissions." In that op-ed, Esty and Porter proposed a carbon charge starting at $5 per ton and rising $5 per ton per year, until it reached $100 per ton in 2030.

A few places have already established a carbon tax. We mentioned the experiment in British Columbia earlier in this book; Ireland and Sweden already have a carbon tax; and more recently another western Canadian province, Alberta – land of the tar sands – adopted one. But what makes the "Conservative Case for Climate Action" so compelling is combining the ideas of a carbon tax with a dividend to the American people, thus bypassing the always tough and politically charged debate on taxation; incorporating export rebates and import fees to ensure the competitiveness of American companies is not impaired; and proposing to eliminate complex environmental regulations such as the Clean Power Plan – and potentially many others like CAFE standards – that would no longer be needed. Carbon tax is not a new concept. The "four pillars" supporting the carbon tax in the op-ed are.[60,61]

With such simple and effective ideas strong and focused governments are made.

Interestingly, there is another constituency that would benefit from a carbon tax that is not mentioned in the op-ed. That would be nuclear power as "base load" for our domestic utilities. Why is this an issue? After all, even though they are aging, our nuclear plants have been producing steady and cheap electricity without being in the news for at least two decades. The potential problem they face comes as an unforeseen consequence of the success stories of both renewables and shale gas in the country. The growth in electricity produced from renewable sources like wind and solar has exceeded all expectations. As recently as 2010, the International Energy Agency (IEA) projected there would be 180 gigawatts of installed solar capacity by 2025. In less than half the time, solar capacity has beaten that estimate by two-thirds and reached 303 gigawatts worldwide in 2016, according to the same IEA. In wind, a similar trend took place, with 487 gigawatts of installed capacity at the end of 2016. Falling costs have made renewables cost competitive with natural gas, even though solar and wind enjoy less than one-third of the subsidies lavished on fossil fuels. Employment in the solar industry in the U.S. has reached 260,000, according to the Solar Foundation, with another 90,000 jobs in wind power, according to the American Wind Energy Association. More Americans work today in solar than at natural gas, oil and coal-fired power plants combined.[62,63,64,65]

This success has created new issues such as how to address the mismatch between renewable supplies and peak demand. Utilities struggle with the trade-off of having too much available power capacity from renewables during the day and the need to have enough capacity during the evening peak hour, when solar power by definition is no longer productive. In cold winters the problem is exacerbated. Nuclear power has been for a while a major component of the utilities' baseload, i.e. running continuously. Today ninety-nine reactors in the U.S. provide about 20% of our electricity, without emitting any greenhouse gases. Increasingly, excess renewables during the day has meant that the whole-sale cost of electricity has gone down to very low levels, hitting negative territory in some cases, which has affected negatively the finances of nuclear plants. As we saw in Chapter 3 on electricity and utilities, the availability of abundant and cheap natural gas from fracking has led to the wholesale replacement of coal-fired plants by new, cleaner natural gas ones, a boon for our environment.

But as nuclear plants age and suffer from very low wholesale electricity rates during the day, utilities are confronted with expensive life-extension proposi-tions, including a lengthy review by the nuclear regulatory commission. An attractive alternative is then to retire nuclear units and replace them with natu-ral gas plants. This is often a popular decision due to entrenched opposition to nuclear power in some quarters. Already five nuclear units have been retired since 2013, in California, Florida, Nebraska, Vermont, and Wisconsin. In Penn-sylvania, Exelon has announced it wants to close the last remaining reactor at its Three Mile Island nuclear plant. Northern California's PG&E is closing its only nuclear unit at Diablo Canyon. Four more nuclear units are also scheduled for retirement in other states. Several more are at risk of closing in the Northeast. All these nuclear reactors are going to be replaced with natural gas-fired units. If this trend continues unabated, emissions from generation of electric power will rise in the country. According to a recent MIT study by Geoffrey Haratyk, if all the at-risk nuclear reactors shut down and were replaced by gas plants, U.S. carbon dioxide emissions would increase by 4.9%, reversing the recent decrease in greenhouse gases from the decline of coal.[66,67,68]

Already some states with ambitious environmental objectives, like Illinois and New York, are resorting to subsidies to keep several local nuclear plants operating, an expensive solution. A carbon tax would solve this problem much more elegantly, putting all zero-carbon dioxide emitting power sources – hydro, nuclear, and renewables – on the same level playing field. Among other things it would make nuclear electricity more competitive relative to natural gas-fired alternatives. This would help us maintain our dams and keep our now smoothly operating nuclear units running. This overview of the recent issues facing our nuclear industry in the U.S. begs the question, do we have too much of a good thing with solar and wind? The answer is no, principally with a carbon tax in place. And a few national initiatives, if pursued effectively, could help our energy sector become more competitive while embracing renewables even further.

In the short-term, we need baseload electricity generating capacity, hopefully with as few carbon dioxide emissions as possible. Medium to long-term, the solution to a more effective utilization of renewables and decreasing reliance on today's baseload power plants is to upgrade our electricity transmission grid to make it more flexible and better integrated across the country. Already the "trifecta" of solar plus wind plus battery (lithium–ion) storage can provide electricity twenty-four hours a day at prices competitive with natural gas fired power plants. But most developments today remain local. We need to start thinking about this at least in regional terms, if not nationwide. Think about Texas: it has a lot of wind capacity, potentially a large excess of it. Yet, from a transmission grid standpoint, Texas is essentially an island, quasi-isolated from the rest of the country. With a flexible, more integrated and efficient grid the intermittency of electricity from renewables would matter less. For example, Texas could sell its excess wind capacity to states using more solar power – like its neighbor New Mexico, and also Arizona and California – during evening peak hours or cloudy days. Mountain states could sell hydropower more effectively to neighbors affected by windless conditions. In Europe, Denmark can afford to generate near 50% of its electricity from wind turbines because its grid is connected to the transmission system in Norway, a country with over abundant hydroelectricity. Germany, on the other hand, lacks high capacity grid connections to its neighbors apart from France. As a result, after it decided to close its nuclear plants, it has had to rely more on French nuclear electricity, and also on its aging fleet of cheap but dirty lignite (brown coal) fired plants. A more flexible grid, "smart" demand–response technologies that can shut down appliances briefly when power supply is low, and advances in electric storage solutions can all help us move to a future where most of our energy comes from renewables.

What will the transmission grid of our future look like?

First, at the national level, existing grid regions such as the California ISO (Independent System Operator), ERCOT (Electric Reliability Council of Texas), and PJM (Pennsylvania Jersey Maryland), will be much better interconnected than today. This will allow much more flexibility in directing the intermittent power from renewables to the areas of largest demand at times of peak supplies. To achieve this requires a national initiative and financing under the direction of the Department of Energy (DOE), in collaboration with the regional transmission system operators, the relevant power producers, and integrated utilities throughout the country.

Second, our transmission grid will have to become not only very flexible but also "smart." A smart grid includes a variety of dynamic energy measurement and end-user demand devices ranging from smart meters, electronic power conditioning, smart appliances (often communicating through what is called "the internet of things"), energy saving assets, and renewable energy resources. Smart grids allow instant communication between suppliers of power and consumers, allowing them to have more flexibility in matching demand loads with supplies. Demand response support adds to this flexibility, allowing generators and users to interact automatically in real time, thus flattening demand spikes (peak leveling) and allowing more productive use of renewable energy sources that are variable in nature. An example of demand response at the industrial level is an aluminum plant that uses its smelter as a short-term source of electricity, like a giant battery. At the residential level, to reduce demand during peak times, the smart grid and assorted internet-connected devices can give utilities the ability to reduce consumption by communicating directly with demand points such as electric car charging stations – stopping them briefly – or air conditioners, shifting their temperature set points. Energy storage, either at the producer or at the end-user level, increases this flexibility even further.

Third, in addition to better interconnection nationwide, the grid of the future will be highly distributed, with power both generated and consumed at thousands of points, contrasting to today's "hub and spoke" centralized grids, the hubs being very large baseload power plants. Think for example of what Tesla is about to power up in Nevada: a giant battery system, storing electricity from solar panels and a wind farm, and capable of providing electricity 24 hours a day to 30,000 homes. Storage innovations like this will both make the grid more flexible and decrease aggregate demands upon it. The future transmission and distribution infrastructure will be able to handle bi-directional energy flows, allowing homes for example to consume electricity in the evening and send power to the grid during day time. This emergence of distributed power, gradually replacing large, centralized power plants, will also help reduce risks of cyber and terrorist attacks on easily identified large targets. Data flow and information management are central to the smart grid. Addition of a new digital layer, with real time integration of power generation, transmission, distribution, and end-user data at millions of demand points, becomes the heart of the transmission grid of the future.[69,70,71]

Are we progressing towards this grid of the future? Well, in typical fashion we are seeing a large number of initiatives from a variety of stakeholders, but with little coordination. Overall, this disorganized set of efforts paints a complex picture that may not lead us where we want to go without a decisive national impetus. Just to mention a few such ongoing initiatives, we have the IntelliGrid architecture provided by the Electric Power Research Institute (EPRI), helping half a dozen utilities such as SoCal Edison and TXU to procure smart meters, distribution automation, and demand response systems. Grid 2030 is a joint vision statement for the U.S. electric system developed by utilities, equipment manufacturers, IT companies, national laboratories, universities, and federal and state government agencies. The Smart Grid Energy Research Center at the University of California, Los Angeles, focuses on large-scale testing of a smart electric vehicle charging network, installed in the territories of local utilities LADWP and SoCal Edison. The Modern Grid Initiative is a joint effort between DOE, the National Energy Technology Laboratory, utilities, and consumer groups to modernize and integrate the U.S. electrical grid. Under this umbrella, DOE has a number of more operational initiatives such as GridWise (developing information technology to modernize the grid) and GridWorks (modernizing key grid components to improve the reliability of the U.S. electric system, with a smart grid demonstration project in the Pacific Northwest). Since 2013, California state government legislation has required local investor-owned utilities to acquire 1.325 gigawatts of power storage capacity by 2020. This includes energy storage installed on both the utility and customer sides of the electric meter. Other state governments, in Hawaii, New York and Texas, have launched similar energy storage initiatives to promote "intelligent" energy storage solutions as part of the mix of new innovations towards a renewable energy future.

If we really want to make progress towards the grid of the future, there needs to be a concerted, focused effort from the federal government. The executive and legislative branches should work together with a group of governors designated by their peers. Half a dozen influential CEOs of large integrated utilities; CEOs of large installed renewable energy farms; technology leaders; academics; environmental NGOs; and the presidents of our largest transmission systems, should all have a seat at the table as well. Clear, straightforward national standards should be developed, so that equipment manufacturers and IT companies can bring to market the devices and information solutions that are needed, with scale, nationwide. Congress and DOE should approve funds to build the additional high-voltage transmission lines required to ensure we have an interconnected national grid with enough flexibility to handle the intermittency challenges posed by renewables. Transition funds should be made available to help our publicly traded utilities manage the gradual change from a centralized power and distribution electricity system to a decentralized, hyper-connected one.[72]

The federal government should also encourage research to tackle the challenge of electricity storage, along the lines of "we went to the moon; are going to Mars; let's discover how to store electricity as well. This will make our daily lives so much easier and will help protect the planet." Better ways to store energy at large should also see research dollars going to them as viable alternatives to the direct storage of electricity. The Department of Energy's Advanced Research Projects Agency-Energy, or ARPA-E, should receive special funds to focus on potential solutions for electricity and energy storage, leveraging a number of technologies briefly outlined in an earlier chapter of this book.

The Department of Homeland Security should be part of this national effort to ensure the future grid is protected from cyber attacks. Homeland Security should also assuage citizens' concerns about privacy, providing for example guidelines for the use of end-user demand data by law enforcement. HHS should educate the population about health concerns such as radio frequency emissions from smart meters. The Federal Energy Regulatory Commission, or FERC, working with consumer organizations, should create simple federal rules that ensure utilities do not use complex, variable, and opaque rate systems to overcharge their customers. Information about the future grid, its generating, transmission and distribution components, should be made public to prevent any ill-intended actor from abusing asymmetry of information – transparency of data is the best vaccination against potential Enrons. The federal government should state clearly that these efforts have a simple and overarching objective, that of making desirable solar and wind power usable even on cold, still evenings, so that the share of renewables in our energy matrix can continue to grow.

Isn't this a lot of big energy decisions to be taken by the government? Shouldn't they be left to the markets? Markets do work a lot better in energy than in health care, for example. A carbon tax will send a decisive signal that will point everyone in the right direction. Having said that, the current hodge-podge of initiatives across government agencies, states, private sector companies, research bodies, and universities seem to indicate that progress towards the energy grid of the future will be halting at best under these efforts. There are some national energy decisions, such as the building of a new, flexible high voltage transmission network, and the wholesale transition towards a smart grid at the distribution level, that the competitive private sector will not make, given the upfront costs, risks and long-term paybacks involved.

Private sector companies will also claim, rightfully, that strategic elements in these long-term decisions such as cyber security, national energy security and climate policy are not their responsibility. Competition will make the new grid of the future work flawlessly, but a public agency has to be responsible, for example, to set the desired amounts of excess generating capacity in the system, since private producers have no incentive at the margin to build excess capacity. The recommendations above focus on clear guidelines and rules, which have to be the same across states and therefore established by the federal government. No new bureaucracy is needed. Existing government agencies can administrate the new guidelines. New federal and state investments are concentrated on the additional high-voltage transmission lines needed to make the grid more flexible, and on incentives and early funding for a couple of targeted research initiatives with long-term reach.

Other countries are moving in this direction: for example, in China and Europe, new high-voltage transmission lines can help leverage wind power generated far away from major cities to supplement renewable energy available in these cities. This way energy intensive data centers can draw their power from grids that have excess renewable energy, even if they are far away. These data centers may also be located in the same remote areas where the renewable energy they consume is being generated, with their data being transmitted over long distances using optical fiber technology. With efficient long-distance transmission grids (and optical fiber networks), these distances can encompass various time zones, and energy demand can be met in places where the sun has already set, with energy generated in areas where the sun is still shining. One can imagine the same dynamic in population and industrial centers with little wind getting energy from distant areas with strong wind power generation. Amazing! But also very efficient from a renewable energy impact standpoint. One day, just like in the former British Empire, "the sun will never set within the renewable energy world."

To summarize the positive impact the grid of the future will have, as well as why the critical decisions involved need to be taken soon, let's quote the environmental leader and innovative thinker Amory Lovins. In a June 12, 2017 article titled, "The Grid Needs a Symphony, not a Shouting Match – We Cannot Afford to Stifle Innovation by Enforcing Outdated Notions of 'Baseload' Power," co-authored with Mark Dyson for the Rocky Mountain Institute e-newsletter Spark, Lovins wrote:[73]

> Today, the grid needs *flexibility* from diverse resources, not baseload power plants. Leveraging market forces to help us decide between options offers the best chance of avoiding the multitrillion-dollar mistake – and giga-tons of carbon emissions – of blindly reinvesting in the past century's technologies . . .
>
> . . . Utilities in the U.S. have had at least a decade of comfortable experi-ence operating grids with a declining share of baseload power relative to low-cost renewable energy. Meanwhile, across the Atlantic, both reliability and renewable energy adoption levels are higher than in the U.S.; notably, the lights failed to go out in England when the U.K. grid recently ran for a full day without any coal power for the first time since 1882, foreshadow-ing its planned phaseout by 2025 . . .
>
> . . . Analytically, scientists working for the Department of Energy 's own world-renowned national laboratories, among others, have consistently shown that grids with moderate-to-high (30–80 percent) shares of renew-able energy, and commensurately lower shares of baseload capacity, work just as reliably and at least as resiliently as fossil fuel-based power systems, but with lower operating costs and risks.
>
> Utility executives, too, increasingly see the writing on the wall that not only is baseload unnecessary for a reliable grid, but it is financially incom-patible with a rapidly changing energy landscape . . .
>
> . . . What's different today, compared to even five years ago, is that the default choices for low-cost energy are, in fact, wind and solar, with long-term fixed prices already outcompeting the costs of new nuclear, coal, and gas plants – or even just the operating costs of old ones. Given those renew-ables' incredibly low and still-falling costs, *flexibility* is even more important than it has been – and luckily, flexibility too is now cheaper, cleaner, and more plentiful than ever before . . .
>
> . . . For example, a utility-scale solar plant in California has shown that many of these ancillary services can be provided as a valuable byproduct of the plant's inverters – extremely reliable solid-state power-electronics

devices already paid for by their primary task of conditioning renewable power to feed into the grid. Aggregators in the PJM grid are controlling fleets of water heaters to balance second-to-second mismatches between demand and supply.

Will the Trump administration listen to this visionary advice, or instead make counter market initiatives such as federal loan guaranties or de-facto subsidies, targeted to help coal-fired and nuclear baseload power plants? Can these potential subsidies prevent the markets from doing their job? Right now the prevailing market winds (no pun intended) are certainly favoring natural gas and renewables, at the expense of existing coal and nuclear plants. Low cost natural gas, in particular, is destroying the commercial viability of many coal-fired power plants. It is also quite conceivable that any new nuclear plant in the U.S. can only be completed if the utility that launched the project receives some type of government help.

What Amory Lovins and Mark Dyson are advocating makes a lot of sense. Since a significant percentage of our fossil fueled electricity generating capacity is only a decade or two away from retirement, we should invest now in the flexibility of a state-of-the-art transmission grid, one that multiplies several fold the potential impact of renewable power. This is the solution to our energy challenges, as opposed to just rebuilding the polluting power plants of yesterdays. It is the way to create an energy future for the U.S. that is reliable, safe, clean, economical, and builds upon our capacity to innovate.

★   ★   ★   ★   ★

High equity capital, transaction taxes, and a tax code without loopholes

In Chapters 4 and 5 (finances and taxes), we explored how complexity in finance, shadow financing and investing instruments devised by people who do not bear their risk amount to a very costly and risky machinery. U.S. taxation, too, with its maze of loopholes, favors the few "cognoscenti" and "insiders" at the expense of the many. Since the 1999 repeal of Glass–Steagall by the Clinton administration, "too big to fail" financial institutions have expanded massively, with assets in the trillions of dollars. Legislation, principally with Dodd–Frank after the global 2008 financial crisis, has made the publicly traded financial system somewhat safer from further meltdowns. But this improved safety carries the cost of great regulatory complexity, quite burdensome for smaller local banks without an army of attorneys and compliance professionals at their disposal. Meanwhile, the shadow financial sector has grown to trillions of dollars, in total opacity, and with little if any regulatory oversight.

Now, under the Trump administration and Congress Republicans, Dodd–Frank has suffered several attacks. The House first voted on legislation that weakened some of the underlying regulations, always in the name of "freeing capital flows and lending." Bank lobbyists were ecstatic – Christmas in June! The U.S. Senate is likely to approve a further weakening of Dodd–Frank after passage of the GOP tax legislation, ostensibly to ease the burden on regional and local banks, early in 2018. More modestly, the U.S. Treasury under former Goldman Sachs partner Steven Mnuchin drafted executive orders for President Trump to sign that nibbled at the edges of Dodd–Frank regulations, without eviscerating them, though. The June 2017 U.S. Treasury report on financial regulation reform accepted in principle such fundamental pillars of Dodd–Frank as equity capital standards; "living wills" for the "too big to fail" institutions; liquidity minima; stress testing for banks; and the Volcker rule. What the report recommended was to apply all these regulations with less stringency, a bias reinforced by the systematic appointment of former Wall Street executives and lawyers at key finance regulatory positions. For example, the Treasury argued that stress tests should apply to banks with more than $50 billion in assets, as opposed to $10 billion today. Banks with higher than required levels of capital could obtain waivers from such stress tests. The Volcker rule should only be applied to very large finance institutions with significant trading operations.[74,75,76]

The Treasury review also asked for changes that would reduce the independence and effectiveness of the Consumers Financial Protection Bureau (CFPB). This makes sense for banks and Wall Street, but none whatsoever for Main Street. After all, the Consumer Bureau is the only federal agency that protects regular Americans in their dealings with banks. Since its inception it has returned over $12 billion to millions of people by reversing fees from phantom accounts (remember Wells Fargo?), moderating predatory fees on loans and mortgages of all kinds, and curtailing abusive debt collection practices. As seen earlier in the book, the appointment in November 2017 of OMB Director Mick Mulvaney to replace departing CFPB director Richard Cordray is likely to dampen significantly the agency's enthusiasm in going after banks, given Mulvaney's declared opposition to the CFPB when it was created. Net net, all the changes recommended by the Treasury lightened the regulatory burden on small and regional banks. They streamlined regulations and reduced the number of overlapping rules. But at what risk to the overall system, and at what cost to consumers?[77,78]

What was not very compelling in the U.S. Treasury report rationale was the argument, often brought forward by bank lobbyists, that Dodd–Frank had undermined the ability of banks to deliver attractively priced credit in sufficient quantity to meet the needs of the economy. The American economy is actually humming along quite nicely. Unemployment is at a record low at 4.1%, and all major Wall Street broad indices, the Dow, the Nasdaq, the S&P 500, the Russells, etc. are at record highs as of late November 2017. Yes, we have a lower percentage of prime aged workers in jobs than France, let alone Germany and Japan, but there is no evidence that any lack of financial credit is behind this. Rather, the economy is not growing as fast as it could because the bottom economic half of the country suffers from too low-paying jobs and does not enjoy enough purchasing power to propel our retail-based economy. The main problem in finance is not lack of credit. It is the lack of simple and effective rules. Since the 2008 meltdown, we appear to be hostages to a regulatory trade-off where we can have on one hand ever more complex regulations, galloping compliance costs, and less systemic risk; or on the other hand streamlined regulations with increased risk. Isn't there a way to extract ourselves from this dilemma and use simple, high level standards and rules that would give us safety in the financial sector without a whole bureaucracy of regulators, lawyers and compliance experts? This is the right time to ask this question. With all financial market indicators in record territory, very high price to earnings rations and volatility indices at record lows, everyone is asleep in terms of worrying about risk. Everyone . . . except several hedge fund billionaires, who are exiting markets and going into cash – could this represent the first clouds before the next storm?

Good news: there are four simple actions that could reduce the overall risk of our financial system while also removing most of the regulatory burden placed today upon the industry to keep it safe.

Raising capital levels, a lot more

The first such action is based upon the Basel set of principles explored earlier in this book, but in a "turbocharged" kind of way. This is a very simple solution to address the problem of the "too big to fail" banks, which most industry observers agree has not been satisfactorily solved, even with Dodd–Frank and the Volcker rule. Today the eight largest U.S. banks have an average equity to total assets ratio – also called leverage ratio – between 6 and 7%. What if the government mandated this leverage ratio to be doubled, or even tripled? And even more, unless the Treasury Department could certify a given bank no longer presented any risk to our financial system? Imagine this. Big banks would face radically lower returns on equity, and then guess what? Wall Street and activist investors would put enormous pressure on them to break themselves apart, separating retail banking assets from their more speculative operations such as derivatives and trading, including proprietary trading done with their own capital. We would wake up with utility banking and the more speculative bits of giant banks spun off into many smaller units, focusing on their specialties. Banking would thus become safer, smaller and much more manageable. Voila!

Is this really a dream? Actually, no – some very serious people have floated this concept of much higher capital levels for banks. Foremost among them is Neel Kashkari, president of the Federal Reserve Bank of Minnesota. Mr. Kashkari can boast of an amazing resume for a relatively young person. He started at Goldman Sachs; worked for the U.S. federal government at the most challenging of times, helping Treasury Secretary Hank Paulson stabilize our financial system during the worst months of the 2008 crisis; then moved to famed bond house Pimco; ran in 2014 as a Republican for the California governorship; and eventually joined the Fed. Under Neel Kashkari's proposal, called the Minneapolis Plan, banks with $250 billion or more in assets would be required to issue equity equal to 23.5% of their risk-weighted assets, leading to a leverage ratio of 15% – about two and a half times today's ratio. The plan does not stop there. If a given bank failed to be certified by the Treasury as no longer posing a threat to the financial system, that bank's level of equity would have to increase by five percentage points every year, up to a maximum of 38% of its risk-weighted assets. Kashkari claims that new financial regulations since 2008 have only reduced the risk of another government bailout for the banking system to 67%, from 84% before the crisis. His proposal, he says, would be expensive for the banks but would cut that risk to 9%:

> The [2008] bailouts violated a core belief that has been handed down from generation to generation in our society that if you take a risk you bear the rewards and consequences of that risk ... We had to tear that up during the crisis because the biggest banks were going to fail and bring down the U.S. economy. And when you violate the core beliefs of society it does lead to anger and a feeling that this wasn't fair.[79,80,81,82]

The Minnesota Fed president is not alone in advocating high equity capital as a simple and effective solution to mitigating the risks of modern finance. Thomas Hoening, Vice-Chairman of the Federal Deposit Insurance Corporation (FDIC), also wants banks to hold more capital instead of returning it to investors through dividends and share buybacks. Jeb Hensarling, the Republican chair of the House financial services committee, has floated a plan requiring higher levels of equity capital, proposing that any bank reaching a leverage ratio of 10% or more could achieve total relief from the Dodd–Frank Act. A number of conservative think tanks such as the Cato Institute support the Minnesota Plan, as does ... Bernie Sanders. Much higher equity capital for banks is clearly a simple, sound idea that could achieve bi-partisan support in our political spectrum and if enacted, could lead to the elimination of many regulations and much government bureaucracy.

Reinstating Glass–Steagall

There is an alternative to the Minnesota Plan, one that is also simple and effective. The reinstatement of Glass–Steagall could lead to the elimination of pretty much all of Dodd–Frank – with the exception of the Consumers Financial Protection Bureau, which needs to stay given what we have seen in retail banking. Over eighty years ago, the very short and to the point Glass–Steagall legislation was enacted to separate traditional commercial (retail) banking from more speculative investment banking. This divide kept the U.S. financial system safe from wholesale meltdowns for sixty-six years, until it was consigned to history by the bi-partisan Gramm – Leach – Bliley Act, signed into law by President Bill Clinton on November 12, 1999. Much has been written how Glass–Steagall would not have prevented the 2008 financial disaster, foremost because the meltdown started with the bankruptcy of Lehman Brothers, a "pure" investment bank without any retail banking activity, and therefore not under the reach of Glass–Steagall. However, right after Lehman Brothers came the giant American International Group (AIG), a multinational insurance company that was duly bailed out amidst much financial and political turmoil. And at least a few voices observed that AIG was bailed out because its principal creditor was no less than Goldman Sachs, which would have been very much at risk should AIG have been allowed to go under like Lehman. After Goldman, also very exposed to AIG, were Morgan Stanley and Bank of America . . .[83,84] Glass–Steagall would have been effective at keeping Goldman Sachs, Morgan Stanley and Bank of America (and many other large financial institutions) as they were before 1999, safer even if making less money. Would the pre-1999 Goldman, a very profitable but also conservative investment bank in the safe hands of its partners, have become as exposed to AIG and subprime mortgages as it had in 2008? Doubtful.

One of Glass–Steagall's greatest appeals, principally for politicians, is that its simplicity makes it very easy to explain to "we the people," us mere mortals not versed in the intricacies of modern finance and sophisticated Wall Street derivative instruments. This is why the two most effective "retail" politicians of the 2016 U.S. presidential campaign, Donald Trump on the right and Bernie Sanders on the left, embraced its return wholeheartedly. This to applauses from tens of thousands of fans at innumerable political rallies. Serious politicians like Jeb Bush and Hillary Clinton said "tsk tsk," we don't get it. Modern finance has become far too complex and integrated for such a simpleton of a law to be effective in modern times. What about Lehman? And what about shadow finance? As seen earlier, "what about Lehman" is a specious argument – superficially plausible but likely wrong. Had Glass–Steagall stayed in place, much of the risks inherent to our financial system at the beginning of the twenty-first century would have probably not existed. The 2008 crisis could have still taken place, like prior crises born out of exaggerated and too speculative uses of derivatives and debt instruments – see Orange County; Long Term Capital Management. But it would have likely been smaller, more contained, and less threatening to the whole economy. So why not reinstate Glass–Steagall? Why not indeed? The 2016 presidential campaign showed a majority of Americans would approve of this, and it worked with exemplary efficiency for well over half a century. Ah, but we forget the giant and ever-expanding shadow finance world. Glass–Steagall could not do anything to mitigate the risks that are starting to proliferate in this brave new opaque world of finance, rightly preceded by the word "shadow." But a couple of actions, even simpler than mandates of high equity capital for banks and the reinstatement of a venerable Depression-era legislation, could help reduce the financial risks that are lurching under these shadows.

Establishing a finance transaction tax

This third proposed action is not a new idea, either. The British stamp duty was enacted in 1694. John Maynard Keynes advocated a tax on all financial transactions in 1936 to curb speculation on Wall Street by financial traders, the main cause of the 1929 crash. In 1972, the economist and Nobel Prize laureate James Tobin proposed a tax on all spot currency transactions, to penalize foreign currency speculation. Later, Tobin commented that his tax would have prevented a number of crises caused by the collapse of currencies in a group of countries (or a single large one), such as the 1997 Asian Financial crisis. The sound rationale Tobin offered is that to deter speculators from shorting the currency of a given country, that country has to boost its money by raising its interest rates dramatically, an action with often disastrous consequences for the local economy. As such, financial transaction tax (FTT) proposals are often called "Tobin tax." Tobin taxes represent a simple, effective and easy to implement instrument. Advocates of a systematic tax on financial transactions, such as 2001 Economics Nobel Prize winner Joseph Stiglitz, argue that a FTT can be collected automatically when banking transactions are settled electronically.

A number of countries already collect some tax on financial transactions, on a somewhat limited scale. About forty countries have a FTT set-up, raising about $40 billion per year. These countries are mostly in Europe, including Belgium, Finland, France, Italy, and Switzerland, with rates typically in the 0.1–0.2% range. All countries in the Eurozone are in favor of such a tax, but not every European Union country is part of the Euro, so this is not yet policy at the E.U. level. Importantly, the countries hosting the most important financial centers of the world are not contemplating a FTT at the moment. No financial transaction tax is being discussed by the Trump administration, by Theresa May's government in the U.K., or by China for Hong Kong and Shanghai – even though there were FTT intentions announced in 2016 as a possibility for curbing speculation in China.[85,86]

Ideally, a FTT would discourage speculation that does not add anything productive to the economy, without affecting useful transactions. Buying stocks because one expects the underlying companies to do well in the long-term; doing the same to build up retirement portfolios for employees; funding expansions of companies into new markets; supporting early stage companies or start-ups – all these actions are speculative in nature, but by and large useful, even fundamental, to the economy. On the other hand, what does algorithmic high frequency trading performed by computers programmed by hedge funds mathematics wizards add to the economy? Not even liquidity, arguably. Who would make the case that an economy built upon high frequency trading would perform better than one built upon companies making goods and services people actually want to buy, supported by state of the art infrastructure? No one.

High frequency trading, so well depicted by Michael Lewis in *Flash Boys: A Wall Street Revolt*, in which stock prices are determined by computers trading with each other, views companies as mere ticker symbols, pawns in a high profit game for a few. This is a harmful type of speculation, since these transactions do not add much liquidity to the system and can be damaging to all the stockholders of a publicly traded company. Regular shareholders are trading at a disadvantage relative to the "flash boys"; companies can go under if computer programs go out of control; employees lose their jobs; and the economy suffers.[87,88]

On May 6, 2010, the New York Stock Exchange experienced a "flash crash," which was actually a brief (thirty-six minutes) but trillion-dollar stock crash. There was much turmoil: for a little while, experts wondered whether they were witnessing "2008 on steroids," until things were brought under control. I remember very well where I was that day, taking off from London to Milano to present my company to groups of potential investors as part of a "road show" to measure institutional investors' interest before our pending IPO on the NYSE. Just as we were taking off and losing cell phone coverage, one of the investment bankers traveling with us said, "something weird is happening to the market in New York." I did not pay much attention, and only learned about the wild ride experienced by the NYSE when we landed in Milano a couple of hours later. All was fine by then, but what if it hadn't been? A single British trader was accused later of having caused the whole debacle, during which well-traded stocks of large blue chip companies such as Accenture basically went down to zero in a matter of minutes – to then go back up to prior levels fairly quickly. That British trader, Navinder Singh Sarao, is being extradited to America. Yes, he played a key role in this disaster. But isn't he also a scapegoat for the "flash boys" community?

How have regulators dealt with the abuses of high frequency trading? The traditional way, I am afraid. First, lawsuits and investigations. By Eric Schneiderman, the New York Attorney General; by the Justice Department under the Obama administration; by the FBI. Then cases opened by regulators, such as the Financial Industry Regulatory Authority, against high frequency traders who flooded U.S. exchanges with thousands of manipulating trades. Such transactions included "wash trades," in which a trader acts as both buyer and seller of a security to create the illusion of volume. Cases were also opened against high frequency traders using "spoofing," orders designed to trick the rest of the market into thinking there are potential buyers or sellers of a stock and move the price of that stock in a direction favorable to the trader. Then some SEC fines were levied in the most egregious cases. Some high frequency trading operations closed, principally when they had been taking place within large and highly visible banks such as Bank of America. But high frequency trading continues to grow, taking advantage of new technologies and dedicated private exchanges established in the "shadow" of the main markets. Traditional regulatory tools, regulators and prosecutors cannot really restrain this type of frivolous but very profitable speculation.

Most proponents of a FTT today defend the tax as an instrument to curb high volumes of trades that can become dangerous for the economy, if left unchecked and in the realm of shadow banking. The types of transactions a FTT is designed to curtail are the above-described computer-driven, high frequency trades in which big transactions occur in fractions of a second. These transactions do not add much liquidity to the system and can cause big crashes, such as the 2010 "flash crash." Beyond the much desirable outcome of curbing high frequency trading, would a FTT levied at the 0.3%-0.5% level be harmful to the economy at large? Not really. Such an FTT would not affect much of the trading in financial markets for sound investment purposes, which takes place over weeks, months, or years. Think of Warren Buffett, who holds on to companies for years, if not decades. Clearly, a financial transaction tax would not increase the cost of his portfolio by much.

What about hedging, used by many businesses to reduce risks – such as airlines hedging against fluctuations on the price of oil – and by investors to minimize fluctuations in their portfolios? These hedges are taken at most a few times per day, most of the time on a monthly or annual basis. For example, a farmer wanting to lock in the price for a corn crop will use hedging once a year, since crops are not more frequent. Hedging with underlying business operating motives is thus quite different from high frequency trading performed for pure speculative reasons, with zero economic benefit and potential destabilizing risks to our financial system.[89]

At what level should a financial transaction tax be set? The answer is simple. Low enough so that it does not discourage sound hedging undertaken for business reasons. High enough so it can be a strong deterrent to purely speculative activities like high frequency trading. In absolute terms, given that "flash" or micro trading relies on thousands, if not more, operations per second, the tax can be quite low in percentage terms and still act as an effective deterrent. The percentages of the FTT should also vary with each type of financial transaction subject to it. The higher the volumes and frequencies involved, the lower the percentage can be without making the tax lose its impact. With this in mind, one might propose the following for an effective FTT:

- 0.5% for equities
- 0.25% for bonds
- 0.5% for options
- 0.05% for foreign currency trades
- 0.05% for futures
- 0.05% for swaps

Exemptions could be made, such as for the purchase of treasury or muni bonds by pension plans. Such a financial transaction tax would definitely provide a strong incentive for our "flash boys" to redirect their talents to more productive areas of our economy. More importantly, it would help reduce a systematic and large component of risk in today's fast-growing shadow banking. A positive by-product of a FTT is that it can also represent an efficient and progressive source of new revenue for the U.S. Treasury, to the tune of several hundred billion dollars per year.

Ending the tax deductibility of interest for businesses

Another large, systemic risk in shadow banking is its extraordinary reliance on debt. The cost of debt is made artificially lower than equity in the U.S. due to the tax deductibility of interest in our tax code. This leads to financial engineering being more important in many company transactions than the actual improvements in operations at these companies. Many private equity groups derive a lot of their returns from the bloated amounts of debt put on the balance sheets of the companies they buy. The financial engineering play-book – actually just as complicated as any NFL playbook, or more – can lead in many cases to transactions summarized as follows: 1) buy company X with some equity and as much debt as possible (this is why such transactions are often called "leveraged" buyouts, or LBOs); 2) pay the new owners a very large dividend from the company's finances; 3) supplement the dividend(s) with all sorts of management and consulting fees paid by X to the owners' group; 4) place a new CEO at the helm of the company, with a clear mandate to make whatever cost cuts and adjustments are needed for the business to survive with the double chains of debt servicing and dividend payments; 5) if everything goes well, sell at a profit within a few years: the return on investment (ROI) on the original equity will be boosted significantly by the debt leverage.

This playbook gets a significant assist from the tax deductibility of the new debt inflicted on the purchased company. In another boost to the private equity owners' profits, the large dividend payments are taxed at a lower rate than regular income. So are the profits they will make on their "carry," by the way, should the company perform well enough to be sold again at a profit. Private equity has been enormously successful, but there are risks, principally in sectors struggling structurally such as fast food and retail. When a bankruptcy occurs, which might have been prevented if the company going under had not been saddled with so much debt, who suffers the most? The private equity owners make less than they could have, of course, but thanks to their dividend and fee payments do not suffer disastrous losses. Debt holders may suffer occasionally, although being sophisticated financial operators they usually have secured covenants that will protect them to some degree. No, it is the laid off employees who take the brunt of the private transaction when things go south, and who speaks for them? But we digress, and should return to the main question at hand about the tax deductibility of business debt: is this good for the economy at large?

The jury may be out today, but only until a financial crisis caused by too much company indebtedness takes place. It is ironic that in a country where so many voices deplore "the amount of debt we are leaving to the next generation," the same voices rarely attack the tax deductibility of interest and the mountains of debt it helps create. Ending the tax deductibility of interest may shift the focus of many private equity groups away from financial engineering towards actual operations of the businesses acquired, which would be a good thing. We might see fewer companies being "flipped" back and forth between different owners at an alarming frequency, and more companies held for long-term operational success. This would also reduce the risks to our financial system as a whole. Multiple defaults on debt can lead to broader economic trouble, if there is a cascade of insolvent companies, bad loans and troubled financial assets happening at the same time.[90,91,92]

Tax deductibility of interest thus distorts financing decisions made by many businesses and can also lead to instability for the economy at large. It features prominently in many profit-shifting arrangements used by multinational corporations to reduce their tax bill in America. It also leads to a significant loss of revenue for the U.S. Treasury, which is why conservative and liberal politicians alike have advocated its elimination. According to estimates by the Federal Reserve, non-financial corporations paid over $450 billion in interest in 2015. The privileged treatment of interest in the U.S. tax code then comes at substantial costs to the Treasury, about $100–150 billion per year up to 2017 – the figure is not easy to calculate, since it depends among other things on the effective tax rate paid by corporations. This actual tax rate varies a lot, among other reasons because of the many loopholes that may benefit some businesses but not others.

To finance the massive tax reduction plan proposed during his 2016 presidential run, Republican senator Marco Rubio proposed eliminating the deductibility of business interest paid, but also to eliminate tax on interest received, essentially treating business interest as a non-tax event. The original House Republicans' Better Way plan sponsored by Paul Ryan before the presidential election also called for ending the deductibility of taxes on business interest. This could be used, for example, to finance the instant depreciation of assets by corporations, instead of spreading it over many years. The late 2017 Republican tax reform only takes a timid step in that direction: it calls for capping interest expense deductions at 30% of corporations' earnings before interest, taxes, depreciation, and amortization (EBITDA). In exchange, it allows corporations to deduct their business investments immediately, instead of spreading their expensing over multiple years. However, lowering the corporate tax rate to 21% will reduce the incentive for businesses to borrow, the resulting tax deductions being worth a lot less.[93]

Ending the tax deductibility of interest for businesses would bring additional stability to our financial system, remove tax code–driven distortions in key business decisions, and increase revenues to the U.S. Treasury. Lots to like about this proposal. The only caveat is that a change of this magnitude should be part of a broader tax reform package, which if properly done could garner strong bipartisan support – unlike the recent GOP tax cuts. In brief outline form, what should be the key elements of such a tax reform package?

We saw in Chapter 5 of this book how exemptions, loopholes, and off-shore havens are used by corporations and wealthy individuals to cut the actual amount of U.S. taxes they pay, way below nominal rates from the tax code. To make our tax code fairer and simpler, the indispensable first step – and arguably the most challenging politically – is to **eliminate the complex mosaic of loopholes** that benefit only those wealthy enough to have expensive tax and legal teams at their disposal. This should be done for taxation on corporations (potentially saving up to $100 billion per year, net of tax deductibility for employer-sponsored health insurance), as well as individuals, with the exception of some tax deductibility for home mortgages, state and local taxes, and exemptions for charity. In terms of timing, the federal government may want to experiment with this removal of deductions and loopholes for a year or two, to measure its impact on treasury revenues. Then, in exchange, corporations should see a lowering of their nominal tax rate (from the 35% rate prevailing through 2017) and an end to the double taxation they theoretically suffer from with their overseas operations; wealthy individuals would continue enjoying lower long-term capital gain tax rates for their investments. The new corporate tax rate should be around the average of our main trading partners, a little lower to increase competitiveness for our companies and remove the strongest incentives for relocations to foreign countries. For reference, the corporate tax rate in Japan is 32% today; in Germany, 30%; in Canada, 26% after federal tax abatement; in the U.K., 20%. A one-time repatriation tax holiday should take place, at a reasonable yet enticing rate, to reset the whole taxation system.

A border tax may have too many drawbacks to be enacted, for our domestic retailers in particular. But U.S. taxation needs to go to a more territorially based system; all businesses should be taxed on their profits from services and goods actually sold in the U.S. This would set a sort of "minimum tax" and prevent the tax avoiding practice of booking profits in offshore tax havens. Our exporters should get some tax relief to make them more competitive relative to competitors benefiting from lax fiscal regimes or governments subsidizing exports. It is worth noting that several tax reform components mentioned above are enacted in the late 2017 GOP tax legislation, albeit with lower tax rates than proposed in this book. Much reduced corporation tax rate, below the average of our main trading partners: check; repatriation tax holiday: check; a more territorially based tax system for business: check. However, the Republicans have ignored pretty much all loopholes favoring large businesses and wealthy individuals, which is one of the main reasons their tax cuts are unfunded and will increase our budget deficits.[94,95]

On another tax related issue, a reasonable "brake" should be applied to galloping CEO compensation, given that despite mounting protests from activists and shareholders, most corporate boards appear unwilling to do anything about it – even in cases of complete disconnect between compensation and performance. Ironically, it was a 1993 initiative to cap the tax deductibility of CEOs and top executives' compensation at $1 million that "turbocharged" the growth in CEO pay, through a well known loophole advantaging both corporations and wealthy individuals. That loophole allowed companies to deduct CEO pay over $1 million as long as it was performance based - think stock options. This drove companies to increase performance based bonuses and stock options on an epic scale: today the median annual CEO compensation is around $15 million, all tax deductible as long as "base pay" does not exceed $1 million. This explosive growth in CEO compensation has prompted many to ask, how much are CEOs in America paid today relative to the employees they manage? To take a very simple example, let's look at a Manhattan company where over 50% of the employees are low-paid clerks or service staff. Assuming the announced 2020 minimum wage of $15 per hour in New York takes hold, and that the median wage at the company is twice that, it would correspond to $60,000 in annual compensation for the median paid worker (for 2,000 hours of work per year). If the CEO of that company earns $15 million a year, then the CEO pay is 250 times that of an employee earning the median wage at the same company. One should also note that the company pays payroll taxes at the full rate for the employee earning median pay. How can anyone justify the tax deductibility of a CEO compensation package worth 250 times as much? Clearly this glaring loophole has to be closed, would it be only to ensure that taxpayers like our employee above are not subsidizing the company's very generous CEO compensation. The elimination of this loophole, a simple remedy, would likely just slow down some of the most egregious abuses, which have been amply documented. But it would at least send a strong signal to corporate boards that it is about time they think seriously about their own measures to ensure CEO compensation does not become a pharaonic entitlement. Today, top CEOs make more than 300 times the average worker, whereas fifty years ago it was 20-to-1, according to a report released by the Economic Policy Institute, mentioned in a June 22, 2015 *Fortune* article.[96]

Finally, a fairer tax code should take into account the strong regressive nature of the payroll tax and raise the full withholding ceiling to above the current $118,500. This would also help ensure Medicare is well financed into the future.[97,98,99]

These simple steps would allow a lowering of some of the rates in the current income tax schedule, although this should focus on the middle-class brackets, where a decrease in taxation will yield the most growth to the economy through increased retail spending. In combination with a universal basic income, the spending power of most of the population would thus be increased significantly, leading to increased growth for our economy. Here is what this **proposed tax plan** could look like:[100]

- Four brackets for income tax rates instead of seven today. The new brackets for individuals would be 10% up to $40,000; 20% up to 200,000; 30% up to 400,000; and 40% above 400,000. For married filing jointly, the initial threshold would be doubled, to $80,000; the $200,000 threshold would become $250,000; and the $400,000 threshold $500,000.
- Federal Earned Income Tax Credit (FEITC) to be doubled, the FEITC being particularly effective in helping low-income working families; Child Tax Credit to be doubled.
- Increase of full withholding ceiling for payroll tax and Medicare from $118,500 to $200,000.
- Elimination of most exemptions in the U.S. tax code, with exceptions made for the tax deductibility of house mortgages (up to $500,000), state and local taxes, and donations to charity. Alternative Minimum Tax (AMT) to be maintained.
- Elimination of most corporate tax exemptions, including tax deductibility for employer-sponsored private health insurance (used to pay for universal health care coverage or "Basic Medicare for All"); elimination of all subsidies for coal, oil, and gas, as well as incentives for renewables.
- Elimination of tax deductibility of interest expense for businesses.
- U.S. corporate tax rate set at 25%; end of double taxation (and corresponding tax credits) on overseas profits for U.S. corporations.
- One-time corporate repatriation tax holiday, at a 15% rate.
- Acceleration of depreciation for industrial corporate assets to one year.
- All profits derived from sales of products and services in the U.S. subject to corporate tax, with corresponding exemptions to American companies to avoid double taxation.

- 10% tax exemption for U.S. exporters of goods and services.
- Establishment of a Carbon Tax, starting at $40 per ton, and increasing by $2.5 a ton per year until it reaches $100 per ton.
- Set up of a Finance Transaction Tax, with the rates mentioned earlier.
- Taxation of the private equity "carried interest" at regular income tax rates, except for funds focusing on "sui generis" start-up companies, which could continue to enjoy long-term capital gains taxation rates.
- Elimination of tax deductibility of total CEO compensation above $1 million per year – including stock options (assessed at current value) and other types of performance based compensation.

During times of solid economic performance and growth, one should pay attention to fiscal responsibility: therefore, this proposed tax reform should not increase our budget deficit. In particular, the lowering of the corporate tax rate from 35% to 25% (costing around $1 trillion over ten years) would be more than compensated by the elimination of most corporate tax exemptions, favorable tax treatments, and the tax deductibility of interest expense for businesses (saving $1.5–2 trillion in aggregate over ten years, given the earlier mentioned estimates).[101] The proposed elements of territorial taxation would help our exporters without adding to the deficit. On the individual and family front, the proposed plan would focus on benefits for the middle-class, through lower rates, higher tax thresholds, and enhanced credits. No benefit would accrue to those individuals earning more than $400,000 per year, while wealthy taxpayers benefiting from lots of exemptions today may end up paying more. Investors (and entrepreneurs) would continue to benefit from the low rates on long-term capital gains, though. The carbon tax proceeds would be returned to all taxpayers via dividend payments, further improving the relative financial situation of our middle classes. The financial transaction tax could be directed to our country's first national wealth fund, so that just like countries as diverse as Chile, Norway and Singapore, we would have national assets saved "for a rainy day." The definition of what would constitute a "rainy day" could include new financial crises; global economic shocks; or severe economic downturns in the country.

With this much simpler taxation, another benefit would accrue to most of us. Tax filings would become very easy to prepare, a far cry from today's tax complexity. Actually, even with today's tax code we could make tax filing a lot simpler. How so?

T.R. Reid, the author of *A Fine Mess: A Global Quest for a Simpler, Fairer, and More Efficient Tax System*, wrote an article called "The I.R.S. Could Be Your Friend" in the *New York Times* on April 14, 2017. Here are some of the comparisons he made on tax preparation between the U.S. and other countries:[102,103]

> Americans will spend more than six billion hours this year gathering records and filling out forms, just to pay their taxes. They will pay some $10 billion to tax preparation firms to help get the job done and spend

$2 billion on tax-preparation software (programs that still require hours of work) . . .

. . . And here's the most maddening thing of all: it doesn't have to be this way.

Parliaments and revenue agencies all over the world have done what Congress seems totally unable to do: They've made paying taxes easy . . .

. . . In the Netherlands, the Algemene Fiscale Politiek (the Dutch I.R.S.) has a slogan: "We can't make paying taxes pleasant, but at least we can make it simple . . ."

. . . In Japan, you get a postcard in early spring from Kokuzeicho (Japan's I.R.S.) that says how much you earned last year, how much tax you owed and how much was withheld. If you disagree, you go into the tax office to work it out. For nearly everybody, though, the numbers are correct, so you never have to file a return.

The author then explains that in many developed countries, computers perform the tax return calculations, using taxpayer data already in the hands of the relevant government agency. All taxpayers have to do is check that their data is accurate. If there is an error, appeal processes are in place to handle discrepancies efficiently. Reid concludes by writing that our own Internal Revenue Service could emulate this simplicity for millions of us, since it has already, electronically, all the relevant wage, dividend, interest, capital gains, and withholding data from our Forms 1040.

Wouldn't that be great?

★   ★   ★   ★   ★

Ambitious government-set standards and private sector innovation

The solutions proposed above in social programs, health care, energy, finance, and taxation share a common theme: replace with very simple legislation a complex set of regulations that most of the time only compliance professionals and lawyers can understand. Regulatory regimes must be simple and focus on addressing the complex attributes of sectors that can significantly contribute to the common good. Whenever possible, clear price signals such as a carbon tax should always take preference over regulations that manage outputs. Regulations that tell the private sector how much of a particular good it can produce, or not, with specific characteristics, are far too intrusive to industry to be effective. Conversely, simple regulations must also exist to prevent the private sector from creating such complex products and services that almost no one understands their risks, leading to economic crises. The list of industries that need special attention from legislators and regulators to protect our economy is mercifully short. Energy and electricity supply; finance; health care; housing;

telecommunications infrastructure; transportation; and water. Generally speaking, many of today's regulations should be replaced by policies emphasizing clear price signals, as opposed to attempts to micromanage industry. The objective is to have government policies set the standards at a high level. These standards should be ambitious, and then the government should get out of the way and let the private sector operate and innovate.

In this book, opacity is a word often used in the same sentence as complexity. There is a reason for this. Opacity is more often than not complexity's faithful companion. Opacity allows complexity and its negative effects to thrive, unchecked by anyone. Conversely, transparency can help expose many complex practices as useless for most people and serving only the interests of a few. When it comes to shady practices, "sunlight is the best disinfectant," as the saying goes. For example, the "dark pools" in finance and their inherent risks represent an illustration of the perils caused by lack of transparency. However, they also add significant complexity to the edifice of modern finance. So do swaps, primarily a gambling tool. And the moral hazard of "too big to fail" banking giants is caused by the complexity of these enormous companies. The "too big to fail" institutions have become giant octopuses of such complexity that there is less and less confidence their management teams can understand them, let alone provide effective control of what they do. To address complexity and opacity, the ideas and solutions proposed in this book are both simple and transparent. In an age where ideas have to fit in a one-minute TV segment or a tweet, any aspiring elected official addressing a crowd can explain all of them clearly.

When it comes to social welfare, which naturally includes health care, it is very important to untangle the far too numerous interfaces between the federal and state governments on one hand, and the private sector on the other. Simplifying and reducing the number of these interfaces can lead to enormous savings for the public purse. These savings can then be used productively to fund simple, effective and nationwide programs. High-level programs such as a Universal Basic Income and a Universal Basic Medicare (UBI-M) should be established to ensure that no American goes hungry, without a roof, or untreated for illness. The private sector, can then take care of the rest and innovate freely to ensure we keep our leadership in advanced medicine and many other areas.

In most of the solutions I am advocating, I have proposed a strong role for the state, which is the only path I see to also having – not a contradiction – a federal government of reduced size. I have also proposed solutions that will lead to a much-needed clarification of where the role of government ends. This should decrease significantly the number of interfaces between the government and the private sector, and reduce costs for both. A government more focused on our health and safety (economic as well as physical), and a private sector free of playing a role in our welfare, will both become more effective as a result.

Beyond health and safety, the simple solutions proposed would limit the role of finance in our economy; create incentives to grow further a "green" economy; curtail abuses in CEO compensation; simplify our tax code; and appeal to politicians from both our major parties who put practicality and tangible results above ideology. Several of these factors have contributed to making our society today much more complex than it used to be. Reversing them will also help us develop a virtuous circle where new, straightforward solutions replace old and complex ones. The solutions in this book focus on a limited number of sectors such as social services, health care, energy, finance, and taxation, where strategic decisions affecting our health, finances and security need to be taken by a strong government for the common good. Far from hampering the private sector, a strong but focused government should help it thrive and create innovative products and services that benefit us all. In the words of *New York Times* columnist David Brooks, at the end of his March 10, 2017 column, "The G.O.P. Health Care Crackup":[104]

> The core of the new era is this: if you want to preserve the market, you have to have a strong state that enables people to thrive in it. If you are pro-market, you have to be pro-state. You can come up with innovative ways to deliver state services, like affordable health care, but you can't just leave people on their own. The social fabric, the safety net and the human capital resources just aren't strong enough.

All of this will help us create a fairer society, more effective as well, and with inequality reduced from today's absurd levels. It should renew our faith in both the private sector and public service. Finally, we should fight complexity and embrace simplicity, but as a means, not an end. A flat tax rate is simpler than even a simple, progressive schedule of taxation. But it defeats all objectives of fairness in a modern society and exacerbates inequality. Going to Mars will be made easier with recoverable rockets, but it still will be no simple quest. As Albert Einstein said, "Everything must be made as simple as possible. But not simpler."

Bibliography

1) Sports

Arantes do Nascimento, Edson: *Pelé, the Autobiography*, with Orlando Duarte and Alex Bellos. Translated from the Portuguese by Daniel Hahn (2007, Simon & Schuster).

Bellos, Alex: *Futebol: The Brazilian Way of Life* (2002, Bloomsbury Publishing).

Foer, Franklin: *How Soccer Explains the World* (2004, Harper Collins).

Kuper, Simon & Szymanski, Stefan: *Soccernomics: Why England Loses, Why Germany and Brazil Win, and Why the U.S., Japan, Australia, Turkey – and Even Iraq – Are Destined to Become the Kings of the World's Most Popular Sport* (2006, Perseus Books).

Lewis, Michael L.: *Moneyball: The Art of Winning an Unfair Game* (2003, W. W. Norton & Company), and *The Blind Side: Evolution of a Game* (2006, same publisher).

2) Health care

Brownlee, Shannon: *Overtreated: Why Too Much Medicine Is Making Us Sicker and Poorer* (2007, Bloomsbury Publishing).

The Dartmouth Institute for Health Care & Clinical Practice: *The Dartmouth Atlas of Health Care* (first published in 1996, American Hospital Publishing, Inc.).

Mann Wall, Barbra: *American Catholic Hospitals: A Century of Changing Markets and Missions* (2011, Rutgers University Press).

Micklethwait, John & Wooldridge, Adrian: *The Fourth Revolution: The Global Race to Reinvent the State* (2014, Penguin Publishing).

Porter, Michael E. & Teisberg, Elizabeth Olmsted: *Redefining Health Care: Creating Value-Based Competition on Results* (2006, Harvard Business School Publishing).

Reid, Thomas Roy III: *The Healing of America: A Global Quest for Better, Cheaper, and Fairer Health Care* (2009, Penguin Books).

Schoonveld, Ed.: *The Price of Global Health: Drug Pricing Strategies to Balance Patient Access and the Funding of Innovation* (2011, Gower Publishing).

Shultz, George P. & Shoven, John B.: *Putting Our House in Order: A Guide to Social Security & Health Care Reform* (2008, W. W. Norton & Company).

3) Electricity and utilities

Gordon, Robert J.: *The Rise and Fall of American Growth: The U.S. Standard of Living since the Civil War* (2016, Princeton University Press).

Klein, Maury: *The Power Makers: Steam, Electricity, and the Men Who Invented Modern America* (2008, Bloomsbury Publishing).

Leclercq, Jacques: *L'Ere Nucléaire* (1988, Hachette).

Nye, David E.: *Electrifying America: Social Meanings of a New Technology* (1992, MIT Press), *Consuming Power: A Social History of American Energies* (1999, same publisher), and *When the Lights Went Out: A History of Blackouts in America* (2010, same publisher).

Sandalow, David: *Freedom From Oil: How the Next President Can End the United States' Oil Addiction* (2007, Brookings Institution Press).

Yergin, Daniel. *The Prize: The Epic Quest for Oil, Money, and Power* (1990, Simon & Schuster).

International Energy Agency: *Electricity Information* and *IEA Statistics* (2015 and 2016).

4) Finance

Bernanke, Ben S.: *The Courage to Act: A Memoir of a Crisis and Its Aftermath* (2015, W.W. Norton & Company).

Lewis, Michael L.: *Liar's Poker: Rising Through the Wreckage on Wall Street* (1989, W. W. Norton & Company), and *The Big Short: Inside the Doomsday Machine* (2010, same publisher).

Piketty, Thomas: *Capital in the Twenty-First Century*. Translated from *Le Capital au XXIe siècle* by Arthur Goldhammer (2013, Editions du Seuil, Harvard University Press).

Piketty, Thomas: *Why Save the Bankers? And Other Essays on Our Economic and Political Crisis.* Translated from the French and annotated by Seth Ackerman (2016, Houghton Mifflin Harcourt).

Rajan, Raghuram G.: *Fault Lines: How Hidden Fractures Still Threaten the World Economy* (2010, Princeton University Press).

Sorkin, Andrew Ross: *Too Big to Fail: The Inside Story of How Wall Street and Washington Fought to Save the Financial System – and Themselves* (2009, Viking Press).

5) Taxation

Freeland, Chrysta: *Plutocrats: The Rise of the New Global Super-Rich and the Fall of Everyone Else* (2012, Penguin Random House).

Reich, Robert B: *Saving Capitalism: For the Many, Not the Few* (2015, Alfred A. Knopf, Penguin Random House).

Stiglitz, Joseph: *The Price of Inequality: How Today's Divided Society Endangers Our Future* (2012, W.W. Norton & Company).

6) Laws and regulations

Crichton, Michael: *Rising Sun* (1992, Alfred A. Knopf).

Gilens, Martin: *Affluence & Influence: Economic Inequality and Political Power in America* (2012, Princeton University Press).

Gore, Albert: *The Assault on Reason* (2007, Penguin Books).

Moore, Kathryn: *The American President: A Complete History* (2013, Fall River Press).

Shultz, George P.: *Issues on My Mind: Strategies for the Future* (2013, The Hoover Institution Press).

7) A winning history of simple tools

Ambrose, Stephen E.: *Nothing Like It in the World: The Men Who Built the Transcontinental Railroad, 1863–1869* (2000, Simon & Schuster).

Baime, Albert. J.: *Go Like Hell: Ford, Ferrari, and Their Battle for Speed and Glory at Le Mans* (2010, Houghton Mifflin Harcourt).

Beschloss, Michael R.: *The Conquerors: Roosevelt, Truman, and Their Destruction of Hitler's Germany* (2001, Paw Prints).

Brokaw, Tom: *The Greatest Generation* (1998, Random House).

De Tocqueville, Alexis: *De la Democratie en Amérique, I and II* (1840).

Descartes, René: *Discours de la Méthode* (1656).

Hobbes, Thomas: *Leviathan* (1651).

Jordan, Jonathan W.: *Brothers. Rivals. Victors: Eisenhower, Patton, Bradley, and the Partnership that Drove the Allied Conquest in Europe* (2014, NAL Caliber).

Larrabee, Eric: *Commander in Chief: Franklin Delano Roosevelt, His Lieutenants, and Their War* (1987, Simon & Schuster).

Locke, John: "*Life, Liberty and Property*" and "*Second Treatise of Government*" (1689 and 1704 respectively).

Montesquieu: *Les Lettres Persanes* (epistolary novel, 1721).

Rousseau, Jean-Jacques: *Du Contrat Social, ou Principes du Droit Politique* (1762, Le Livre de Poche Classique).

Shultz, George P.: *Turmoil and Triumph: My Years as Secretary of State* (1993, Scribners, Macmillan Publishing Company).

Voltaire: *Candide* (1759, Le Livre de Poche Classique).

8) Technology defeats complexity . . . sometimes

Isaacson, Walter: *Steve Jobs* (2011, Simon & Schuster).

Keynes, John Maynard: *Economic Possibilities for Our Grandchildren* (1930).

Shultz, George P. & Armstrong, Robert C.: *Game Changers, Energy on the Move* (2014, Hoover Institution Press).

Vance, Ashlee: *Elon Musk: Tesla, Space X, and the Quest for a Fantastic Future* (2015, Harper Collins).

9) How did we get here?

Milanovic, Branko: *Global Inequality: A New Approach for the Age of Globalization* (2017, Harvard University Press).

10) Proposed solutions to improve our lives

Friedman, Gerald: *Physicians for a National Health Program*, PNHP and *Healthcare-Now!* July 31, 2013.

Herzlinger, Regina: *Who Killed Healthcare? America's $2 Trillion Medical Problem and the Consumer Driven Cure* (2007, McGraw-Hill).

International Energy Agency (IEA): *Key World Energy Statistics* (2016, IEA).

Lewis, Michael L.: *Flash Boys: A Wall Street Revolt* (2014, W.W. Norton & Company).

Lovins, Amory & Dyson, Mark: *The Grid Needs a Symphony, Not a Shouting Match.* (2017, *Spark*, The Rocky Mountain Institute.

Paine, Thomas: *Agrarian Justice* (1797, A Thomas Paine Book).

Reid, Thomas Roy III: *A Fine Mess: A Global Quest for a Simpler, Fairer, and More Efficient Tax System* (2017, Penguin Random House).

Stern, Andy & Kravitz, Lee: *Raising the Floor: How a Universal Basic Income Can Renew Our Economy and Rebuild the American Dream* (2016, Public Affairs Books).

Notes

Chapter 1

1 "'Snow Bowl:' New England Raiders 2001/2 playoff game," *AP*, January 2015.
2 "Tuck Rule Hard to Grasp," by Mark Maske, *The Washington Post*, October 15, 2005.
3 Reference "Chancellor's Big Play Allows Seattle to Beat Detroit 13–10," by Tim Booth, AP Sports Writer, October 6, 2015.
4 "The NFL Rule Book has 244 pages," Quora, 2016.
5 Rule 8, Section 1, "Articles 3–4, Completing a Catch," in *NFL Rule Book, 2016*, from the NFL Football Operations, in section including "Article 3. Completed or Intercepted Pass," and "Article 4. Incomplete Pass."
6 Reference "Here's an Idea: A Catch Should Be a Catch," by Greg. A. Bedard, *MMQB*, January 12, 2015.
7 "Basic NFL Rule Seems Impossible to Grasp: Fans and Experts Struggle to Define a Catch," by John Branch, *The New York Times*, February 2, 2016.
8 "Baseball: It's a Complex Sport," *Education Baseball Radio*, July 25, 2015.
9 Reference "World Series: Why Kids Aren't Watching Baseball," by Matthew Futterman, *The Wall Street Journal*, October 30, 2013.
10 Reference "Don't Let Statistics Ruin Baseball," by Steve Kettman, in a *New York Times* column on April 8, 2015.
11 *Moneyball: The Art of Winning an Unfair Game*, by Michael L. Lewis (2003, W. W. Norton & Company).
12 "Baseball Is More Than Data," by Lance Fortnow, commenting on the April 8, 2015, Steve Kettman, *The New York Times* op-ed. More online comments followed Kettman's column, several under the title "Don't Let 'Op Eds' Ruin Baseball."
13 "How Major League Baseball Lost Its Way," by Sean Evans and Gavin Evans, March 31, 2013.
14 *Pelé, the Autobiography*, by Edson Arantes do Nascimento, *with* Orlando Duarte *and* Alex Bellos. Translated from the Portuguese by Daniel Hahn (2007, Simon & Schuster).
15 Even though its focus is on the role of economics, why certain countries win or lose in world cups, and the business of soccer, few books illustrate the universality of soccer as well as the book by *Financial Times* journalist Simon Kuper and sports economist Stefan Szymanski: *Soccernomics: Why England Loses, Why Germany and Brazil Win, and Why the U.S., Japan, Australia, Turkey – and Even Iraq – Are Destined to Become the Kings of the World's Most Popular Sport* (2006, Perseus Books).
16 The elimination of Italy, the "Squadra Azzurra" (Blue squad), from the 2018 World Cup in Russia hit this soccer-crazed country like a national cataclysm. "Apocalisse Azzurra!" cried the daily *La Stampa*; "Fuori Tutti!" (Fire them all!) was the title in the daily *Corriere dello Sport*.
17 "Official Rules of Major League Baseball (240 pages) vs. Official Rules of Soccer: 152 pages vs. Laws of the Game (FIFA): 143 pages," Quora.

18 "Baseball or Soccer?" Op-ed by David Brooks, *The New York Times*, July 10, 2014.

19 The 2014 World Cup in Brazil, with a very decent participation by team USA (which passed the first round of play after three matches and was eliminated by Belgium in the playoff round of 16), motivated many columnists to write. If David Brooks in his July 10, 2014, *New York Times* opinion piece was resolutely "pro" soccer, others on his right were not. Hence what we could call "the Tea Party's view of soccer": for example, on July 2, 2014, Ann Coulter wrote a provocative opinion in the *Clarion-Ledger* titled, "Any Growing Interest in Soccer a Sign of Nation's Moral Decay."

20 "Soccer Versus Baseball: Which Is the Best Analogy for Data Governance?" by Carol Newcomb, Data Management Consultant, SAS Institute, Inc., December 1, 2015.

Chapter 2

1 In these introductory pages I used sample statistics from a lot of databases and sources: the World Health Organization (WHO); the WHO's Global Health Observatory data repository; the Organization for Economic Co-Operation and Development (OECD); the World Bank; Bloomberg; the U.S. Department of Health and Human Services (HHS); the U.S. Centers for Medicare and Medicaid Services (CMS); and specific countries' official statistics, among others. All data sources and databases are directly referenced in the text of this chapter. Most importantly, to ensure that the data referenced in this chapter was not accidentally a "one-year outlier," I performed the same analyses with data from the years 2013, 2014, and 2015. The resulting data did not change in a material way, especially when looking at the U.S. rankings, the main topic at hand. So, I used the most recent full set of data available at the time of writing of this book, that of 2015. For example, Exhibit 2.1 of this health care chapter shows the 2015 health care costs per capita of thirty-five OECD economies, in descending order, using sample data from a comprehensive OECD database. It also shows for each country the health care costs as percentage of GDP, using a small sample of GDP per capita at PPP (current international dollars) to calculate this for the same countries, from the 2015 World Bank International Comparison Program.

GDP per capita data from the same World Bank database is also available for 2016, but since I could not match it with 2016 health care costs per capita figures (not yet available from the OECD), I kept all data shown in this chapter from the year 2015. From what I have read recently in terms of available statistics, the data coming up for 2016 within the next few months should not show any material change relative to what I show in this chapter, in terms of comparative health care costs and outcomes in OECD countries.

2 Exhibit 2.1: See note 1.

3 "The Most Efficient Health Care Systems in The World," by Kavitha A. Davidson, *The Huffington Post*, August 30, 2013.

4 "Bloomberg: US healthcare system near bottom on efficiency," by Meg Bryant, *HealthcareDive*, September 30, 2016.

5 Exhibit 2.2 shows life expectancy data by country in 2015 and the WHO's ranking of the world's health systems (in parentheses) for thirty-five OECD countries (World Health Organization, Global Health Observation data repository).

6 "Explaining High Health Care Spending in the United States: An International Comparison of Supply, Utilization, Prices, and Quality," by David A. Squires, *The Commonwealth Fund*, May 2012.

7 "The Health Care Century," by Jean P. Drouin, Viktor Hediger, Nicolaus Henke, Ludwig Kanzler, Eoin F. Leydon, and Paolo De Santis, *The McKinsey Quarterly*, 2007.

8 "The Best That *Limited Money* Can Buy," by Martin Markus and Sorcha McKenna, *McKinsey Health International*, Number 6.

9 These pages describe the types of health care systems in Germany, Japan, and my native France. Although I have enjoyed first-hand excellent care in all three countries and had all the required high-level data and personal experiences, I need to reference for

this narrative the excellent book by longtime *Washington Post* correspondent T.R. Reid, titled: *The Healing of America: A Global Quest for Better, Cheaper, and Fairer Health Care* (2009, Penguin Books). In particular, Reid's chapters on France ("The Vital Card"); Germany ("Applied Christianity"); and Japan ("Bismarck on Rice") are excellent accounts of his patient experiences in these three countries.

10 Ditto note 9, with reference to the chapters on the U.K. ("Universal Coverage, No Bills") and Canada ("Sorry to Keep You Waiting") in T. R. Reid's book.

11 "69 Years Ago, a President Pitches His Idea for National Health Care," by Dr. Howard Markel, *PBS NewsHour, KQED*, November 19, 2014.

12 "A Brief History: Universal Care Efforts in the U.S." *Physicians for a National Health Program*, transcribed from a talk given by Karen S. Palmer in San Francisco at the Spring, 1999 PNHP meeting.

13 Exhibit 2.3 shows the State Medicaid and CHIP Income Eligibility Standards for all fifty states, expressed in monthly income for a household size of four, from the Center for Medicare and Medicaid Services (CMS), 2015.

14 "Historical National Health Expenditure (NHE) Data, 2016," NHE Fact Sheet, Centers for Medicare & Medicaid Services, CMS.gov.

15 "List of University Hospitals in the U.S.," in the *U.S. News and World Report*'s Best Hospitals.

16 "Sister Carol Keehan, President of CHA," *Zenit.org*.

17 Kaiser.org website; websites of Catholic hospital systems.

18 "Health Care Costs in the U.S. in 2015 and 2016," by the U.S. Department of Health and Human Services (HHS).

19 "National Health Expenditure Data, Highlights, 2016," by the Centers for Medicare and Medicaid Services (CMS). The share of health care spending by the federal government is under the header "Health Spending by Type of Sponsor," with the following footnote: "Type of sponsor is defined as the entity that is ultimately responsible for financing the health care bill, such as private businesses, households, and governments. These sponsors pay health insurance premiums, and out-of-pocket costs, or finance healthcare through dedicated taxes and / or general revenues." This slightly restrictive definition (it focuses only on the payer side) explains why the $935 billion total mentioned for federal spending in 2016 is a lower number than the aggregate federal government spending for Medicare, Medicaid, the VA, Department of Defense TRICARE, CHIP, etc.

20 "National Health Expenditure (NHE) Fact Sheet – 2015 and 2016 Total U.S. Health Care Spending," by the Centers for Medicare and Medicaid Services (CMS), June 14, 2017.

21 Exhibit 2.4 shows an unidentified hospital in the U.S. with about $600 million in annual net patient revenue and its half-year statement of revenues and expenses for the first half of 2015.

22 "One Percent of the Population With the Highest Spending Accounted for 27% of Aggregate Health Care Spending in 2009," study by the Agency for Health Care Research and Quality.

23 "Health, United States 2014, with Special Feature on Adults Aged 55–64," by the U.S. Department of Health and Human Services, Centers for Disease Control and Prevention, and National Center for Health Statistics.

24 "The Big Idea: How to Solve the Cost Crisis in Health Care," by Michael E. Porter and Robert S. Kaplan, *Harvard Business Review*, September 2011.

25 "Why Medical Bills Are a Mystery," by Michael E. Porter and Robert S. Kaplan, *The New York Times*, April 14, 2012.

26 "Kaplan and Porter's Misguided Microanalysis of Costs," posted by Don McCanne, MD, in *Quote of the Day* (QotD), on April 16, 2012.

27 "Study: Health IT Spending to Top $34.5B," by Diana Manos, Healthcare IT News (from Technology Business Research Inc.'s Source IT Healthcare Report), August 29, 2013.

28 "IT Spending in Healthcare on the Rise, Growing Fast Towards 2019," by Colson Steber, *Communications for Research (CFR)*, September 17 2015.
29 *Overtreated: Why Too Much Medicine Is Making Us Sicker and Poorer*, by Sharon Brownlee (2007, Bloomsbury Publishing).
30 "Drug Executive Arrest Gives Others a Shield," *The New York Times*, December 18, 2015.
31 "Shkreli and the True Cost of High Drug Prices," *The Financial Times*, December 23, 2015.
32 "Accounting for the Cost of US Health Care: A New Look at Why Americans Spend More," by Diana Farrell, Eric Jensen, Bob Kocher, MD, Nick Lovegrove, Fareed Melhem, Lenny Mendonca, Beth Parish, *McKinsey Global Institute*, December 2008.
33 "Drug Prices Keep Rising Despite Intense Criticism," by Katie Thomas, *The New York Times*, April 27, 2016.
34 "The Dartmouth Atlas of Health Care," by the Dartmouth Institute for Health Care and Clinical Practice, American Hospital Publishing, Inc.
35 "Reflections on Variations," by The Dartmouth Institute for Health Care and Clinical Practice, *Dartmouth Atlas of Health Care*, 2017.
36 "Perspective: Practice Variations and Health Care Reform: Connecting the Dots," by John E. Wennberg, *Health Affairs*, October 7, 2004.
37 "Variation Matters. But Its Elimination Is More Critical to Improve Outcomes Than Saving Money," by Merrill Goozner, *Modern Healthcare*, June 1, 2013.
38 "Doubt Is Cast About a Health Care Gauge," The Upshot, *The New York Times*, December 15, 2015.
39 "Supply-Sensitive Care. Unwarranted Variation: The Overuse, Underuse, and Misuse of Care," a Dartmouth Atlas Project Topic Brief, 2005.
40 "Reflections on Geographic Variations in U.S. Health Care," by Elliott S. Fisher and Jonathan Skinner, The Dartmouth Institute for Health Policy and Clinical Practice, May 12, 2010.

Chapter 3

1 Reference the book *The Power Makers: Steam, Electricity, and the Men Who Invented Modern America*, by Maury Klein (2008, Bloomsbury Press).
2 "Goodbye, Golden Age of Growth," *Bloomberg View*, January 26, 2016.
3 Reference the book *The Rise and Fall of American Growth – The U.S. Standard of Living Since the Civil War*, by Robert J. Gordon (January 2016, Princeton University Press).
4 "George Westinghouse," by the IEEE Global History Network.
5 Reference the book *Electrifying America: Social Meanings of a New Technology, 1880–1940*, by David E. Nye (1992, The MIT Press).
6 "Rural Electrification Administration," by Robert Whaples, 2008.
7 *FDR: The New Deal Years, 1933–1937*, by Kenneth S. Davis (1986, Random House).
8 "Mr. TVA: Grass-Roots Development, and the Rise and Fall of the Tennessee Valley Authority as a Symbol for U.S. Overseas Development, 1933–1973," *The Diplomatic History*, Vol. 26, Issue 3, 2002.
9 Reference the book *Consuming Power: A Social History of American Energies*, by David E. Nye (1999, The MIT Press).
10 "U.S. Electric Utility Industry Statistics," publicpower.org.
11 "Largest Electric Utilities in the U.S.," by Martin Rosenberg, *The Energy Times*, 2015.
12 "50 Years of Nuclear Energy," by the International Atomic Energy Agency (IAEA).
13 "List of Nuclear Units in the U.S. by Utility Owner," by the U.S. Nuclear Regulatory Commission, Map of Power Reactor Sites, *Information Digest*, 2015.
14 Reference the book *L'Ere Nucléaire*, by Jacques Leclercq (1988, Hachette).
15 "Nuclear Power in France," by the World Nuclear Association, 2014, updated 2017.
16 "International Energy Statistics – Nuclear Electricity Net generation by Country," by the U.S. Energy Information Administration.

17 *Three Mile Island: A Nuclear Crisis in Historical Perspective*, by Samuel J. Walker (2004, University of California Press).

18 "Findings: Energy Lessons," by John Tierney, *The New York Times*, October 6, 2008.

19 "Barbara Boxer Wants U.S. Probe on San Onofre," *Associated Press (AP)*, May 28, 2013.

20 "San Onofre Nuclear Plant to Shut Down," by Steven Mufson, *The Washington Post*, June 8, 2013.

21 "Nuclear Follies," *Forbes*, February 11, 1985.

22 "The Accidental Century – Prominent Energy Accidents in the Last 100 Years," by Benjamin Sovacool, 2009.

23 "The Blackout of 2003: The Context; Failure Reveals Creaky System, Experts Believe," by David Firestone and Richard Pérez-Peña, *The New York Times*, August 15, 2003.

24 "U.S. Electricity Blackouts Skyrocketing," by Thom Patterson, *CNN*, October 15, 2010.

25 Reference the book *When the Lights Went Out: A History of Blackouts in America*, by David E. Nye (2010, The MIT Press). Blackouts in the U.S. make news, in the country and also internationally. So, I have "lived" all our important blackouts since 1977, principally the huge one in 2003. We just could not believe the satellite photos with this huge chunk of America pitch black, a genuine dark hole in the globe! It made the U.S. look as if its entire northeastern coastline had been replaced by a gigantic new Gulf (of the Atlantic?), from Baltimore to Boston, going as far west as Columbus. Before writing these pages, I had great pleasure in reading Nye's book, a powerful narrative of these real life stories, and who inspired me a great deal.

26 "The California Electricity Crisis: Causes and Policy Options," by Christopher Weare, *Public Policy Institute of California*, 2003.

27 *Enron: Corporate Fiascos and Their Implications*, by William R. Bufkins and Bala Dharan (2004, Foundation).

28 *The Smartest Guys in the Room*, by Peter Elkind and Bethany McLean (2003, Portfolio Trade).

29 Reference the book *Nuclear Implosions: The Rise and Fall of the Washington Public Power Supply System*, by Daniel Pope (2008, Cambridge University Press).

30 "Energy Future Holdings Offers Bankruptcy Plan," *The New York Times*, April 15, 2013.

31 "Energy Future Holdings files for Chapter 11 Bankruptcy," by Jim Fuquay and Steve Kaskovich, *Fort Worth Star–Telegram*, April 28, 2014.

32 "TXU, Oncor Owners File for Bankruptcy," by Ramit Plushnick-Masti, *NBC News Dallas–Fort Worth*, April 28, 2014.

33 "Energy Future Holdings Files for Bankruptcy," by Jim Malewitz, *The Texas Tribune*, April 29, 2014.

34 "Biggest LBO Failure Is Energy Future Purgatory for KKR," by David Carey, *Bloomberg News*, 2014.

Chapter 4

1 "The 2008 Financial Crisis Timeline: The 33 Most Critical Events in the Worst Crisis Since the Depression," by Kimberly Amadeo, *The Balance*, 2013, updated March 14, 2017.

2 "AIG Bailout: Cost, Timeline, Bonuses, Causes, Effects: Why It Made Bernanke Angrier Than Anything Else in the Recession," by Kimberly Amadeo, *The Balance*, 2013, updated April 11, 2017.

3 "2009 Financial Crisis: Explanation, Timeline, Bailouts: How They Stopped the Madness," by Kimberly Amadeo, *The Balance*, 2013, updated November 9, 2016.

4 "Ben Bernanke: The 2008 Financial Crisis Was Worse Than the Great Depression," by Tim Worstall, *Forbes*, August 27, 2014.

5 Ditto.

6 "Banking Collapse of 2008: Three Weeks That Changed the World," by Nick Mathiason and Heather Stewart, *The Guardian*, December 27, 2008.

7 "The Biggest One-Day Declines in the Dow Jones Industrial Average: Economic and Political Turmoil Often Result in Wild Swings of Stock Prices," by Beth Rowen, *Stock Market*, July 26, 2016.

8 "The Origins of the Financial Crisis. Crash Course: The Effects of the Financial Crisis Are Still Being Felt Five Years After," *The Economist*, September 7, 2013.

9 "The 2008 Financial Crisis: A Look at the Causes, Costs and Weighing the Chances of It Happening Again," by Kimberly Amadeo, *The Balance*, 2013, updated July 1, 2017.

10 *The Big Short: Inside the Doomsday Machine*, by Michael Lewis (2010, W. W. Norton & Company).

11 "Orange County Bankruptcy, the Overview: Orange County Crisis Jolts Bond Market," by Floyd Norris, *The New York Times*, December 8, 1994.

12 "A Default by Orange County," by Sallie Hofmeister, *The New York Times*, December 9, 1994.

13 "The Culprits of Orange County," by Carol J. Loomis, *Fortune*, November 21, 2012.

14 "Ending Suit, Merrill Lynch to Pay California County $400 Million," by Andrew Pollack with Leslie Wayne, *The New York Times*, June 3, 1998.

15 "We're Out! Orange County Pays Final Bankruptcy Bill on July 1st. The Ride's Been Wild," by Teri Sforza, *Orange County Register*, June 30, 2017.

16 "What Is Securitization," by Chris Gallant, *Investopedia*, May 4, 2017.

17 "Credit Default Swap (CDS) Definition," *Investopedia*, 2017.

18 "Synthetic CDO Definition," *Investopedia*, 2017.

19 "What Is a 'Swap'?" and "Interest Rate Swap," definitions and case example in *Investopedia*. The case example and calculations in my chapter on finance describing company X issuing five-year bonds and engaging in a swap with company A is taken directly from this Investopedia example, shown under the headline "BREAKING DOWN 'Swap': Interest Rate Swaps," in 2017. I just changed the letter acronyms from the two companies involved (e.g. "ABC" is "X" in my book), made millions of dollars billions (what are mere millions in modern finance?), and replaced the London Interbank Offered Rate (LIBOR) by one-year U.S. T-bills, to speak more to a U.S. audience. I felt this example was an excellent illustration of the sophisticated "mental gymnastics" finance professionals engage in routinely, which is why I decided to use it almost verbatim from its source.

20 "An Introduction to Dark Pools," by Elvis Picardo, *Investopedia*, updated May 5, 2017.

21 "Banks Reduce Dark Pool Trading as Brexit Slams U.S. Markets," *Bloomberg*, June 24, 2016.

22 "Shadow Banking System Definition," *Investopedia*, 2017.

23 "Complexity, Not Size, Is the Real Danger in Banking," op-ed by John Kay in the April 13, 2016 edition of the *Financial Times*.

24 "Obama to Sign Dodd-Frank Financial Regulatory Reform Bill Into Law Today," *The Washington Independent*, July 21, 2010.

25 "Dodd-Frank Act Becomes Law," *The Harvard Law School Forum on Corporate Governance and Financial Regulation*, July 21, 2010.

26 "The Dodd Frank Act: A Cheat Sheet," by Morrison and Foerster, 2010: "The Dodd–Frank Wall Street Reform and Consumer Protection Act, or Dodd–Frank Act, represents the most comprehensive financial regulatory reform measures taken since the great depression."

27 "Rules for 'Too Big to Fail' Insurance Firms Coming Soon: Fed Official," by Lisa Lambert, *Reuters Business News*.

28 "MetLife Ruled Not Too Big to Fail," by Lucinda Shen, *Fortune*, March 30, 2016.

29 "Consumer Financial Protection Bureau Fines Wells Fargo $100 Million for Widespread Illegal Practice of Secretly Opening Unauthorized Accounts: Bank Incentives to Boost Sales Figures Spurred Employees to Secretly Open Deposit and Credit Card Accounts," Consumer Financial Protection Bureau, September 8, 2016.

30 "CFPB Architect Blasts Wells Fargo CEO for Lax Financial Oversight: Warren Calls Out Stumpf's 'gutless leadership'," by Jacob Gaffney, *Housing Wire*, September 20, 2016.

31 "Wells Fargo CEO refuses to push for exec pay clawback," by Nathan Bomey, *USA Today*, September 20, 2016.

32 "Wells Fargo Claws Back Millions from CEO After Scandal," *The Wall Street Journal*, September 27, 2016.

33 "Wells Fargo Claws Back Part of CEO, Other Executive's Salary," *ABC News*, September 27, 2016.

34 "Warren Buffett on Wells Fargo: 'There's never just one cockroach in the kitchen.' Buffett says when one puts a spotlight on a large financial institution like Wells Fargo, they're likely to find something. 'What you find is there's never just one cockroach in the kitchen when you start looking around,' he says," by Berkeley Lovelace Jr., *CNBC*, August 31, 2017.

35 *Too Big to Fail: The Inside Story of How Wall Street and Washington Fought to Save the Financial System – and Themselves*, by Andrew Ross Sorkin (2009, Viking Press).

36 "What Was the Glass–Steagall Act?" Reem Heakal, *Investopedia*, updated November 16, 2015.

37 "What the Heck Is the Controversial Glass–Steagall Act?" Heather Long, *CNN MoneyStream*, October 14, 2015.

38 "One of Elizabeth Warren's Key Ideas Slid Into the Official GOP Platform: Reinstating Glass Steagall," by Max Ehrenfreund, *The Washington Post*, July 19, 2016.

39 "Banking Act of 1933, Commonly Called Glass–Steagall: A Detailed Essay on an Important Event in the History of the Federal Reserve," by Julia Maues, Federal Reserve Bank of St, Louis.

40 "In Financial Reform, Keep It Simple Like Glass–Steagall: Central Bankers Are Starting to Realize That Complex Regulation Can Defeat the Regulation's Purpose," by Brendan Greeley, *Bloomberg Businessweek*, April 12, 2013.

41 "Dodd–Frank Versus Glass–Steagall: How Do They Compare?" Pam Martens and Russ Martens, *Wall Street on Parade: A Citizen Guide to Wall Street*, August 7, 2014.

42 "What Are BASEL 1, 2 and 3 Norms? What Are the Basic Differences Between These Norms?" Vinod Gattani, *Idea Cellular* (via Quora), May 2, 2014.

43 "Basel III: International Regulatory Framework for Banks," the Bank for International Settlements.

44 "How to Rein Wall Street," by Hillary Clinton, *The New York Times*, December 7, 2015.

45 "Mervyn King: New Financial Crisis Is 'Certain' Without Reform of Banks," *The Guardian*, February 28, 2016.

46 "Too Dull to Fail? Post-Crisis Regulators Wanted Banks to Behave More Like Utilities to End the 'Too Big to Fail' Culture. Now, With Valuations and Profit Levels Converging, What Does This Shift Mean for the Sector?" Patrick Jenkins, *The Financial Times*, September 7, 2016.

47 "Lord Adair Turner on the 'Largely Fictional' World of Finance," by Matt Phillips, *Quartz Media*, January 20, 2016.

48 "Adair Turner: The Clearest Explanation of the Cause of Financial Crisis," by Mira Tekelova, *Positive Money*, November 7, 2012.

49 "The Only Thing Useful Banks Have Invented in 20 Years Is the ATM," by Paul Volcker, in a speech at the December 2009 *Wall Street Journal* Future of Finance Initiative conference in the U.K. As reported in a December 13, 2009 *New York Post* article, the former Chairman of the Federal Reserve under Presidents Carter and Reagan started his remarks with, "you are not going to be very happy with my response," when asked to offer ideas about reforms in financial services. In his speech, he also said: "I found myself sitting next to one of the inventors of financial engineering . . . he had won a Nobel Prize, and I nudged him and asked what all the financial engineering does for the economy and what it does for productivity. Much to my surprise he leaned over and whispered in my ear that it does nothing. I asked him what it did do and he said that it moves around the rents in the financial system and besides that it was a lot of intellectual fun."

50 "Simplicity Is the Key to a Resilient Banking Regime" – "Setting the Level of Equity Banks Must Hold is a Judgment Call," Opinion column in the February 16, 2016 issue of the *Financial Times*.
51 "The Only Thing Useful Banks Have Invented in 20 Years Is the ATM," by Paul Volcker," reported in a December 13, 2009 *New York Post* article (Note 49). Paul Volcker commented on finance "taking all our best young talent." Just before this, he explained why: "Now, I have no doubts that it [financial engineering] moves around the rents in the financial system, but not only this as it seems to have vastly increased them. How do I respond to a Congressman who asks if the financial sector in the United States is so important that it generates 40% of all the profits in the country, 40% after all the bonuses and pay? Is it really a true reflection on the financial sector that it rose from two-and-a-half percent of value added according to GDP numbers to six-and-a-half percent in the last decade?"

Just before the beginning of chapter 5 on taxation, at the end of the first section of photos in this book, I displayed two charts (Images 5.1 and 5.2) from the Tax Foundation in Washington DC (thank you to the Tax Foundation for the permission to reproduce these charts in my book), showing maps of the U.S. with tax rates across the fifty states. I chose them to illustrate the wide differences in state income and property tax rates across the country and also the impact of Proposition 13 on property taxes, which is discussed in chapter 5. The title of the first chart (Image 5.1) is: "Top state marginal individual income tax rates, 2016." The title of the second chart (Image 5.2) is: "Mean effective property tax rates on owner occupied housing by state, 2016."

Chapter 5

1 "Taxes Are the Price We Pay for Civilization," a 1927 quote by U.S. Supreme Court Justice Oliver Wendell Holmes.
2 *Mr. Justice Holmes and the Supreme Court*, by Felix Frankfurter (1938, Harvard University Press).
3 "Look at How Many Pages Are in the Federal Tax Code," by Jason Russell, *The Washington Examiner*, Wednesday, August 30, 2017.
4 "Buffett Says He's Still Paying Lower Tax Rate Than His Secretary," by Chris Isidore, *CNN Money*, March 4, 2013.
5 "The Progressive Income Tax in U.S. History," by Burton W. Folsom, *Foundation for Economic Education*, May 1, 2003.
6 "The Annual RPI and Average Earnings for Britain, 1209 to Present," by Gregory Clark, *Measuring Worth*, 2016.
7 "A Tax to Beat Napoléon," Her Majesty's Revenue and Customs, 2007.
8 "The Politics of Income Inequality," by Eduardo Porter, *The New York Times*, May 13, 2014.
9 "The Hidden Progressive History of Income Tax," by Erik Loomis, *AlterNet*, September 7, 2012.
10 "Historical Effective Federal Tax Rates: 1979 to 2004," the Congressional Budget Office, December 2006.
11 *Capital in the Twenty-First Century [Le Capital au XXIe siècle]*, by Thomas Piketty translated by Arthur Goldhammer (April 2014, Harvard University Press).
12 "What Are Payroll Tax and Who Pays Them," by John Olson, the Tax Foundation, July 25, 2016.
13 "State Income Tax Rates and Brackets for 2017," by Morgan Scarboro, the Tax Foundation, March 9, 2017.
14 "State Income Tax Rates and Brackets for 2016," by Nicole Kaeding, the Tax Foundation, February 8, 2016.
15 "State Tax Collection Data: Income, Sales, License, Other Taxes," sourced from: Governing: The States and Localities, 2016.

16 "Who Pays? A Distributional Analysis of the Tax Systems in All 50 States," by Carl Davis, Kelly Davis, Matthew Gardner, Robert S. McIntyre, Jeff McLynch, and Alla Sapozhnikova, Institute on Taxation and Economic Policy, November 2009.

17 "Mean Effective Property Tax Rates on Owner Occupied Housing," The Tax Foundation, 2016.

18 *Tax Revolt: Something for Nothing in California*, by Jack Citrin and David Sears (1982, Harvard University Press).

19 "Prop. 13 Remains Controversial After a Quarter of a Century," by Carolyn Lochhead, *San Francisco Chronicle*, August 16, 2003.

20 "Californians Approve Massive Tax Hike on the Wealthy," by Tami Luhby, *CNN Money*, November 7, 2012.

21 "An Experienced Jerry Brown Vows to Build on What He's Already Done," *The Los Angeles Times*, October 19, 2014.

22 "History of Statewide Sales and Use Tax Rates," California State Board of Equalization, 2015.

23 "Let's Look at How Much Apple's Overseas Cash Hoard Has Grown in the Last 8 Years," by Jeff Dunn, *Business Insider*, August 25, 2016.

24 "$2.1 Trillion in Corporate Profits Held Offshore: A Comparison of International Tax Proposals," by the U.S. PIRG Education Fund and Citizens for Tax Justice (CTJ), July 15, 2015.

25 "Ireland Resists Closing Corporation Tax 'Loophole' – Tech Firms Lobbied Noonan Not to Adopt New OECD Rules About Where They Pay Tax," by Jack Power, *The Irish Times*, November 10, 2017.

26 "Companies Avoiding Taxes," by David Leonhardt, *New York Times*, 2016.

27 *Corporate Tax Reform: Taxing Profits in the 21st Century*, by Martin A. Sullivan (2011, Apress).

28 "Why the EU Says Apple Must Pay Ireland $14.5 Billion in Tax," by Tom Bergin, *Reuters Business News*, August 30, 2016.

29 "Apple Slapped With Fine Up to $14.5 Billion by the European Union," *SteelersLounge*, August 2016.

30 "Apple Ordered to Pay Up to 13b Euros After EU Rules Ireland Broke State Aid Laws," by Sean Farrell and Henry McDonald, *The Guardian*, August 30, 2016.

31 "How Apple Could Bring Overseas Cash Home to Help Fix America's Crumbling Infrastructure," by Clara Linnane, *MarketWatch*, October 17, 2016.

32 "Report: Repatriation Tax Holiday a 'Failed' Policy," by Kristina Peterson, *The Wall Street Journal*, October 10, 2011.

33 "Mitt Romney Releases Tax Return for 2011, Showing He Paid 14.1 Percent Tax Rate," *The Washington Post*, 2012.

34 "What You Need to Know About Mitt Romney's 2011 Tax Return," *The Atlantic*, 2012.

35 "The Case for Higher Taxes," by Rana Foroohar, *The Financial Times*, May 22, 2017.

36 "Panama Papers Show How Rich United States Clients Hid Millions Abroad," by Eric Lipton and Julie Creswell, *The New York Times*, June 5, 2016.

37 "Panama Papers: UBS, HSBC Offshore Dealings Thrust Into Spotlight," *Bloomberg*, May 2016.

38 "Farewell to the Woman They Called the Queen of Mean: Leona Helmsley Dies at 87," by Ed Pilkington, *The Guardian*, August 20, 2007.

39 "Vouchercare Is Not Medicare," op-ed by Paul Krugman, *The New York Times*, June 5, 2011.

40 "Chile's Retirees Find Shortfall in Private Plan," by Larry Rohter, *The New York Times*, January 27, 2005.

41 "Chile's Privatized Social Security System, Beloved by U.S. Conservatives, Is Falling Apart," op-ed by Michael Hiltzik, *The Los Angeles Times*, August 12, 2016.

42 "The Republican Tax Plan Would Add $1.7 Trillion to Federal Deficits," by Nash Jenkins, *Time*, November 9, 2017.

43 "Trump Tax Plan Revealed: Three Big Changes to Look For," by Tony Nitti, *Forbes*, September 27, 2017.

44 "Gary Cohn: Trickle-Down Is Good for the Economy. A Year Ago, I Was Advising Companies to Move Out of the US," November 9, 2017 interview with *CNBC's* John Harwood.

45 "Gary Cohn Had an Awkward Moment When CEOs Appeared to Shoot Down One of the Biggest Arguments for the GOP Tax Plan," by Bob Bryan, *Business Insider*, November 14, 2017.

46 "More Than 400 Millionaires Tell Congress: Don't Cut Our Taxes," by Heather Long, *The Washington Post*, November 12, 2017.

47 Joseph E. Stiglitz, quoted in "Trump Tax Plan May Free Up Corporate Dollars, But Then What? Trump Has Big Tax Plans, But Evasion Eludes Limits," by Patricia Cohen, *The New York Times*, August 29, 2017.

48 "The Republican Tax Plan Built for Plutocrats," by Martin Wolf, *The Financial Times*, November 22, 2017. .

Chapter 6

1 *Issues on My Mind: Strategies for the Future*: Chapter 4 ("A Better Energy Future"), and Appendix 4, by George P. Shultz (2013, Hoover Institution Press).

2 The original title of Miguel de Cervantes' illustrous novel is *El Ingenioso Hidalgo Don Quijote de la Mancha*, or *The Ingenious Nobleman Don Quixote of la Mancha* in English.

3 "American Wind Energy Association (AWEA) Texas Fact Sheet," April 3, 2017.

4 "U.S. Number One in the World in Wind Energy Production," American Wind Energy Association, 2017.

5 "Total System Electric Generation," California Energy Commission, 2017.

6 "Germany: The World's First Major Renewable Energy Economy," by Jane Burgermeister, *Renewable Energy World*, April 3, 2009.

7 "Germany Leads Way on Renewables, Sets 45% Target by 2030," Worldwatch Institute, September 3, 2017.

8 "Net Generation by Energy Source: Total (All Sectors), 2007 – June 2017," U.S. Energy Information Administration, 2017.

9 "U.S. Field Production of Crude Oil, 1920–2017," U.S. Energy Information Administration, 2017.

10 "U.S. Oil Imports From OPEC Have Plunged to a 28-Year Low," *Bloomberg Finance*, 2016.

11 "Weekly U.S. Imports of Crude Oil, 1990 – June 2017," U.S. Energy Information Administration, 2017.

12 "CAFE Overview," NHTSA, 2009.

13 "Gas Guzzler Tax," U.S. Environmental Protection Agency (EPA), 2014.

14 "CAFE 2011–2016 Final Rule," NHTSA, 2011.

15 "Reducing CO2 Emissions From Passenger Cars: Policies and Climate Action," European Commission, 2011.

16 "From 10–15 to JC08: Japan's New Economy Formula," Japan Automobile Manufacturers Association (JAMA), 2009.

17 "Carbon Trading: How Does It Work," *BBC News*, September 25, 2015.

18 "UK Calls for Major Changes to EU's 'Cap and Trade' Emissions System," the U.K. Department of Energy and Climate Change, part of "Climate Change International Action, Low Carbon Technologies, and Greenhouse Gas Emissions," July 16, 2014.

19 "The End of the EU's Cap-and-Trade Affair: This Could Turn Out to Be Very Good News for the World's Climate," Op. Ed. by Bjorn Lomborg, *The Wall Street Journal*, April 21, 2013.

20 "Europe's Carbon Market Crisis: Why Does It Matter," by Thomas Grose, *National Geographic News*, April 20, 2013.

21 "Proposition 23: Backers Were Outspent, Out-organized," *The Los Angeles Times*, November 3, 2010.

22 "Jerry Brown Defends Embattled State Climate Law But Is Open to 'Adjustments'," by Colin Sullivan, *The New York Times*, 30 Apr, 2010.

23 "California's Cap-and-trade Program Faces Daunting Hurdles to Avoid Collapse," by Chris Megerian and Ralph Vartabedian, *The Los Angeles Times*, June 14, 2016.

24 "California Cap-and-trade Program Has Cut Pollution. So Why Do Critics Keep Calling it a Failure?" Michael Hiltzik, *The Los Angeles Times*, July 29, 2016.

25 "California's Cap-and-Trade Bubble," *The Wall Street Journal*, July 2016.

26 "California's Cap-and-trade Carbon Program Sputters Again," *The Sacramento Bee*, July 2016.

27 "Washington Voters Reject Initiative to Impose Carbon Tax on Fossil Fuels," by Lewis Kamb, *The Seattle Times*, November 8–9, 2016.

28 "A Price Tag on Carbon as a Climate Rescue Plan," by Justin Gillis, *The New York Times*, May 30, 2014.

29 "Carbon Tax v Cap-and-trade: Which is Better?" The Grantham Research Institute on Climate Change and the Environment, quoted in *The Guardian*, January 31, 2013.

30 "Which is Better: Carbon Tax or Cap-and-trade?" The Grantham Research Institute on Climate Change and the Environment, March 21, 2014.

31 "Trump's Decision to Kill TPP Leaves Door Open for China," by Charles Riley, *CNN*, January 23, 2017.

32 "U.S. Allies See Trans-Pacific Partnership as a Check on China," by Jane Perlez, *The New York Times*, October 6, 2015.

33 "U.S. and 11 Nations Seal Pacific Trade Deal," *The Financial Times*, February 5, 2016.

34 "Forget NAFTA, the TPP Is the New 'Gold Standard' of Global Trade," by Gordon Isfeld, *Toronto's National Post*, October 12, 2015.

35 "Trading Down: Unemployment, Inequality and Other Risks of the Trans-Pacific Partnership Agreement," by J. Capaldo and A. Izurieta, Global Development and Economic Institute, January 16, 2016.

36 "The Trans-Pacific Partnership Clause Everyone Should Oppose," op-ed by Elizabeth Warren, *The Washington Post*, February 25, 2015.

37 "TPP: What Is it and Why Does It Matter?" *BBC News*, January 23, 2017.

38 "What Is TPP? Behind the Trade Deal That Died," by Kevin Granville, *The New York Times*, January 23, 2017.

39 "Donald Trump and the History of Tariffs and Trade," by Lana Ulrich, *Constitution Daily*, January 18, 2017.

40 "Life Expectancy for White Americans Declines," by Betsy McKay, *The Wall Street Journal*, April 20, 2016.

41 "My Take on the Republicans' New Interesting Corporate Tax Plan," by Jared Bernstein, *The Washington Post*, December 30, 2016.

42 "Federal Regulatory Agencies of the United States Government," *eInvestigator.com*, 2016.

43 "Employee Profiles at the FCC," FCC, January 4, 2016.

44 "FY 2017 Congressional Budget Justification," U.S. Securities and Exchange Commission, 2016.

45 "Federal Deposit Insurance Corporation (FDIC); Federal Energy Regulatory Commission (FERC); Federal Trade Commission (FTC); and Food and Drug Administration (FDA)," *AllGov: Everything Our Government Really Does*, 2016.

46 "EPA's Budget and Spending," the Environmental Protection Agency, January 12, 2017.

47 "NRC: Our Plans, Budget, & Performance," the Nuclear Regulatory Commission, 2016.

48 "Mary Jo White to Rejoin Debevoise & Plimpton," by Elizabeth Olson, *The New York Times*, February 15, 2017.

49 "Sen Warren Urges Obama to Remove Mary Jo White as SEC Chair," by Antonio José Vielma, *CNBC Business News and Finance*, October 14, 2016.

50 "White House Is Sticking With SEC Chief Mary Jo White," *The Wall Street Journal*, October 14, 2016.

51 "Lawyers per capita by State," the *Last Gen X American*, 2016.

52 *The American President: A Complete History*, by Kathryn Moore (2007, Fall River Press).

53 "Wilbur Ross Tries to Turn Around US Heartland," *The Financial Times*, November 25, 2016.

54 "Who Are the Democratic Superdelegates," by Drew DeSilver, Pew Research Center, May 5, 2016.

55 "Cruz Allies Prevail in North Dakota Delegate Race," by Phil Mattingly and Tom LoBianco, *CNN*, April 4, 2016.

56 "Colorado GOP Blundered on 2016 Presidential Caucus," *The Denver Post*, February 26, 2016 (1/2).

57 "Ted Cruz Wins All Colorado Delegates at Convention," *Election Central*, April 2016.

58 "Colorado GOP Blundered on 2016 Presidential Caucus," *The Denver Post*, February 26, 2016 (2/2).

59 "Ted Cruz Gains in Louisiana After Loss There to Donald Trump," *The Wall Street Journal*, March 24, 2016.

60 *Disconnecting Parties: Managing the Bell System Break-Up, an Inside View*, by Brooke Tunstall (1985, McGraw-Hill).

61 "AT&T–Time Warner Proposed Merger Is Compared to Comcast Deal," by Jim Zarroli, *National Public Radio*, October 26, 2016.

62 *Issues on My Mind: Strategies for the Future*, by George P. Shultz (2013, Hoover Institution Press): Chapter Four, "A Better Energy Future," pages 50 and 51, and Appendix 4, pages 204–206, "Why We Support a Revenue-Neutral Carbon Tax," by George P. Shultz and Gary S. Becker, reproduced from an op-ed in the *Wall Street Journal*, April 7, 2013.

Chapter 7

1 "Les constitutions en France (de 1791 à nos jours)," ["The Constitutions in France (from 1791 to our time)"], by Laurent Albaret, *Les Clionautes*; Informations by Claude Robinot, Pierre Borgo and Dominique Chathuant, extracted from France's "Conseil Constitutionnel" website.

2 "The Constitution of the United States" and "The Bill of Rights & All Amendments," *Constitutionus.com*.

3 "A Note on Brevity (of the US Constitution)," *The Economist*, July 1, 2009.

4 "Who Wrote the Constitution?" *Laws.com*.

5 "America's Founding Fathers – Delegates to the Constitutional Convention," the U.S. National Archives and Records Administration.

6 "Foundations of American Government – French and English Influences," ushistory.org.

7 "Democracy and the Origins of the US Constitution," by Lewis Loflin, *Sullivan-county.com*.

8 "Montesquieu, Separation of Powers, the Constitution, and the Founding Fathers," *America's Survival Guide*.

9 "In What Ways Did Baron de Montesquieu Influence the Constitution of the United States?" Aatif Rashid, *The Classroom*.

10 "France and the Origins of American Political Culture," by James Banner, *vqronline.com*, Autumn 1988 issue.

11 "Hobbes, Locke, Montesquieu, and Rousseau on Government," Constitutional Rights Foundation, Spring 2004.

12 "Enlightenment Influences on American Politics," by Shad Mickelberry, February 19, 2009.

13 "The United States Constitution: Beauty in Ambiguity; Logic in Simplicity," by Gary Nolan, *The Logical Libertarian*, March 21, 2014.

14 "Principles of Law: Simplicity is Beautiful," by Ryan Young, *The Competitive Enterprise Institute*, February 10, 2012.

15 "Like it Or Not, Complexity Is Something We Can No Longer Ignore," *Forbes*, September 9, 2016.

16 "What Would Alexis de Tocqueville Have Made of the 2016 US Presidential Election," by Arthur Goldhammer, *The Nation*, September 28, 2016.

17 "Even God Quotes Tocqueville," by Christopher Caldwell, *The New York Times* (Review of Books by Hugh Brogan and Joseph Epstein), July 8, 2007.

18 *De la Démocratie en Amérique, Volumes I & II*, by Alexis de Tocqueville, 1835 (Volume I) and 1840 (Volume II).

19 "Tocqueville Reminds Us That Local Communities Make Democracy Work, But Not in The Way You Think," by Pascal-Emmanuel Gobry, *The Federalist*, January 7, 2014.

20 "Tocqueville in America," *The New Yorker*, May 17, 2010.

21 "Inventors and Inventions from 1851–1900 – the Second Half of the Nineteenth Century," *EnchantedLearning.com*.

22 "Early Twentieth Century Inventors and Inventions," *EnchantedLearning.com*.

23 "The Advent of the Steel Rail, 1857–1914," by David Brooke, *Journal of Transport History*, 1986.

24 "Andrew Carnegie," *ExplorePaHistory.com*.

25 *The Rise and Fall of the Great Powers*, by Paul Kennedy (1987, Random House).

26 "10 Moments That made American Business," by John Steele Gordon, *American Heritage*, 2007.

27 *Henry Ford*, by Vincent Curcio (2013, Oxford University Press).

28 This entertaining story was beautifully narrated in the book *Go Like Hell: Ford, Ferrari, and Their Battle for Speed and Glory at Le Mans*, by A. J. Baime (2010, Houghton Mifflin Harcourt).

29 *Nothing Like It in the World: The Men Who Built the Transcontinental Railroad, 1863–1869*, by Stephen E. Ambrose (2000, Simon & Schuster).

30 *Encyclopedia of American Railroads*, edited by William D. Middleton, Rick Morgan, and Roberta L. Diehl (2007, Indiana University Press).

31 "Pullman Sleeping Cars Add Comfort to Overnight Travel," *RailsWest.com*, 2002.

32 *Travel by Pullman: A Century of Service*, by Joe Welsh and Bill Howes (2004, MBI).

33 "America on the Move: Railroads' Role, 1950–2000," National Museum of American History, 2000.

34 "Freight Rail Overview," by the Federal Railroad Administration, U.S. Department of Transportation, 2012.

35 "U.S. Ton-Miles of Freight, 1980–2015," from the U.S. Bureau of Transportation Statistics, 2016 (1/2).

36 "North American Freight Rail Industry," Transportation Research Board, Association of American Railroads, March 14, 2014.

37 "U.S. Ton-Miles of Freight," U.S. Bureau of Transportation Statistics, 2016 (2/2).

38 "Country Comparison: Railways," World Factbook, Central Intelligence Agency, 2016.

39 "Freight Transport Statistics," Eurostat – Statistics Explained, 2017.

40 "China Statistical Yearbook 2016" and "Railway Statistical Bulletin," 2015.

41 "City of New Orleans," written by Steve Goodman; recorded by Arlo Guthrie in 1972 and Willie Nelson in 1985.

42 *The Greatest Generation*, by Tom Brokaw (1998, Random House).

43 *Commander in Chief: Franklin Delano Roosevelt, His Lieutenants, and Their War*, by Eric Larrabee (1987, Simon & Schuster).

44 "The Jeep, the Dakota, and the Landing Craft Were the Three Tools That Won the War," quote from Dwight D. Eisenhower, reported by David Stubblebine in World War II Database.

45 "The Iconic M1 Garand," by Garry James, *Guns and Ammo*, April 11, 2016.

46 "Jeep," by David Stubblebine, in World War II Database.

47 "GMC Trucks Helped Win World War II," compiled by Donald E. Meyer, GMC Truck Historian, first published in American Truck Historical Society.

48 "How GM's Divisions Tackled the War Effort," by Ward Carroll, *Military.com*.

49 *U.S. Military Wheeled Vehicles*, by Fred W. Crismon (2001, Victory WWII).

50 "The Bazooka: A History," by Paul Huard, *RealClear Defense*, March 13, 2015.

51 *The Bazooka*, by Gordon L. Rottman (2012, Osprey Publishing).

52 "Medium Tank M4 Sherman," *Tank Encyclopedia*, November 28, 2014.

53 *T-34–85 vs. M26 Pershing: Korea 1950*, by Steven Zaloga (2010, Osprey Publishing).

54 *Tank Tactics: From Normandy to Lorraine*, by Roman Jarymowycz (2008, Stackpole Books).

55 *Freedom's Forge: How American Business Produced Victory in World War II*, by Arthur Herman (2012, Random House).

56 "How Parachute Is Made: Material, Manufacture, Making, History, Used, Parts, Components, Structure, Machine, History," How Products Are Made.

57 "Polymer Advances in the Interwar Period: The Impact of Science on World War II," by Major Paul Wakefield, *The Army Logistician*, Volume 39, Issue 2.

58 "Douglas C-47 (Skytrain/Dakota) Medium Transport Aircraft." Authored by Staff Writer: Content@www.MilitaryFactory.com, 2017.

59 "History: Douglas C-47 Skytrain Military Transport," Boeing, 2015.

60 *The World's Greatest Aircraft*, by Len Cacutt (1988, Amber Books).

61 "B-17 Flying Fortress: Historical Snapshot," Boeing.

62 "15 Things You Never Knew About The B-17 Flying Fortress," by Martin Swayne, November 3, 2015.

63 *The Liberty Ships: The History of the 'Emergency' Type Cargo Ships Constructed in the United States During the Second World War*, by L.A. Sawyer and W. H. Mitchell (1985, Informa Pub).

64 *How the War Was Won*, by Payson Phillips O'Brien (2015, Cambridge University Press).

65 "Apollo 17," by Mark Wade, *Encyclopedia Astronautica*.

66 "Eugene Cernan: Last Man on the Moon," by Elizabeth Howell, Space.com Contributor, January 16, 2017.

67 "The Cold War Timeline," Timelines, in *History on the Net*.

68 "Cold War Timeline," Events – Timelines, in *datesandevents.org*, 2003.

69 "The Cuban Missile Crisis: What You Know Is Wrong," by Alex Beam, *The New York Times*, June 13, 2008.

70 "Foreign Affairs, Missiles and Pacifists," by Flora Lewis, *The New York Times*, November 18, 1983.

71 "CIA Admits Involvement in Chile," by David Briscoe, *ABC News*, September 20, 2000.

72 "The 1964 'Made in Brazil' Coup and U.S. Contingency Support-plan If the Plot Stalled," MercoPress, *South Atlantic News Agency*, April 15, 2012.

73 "America's Role in Argentina's Dirty War," Editorial Board, *The New York Times*, March 17, 2016.

74 "The Battle Over Angola," *Time*, December 29, 1975.

75 *Turmoil and Triumph: My Years as Secretary of State*, by George P. Shultz (1993, Scribners, McMillan Publishing Company).

Chapter 8

1 *A Year in Provence*, by Peter Mayle (1989, Hamish Hamilton).

2 "Tech Time Warp of the Week: Watch Jeff Goldblum Sell the World on Apple . . . And This Crazy Email Thing," *Wired*.

3 "The 8 Best 'Drunk Jeff Goldblum' Videos," by Lindsay Robertson, *Stereogum*, 2009.

4 "How it Works: The Technology of Touch Screens," by Alfred Poor, *Computerworld*, October 17, 2012.

5 *Steve Jobs*, by Walter Isaacson (2011, Simon & Schuster).

6 "Hi. I'm Andy Rubin. Co-founder of Android. Today I'm Launching a New Kind of Company." Advertisement page in *The Wall Street Journal*, May 30, 2017.

7 "Egypt and Tunisia's New 'Arab Winter'," *Euro News*, October 22, 2014.

8 *Elon Musk: Tesla, Space X, and the Quest for a Fantastic Future*, by Ashlee Vance (2015, Harper Collins).

9   "Tesla Q3 2017 Vehicle Production and Deliveries," in a press release by Tesla, Inc. on October 2, 2017.

10 "How 11 Countries Are Leading the Shift to Renewable Energy," *cleantechnica.com*, from Climate Reality Project, February 4, 2016 – using 2015 International Energy Agency (IEA) data on wind and solar capacity.

11 "Top 5 Countries in Renewable Energies," *activesustainability.com*, 2016.

12 "These 10 Countries Are Ramping Up Clean Energy More than Any Others," by Rebecca Harrington, *Tech Insider*, March 29, 2016.

13 "The Top Countries in Wind and Solar Energy Per Capita," by Sophie Vorrath, *Renew Economy*, August 8, 2012.

14 "Solar: Chinese Efficiency vs. U.S. Innovation," *The Seattle Times*, October 25, 2011.

15 "Why Concentration of the Solar Industry in China Will Stunt Innovation," by Varum Sivaram, *corporateecoforum.com*, July 26, 2015.

16 "How Wall Street Once Killed the U.S. Solar Industry . . . and How It Could Happen Again," by Robinson Meyer, *The Atlantic*, April 17, 2017.

17 "American Solar Industry's Secret Sauce: Innovation," by Ucilia Wang, *greentechmedia. com*, December 12, 2008.

18 "The Future of Wind Power: 9 Cool Innovations," by Derek Markham, *TreeHugger*, April 4, 2012.

19 "Six Innovative Wind Turbine Designs," by Cat DiStasio, *engadget.com*, November 5, 2016.

20 "Where Is the Real Innovation in Wind Energy," by Michael Barnard, *cleantechnica.com*, April 21, 2014.

21 *Game Changers, Energy on the Move*, by George P. Shultz and Robert C. Armstrong (2014, Hoover Institution Press).

22 "Economic Possibilities," essay by John Maynard Keynes, 1930.

23 "How the Five Day Weekend Works," by Josh Clark, in *HowStuffWorks*.

24 "Trump Labor Secretary Pick Andy Puzder Talked About Replacing Workers with Robots," by Tonya Garcia, *MarketWatch*, 12/10/2016.

25 "Amazon Now Employs Over Half a Million People, and It Plans to Hire Thousands More," by Julie Bort, *Inc.* post on *Business Insider*, October 27, 2017

26 The protectionist tendencies shown by some members of the Trump administration, and their focus on bi-lateral trade deficits, make me think of the wonderful quote, "Everything you need to know about trade economics, in 70 words," by George P. Shultz and Martin S. Feldstein, *The Washington Post*, May 5, 2017 ("If a country consumes more than it produces, it must import more than it exports. That's not a rip-off; that's arithmetic. If we manage to negotiate a reduction in the Chinese trade surplus with the United States, we will have an increased trade deficit with some other country. Federal deficit spending, a massive and continuing act of dissaving, is the culprit. Control that spending and you will control trade deficits.").

27 "Earnings Gap Over U.S. Workers Grow For S&P 500 CEOs. CEO Pay Still Dwarfing Pay of U.S. Workers: Union Report," by Ross Kerber and Peter Szekely, *Reuters*, May 9 2017.

28 "Could AI Solve the World's Biggest Problems?" Will Knight, *MIT Technology Review*, January 12, 2016.

29 "Solutions to the World's Biggest Problems Are Within Our Reach," by Darlene Damm and Nicholas Haan, *SingularityHub*, August 17, 2016.

30 "22 Amazing Ways to Solve Problems With Technology (Simple)," by Jesai Shethna, *educba.com*, 2015.

31 "4 Innovations that Use Technology to Solve Social Issues," *goodnet.org*, September 9, 2015.

32 "How Great Technologies Can Help Solve the World's Problems," by T. J. Cook, Innovation Insights, *Wired*, April 2, 2014.

33 "This Ingenious Machine Turns Feces Into Drinking Water," by Bill Gates, January 5, 2015.

34 "Bill Gates' Plan to Help the Developing World Profit from Its Sewage," by Davey Alba, *Wired*, January 6, 2015.

35 "Report: Uber and Lyft Bloating SF Traffic by 15–20 Percent," by Joe Kukura, *SFist News*, September 8, 2017.
36 Ditto.

Chapter 9

1 "69 Years Ago, a President Pitches His Idea for National Health Care," by Dr. Howard Markel, *PBS NewsHour, KQED*, November 19, 2014.
2 "History Lesson: Votes Cast For/Against 1935 Social Security Act and 1965 Medicare Bill," by Tamara Sheperd, *Knox Views*, January 23, 2010.
3 "Taxing," by John Cassidy, *The New Yorker*, January 18, 2004.
4 "Six Years After Cheney Said 'Deficits Don't Matter,' The National Debt Hits a 50-Year High," by Pat Garofalo, *ThinkProgress*, 2008.
5 "Trump Team Stands by Budget's $2 Trillion Math Error," by Ben Popken, *NBC News*, May 24, 2017.
6 "Trump Budget Based on $2 Trillion Math Error," by Jonathan Chait, *The Daily Intelligencer*, May 23, 2017.
7 "The Unworkable Math of Trump's Budget," by Alana Semuels, *The Atlantic*, May 23, 2017.
8 "President Trump's Budget Includes a $2 Trillion Math Mistake: It's Called 'Double Counting'," by Ryan Teague Beckwith, *Time*, May 24, 2017.
9 "Germany Exports, Percent of GDP," *TheGlobalEconomy*, 2016.
10 "Exports of Goods and Services (% of GDP)," World Bank Data, the World Bank Group, 2016.
11 *Global Inequality: A New Approach for the Age of Globalization*, by Branko Milanovic (2017, Harvard University Press). This is one of the best books explaining the relationship between inequality and globalization: inequality has both fallen across nations and soared within the developed world, as middle-class incomes in China (and Brazil, India, and other developing countries) have grown significantly, while middle-class incomes have stagnated in the U.S., the U.K., Continental Europe, and Japan.
12 "A Look at the Shocking U.S. Student Loan Debt Statistics for 2017," *studentloanhero.com*, September 13, 2017.
13 "How Many Americans Have a Passport," *The Expeditioner*, December 11, 2016.
14 "The Great American Passport Myth: Why Just 3.5% Of Us Travel Overseas," by William D. Chalmers, *The Huffington Post*, November 29, 2012.
15 "Medicare and Veterans Affairs (VA) Benefits," *Medicare Interactive*, 2017.
16 "Medicare vs. Medicaid," *eHealth Medicare*, 2017.
17 "A Whistle-Blower Tells of Health Insurers Bilking Medicare," by Mary Williams Walsh, *The New York Times*, May 15, 2017.
18 "UnitedHealth Overbilled Medicare by Billions, U.S. Says in Suit," by Mary Williams Walsh, *The New York Times*, May 19, 2017.
19 "UnitedHealth Requests Federal Court Dismiss Medicare Advantage Lawsuit," by Les Masterson, *Healthcare Dive*, July 17, 2107.
20 "Medicare Advantage Money Grab – Whistleblowers: UnitedHealthcare Hid Complaints About Medicare Advantage," by Fred Schulte, the Center for Public Integrity and Kaiser Health News, July 28, 2017.
21 "AntiFraud – Federal Judge Dismisses Medicare Advantage Fraud Suit Against UnitedHealthcare," by Paige Minemyer, *FierceHealthcare*, October 6, 2017.

Chapter 10

1 "Universal Basic Income Would Pay Everyone to Improve Quality of Life," by Marisa Kendall, *The Mercury News*, June 4, 2017.
2 "Agrarian Justice," by Thomas Paine (1797, A Thomas Paine Book).
3 *Raising the Floor: How a Universal Basic Income Can Renew Our Economy and Rebuild the American Dream*, by Andy Stern, with Lee Kravitz (2016, Public Affairs Books).

4   "The Indestructible Idea of the Basic Income," by Jesse Walker, *reason.com*, June 3, 2017.

5   "Universal Basic Income: The Answer to Automation?" *infographic.com*, 2017.

6   "A Basic Income for Everyone? Yes, Finland Shows It Really Can Work," by Aditya Chakrabortty, *The Guardian*, October 31, 2017.

7   "What Is Basic Income?" Basic Income Earth Network (BIEN), 2017.

8   Note from author: A rough calculation for this estimate is as follows, with 2016 census numbers: 74 million children (under 18); 61 million receiving social security; 25 million undocumented and green card holders; and about 30 million earning more than $100,000 per year, or about 190 million people (59% of our population).

9   "Federal Government Programs Helping the Poor," United States Census Bureau, 2017.

10   "Safety Net Programs – Federal Safety Net," *federalsafetynet.com*, 2017.

11   "These programs spent $361 billion and $373 billion in 2015 and 2016, respectively. The welfare budget also includes the Medicaid Program (health care for the low-income Americans). With the inclusion of Medicaid the overall spending on welfare totaled $711 billion in fiscal year 2015 and $740 billion in 2016." From the Welfare Budget – Federal Safety Net in 2017, federalsafetynet.com.

12   "California's Would-be Governor Prepares for Battle Against Job-killing Robots," by Paul Lewis, *The Guardian*, June 5, 2017.

13   "Message from Seth Moulton," Andover Democratic Town Committee, andoverdemocrats.org, May 7, 2017.

14   "GOP Senators Hold Press Conference to Demand Assurances that GOP Health Plan Does Not Become Law," by Lydia Ramsey, *Business Insider*, July 27, 2017.

15   "GOP Obamacare Repeal Bill Fails in Dramatic Late-Night Vote," by MJ Lee, Lauren Fox, Ted Barnett, Phil Mattingly and Ashley Killough, *CNN*, July 28, 2017.

16   "National Health Expenditure Accounts: Methodology Paper, 2016 – Exhibit 1: National Health Expenditures by Type of Expenditures and Program: Calendar Year 2016," CMS Research, Statistics, Data, Trends and Reports.

17   "Government Funds Nearly Two-Thirds of U.S. Health Care Costs: American Journal of Public Health Study," by Mark Almberg, Physicians for a National Health Program (PNHP), January 21, 2016.

18   *Who Killed Healthcare? America's $2 Trillion Medical Problem – and the Consumer Driven Cure*, by Regina Herzlinger (2007, McGraw-Hill).

19   "Friedman Analysis of HR 676: Medicare for All Would Save Billions," study by Gerald Friedman, Physicians for a National Health Program, July 31, 2013.

20   "NHS Waiting Times 'driving people to turn to private treatment'," by Denis Campbell, *The Guardian*, September 10, 2017.

21   "Friedman Analysis of HR 676: Medicare for All Would Save Billions," see note 19.

22   "Friedman Responds to Thorpe on Single-Payer," by Gerald Friedman, *the D&S Blog*, 2016.

23   "Key Elements of the U.S. Tax System: How Does the Tax Exclusion for Employer-Sponsored Health Insurance Work?" The Tax Policy Center, April 11, 2017.

24   "Tax Subsidies for Private Health Insurance," by Matthew Rae, Gary Claxton, Nirmita Panchal, and Larry Levitt, the Kaiser Family Foundation, October 27, 2014.

25   "Medicare Part D Spotlight: Part D Plan Availability in 2010 and Key Changes since 2006," the Henry J. Kaiser Family Foundation, November 2009.

26   "Californians in individual Market Spent $2,500 Less on Care in 2015 Than Before the ACA," by Amy Adams, *CHCF.org*, April 17, 2017.

27   "Medicaid Enrollment & Spending Growth: FY 2015 & 2016," by Robin Rudowitz, Laura Snyder, and Vernon K. Smith, the Henry J. Kaiser Family Foundation, October 15, 2015.

28   "Total Number of Medicare Beneficiaries," the Henry J. Kaiser Family Foundation, 2016.

29   "State and Federal Spending Under the ACA," *macpac.gov*, 2016.

30 "The Surprising News About 2017 Medicare Premiums and Deductibles You May Have Missed," by Philip Moeller, November 18, 2016, *PBS NewsHour, KQED*.

31 "Modern Era Medicaid: Findings from a 50-State Survey of Eligibility, Enrollment, Renewal, and Cost-Sharing Policies in Medicaid and CHIP as of January 2015," by Tricia Brooks, Joe Touschner, and Samantha Artiga, the Henry J. Kaiser Family Foundation, January 20, 2015.

32 "The VA by the Numbers: How Big is It and Who Uses It?" *NBC News*, 2016.

33 "Do the Majority of Americans Still Get Health Insurance Through Work?" Jordan Jolley, *ZaneBenefits*, January 14, 2015.

34 "Vast Majority of Obamacare Enrollees Still Receiving Subsidies," by Bob Herman, *Modern Healthcare*, March 11, 2016.

35 "State Single Payer Legislation," *Healthcare-Now*, 2017.

36 "'Medicare for All' Would Cover Everyone, Save Billions in First Year," *Healthcare-Now*, 2016.

37 "New York's Single-payer Healthcare Plan Passes in State Assembly," by Jonathan LaMantia, *Modern Healthcare*, May 17, 2017.

38 "New York Assembly Passes Universal Healthcare Bill," *Healthcare-Now*, May 27, 2017.

39 "Rockland, Westchester Lawmakers Push for New York Health Act's Single-Payer Bill," by David Robinson, LoHud.com, December 7, 2017.

40 "Economist Shows That Single-payer Health Care in California Would Protect Business and Save the Public Money," by Steven Rosenfeld, *AlterNet*, May 31, 2017.

41 "Single-payer Plan Would Save California $37 Billion Per Year, Study Says," by Kathy Murphy, *The Mercury News*, May 31, 2017.

42 "California's New Single-Payer Proposal Embraces Some Costly Old Ways," *U.S. News and World Report*, June 1, 2017.

43 "Single-payer Health Care Bill Passes State Senate, Heads to Assembly," by Melody Gutierrez, *SFGate*, June 1, 2017.

44 "California Senate Committee Approves Single-Payer Health Care Bill," by Mark Gruenberg, *People's World*, June 2, 2017.

45 "Single-Payer Healthcare Plan Advances in California Senate – Without a Way to Pay Its $400 Billion Tab," by Patrick McGreevy, *The Los Angeles Times*, June 1, 2017.

46 "What would California's Proposed Single-Payer Healthcare System Mean for Me?" Melanie Mason, *The Los Angeles Times*, June 1, 2017.

47 "Nevada May Become First State to Offer Medicaid To All, Regardless of Income," by Alison Kodjak, *All Things Considered, National Public Radio*, June 13, 2017.

48 "Nevada Moves Closer to a Landmark Medicaid-for-All Healthcare Model," by David Montero, *The Los Angeles Times*, June 8, 2017.

49 Ditto.

50 "Nevada Governor Vetoes Medicaid-for-all Bill," by David Montero, *The Los Angeles Times*, June 17, 2017.

51 "Time for Democrats to Unite Around Medicare For All," *The Washington Post*, June 6, 2017.

52 "How a Sanders Medicare-For-All Plan Can Be Affordable and Appeal to Republicans," by Laurence Kotlikoff, *Forbes*, February 17, 2016.

53 "Medicare For All – Use Formula to Replace ACA," by Roseann Demoro, *TheHill*, January 9, 2017.

54 "What Comes Next for Obamacare? The Case for Medicare for All," by Robert H. Frank, *The New York Times*, March 24, 2017.

55 "The Growing Appeal of 'Medicare' For All," by Catherine Rampell, *San Francisco Chronicle*, April 18, 2017.

56 "Sanders Will Introduce Universal Health Care, Backed by 15 Democrats," by David Weigel, *The Washington Post*, September 12, 2017.

57 "Why We Need Medicare For All," op-ed by Bernie Sanders, *The New York Times*, September 13, 2017.

58 "Sanders Offers Possible Tax Hikes That Could Pay for Universal Medicare," by David Weigel, *The Washington Post*, September 13, 2017.

59 "A Conservative Case for Climate Action," by Martin S. Feldstein, N. Gregory Mankiw, and Ted Halstead (with co-authors James A. Baker III, Henry M. Paulson Jr., George P. Shultz, Thomas Stephenson, and Rob Walton), op-ed in *The New York Times*, February 8, 2017. Copyright permission obtained through PARS, The New York Times information REF # 000051888.

60 "Pain at the Pump? Try a Charge on Carbon Emissions," by Michael E. Porter and Daniel C. Esty, op-ed in *The New York Times*, April 27, 2011.

61 "Esty's Reflections on 'A Conservative Case for Climate Action'," by Professor Dan Esty, Yale Center for Environmental Law and Policy, February 15, 2017.

62 "IEA: Global Installed PV Capacity Leaps to 303 Gigawatts," by Eric Wesoff, *greentechmedia.com*, April 27, 2017.

63 "U.S. Wind Power Jobs Hit Record, Up 20 Percent in 2016," American Wind Energy Association, *U.S. Wind Industry Annual Market Report, Year Ending 2015*, April 12, 2016.

64 "U.S. Solar Jobs Jumped Almost 25% In the Past Year," by Kirsten Korosec, *Fortune*, February 7, 2017.

65 "Global Wind Report Annual Market Update," *Gwec.net*, 2017.

66 "Renewable Percentages in California," California Energy Commission, 2017.

67 "Barriers to Renewable Energy Siting Impede State Climate Goals: Innovative Policy Can Help," an interview with Eleanor Stein, *Forbes*, April 12, 2017.

68 "Renewable Subsidies Are Killing Nuclear and Threatening Climate Progress (Intermittent Solar and Wind Must Be Backed Up by Fossil Fuels Like Methane)," by Will Boisvert, *Environmental Progress*, June 18, 2016.

69 "Improving Infrastructure through Smart Grid Technology," by Patrick Fiorenza, *GovLoop*, 2012.

70 "The Pros and Cons of Smart Grid Technology," by Barbara Wichmann, *Artemia*, December 17, 2014.

71 "Current Grid vs. Smart Grid," *Smart Grid Technology*, 2016.

72 "What Is the Difference Between a Microgrid and a Smartgrid?" Masoud Zebarjadi, *ResearchGate*, 2016.

73 "The Grid Needs a Symphony, Not a Shouting Match – We Cannot Afford to Stifle Innovation by Enforcing Outdated Notions of 'Baseload'," by Mark Dyson and Amory Lovins, *Spark*, The Rocky Mountain Institute, June 12, 2017.

74 "What Treasury's Financial Regulation Report Gets Right – and Where It Goes Too Far," by Nellie Liang, *Brookings*, June 13, 2017.

75 "Here's the Trump Treasury Department's Plan to Change American Financial Regulations," *Fortune*, June 13, 2017.

76 "U.S. Treasury Unveils Financial Reforms, Critics Attack," by Pete Schroeder and Lisa Lambert, *Reuters*, June 13, 2017.

77 "The Financial System Is Still Blinking Red. We Need Reform More Than Ever," by Rana Foroohar, *The Guardian*, September 14, 2017.

78 "Republicans Want to Sideline This Regulator. But It May Be Too Popular," by Steve Elder, *The New York Times*, August 31 2017.

79 "President Kashkari Announces Initiative to End Too Big to Fail (TBTF) at the Brookings Institution," Alyssa Augustine, The Federal Reserve Bank of Minneapolis, February 16, 2016.

80 "Minneapolis Fed's New President Is Making Waves With Plan to Scrutinize the Power of the Nation's Biggest Banks," by Dave Beal, *MinnPost*, April 1, 2016.

81 "Fed's Kashkari Releases Plan to End 'Too Big to Fail', Compares Banks to Terrorists," by Richard Bowen, December 1, 2016.

82 "Neel Kashkari on Banking, Bailouts, Blind Spots, Jamie Dimon and Donald Trump," by Burl Gilyard, *MinnPost*, June 9, 2017.

83 "Goldman Sachs Got Billions From AIG For Its Own Account, Crisis Panel Finds," by Shahien Nasiripour, *The Huffington Post*, March 25, 2011.

84 "The AIG Bailout Scandal," by William Greider, *The Nation*, August 6, 2010.

85 "How a Financial Transaction Tax Would Benefit Us All," by Paul Wilmott, *World Economic Forum*, May 22, 2017.

86 "A Financial Transaction Tax Would Help Ensure Wall Street Works for Main Street," by Josh Bivens and Hunter Blair, Economic Policy Institute, July 28, 2016.

87 *Flash Boys: A Wall Street Revolt*, by Michael Lewis (2014, W. W. Norton & Company).

88 "Michael Lewis Reflects on Flash Boys," *Vanity Fair*, March 2015.

89 "Financial Transaction Taxes in Theory and Practice," by Leonard E. Burman, William G. Gale, Sarah Gault, Bryan Kim, Jim Nunns, and Steve Rosenthal, *Brookings*, February 29, 2016.

90 "Republican Tax Reform Seen Shrinking Corporate Bond Market – Elimination of Interest Tax Deductions," by Claire Boston, *Bloomberg Markets*, December 16, 2016.

91 "The Next Tax Battle Is Here, and It's a Bigger Chunk of Money Than Border Adjustment," *CNBC*, March 15, 2017.

92 "Interest Deductibility: Issues and Reforms," by Alan Cole, *taxfoundation.org*, May 4, 2017.

93 "The GOP Tax Plan: 3 Big Wins for Business," by Shawn Tully, *Fortune*, November 2, 2017.

94 "Our Complex Tax Code is Crippling America," by Chris Edwards, *Time*, April 11, 2016.

95 "A Lesson for Trump: The Best Tax Reforms Are the Stealthiest," op-ed by John Kay, *The Financial Times*, September 2, 2017.

96 "Top CEOs Make More than 300 Times the Average Worker," by Paul Hodgson, *Fortune*, June 22, 2015.

97 "It's a Myth That Corporate Tax Cuts Mean More Jobs," by Sarah Anderson, *The New York Times*, August 30, 2017.

98 "There's Little Evidence that Cutting Corporate Taxes Creates Jobs," by John W. Schoen, *CNBC*, August 30, 2017.

99 "We Need Higher Taxes," by Robert Samuelson, *The Washington Post*, August 27, 2017.

100 "Tax Brackets in 2017," by Kyle Pomerleau, *taxfoundation.org*, November 10, 2016.

101 "Biggest Tax Cuts and Tax Increases in House G.O.P. Bill," by Alicia Parlapiano and Adam Pearce, *The New York Times*, November 16, 2017.

102 *A Fine Mess: A Global Quest for a Simpler, Fairer, and More Efficient Tax System*, by T.R. Reid (2017, Penguin Random House).

103 "The I.R.S. Could Be Your Friend," by T.R. Reid, *The New York Times*, April 14, 2017.

104 "The G.O.P. Health Care Crackup," op-ed by David Brooks, *The New York Times*, March 10, 2017.

Index

Note: Page numbers in *italic* indicate a figure on the corresponding page.